GW01417541

0   10   20km

Exeter

Torbay

Plymouth

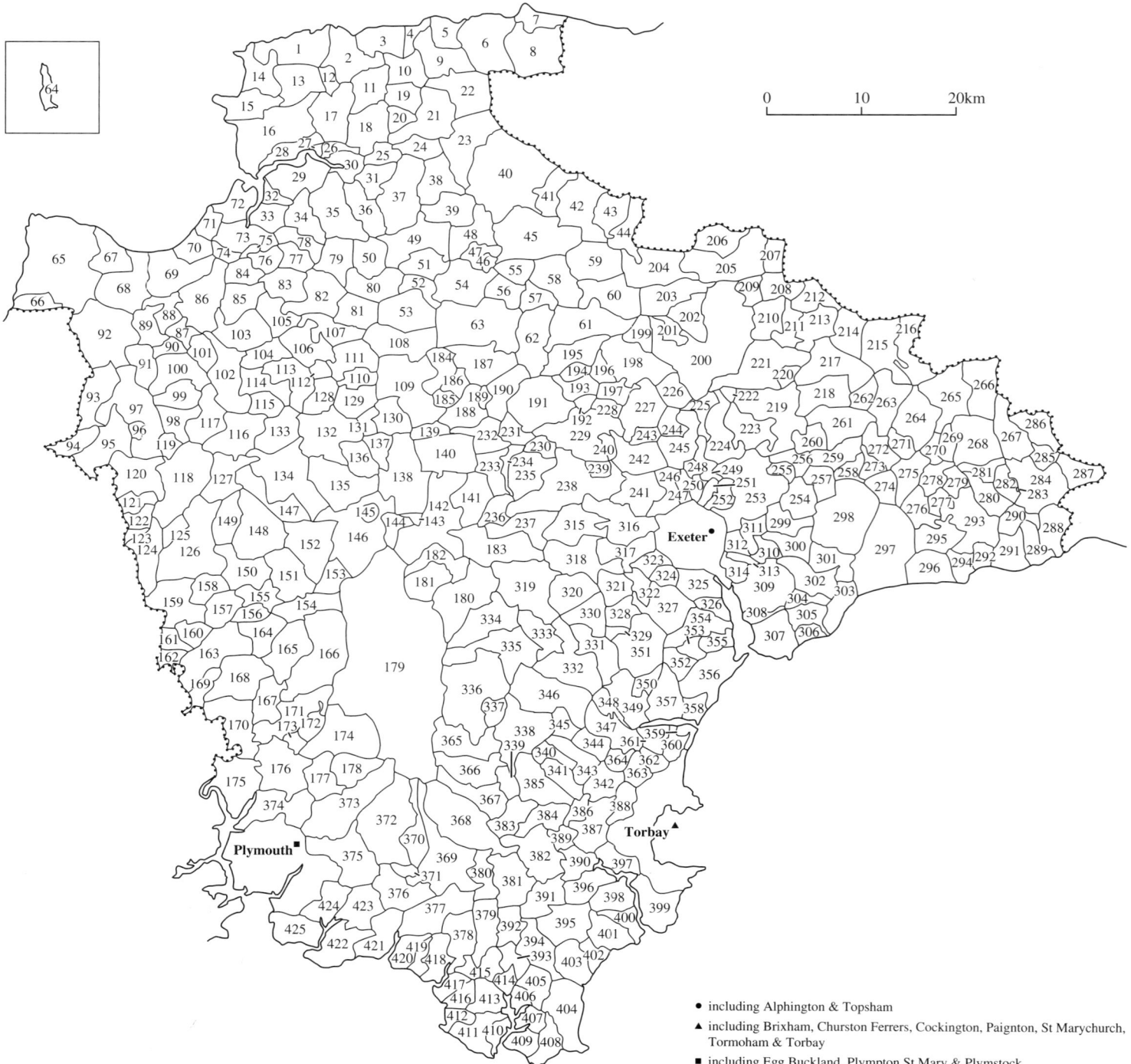

• including Alphington & Topsham
▲ including Brixham, Churston Ferrers, Cockington, Paignton, St Marychurch, Tormoham & Torbay
■ including Egg Buckland, Plympton St Mary & Plymstock

1 Ilfracombe
2 Berrynarbor
3 Combe Martin
4 Trentishoe
5 Martinhoe
6 Lynton & Lynmouth
7 Countisbury
8 Brendon
9 Parracombe
10 Kentisbury
11 East Down
12 Bittadon
13 West Down
14 Mortehoe
15 Georgeham
16 Braunton
17 Marwood
18 Shirwell
19 Arlington
20 Loxhore
21 Bratton Fleming
22 Challacombe
23 Brayford (including Charles & High Bray)
24 Stoke Rivers
25 Goodleigh
26 Pilton West
27 Ashford
28 Heanton Punchardon
29 Fremington
30 Barnstaple
31 Landkey
32 Instow
33 Westleigh
34 Horwood, Lovacott, Newton Tracey
35 Tawstock
36 Bishop's Tawton
37 Swimbridge
38 East & West Buckland
39 Filleigh
40 North Molton
41 Twitchen
42 Molland
43 West Anstey
44 East Anstey
45 Bishop's Nympton
46 Queen's Nympton
47 George Nympton
48 South Molton
49 Chittlehampton
50 Atherington
51 Satterleigh & Warkleigh
52 Chittlehamholt
53 Burrington
54 King's Nympton
55 Mariansleigh
56 Romansleigh
57 Meshaw
58 Rose Ash
59 Knowstone
60 Rackenford
61 Witheridge
62 East Worlington
63 Chulmleigh
64 Lundy
65 Hartland
66 Welcombe
67 Clovelly
68 Woolfardisworthy
69 Parkham
70 Alwington
71 Abbotsham

72 Northam
73 Bideford
74 Littleham
75 Landcross
76 Weare Giffard
77 Huntshaw
78 Alverdiscott
79 Yarnscombe
80 High Bickington
81 Roborough
82 St Giles in the Wood
83 Great Torrington
84 Monkleigh
85 Frithelstock
86 Buckland Brewer
87 Bulkworthy
88 East Putford
89 West Putford
90 Abbots Bickington
91 Sutcombe
92 Bradworthy
93 Pancrasweek
94 Bridgerule
95 Pyworthy
96 Holsworthy
97 Holsworthy Hamlets
98 Cookbury
99 Thornbury
100 Milton Damerel
101 Newton St Petrock
102 Shebbear
103 Langtree
104 Peters Marland
105 Little Torrington
106 Merton
107 Beaford
108 Ashreigney
109 Winkleigh
110 Dowland
111 Dolton
112 Huish
113 Petrockstowe
114 Buckland Filleigh
115 Sheepwash
116 Black Torrington
117 Bradford
118 Ashwater
119 Hollacombe
120 Clawton
121 Tetcott
122 Luffincott
123 Northcott
124 St Giles on the Heath
125 Virginstow
126 Broadwoodwidger
127 Halwill
128 Meeth
129 Iddesleigh
130 Broadwoodkelly
131 Monkokehampton
132 Hatherleigh
133 Highampton
134 Northlew
135 Inwardleigh
136 Jacobstowe
137 Exbourne
138 Sampford Courtenay (including Honeychurch)
139 Bondleigh
140 North Tawton
141 Spreyton
142 South Tawton
143 Sticklepath

144 Belstone
145 Okehampton
146 Okehampton Hamlets
147 Beaworthy
148 Bratton Clovelly
149 Germansweek
150 Thruselton
151 Bridestowe
152 Sourton
153 Common to Bridestowe & Sourton
154 Lydford
155 Lewtrenchard
156 Coryton
157 Marystow
158 Stowford
159 Lifton
160 Kelly
161 Bradstone
162 Dunterton
163 Milton Abbot
164 Brentor
165 Mary Tavy
166 Peter Tavy
167 Tavistock
168 Lamerton
169 Sydenham Damerel
170 Gulworthy
171 Whitchurch
172 Sampford Spiney
173 Horrabridge
174 Walkhampton
175 Bere Ferrers
176 Buckland Monachorum
177 Meavy
178 Sheepstor
179 Dartmoor Forest
180 Chagford
181 Gidleigh
182 Throwleigh
183 Drewsteignton
184 Wembworthy
185 Brushford
186 Eggesford
187 Chawleigh
188 Coldridge
189 Nymet Rowland
190 Lapford
191 Morchard Bishop
192 Kennerleigh
193 Woolfardisworthy
194 Washford Pyne
195 Thelbridge
196 Puddington
197 Poughill
198 Cruwys Morchard
199 Templeton
200 Tiverton
201 Loxbeare
202 Washfield
203 Stoodleigh
204 Oakford
205 Bampton
206 Morebath
207 Clayhanger
208 Hockworthy
209 Huntsham
210 Uplowman
211 Sampford Peverell
212 Holcombe Rogus
213 Burlescombe
214 Culmstock
215 Hemyock

216 Clayhidon
217 Uffculme
218 Kentisbeare
219 Cullompton
220 Willand
221 Halberton
222 Butterleigh
223 Bradninch
224 Silverton
225 Bickleigh
226 Cadeleigh
227 Cheriton Fitzpaine
228 Stockleigh English
229 Sandford
230 Copplestone
231 Down St Mary
232 Zeal Monachorum
233 Bow
234 Clannaborough
235 Colebrooke
236 Hittisleigh
237 Cheriton Bishop
238 Crediton Hamlets
239 Crediton
240 Upton Hellions
241 Newton St Cyres
242 Shobrooke
243 Stockleigh Pomeroy
244 Cadbury
245 Thorverton
246 Upton Pyne
247 Brampford Speke
248 Nether Exe
249 Rewe
250 Stoke Canon
251 Huxham
252 Poltimore
253 Broadclyst
254 Whimple
255 Clyst St Lawrence
256 Clyst Hydon
257 Talaton
258 Feniton
259 Payhembury
260 Plymtree
261 Broadhembury
262 Sheldon
263 Dunkeswell
264 Luppitt
265 Upottery
266 Yarcombe
267 Membury
268 Stockland
269 Cotleigh
270 Monkton
271 Combe Raleigh
272 Awliscombe
273 Buckerell
274 Gittisham
275 Honiton
276 Farway
277 Northleigh
278 Offwell
279 Widworthy
280 Shute
281 Dalwood
282 Kilmington
283 Common to Axminster & Kilmington
284 Axminster
285 All Saints
286 Chardstock
287 Hawkchurch

288 Uplyme
289 Combpyne Rousdon
290 Musbury
291 Axmouth
292 Seaton
293 Colyton
294 Beer
295 Southleigh
296 Branscombe
297 Sidmouth (including Salcombe Regis & Sidbury)
298 Ottery St Mary
299 Rockbeare
300 Aylesbeare
301 Newton Poppleford & Harpford
302 Colaton Raleigh
303 Otterton
304 Bicton
305 East Budleigh
306 Budleigh Salterton
307 Exmouth (including Littleham & Withycombe Raleigh)
308 Lympstone
309 Woodbury
310 Farringdon
311 Clyst Honiton
312 Sowton
313 Clyst St Mary
314 Clyst St George
315 Tedburn St Mary
316 Whitestone
317 Holcombe Burnell
318 Dunsford
319 Moretonhampstead
320 Bridford
321 Doddiscombsleigh
322 Dunchideock
323 Ide
324 Shillingford St George
325 Exminster
326 Powderham
327 Kenn
328 Ashton
329 Trusham
330 Christow
331 Hennock
332 Bovey Tracey
333 Lustleigh
334 North Bovey
335 Manaton
336 Widecombe in the Moor
337 Buckland in the Moor
338 Ashburton
339 Buckfastleigh
340 Woodland
341 Broadhempston
342 Ipplepen
343 Torbryan
344 Ogwell
345 Bickington
346 Ilsington
347 Newton Abbot (including Highweek & Wolborough)
348 Teigngrace
349 Kingsteignton
350 Ideford
351 Chudleigh
352 Ashcombe
353 Mamhead
354 Kenton
355 Starcross

356 Dawlish
357 Bishopsteignton
358 Teignmouth
359 Shaldon
360 Stokeinteignhead
361 Haccombe with Combe (Combeinteignhead)
362 Coffinswell
363 Kingskerswell
364 Abbotskerswell
365 Holne
366 West Buckfastleigh
367 Dean Prior
368 South Brent
369 Ugborough
370 Harford
371 Ivybridge
372 Cornwood
373 Shaugh Prior
374 Bickleigh
375 Sparkwell
376 Ermington
377 Modbury
378 Aveton Gifford
379 Loddiswell
380 North Huish
381 Diptford
382 Harberton
383 Rattery
384 Dartington
385 Staverton
386 Littlehempston
387 Berry Pomeroy
388 Marldon
389 Totnes
390 Ashprington
391 Halwell & Moreleigh
392 Woodleigh
393 Buckland-tout-Saints
394 East Allington
395 Blackawton
396 Cornworthy
397 Stoke Gabriel
398 Dittisham
399 Kingswear
400 Dartmouth
401 Stoke Fleming
402 Strete
403 Slapton
404 Stokenham
405 Frogmore & Sherford
406 Charleton
407 South Pool
408 Chivelstone
409 East Portlemouth
410 Salcombe
411 Malborough
412 South Huish
413 West Alvington
414 Kingsbridge (including Dodbrooke)
415 Churchstow
416 South Milton
417 Thurlestone
418 Bigbury
419 Ringmore
420 Kingston
421 Holbeton
422 Newton & Noss (Newton Ferrers)
423 Yealmpton
424 Brixton
425 Wembury

DEVON AND CORNWALL RECORD SOCIETY

New Series, Volume 45

Issued to members of the society for the year 2002

Devon and Cornwall Record Society

New Series, Volume 45

DEVON MAPS AND MAP-MAKERS: MANUSCRIPT MAPS BEFORE 1840

Two volumes

Part II

Edited with an Introduction by

Mary R. Ravenhill and Margery M. Rowe

Exeter

2002

© Devon and Cornwall Record Society,
Mary R. Ravenhill and Margery M. Rowe 2002

No part of this publication may be reproduced, stored in a retrieval system, or
transmitted in any form or by any means, electronic, mechanical, photocopying,
recording or otherwise, without the prior permission of the copyright holders.

ISBN 0 901853 45 3

Designed and typeset by Mike Dobson, Quince Typesetting
Times New Roman 9/12

Printed and bound in Great Britain
by Short Run Press Ltd, Exeter

Contents

Part II

CARTO-BIBLIOGRAPHY

Parishes F–Z

6/1/1

FARRINGDON
1714   King's College Cambridge Archive SJP 227

Creely Barton SY 002905

TITLE: 'A Map of Creely Barton' 'Surveyed and plotted [per] Nicho Thomas 1714'

SURVEYOR: Nicholas Thomas

SCALE: 'A Scale of Chains'; scale bar; 1"=3 chains; 1:2376

MATERIAL, SIZE & ORIENTATION: parchment, coloured; 77.5cms EW x 59.6cms NS; north to top

CONTENT: streams, pond, blue; 'Grindal Brook' named; fields outlined by double ink lines with green hedge symbols between; alphabetic reference to list giving field names and content; hedgerow trees described in words, e.g., 5 Elms, 5 Poll Elms, 6 Poll Oaks etc; green tree symbols showing orchards, copse and woods which are also stippled green; moor, green with brown stippling; formal gardens in plan; marl pit, roads, brown; 'Road from Exon' named; gate across road to Creely; buildings in elevation; peripheral owners named and boundaries between their lands at the edge of Creely Barton indicated by an arrow at right angles; fields forming 'Part of Mary Clist P'ish' named

DECORATION: title inscribed on yellow ribbon; arms of King's College in black, blue and red embellished by crudely-drawn acanthus leaves coloured yellow with shell at top; 8 point compass rose, blue/red, blue centre; north marked by yellow fleur-de-lys

ENDORSEMENT: St James's Priory Estate called Creely by No Thomas 1714

6/1/2

FARRINGDON
1798   Z17/3/7

See entry under Dunsford, 4/13/5

In this leather-bound volume of estate maps map number 8 of Hobshayes in Farringdon Parish is missing, although referred to

6/1/3

FARRINGDON
1802   5292F/A53(MAP 2)

Spain Farm SY 004926

TITLE: 'Map of a Tenement called Potter's Charity in Farringdon. Devon.'

SURVEYOR: 'J. Coldridge 1802'

SCALE: 'Scale of Chains containing 66 Feet each'; scale bar; 1"=1.5 chains; 1:1188

MATERIAL, SIZE & ORIENTATION: parchment, coloured; approx. 48.5cms EW x 38cms NS [bound into volume and folded]; north to top

CONTENT: pond, grey; fields outlined in grey, with field names; alpha-numeric reference to table giving field names, content of arable, waste, hedges and total content; gates; tree symbols showing orchards; roads, buff; direction given; footpaths, buff, pecked lines; buildings in plan, red; peripheral parish [Honiton Clyst], owners and estates named

DECORATION: title cartouche: view of castle, river, mountains and trees, black/yellow [connection with Farringdon not obvious]; 8 point compass rose, grey/black; north marked by fleur-de-lys and east by symbol

ASSOCIATED DOCUMENT: in the accounts section of the same volume is the record of the payment to J. Coldridge for surveying and mapping the Farringdon Estate, £1. 5s 6½d, 7 July 1802

6/1/4

FARRINGDON
1814   50/3/1/3

Creely Barton SY 002905

TITLE: 'Sketch of the Estate of Creely Barton the Property of Mrs Hawtrey 1814'

SURVEYOR: not named

SCALE: not given

MATERIAL, SIZE & ORIENTATION: paper, ink; 56.5cms x 43.6cms; no direction

CONTENT: fields outlined in ink, some shaded grey, with field names and alpha-numeric reference [to Survey Book]; tree symbols showing orchards and isolated trees; tree symbols with stippling marking coppice; roads, directions given; footpaths, pecked lines; buildings in plan, black; peripheral owners named

FARRINGDON see also C71–72

6/2/1

FARWAY
1728   1585F/19/1

Radish Plantantion SY 181918
See entry under Branscombe, 2/26/1

6/2/2

FARWAY
1781   281M/E5

Farway Church SY 182957
See entry under Colyton, 3/27/7

6/2/3

FARWAY
*c.*1820   SRO DD/WY/Box 121

Widcombe Barton SY 183948
TITLE: 'Widcombe, Cotshay, Idehill and Lambrook; Estates in Farway, Devon'
SURVEYOR: not named
SCALE: 'Scale Chains'; scale bar; 1"=6 chains; 1:4752
MATERIAL, SIZE & ORIENTATION: paper, coloured; 52.2cms EW x 41.2cms NS; north to top
CONTENT: river, spring, blue; fields in various colours, with numeric reference [to table]; tree symbols showing woods; roads, buff, directions given; footpaths, pecked lines; buildings in plan, red or black; peripheral owners named
Inset: Cotshay which is detached
DECORATION: 4 point compass indicator; north marked by an arrow

6/2/4

FARWAY
1826   5556Z/ME1

NORTHLEIGH/OFFWELL/SOUTHLEIGH/WIDWORTHY
Farway Church SY 182957 Offwell Church SY 195996 Northleigh Church SY 196959
Southleigh Church SY 204934 Widworthy Church SY 213993
Leather-bound volume, 25cms x 30cms, has general map followed by 29 maps and accompanying tables, index, abstract and summary
TITLE: 'Maps and Particulars of Lands situate in the Parishes of Farway, Offwell, Widworthy, Northleigh and Southleigh in the County of Devon Property of Sir John Prideaux Bart. 1826'
SURVEYOR: 'G.A. Boyce Tiverton 1826'
General Map: Title and surveyor as above
SCALE: 'Scale'; scale bar; 1"=16 chains; 1:12672
MATERIAL, SIZE & ORIENTATION: parchment, coloured; 46.3cms EW x 44.8cms NS; north to top
CONTENT: streams, ponds, form lines, black; fields, 'those held in fee are full coloured [and] those of which Sir J.W. Prideaux holds an undivided Portion are outlined only'; other fields, plain; tree symbols showing ?orchard or coppice; stippling marking downs; roads, fenced and unfenced, directions given; buildings in plan, black; churches in elevation; peripheral owners named
DECORATION: 8 point compass rose, shaded lines; north marked by fleur-de-lys; names in variety of scripts
INDIVIDUAL MAPS: – Farway, 18maps; Offwell, 3 maps; Widworthy, 2 maps; Northleigh 5 maps; Southleigh, 1 map
SCALE: variable between 1"=3 chains, 1:2376 and 1"=16 chains, 1:12672
GENERAL CONTENT: streams, ponds; fields outlined with hedge symbols; alpha-numeric reference to table on preceding page giving field names, land use and content; parallel lines indicating arable; tree symbols showing orchard and coppice; gardens including walled garden at Netherton Barton in Farway; roads, fenced and unfenced; peripheral owners named

6/3/1

FENITON
1770 [later copy]   1324A/PF4

Feniton Church SY 108994
TITLE: 'A Survey of the Mannor of Feniton in the Year 1770'
SURVEYOR: not named

SCALE: not given

MATERIAL, SIZE & ORIENTATION: paper [torn], watermark 1814, ink; 31.9cms EW x 20.2cms NS; north to top

CONTENT: 'River Otter' and leat; fields, some named with owners; numeric reference to table giving field names and content; roads, directions given; mills; 'scool of Broadhembury'

ASSOCIATED DOCUMENTS: relate to Burrough's gift. The Reverend John Burrough gave £40 in his Will for the support of a schoolmaster and his executors purchased an acre of ground in the parish of Feniton

6/3/2

FENITON
| 1795 | 961M/E25, E26 |

Escot House SY 082981

TITLE: 'A Plan of Roads at Escot for Sir John Kennaway Bart. Septr 21st 1795'

SURVEYOR: not named; [John Veitch]

SCALE: 'A Scale of Ten Chains being a Furlong'; scale bar; 1"= 3 chains; 1:2376

MATERIAL, SIZE & ORIENTATION: paper, slight colour; 109.5cms x 54.5cms; no direction

CONTENT: roads, yellow and green; various points referred by letter to statement giving measurements and perceived advantages of new road; principal features on either side of the road distinguished by name; Escot House, Fair Mile Inn and Talaton Farm House in plan, hatched black

ENDORSEMENT: Vetchs plan for turning Talaton Road 1790–1800

NOTE: 961M/E26 is a copy of 961M/E25 with slight differences. Roads are coloured yellow and grey

ENDORSEMENT: Talaton Roads by Great Copse etc

PUBLICATION: Todd Gray *The Garden History of Devon* (Exeter, 1995), 99

6/3/3

FENITON
| 1823/5 | 961M add/M/E2 |

Escot House SY 082981

Leather-covered volume tooled in gold, 26.7cms x 37.5cms, with Escot bookplate

TITLE: 'Plans of Manors and Lands in the County of Devon The Property of Sir John Kennaway Bart Robert Dymond Land Surveyor, Exeter. 1825'

SURVEYOR: pencil annotation on page 13 dated July 23 1845 'From the commencement of the Book to this page inclusive the maps were made by Tozer – Marldon – p.14 (lands in Sidmouth) by Coldridge – the remr by Dymond to p.42 inclusive'

SCALE: General Index listing 42 maps preceded by 'A Map of the Country on a Scale of One Inch to a Mile'; this was taken from the O.S. map of 1809 with additional features named and areas belonging to the estate coloured green.' 'Scale of Two Miles'; 1"=1 mile; 1:63360; this map signed by C. Tozer

MATERIAL, SIZE & ORIENTATION: paper, coloured; single page for each map; no direction indicated but arrow pointing to top on title page

MAPS 1–13

These maps cover the areas around Escot, Talaton and the Manor of Tale in the Parish of Payhembury.

CONTENT: rivers, leats, ponds, blue; arrows indicating direction of flow; weir; fields outlined in various colours, some with hedge symbols; numeric reference to table on opposite page giving field names and content; asterisks indicating hedge ownership; gateways; moors and commons, plain with ink stippling; tree symbols showing orchards; woods and coppices stippled in 3 shades of green; roads, directions given; footpaths, pecked lines; buildings in plan, red; peripheral parishes named

Pencil construction grid

MAP 14

Lands in Sidmouth

SURVEYOR: [J or S] Coldridge

SCALE: 'Scale of Chains containing 66 Feet each'; scale bar; 1"=4 chains; 1:3168

MATERIAL etc as above

CONTENT: Sidmouth beach named; stream lines indicating sea; stream, blue; fields in various colours, some named; alphabetic reference to table on opposite page giving owners' names with their holding and its content; gates; gardens; other landowners named; roads, footpaths, pecked lines; tree symbols showing isolated trees; buildings in plan, grey; peripheral owners named

| MAPS 15–42 | [Maps 35–42 dated 1825] |

These maps cover areas around Straightgate (dated 1823), Mount Olditch, Lands in the Parish of Whimple and the Parish of Ottery St Mary

SURVEYOR: maps signed individually by 'Robert Dymond, Land Surveyor Exeter 1823' and '1825'

SCALE: 'Scale of Chains'; scale bar; variable scales, between 1"=2 chains and 1"=9 chains; 1:1584 and 1:7128

MATERIAL etc as above

CONTENT: pond, blue; fields outlined in colour; alpha-numeric reference to table on opposite page giving landholders' names, field names, 'Clear Content', 'Hedges & Ditches', 'Total Content'; tree symbols showing orchards; roads, buff, fenced and unfenced; directions given; buildings in plan, black/pink; peripheral owners named

Map 32 in rough plan only on a separate sheet

FENITON see also SUPPLEMENT S2

6/4/1

FILLEIGH
late 18th cent.   1262M/E22/5

Castle Hill SS 673284

TITLE: not given [shows Castle Hill mansion, grounds and estate]

SURVEYOR: not named [Robert Ballment]

SCALE: no unit of measurement stated; scale bar; 1"=2.5 ?chains; 1:1980

MATERIAL, SIZE & ORIENTATION: paper, ink, repaired; irregular shape, c.177cms x 112cms; no direction

CONTENT: river, ponds; fields, named with content, 2 figures given inclusive and exclusive of hedges and waste; some land use indicated; numeric reference [to Survey Book]; gates; farmyard, kitchen gardens and courtlages; tree symbols showing ornamental avenues, grouped plantings, isolated trees; with stippling marking woods and plantations; roads, bridge; footpaths, pecked lines; buildings in plan including a 'Menagery' and 'Castle'

Pencil construction grid

NOTE: the impression given by this map is of a plan for the development of a landscaped estate

PUBLICATIONS: Hugh Fortescue, *A Chronicle of Castle Hill 1454–1918* (Privately printed, 1929), mentions a map of 1763 but this map appears to be later; Todd Gray, *The Garden History of Devon* (Exeter, 1995) shows a portion of the map on page 24

6/4/2

FILLEIGH
18th cent.   1262M/E22/3

Heddon SS 648287

TITLE: not given [area surrounding Heddon and Broompark]

SURVEYOR: not named [same hand as 1262M/E22/27]

SCALE: no unit of measurement stated; 1"=3.5 ?chains; 1:2772

MATERIAL, SIZE & ORIENTATION: paper, badly damaged, slight colour; c.87.5cms x 83.5cms; no direction

CONTENT: fields, some outlined in colour; named with content; alpha-numeric reference [to Survey Book]; asterisks indicating hedge ownership; gates; courtlages and gardens; stippled areas named 'Alders, Orchards, Timber, Coppice'; quarry; roads; buildings in plan, grey; peripheral owners and parishes named

6/4/3

FILLEIGH
18th cent.   1262M/E22/4

Heddon SS 648287

TITLE: not given [area near to and south-east of Heddon]

SURVEYOR: not named

SCALE: not given

MATERIAL, SIZE & ORIENTATION: paper, ink; 72.3cms x 82.5cms; no direction

CONTENT: fields, named, some with occupiers' names; gates; glebe; roads, directions given; buildings in elevation

6/4/4

FILLEIGH
1810   1262M/E1/42

Filleigh Church SS 663280

TITLE: 'A Plan of the Poor Houses Built by the Right Honble Earl Fortescue in the Year 1809. – with the Garden Ground allotted to the same, taken ye 19th March 1810 by Robt Ballment'

SURVEYOR: Robert Ballment

SCALE: 'A Scale of Chains each containing Four Statute Perches'; scale bar; 1"=1 chain; 1:792

MATERIAL, SIZE & ORIENTATION: paper, ink; 26.6cms EW x 35.3cms NS; true and magnetic south marked; north to top

CONTENT: fields, gardens and houses outlined in solid and dotted ink lines, with numeric reference [to Survey Book] and with some field names; roads, directions given

ENDORSEMENT: A Plan of the Out Barton Poor Houses and Gardens

6/5/1

FREMINGTON
1776   NDRO 1142B/EP15

Bickington SS 535325

TITLE: 'Plan of an Estate in Bickington called Monjoy Tenement in the Parish of Fremington'

SURVEYOR: John Tamlyn

SCALE: no unit of measurement indicated; scale bar; 1"=3 ?chains; 1:2376

MATERIAL, SIZE & ORIENTATION: paper, mounted on linen, coloured; 62.2cms EW x 48.4cms NS; north to top

CONTENT: fields outlined in colour and lighter wash of green or yellow, named; alphabetic reference to table giving content; asterisks indicating hedge ownership; gardens and courtlages; tree symbols on field boundaries; roads, buff; directions given; buildings in plan, hatched

DECORATION: 32 point compass rose, ink shading; triple outer circle; north marked by fleur-de-lys, east by bar

ENDORSEMENT: June 7th 1776 Plan of an Estate in Bickington called Monjoys Tenement in the Parish of Fremington

6/5/2

FREMINGTON
1779/1822   NDRO TD146/E1

Fremington Church SS 512326
See entry under Barnstaple, 2/2/4

6/5/3

FREMINGTON
1784   NDRO B1 A 11A

Bickington SS 535325

TITLE: 'Survey of Collibears' Tenement together with Brownings Close & Muddle Bridge Field all lying in or near Bickington within the Parish of Fremington in the County of Devon belonging to Mr John Thorn A:D: 1784'

SURVEYOR: not named

SCALE: 'Scale of Chains'; scale bar; 1"=3 chains; 1:2376

MATERIAL, SIZE & ORIENTATION: parchment, coloured; 70cms EW x 59.8cms NS; north to top

CONTENT: river, stream lines; arrows indicating direction of flow; Muddle Bridge and Quay named; fields outlined in colour, named; contents listed in table; crosses indicating hedge ownership; gates, red; roads, green margins; directions given; buildings in plan, keyed by letter to list headed 'Houses'; peripheral owners named

INSET: maps of Muddle Bridge and Brownings Close

DECORATION: title, scale, insets and tables enclosed in triple-lined rectangular panel; 16 point compass rose, plain/red; triple outer circle; north marked by fleur-de-lys

6/5/4

FREMINGTON
1791   NDRO 1142B/EP16

Fremington Church SS 512326

TITLE: 'A Field Map or Plan of an Estate in the Parish of Frimengton [sic] and County of Devon called Giless the Land of Mr Henry Drake taken ye 29th of March 1791 by Robt Ballment'

SURVEYOR: Robert Ballment

SCALE: no unit of measurement stated; 2 lines of figures to be read from opposite sides of the map

MATERIAL, SIZE & ORIENTATION: paper, ink; 42.7cms x 96.5cms; no direction

CONTENT: fields named with content; alpha-numeric reference to table giving names of fields or parcels, land use and content; asterisks indicating hedge ownership; roads named; footpaths, pecked lines; houses in elevation; peripheral owners named

6/5/5

FREMINGTON
1798   4163M/E1

Fremington Church SS 512336
See entry under Alverdiscott, 1/5/2

6/5/6

FREMINGTON
1798   NDRO B354 add3/2

Fremington Church SS 512336
TITLE: 'A Map of East-Hayes in the Parish of Firmington (sic) and County
    of Devon'
SURVEYOR: 'Survey'd, 1798 By David Palmer'
SCALE: 'A Scale of Statute Chains'; scale bar; 1"=3.5 chains; 1:2772
MATERIAL, SIZE & ORIENTATION: parchment, coloured; 60.7cms EW x
    70.9cms NS; north to top
CONTENT: fields outlined in various colours with numeric reference to
    'Referential Table' giving field names and content, arranged under
    tenement; asterisks indicating boundary ownership; black tree sym-
    bols showing orchard and coppice; stippling marking moor; roads.
    plain; buildings in plan, outlined in black; peripheral owners named
DECORATION: title cartouche: tree and fence; 'cross-stitch' effect on some
    lettering; a ?goblet surmounting the 'Referential Table'; 8 point
    compass rose, black lines; north marked by fleur-de-lys

6/5/7

FREMINGTON
1799   NDRO 1142B/EP17

Lower Yelland SS 493322
TITLE: 'A Map of Thomas Treble's Estate in the Village of Yealand in
    Fremington. In this Map it is to be understood that the Names of the
    People written, denotes that such Persons are the Proprietors of such
    Hedges as their Names leads off from – And the Dashes aCross the
    hedge, denotes that it is a such Persons Hedge so far as that Dash and
    no further'
SURVEYOR: not named
SCALE: not given
MATERIAL, SIZE & ORIENTATION: paper, watermark, ink; 38.5cms EW x
    48cms NS; north to top
CONTENT: river, shaded; low water mark; fields outlined with double ink
    line; named; alphabetic reference [to Survey Book]; gates; rough
    tree symbols in named coppice; roads, named; house and garden in
    plan; peripheral owners named
DECORATION: 16 point compass rose; north marked by fleur-de-lys
ENDORSEMENT: Prepared 1799 a 1800

FREMINGTON see also C73

FRITHELSTOCK see C74, C110

7/1/1

GEORGEHAM/MORTEHOE
late 17th cent.   NDRO 3704M/E2/1

Croyde Village SS 445392   Putsborough SS 449403
TITLE: not given
SURVEYOR: not named; [– Cornish]
SCALE: not given
MATERIAL, SIZE & ORIENTATION: parchment, coloured; 43.7cms EW x
    59.4cms NS; west to top
CONTENT: sea, green wave lines; Lanes Well, green; 'Putburroug Sands,
    Wollacomb and Cride Sands' named, buff; high and low water
    marked; cliffs and off-shore rocks in profile, named; 'Isle of Lunday';
    roads, buff, named; 'the Kings High Way', 'the Sea Gate Maytained
    by ye Mannor' with gate symbol across the road; buildings in
    elevation, named; 'Pickwell House, Cride Village, Putsburrough,
    Moorthowe Church, Lime Killn House'; 'Cride Beakon'; parish
    boundaries, some in colour, some pecked lines
DECORATION: 32 point compass rose; north marked by fleur-de-lys, NSEW
    by letter
ASSOCIATED DOCUMENT: An account dated 12 Sept. 1690 of Henry Jones
    to Captain Incledon includes the item 'pd Cornish for culloringe the
    Mapp 1s' [NDRO 3704M/LL8] may relate to this or one of the two
    following maps
PUBLICATION: Mary R Ravenhill and Margery M Rowe, eds, *Early Devon
    Maps* (Exeter, 2000), 24

7/1/2

GEORGEHAM/MORTEHOE
late 17th cent.   NDRO 3704M/E2/2

Croyde Village SS 445392
TITLE: not given
SURVEYOR: not named; [– Cornish]
SCALE: not given

MATERIAL, SIZE & ORIENTATION: parchment, ink and ochre colour; 42.7cms
EW x 53.8cms NS; west to top
CONTENT: sea coast, cliffs marked by cross hatching; 'Baggy Poynt,
Moozt Stone Poynt' named; rocks; 'Lowe watter marke and Sand
ridge' named; 'Lunday' with anchor marking anchorage; 'Lanes
Well'; roads named around Croyde and Putsborough; 'Cride Becon';
buildings crudely drawn, part plan, part elevation; 'Invention House'
named; parish and manor boundaries
DECORATION: 16 point compass rose, elaborately decorated in ochre and
cream; double outer circle; rhumb lines
ENDORSEMENT: the Mapp of cride

7/1/3

GEORGEHAM/MORETHOE

late 17th cent.   NDRO 3704M/E2/3

Croyde Village SS 445392
TITLE: not given [covers area of Croyde, Saunton and Woolacombe]
SURVEYOR: not named; [– Cornish]
SCALE: 'A Scale of One Mile'; scale bar; 1"=½ mile; 1:15840
MATERIAL, SIZE & ORIENTATION: paper, coloured; 48cms EW x 61.8cms
NS; west to top
CONTENT: sea, blue; 'Saunton, Cryde, Pickwell and Wollacoombe Sands',
yellow; low water mark; cliffs, dark grey with cross hatching; rocks,
black; 'Lundy Isle' and anchorage marked; roads, named; 'Manor
Gate' across the 'Highway to the Lands'; 'Cryde' Beacon; houses in
detailed elevation drawn on opposing horizons, varying in size;
bartons and manors named, black; parishes named, red; lands of the
plaintiff, Mr Webber, named; shown with wide bands of colour, blue
and red on south, light and dark blue on north
DECORATION: two 32 point compass roses, red; 4 concentric circles; north
marked by fleur-de-lys, east by arrowhead, NSEW by letter; rhumb
lines

7/1/4

GEORGEHAM

1779   NDRO TD/146/E1

Darracott SS 472392
See entry under Barnstaple, 2/2/4

7/1/5

GEORGEHAM

1818   NDRO 1142B/WP23

Georgeham Church SS 465399
TITLE: 'A Map of Several Estates called Darracott's consisting of
Clement's late Rudd's, Edulph's late Ward's, and Dean's late Rudd's,
with Crowbury all situate in the Parish of Georgeham in the County
of Devon The Land of Robert Hole Esquire 1818'
SURVEYOR: 'By Thomas Shearm, Land & Timber Surveyor, Stratton,
Cornwall'
SCALE: 'Scale of Chains, 22 Yards each'; scale bar; 1"=4 chains; 1:3168
MATERIAL, SIZE & ORIENTATION: parchment, coloured; 67.5cms EW x
77.5cms NS; north to top
CONTENT: watercourse, blue; relief shown by hill shading; fields,
coloured, named; hedge symbols indicating ownership; numeric
reference to lists repeating field names with content, grouped by
landholding and tenant; colour reference to that used on map and to
'Explanation'; gates; tree symbols showing woods and orchards;
roads, buff, fenced and unfenced; directions given; houses in plan,
red; other buildings black; land belonging to schools named; peripheral owners named
DECORATION: 8 point compass rose, plain/black; north marked by fleur-
de-lys, double outer circle

7/1/6

GEORGEHAM

1833   1262M/E22/33

Pickwell SS 456410
TITLE: 'Map of Pickwell Barton in the Parish of Georgeham in the County
of Devon the property of the Right Honble Earl Fortescue. 1833'
SURVEYOR: 'Robert Bowman Landsurveyor'
SCALE: 'Statute Chains'; scale bar; 1"=6 chains; 1:4752
MATERIAL, SIZE & ORIENTATION: paper, mounted on linen, slight colour;
64.6cms EW x 82.5cms NS; east to top
CONTENT: stream, pond, blue; fields outlined in black and blue, note that
'The Black line represents the Ditch and the Blue line shade the
Fence'; arable land, parallel stippled lines; stippled fields indicate
meadow; numeric reference to table giving field names and content;
tree symbols showing orchards, plantations and woods; gardens;
roads, directions given; footpaths, bridle paths pricked lines; buildings
in plan, red; quarries; lime kiln; peripheral owners named

DECORATION: title embellished with flourishes; 8 point compass rose, shaded line decoration; north marked by elaborate fleur-de-lys; border: running pattern in blue with flowers and circles

7/2/1

GEORGE NYMPTON
1757   1148M add/6/1

George Nympton Church SS 701229
See entry under Chulmleigh Maps XIV–XVI with terriers, 3/15/2

7/2/2

GEORGE NYMPTON
1774   NDRO B 229/7

George Nympton Church SS 701229
TITLE: 'A Plan of Hayne and Culverhill laying in the Parish of George Nympton in the County of Devon Lands belonging to the Revd Mr Jno Karslake'
SURVEYOR: 'Simon Woolcott Surveyor'
SCALE: 'A Scale of Chains'; scale bar; 1"=3 chains; 1:2376
MATERIAL, SIZE & ORIENTATION: parchment, coloured; 94cms EW x 68.2cms NS; north to top
CONTENT: 'River Hole', brook, pond, blue; arrow indicating direction of flow; fields outlined in green or yellow with colour wash; alphanumeric reference to table giving field names and content; ownership of boundary hedges indicated by letter referring to table; gates; green tree symbols showing orchards and isolated trees; roads, buff; directions given; buildings in plan, grey; Culverhill Court named; peripheral owners named'
DECORATION: title cartouche: rococo, ruched fabric with some stylised leaf forms; scale: rococo, leaf and scroll design with shell at top; 32 point compass rose, pink/plain, yellow/plain; yellow outer circle; north marked by fleur-de-lys, east by cross; wide yellow border

7/2/3

GEORGE NYMPTON
1797   NDRO 2309 add 2

George Nympton Church SS 701229
TITLE: 'A Map of the Manor of Arnold Devon belonging to the Right Honourable Lord Clinton for Explanation see Heanton Map Wm White 1797'
SURVEYOR: William White
SCALE: no unit of measurement stated; scale bar shows chains; 1"=4 chains; 1:3168
MATERIAL, SIZE & ORIENTATION: paper, slight colour; 49.6cms EW x 35.8cms NS; north to top
CONTENT: river, grey margins; arrow indicating direction of flow; fields outlined in colour with hedge symbols; numeric reference to Survey book; fields shaded to show land use [no key]; gates; tree symbols; roads, fenced; footpaths, pecked lines; buildings in plan, black; George Nympton Church in elevation and distances from it of areas mapped indicated
DECORATION: 8 point compass rose; north marked by fleur-de-lys, SEW by letter
ASSOCIATED DOCUMENT: Survey Book of 1793 under same reference

7/3/1

GERMANSWEEK
*c.*1833*   314M/E143

Hennard Jefford SX 429924 (now part of Roadford Reservoir)
TITLE: 'Hennard Gifford and Hennard Village in Germansweek'
SURVEYOR: not named
SCALE: not given
MATERIAL, SIZE & ORIENTATION: paper, slight colour, 52.7cms EW x 44.2cms NS; north to top
CONTENT: streams, including mill stream, blue; fields outlined in various colours with numeric reference to table giving field names, content in statute and customary measure; content of hedges and waste; gates; tree symbols showing orchards; roads, directions given; buildings in plan, various colours; mill; peripheral owners and estates named
DECORATION: 8 point compass indicator, shaded lines; north marked by fleur-de-lys, E by letter

* date taken from DRO catalogue

7/4/1

GIDLEIGH

1639   1306B/EP1

Gidleigh Common SX 650875

TITLE: 'Gidley common taken in a Perambulation 1639'

SURVEYOR: not named

SCALE: not given

MATERIAL, SIZE & ORIENTATION: paper, watermark, ink; 31.7cms x 40.9cms; no direction

CONTENT: 'River Teign', brooks marked; principal features named, 'Brimstone Down, Battary, South Creaber, North Creaber, Thowell moor, Moortown Gate; line of 'suppos'd encroachment'; boundary marks named and distances between them; 'Gidley Church' in elevation

7/4/2

GIDLEIGH

1798   1306B/EP2

Gidleigh Common SX 650875

TITLE: 'A Map of Gidley Commons taken at a Perambulation in Rogation Week 1639'

SURVEYOR: not named

SCALE: 'A Scale' but no unit of measurement stated; scale bar

MATERIAL, SIZE & ORIENTATION: paper, ink; 43.5cms EW x 53.5cms NS; north to top

CONTENT: ink and green line indicating boundary of Common with numbered points referred to a 'Reference List' where boundary stones listed and yards between each noted; some features named 'Brimson Down, Baddery, Scorwell, Southway, Creabeere, North Way, North Creabeere, Thewell Moor, Mooretown Gate, Answorthy'

DECORATION: 4 point compass indicator; north marked by fleur-de-lys

ENDORSEMENT: A True Copy of the Original Drawing made this Tenth Day of August 1798

7/5/1

GITTISHAM

1772   1077 6/15

Deer Park Hotel ST 131001

TITLE: 'A Plan of all that Part of Deerpark-Ham lying within the Parish

of Gittisham in the County of Devon made and taken by us Francis King and James Channon between Thomas Putt and Henry Fry Esqrs shewing their respective Properties in the said Ham in Pursuance of their Agreement; and after two small Plots lying at the eastern end of the said Ham in Buckerel belonging to Sir John Elwill Bart and the said Henry Fry. Witness our Hands the Twenty Ninth Day of September one thousand seven hundred and seventy two'

SURVEYORS:: Francis King and James Channon of Honiton

SCALE: 'A Scale of Chains'; scale bar; 1"=2 chains; 1:1584

MATERIAL, SIZE & ORIENTATION: parchment, coloured; 51.7cms EW x 30.5cms NS; north to top

CONTENT: River Otter named, grey margins; arrows indicating direction of flow; land allotted to Thomas Putt outlined by broad green band; land allotted to Henry Fry outlined by narrow green band; Sir John Elwill's land outlined in yellow; gates; grey tree symbols showing woodland; isolated trees named and where marking parish boundary this is indicated; road leading to 'Deerpark House', fenced and unfenced; boundary between Gittisham and Buckerell parishes clearly defined by named trees and boundary stones

Top right: legal agreement between Thomas Putt and Henry Fry separating and dividing their shares in the property, signed and witnessed

DECORATION: 8 point compass rose, grey/plain; north marked by fleur-de-lys, SEW by letter

7/5/2

GITTISHAM

1780   1508M Devon/Surveys/V4

Gittisham Church SY 134983

See entry under Combe Raleigh, 3/29/1

7/5/3

GITTISHAM

1780   Private hands

Gittisham Church SY 134983

See entry under Honiton, 8/21/4

7/5/4

GITTISHAM
c.1788*   Private hands

Combe House SY 143979

TITLE: 'A Map of Combe Barton, in the Parish of Gittisham, in the County
of Devon; Belonging to the Representatives of Thos Putt Esqr: Decd:
Wm Pearse Surveyor'

SURVEYOR: William Pearse

SCALE: '80 poles 5½ yards each'; scale bar; 1"=16 perches; 1:3168

MATERIAL, SIZE & ORIENTATION: parchment, coloured, framed; 68cms x
90.5cms; south-west to top

CONTENT: river, ponds, buff; shading indicating slopes; fields outlined
in colour, named; parallel lines indicating arable; gates, buff; gardens;
green tree symbols marking orchards, copses, avenues and isolated
trees; roads, fenced and unfenced, directions given; buildings in plan,
grey; quarries (marl pits)

Explanation identifying roads, land use, orchards, copses and
waters

DECORATION: title cartouche: medallion of bead and leaf design
surmounted by urn with festoons of leaves and with rural scene of
cows and sheep below; 32 point compass rose, plain/grey; north
marked by fleur-de-lys, SEW by letter; border: running leaf pattern

INSETS:

a) view of Combe House

b) 'A Plan of Combe House and Gardens'; Scale: 1"=5 poles; 1:985;
shows detailed plan of the gardens – the flower garden, the higher
garden, etc and alphabetical reference to Explanation naming various
features

* Thomas Putt died in 1787

GITTISHAM see also C75–77

8/1/1

HACCOMBE
[*c*.1600]   Private hands

Haccombe House SX 898702

TITLE: not given [shows village of Haccombe and Haccombe House].
This appears to be a 19th century copy of an original map on
parchment, now missing

SURVEYOR: not named

SCALE: not given

MATERIAL, SIZE & ORIENTATION: paper, mounted on silk, coloured; 45.7cms
EW x *c*.69cms NS; directions North, East and West on margins; east
to top

CONTENT: leats, named, irrigation channels, mill pools and fish ponds,
blue; bridges; some indication of relief; fields coloured shades of
green or brown and outlined with green hedge symbols; some fences
in profile; gardens in plan and with parks and meadows, named;
gates; green tree symbols showing orchards, coppice and hedgerow
trees; 'The Coppes' named; roads, buff, named; directions given;
fences and gates across road by 'Hackcombe House'; buildings,
including church, in elevation, red or blue roofs; 'Haccombe House'
with walled courtyard, 'Parsonage House and Haccombe Mill'
named; 2nd mill shown; 'The Village of Hackcombe' named

PUBLICATION: Todd Gray, *The Garden History of Devon* (Exeter, 1995),
23. Detail of map reproduced in Sale Particulars of 1942, claiming
to be a 'facsimile of a very old map on skin'. This is similar to the
map described above but with some additions and omissions. Sale
Particulars are at Z18/64.

8/1/2

HACCOMBE
18th cent.   2723M (B9)

Haccombe House SX 898702

TITLE: not given [relates to lands in disputed ownership]

SURVEYOR: not named

SCALE: 'Scale is 4½ Chains to an Inch'; 1"=4.5 chains; 1:3564

MATERIAL, SIZE & ORIENTATION: paper, coloured; 46.8cms EW x 63.1cms
NS; south to top

CONTENT: estates in different ownerships in various colours, content given
in table; roads, plain or buff; turnpike road from Newton to Torquay;
footpaths, pecked lines; peripheral owners, estates and parishes named

DECORATION: 4 point compass indicator; north marked by fleur-de-lys

NOTE: map is in 2 pieces, with a possible third section missing

8/1/3

HACCOMBE et al.

1808   MFM 35

Estate atlas of Carew family property. The original was sold at the same time as the Manor and Lordship of Haccombe in the 1980s but the Devon Record office had microfilmed it in black and white before the sale. Unfortunately the size was not indicated and therefore the representative fraction could not be computed. There are also some coloured photographic prints in the DRO of portions of the maps. There is an index in the front of the volume to the first 14 maps. J. Coldridge signs some of the maps which are not in the index but the style of all maps in the volume seems similar.

TITLES: follow

SURVEYOR: [assumed to be John Coldridge]

SCALE: 'Scale of Chains'

MATERIAL, SIZE & ORIENTATION: volume with leather covers, not known whether paper or parchment, coloured; size not known; east to top

CONTENT: fields in various colours with alpha-numeric reference to Abstract which is part of the volume; tree symbols showing hedgerows and ?orchards; buildings in plan; peripheral owners named

DECORATION: 4 point compass indicator; north marked by fleur-de-lys

LIST OF MAPS:-

p.21   'Manor of Haccombe in the Parishes of Haccombe and Combe-inteignhead and County of Devon'

p.22   Untitled map but referred to as 'Milbourne Down' in index

p.23   'West a borough, Langs, Gotbeds etc in the Parish of Combein-teignhead'

p.24   'Burts'

p.25 and 26 'Part of the Manor of Webberton in the Parish of Loddiswell'

p.27   Blank

p.28   'A Plan of Shortridges part of the Manor of Tiverton'

p.29   'Lower Knightshayes in the Manor of Tiverton'

p.30   Blank

p.31   'East Bartons part of the Manor of Tiverton' p.32 'A Plan of Wormsland & Maplehold part of the Manor of Tiverton'

p.33   'A Plan of Lower Prescott part of the Manor of Tiverton'

p.34   'A Plan of Yewings or Lower Yerlstone & Lovels & Landbote Lukeslade or Nether Yerlstone Evans's House and fields late the New Inn Motts House and Fields or Old New Inn Cullombs or Dunns Plaistery'

No page references to the following maps:-

'Plan of Gogwell part of the Manor of Tiverton and Higher Rode part of the Manor of Woobournford'

'Plan of Netherford & Hannabuss's'

'Plan of Lower Rode part of the Manor of Woobournford'

'Plan of Clarkes & Moyles part of the Manor of Woobournford'

'Map of Bickleigh Court Barton' signed by J. Coldridge, 1808

'Horethorne, part of the Manor of Bickleigh', signed by J. Coldridge, 1808

'Glebe Clamourcleve part of the Manor of Bickleigh' signed by J. Coldridge, 1808

'Wills's, Two Wells and Well Place, Burnhayes Two Cottages part of the Manor of Bickleigh' signed by J. Coldridge, 1808

'Shotash Little Burn Lower and Higher Brithayes part of the Manor of Bickleigh' signed by J. Coldridge, 1808

'Henbeer and Exland part of the Manor of Bickleigh'

'Tiverton Castle' (not by Coldridge)

Untitled plan of dwelling houses, and cottages etc

HACCOMBE see also C176

8/2/1

HALBERTON

[1603–1608]   6065Z/E1

Waye Mill SS 993090 Moorstone Barton ST 016099

TITLE: not given

SURVEYOR: not named

SCALE: not given

MATERIAL, SIZE & ORIENTATION: paper, mounted on board, 131cms EW x 43.2cms NS; west to top

CONTENT: river rising from 3 springs, green with stream lines; sluices/flood hatches controlling diversions for irrigation, shown diminishing into small ditches; fords and bridges; information as to who was diverting the water and where ; fields and strips coloured in shades of green, marked with lord's, tenants' and field names; tree and hedge symbols; woods named; roads, buff, named; directions given; houses in elevation of various sizes with owners' names; 'Moorston House' within walled enclosure; mill, barn

DECORATION: 32 point compass rose, light and mid green on pink background; NSEW by letter

ASSOCIATED DOCUMENTS: The Manor of Moreston passed to the Wyndham family on the marriage of Sir John Wyndham (d.1574) and Elizabeth Sydenham. The map appears to be contemporary with a Chancery

Case, John Wyndham versus Abraham Turner concerning the manor of 'Mourston', Devon and the diversion of a watercourse and which dates from 1603–1608. Depositions in the case, which are in the Somerset Record office (ref. DD/WY/22/1), mention the three springs or heads of water, the path from Pitt Wood and Waye Mill and Ford House, all of which are visible on the map. A later record in the same office (ref. DD/WY Box 22/3) relating to a case between Sir John Wyndham v John Harris mentions 'taking away the earth of a certain bank of the said Sir John Wyndham of the ancient leat part of Moorstone Barton and the close called Camplehays'. Harris promises to repair the banks and fill up the undermined trench with earth, January 1617/18.

The map was formerly in Taunton Museum, see *DCNQ* XVII, No.200 (1932–3), but was presented to Exeter City Library by Mr Wyndham in May 1934.

PUBLICATION: Mary R Ravenhill and Margery M Rowe, eds, *Early Devon Maps* (Exeter, 2000), 28

8/2/2

HALBERTON
1739 or earlier   ECA Book 58

Sellake ST 003141
See entry under Exeter Chamber Map Book, 5/3/50

8/2/3

HALBERTON
1788–1789   6107

Halberton Church ST 006129
See entry under Bridestowe, 2/35/6

8/2/4

HALBERTON
1812   50/7/1/7a

Canal Bridge at Halberton ST 011131
TITLE: not given
SURVEYOR: not named
SCALE: not given

MATERIAL, SIZE & ORIENTATION: paper, ink, slight colour; 32.2cms EW x 29cms NS; north to top
CONTENT: line of Grand Western Canal shown by broken red lines and grey margins; bridge; fields named with content; owners identified; road; proposed new road crossing canal, broken line, red
DECORATION: 4 point compass indicator; north marked by symbol
ASSOCIATED DOCUMENTS: 50/7/1/7b,c details, exchange of land between the owners, Charles Chichester and Henry Cook and the Grand Western Canal Company

8/2/5

HALBERTON
1813   2062B/T15

Greenway Bridge ST 008132
TITLE: not given [shows area north of Halberton and proposed route of Great Western Canal]
SURVEYOR: not named
SCALE: not given
MATERIAL, SIZE & ORIENTATION: parchment, coloured; 15.5cms EW x 16.8cms NS; north to top
CONTENT: 3 fields outlined in ink, coloured blue or buff; named with content; some adjoining fields named; owners also named; roads, directions given; proposed route of canal, broken lines with new bridge shown
DECORATION: 4 point compass indicator; north marked by symbol, SEW by letter
ASSOCIATED DOCUMENT: plan forms part of Conveyance from Thomas Babb, yeoman of Washfield to Henry Skinner of Cullompton

8/2/6

HALBERTON
1814   2062B/T19

Canal SS 996139
TITLE: not given [shows area north of Halberton and proposed route of Great Western Canal]
SURVEYOR: not named
SCALE: not given
MATERIAL, SIZE & ORIENTATION: parchment, slight colour; 22.4cms x 25.5cms; north-west to top

CONTENT: fields outlined in ink, named and numbered; owners of adjoining fields named; one field coloured and parts of others where canal to be constructed also coloured, all with content; road, directions given; proposed route of canal, broken lines

DECORATION: 4 point compass indicator; north marked by symbol, SEW by letter

ASSOCIATED DOCUMENT: plan forms part of Conveyance from Samuel Archer to Henry Skinner of Cullompton

8/2/7

HALBERTON
1814   Bristol RO, DC/E/12/7

Halberton Church ST 006129

TITLE: 'A Reduced Plan of the Parish of Halberton in the County of Devon'

SURVEYOR: 'Richard King Finnimore, Surveyor, Halberton'

SCALE: 'Scale of Chains'; scale bar; 1"=8 chains; 1:6336

MATERIAL, SIZE & ORIENTATION: paper, coloured; 185.8cms EW x 98.5cms NS (on rollers); north to top

CONTENT: rivers, blue; ponds, black lines; relief shown by hill shading; fields, various shades of green with numeric reference to survey giving names of proprietors and occupiers, premises, 'quality' (land use), acreage in statute measure and key to colour for land use; hedge symbols indicating ownership; green tree symbols showing orchards and woods; roads, buff, some directions given; buildings in plan, black; peripheral parishes named

INSETS: 'Tythings of Chief Loman' and 'Burliscombe and Sampford Tything'

DECORATION: 8 point compass rose, black/grey; north marked by fleur-de-lys, SEW by letter

ASSOCIATED DOCUMENT: survey (DC/E/12/8)

8/2/8

HALBERTON
1815   2062B/T22

Area not identified

TITLE: not given [2 small maps of proposed route of Great Western Canal]

SURVEYOR: not named

SCALE: not given

MATERIAL, SIZE & ORIENTATION: parchment, slight colour; map 1: 13cms EW x 13.5cms NS; north to top; map 2: 13.2cms x 26cms; north-west to top

CONTENT: fields, some pink with content; other fields plain and with the fields adjoining owners' names given; proposed route of canal, broken line; roads, plain; proposed new road, pink; directions given

DECORATION: 4 point compass indicators [3]; north marked by arrowheads, SEW by letter

ASSOCIATED DOCUMENT: plans form part of Conveyance from Christopher Laroche to Henry Skinner of Cullompton

8/2/9

HALBERTON
1815   2062B/T26

Greenway bridge ST 008132

TITLE: not given

SURVEYOR: not named

SCALE: not given

MATERIAL, SIZE & ORIENTATION: parchment, slight colour; 16.9cms EW x 18.6cms NS; north to top

CONTENT: proposed canal in outline; fields outlined in ink with field names and tithe map references added later in pencil; plots to be conveyed marked in red with content given; roads, directions given; peripheral owners named

DECORATION: 4 point compass indicator; north marked by symbol, SEW by letter

ASSOCIATED DOCUMENT: plan is part of Conveyance of strips of land by Thomas Babb, yeoman, to Grand Western Canal Company, dated 24 June 1815

NOTE: see also 2062B/T15

8/2/10

HALBERTON
1817   2062B/T29

Greenway Bridge ST 008132

TITLE: not given

SURVEYOR: not named

SCALE: not given

MATERIAL, SIZE & ORIENTATION: parchment, slight colour; 17.3cms EW x 19.1cms NS; north to top

CONTENT: field in outline, with 2 plots to be conveyed for making the canal and towpaths coloured red; road from Tiverton to Wellington

DECORATION: 4 point compass indicator; north marked by arrow, SEW by letter

ASSOCIATED DOCUMENT: plan is part of Conveyance of land by Francis Cowler Wood to Grand Western Canal Company dated 21 October 1817

8/2/11

HALBERTON
1821   SRO DD/WY/(Devon Maps)

Moorstone Barton ST 016099
See entry under Burlescombe, 2/51/4

8/2/12

HALBERTON
1839   50/7/1/16

Battens Farm ST 025134

TITLE: 'Map of an Estate called Battens in the Parish of Halberton Devon 1839'

SURVEYOR: 'T. Parker Land Surveyor, Willand, Devon'

SCALE: no unit of measurement stated; scale bar; 1"= ?3 chains; 1:?2376

MATERIAL, SIZE & ORIENTATION: paper, ink, slight colour; 57.5cms EW x 36cms NS; north to top

CONTENT: ponds, canal, blue; bridge; towpath; fields outlined in ink and some hedge symbols; numeric reference [to Survey Book]; gates; tree symbols showing ?orchards; roads; footpaths, pecked lines; buildings in plan, red or grey

DECORATION: 4 point compass indicator; north marked by arrowhead

8/2/13

HALBERTON
19th cent.   SRO DD/SAS/C1540

Whitedown Cross SS 982102   12, part 2 of 2
TITLE: not given [Whitedown]
SURVEYOR: not named
SCALE: not given

MATERIAL, SIZE & ORIENTATION: paper, mounted on linen, ink; 38.2cms EW x 47.5cms NS; north to top

CONTENT: fields outlined in ink, some with content; asterisks indicating fence ownership; roads, directions given; footpaths, pecked lines; note of Bampton and Halberton Highways

NOTE: by John Webber that he has examined the plans and approves of the allotments as they are delineated; some owners' names added later in pencil

DECORATION: 4 point compass indicator; north marked by an arrow

8/2/14

HALBERTON
19th cent.   50/3/1/2

Selgars Mill ST 052116
TITLE: 'Halberton and Willand Inclosure Plan of Commons'
SURVEYOR: not named
SCALE: 'Scale of Chains'; scale bar; 1"=4 chains; 1:3168

MATERIAL, SIZE & ORIENTATION: paper, watermark 1832, ink, slight colour; 75.7cms x 49.4cms; north-west to top

CONTENT: stream and mill pool, blue; allotments outlined in ink with new owners' names or Lot numbers; numeric reference, red, in some allotments [to Survey Book]; roads, some named; directions given; new roads, red, distances indicated; quarries; buildings in plan, hatched black, named

INSET: allotment at Dean Hill

DECORATION: 8 point compass rose; north marked by diamond symbol

NOTE: 'I have examined this plan and approve of the allotments as they are here delineated John Webber'

ENDORSEMENT: Halberton and Willand Commons

HALBERTON see also C78

HALWELL see C113

8/3/1

HALWILL
1788–1789   6107

Halwill Church SX 427994
See entry under Bridestowe, 2/35/6

8/4/1

HARBERTON
1786–1808   Z17/3/20–21

Harberton Church SX 778587
See entry under Ashburton, 1/8/2

8/4/2

HARBERTON
1800   118M/F3

Harberton Church SX 778587
See entry under Ashprington, 1/10/3

8/4/3

HARBERTON
early 19th cent.   1352A/PFB20

Peak Cross SX 789591
TITLE: 'A Plan and Measurement of the Road leading from Follaton
    Cross to Peak Cross in the Parishes of Totnes and Harberton Devon.
    by J Foster'
SURVEYOR: James Foster
SCALE: not given
MATERIAL, SIZE & ORIENTATION: paper, mounted on linen, slight colour;
    27.3cms x 21.8cms; no direction
CONTENT: roads, buff and outlined in dark green; directions given and
    numeric references to stretches of road; list of those responsible for
    the repair of sections of the road
ENDORSEMENT: The Vicar of Harberton. Found among the Chancellors
    papers with accompanying document of Alteration before the Justices
    of the Peace in Exeter 1824
ASSOCIATED DOCUMENT: Order of Quarter Sessions dated 15 June 1824

as to the division for the repair of the road by the Parishes of Harberton
and Totnes in Jackmans Lane

8/4/4

HARBERTON
1817   Ex. D&C Ch. Comm. 98/8791

Harberton Church SX 778587
See entry under Aylesbeare, 1/18/2

HARBERTON see also C79

8/5/1

HARFORD
[1794]   51/7/7/2

See entry under Dartmoor, 4/3/5

8/5/2

HARFORD
c.1800   PWDRO 1403/28

Harford Church SX 638595
TITLE: not given
SURVEYOR: not named
SCALE: not given
MATERIAL, SIZE & ORIENTATION: paper, backed with linen and repaired;
    slight colour; 222cms x 52.3cms; no direction
CONTENT: 'River Erme', Henglake', 'mouth of Knocking Hill Lake',
    'Dry Lake or Thorn Lake', 'Black Pool' all named; 'Ugborough Moor
    or Langford Leister', 'Cornwood Moor', 'East Harford Moor',
    'Forest of Dartmoor', 'Brent Moor', 'Detached part of Ugborough
    Moor', all named; bound stones; Peter's Cross alias Wester Whit-
    borough marked by a cross; 'Erm Pound'; gates; roads, unfenced,
    buff; some directions given; footpaths, single lines in various colours;
    Harford Church and Parsonage in elevation; sites of ruined houses
    marked; peripheral estates named
NOTE: because of the prominence of East Harford Moor on the map, it
    may date from 1794 (see document of that date filed under Dartmoor).

8/6/1

HARPFORD

1763   96M/Box 18/1&2

Harpford Wood SY 100903

TITLE: 'Three Plots of coppice, parts of Harpford Wood Map'd 15th sepr 1763'

SURVEYOR: not named

SCALE: not given

MATERIAL, SIZE & ORIENTATION: paper, ink; 40.2cms x 32cms; no direction

CONTENT: 3 areas outlined in ink; named and with content

8/6/2

HARPFORD

1765   96M/Box 18/1&2

Harpford Wood SY 100903

TITLE: 'A Plot of Coppice at the West-end of Hill-Close Ball in Harpford Wood containing 25A:2R:8P Statute measure Map'd ye 25th April 1765'

SURVEYOR: not named

SCALE: not given

MATERIAL, SIZE & ORIENTATION: paper, ink; 40.4cms EW x 32.4cms NS; north to top

CONTENT: river, stream lines; bridge; one area outlined in ink with hedge indicated; gate; footpath, pecked lines

8/7/1

HARTLAND

early 18th cent.   Private hands

Hartland Abbey SS 241248

TITLE:

SURVEYOR:

SCALE:

MATERIAL, SIZE & ORIENTATION: parchment, coloured; approx. 91.5cms x 91.5cms (framed); probably east to top

CONTENT: fields, diagrammatic, named with content and those 'in hand' noted; formal gardens in detail; tree symbols showing orchards and isolated trees; house in elevation

NOTE: dated from the reconstruction of the Abbey and grounds

undertaken by Paul Orchard who married Mary Luttrell the Abbey estate's heiress

Information from *Hartland Abbey circa 1157* Guide Book

8/7/2

HARTLAND

1779/1822   NDRO TD/146/E1

Titchbury SS 244270 Hartland Church SS 235247

See entry under Barnstaple, 2/2/4

8/7/3

HARTLAND

1783/1794   NDRO B170/180RT

Galsham SS 245227

TITLE: 'A Map or Plan of the Estates called Callsham and Greenleek situate in the Parish of Hartland in the County of Devon the Lands of Mrs Anne Hamlyn Widow Survey'd and Plann'd in 1783 by Mr William Harris and Mapp'd in 1794 by Robert Ballment'

SURVEYORS:: William Harris and Robert Ballment

SCALE: 'A Scale of Chains each containing Four Statute Perches'; scale bar; 1"=2 chains; 1:1584

MATERIAL, SIZE & ORIENTATION: parchment, coloured; 88cms EW x 66cms NS; north to top

CONTENT: river, grey/bue; arrows marking direction of flow; fields outlined in green or yellow; where named are owned by others; alpha-numeric reference [to survey Book]; 'asterisms' indicating hedge ownership; gates; tree symbols; roads, buff, fenced and unfenced; directions given; lanes narrower; footpaths, pecked lines; buildings in plan, pink, outlined in red; peripheral owners named

DECORATION: 8 point compass rose, plain/shaded grey; north marked by fleur-de-lys, east by cross

8/7/4

HARTLAND

1796   LMA 1876/MP/06/05a

Baxworthy Corner SS 284223 Staddon SS 268221

TITLE: 'A Map of two Estates called Baxworthy and Staddon in the

Parish of Hartland in the County of Devon the Property of the Right Honourable the Governors of the Charterhouse Surveyed and Delineated by John Prickett of Highgate Middlesex 1796'

SURVEYOR: John Prickett

SCALE: 'Poles'; scale bar; 1"=16 poles; 1:3168

MATERIAL, SIZE & ORIENTATION: parchment, coloured; 84.8cms EW x 58.9cms NS; north to top

CONTENT: river, blue; fields outlined in turquoise (Baxworthy) or green (Staddon) with hedgerow symbols; some fields with brown parallel lines; numeric reference to list giving field names and content; green or turquoise tree symbols marking isolated trees; garden, yellow; roads, buff, directions given; buildings in plan, grey or pink; peripheral owners, tenants and estates named

DECORATION: 16 point compass rose, grey; north marked by fleur-de-lys

8/7/5

HARTLAND
1796   LMA 1876/MP/06/05b

Milford SS 233226

TITLE: 'A Map of and Estate called Millford in the Parish of Hartland in the County of Devon the Property of the Right Honourable the Governors of the Charter House Surveyed and Delineated by John Prickett of Highgate Middlesex 1796'

SURVEYOR: John Prickett

SCALE: 'Poles'; scale bar; 1"=16 poles; 1:3168

MATERIAL, SIZE & ORIENTATION: parchment, coloured; 50.9cms EW x 73.4cms NS; north to top

CONTENT: 'The Sea', blue with coastline marked in a deeper blue; streams, blue; cascade; bridges; fields, green, some with brown parallel lines showning cultivation; numeric reference to table giving field names and content; green hedge symbols indicating ownership; garden; green tree symbols marking ?coppice; 'The Green'; roads, buff, some directions given; a sand road, buff; 'A Mill'; buildings in plan, red or grey; peripheral owners and estates named; note that an individual moiety of Beckamore belongs to Mr Martyn and that Milford Common contains 90 acres on which this estate has a right to depasture

DECORATION: 8 point compass rose, shaded grey/black; north marked by fleur-de-lys

8/7/6

HARTLAND
1796   LMA 1876/MP/06/05c

Hartland Point SS 230278

TITLE: 'A Map of an Estate called Harty Point or Blagdon's in the Parish of Hartland in the County of Devon the Property of the Right Honourable the Governors of the Charter-House'

SURVEYOR: 'Surveyed AD 1796 by Jno Prickett of Highgate Middx'

SCALE: not given

MATERIAL, SIZE & ORIENTATION: parchment, coloured; 49.5cms EW x 67.7cms NS; north to top

CONTENT: coastline, deep blue; 'The Sea and a High Clift', 'Hartland Point', 'Bristol Channel' named; streams, blue; fields outlined in dark green with numeric reference to table giving field names and content; hedge symbols indicating ownership; brown parallel lines indicating cultivated land; gardens in detail; road, buff; sand road, dashed line; buildings in plan, red; peripheral owners and estates named

DECORATION: 8 point compass rose, shaded black/grey; north marked by fleur-de-lys

ENDORSEMENT: Harty Point

8/7/7

HARTLAND
1796   LMA 1876/MP/06/04a

Hartland Church SS 260244

TITLE: 'A Plan of North Gate and Chubacroft in the Borough of Harton, in the Parish of Hartland Devon'

SURVEYOR: 'J. Blake Feby 1796'

SCALE: 'A Scale of Gunter's Chains'; scale bar'; 1"=1.25 chains; 1:980

MATERIAL, SIZE & ORIENTATION: parchment, slight colour; 50.6cms EW x 51cms NS; north to top

CONTENT: fields and tenements, plain with numeric reference to 'Explan-ation' giving description and content; gates; hedge symbols, green or yellow; fence symbols indicating ownership; garden in detail; green tree symbols marking isolated trees; roads, grey; Market Place, Church Land and New Inn Garden named; peripheral owners named

DECORATION: title cartouche: rococo style with scrolls, leaves and flowers; 8 point compass rose, black/white; north marked by fleur-de-lys, east by cross

8/7/8

HARTLAND

[1796]   LMA 1876/MP/06/04b

Hartland Church SS 260244

TITLE: 'A Plan of North Gate Harton Borough'

SURVEYOR: [J. Blake]

SCALE: 'A Scale of Gunter's Chains'; scale bar; 1"=1.25 chains; 1":980

MATERIAL, SIZE & ORIENTATION: parchment, slight colour; 36.6cms x 38.9cms; no direction

CONTENT: area of land with hedge symbols, black, showing boundaries; black tree symbols showing isolated trees; roads, plain, named; buildings in plan, outlined in red; Market Place, old malthouse and New Inn named; peripheral owners named

DECORATION: elevation and ground plan of house, the latter 'at a scale of 40ft'; title cartouche: rococo style with leaves

8/7/9

HARTLAND

1797   LMA 1876/MP/06/07d

Farford SS 271233

TITLE: 'A Map of two Estates called Higher and Lower Farford in Hartland Devon the Property of Mr Thos. Chope in the occupation of Mr Richd Westlake and Wm Nichol taken from a map made in, or about the Year 1790 and carefully corrected to the present Scale by taking the Roads in 1797'

SURVEYOR: not named

SCALE: 'Poles'; scale bar; 1"=16 poles; 1:3168

MATERIAL, SIZE & ORIENTATION: paper, slight colour; 58.5cms EW x 47.5cms NS; north to top

CONTENT: stream, blue; fields outlined in various shades of green; numeric reference in 2 colours to lists for Lower Farford and Higher Farford respectively, giving field names and content; gates; roads, buff; peripheral owners and estates named

DECORATION: 16 point compass rose, light grey/dark grey; north marked by fleur-de-lys

8/7/10

HARTLAND

1799   LMA 1876/MP/06/07a

Bursdon Moor SS 267201

TITLE: 'A Map of Bursdon-Moor, and other Lands thereunto adjoining in the Parish of Hartland in the County of Devon 1799'

SURVEYOR: not named

SCALE: 'Poles'; scale bar; 1"=16 poles; 1:3168

MATERIAL, SIZE & ORIENTATION: paper, coloured; 81.5cms EW x 67.7cms NS; north to top

CONTENT: fields outlined in various colours; numeric reference to Westerns Tenement giving field names, content; land use and quality indicated; Bursdon Common Moor, green wash with green shading; gardens; black tree symbols; roads, fenced and unfenced, buff, directions given; buildings in plan, hatched red; peripheral owners named; one boundary of the moor indicated as neglected

DECORATION: 16 point compass rose, plain/shaded grey; north marked by fleur-de-lys

8/7/11

HARTLAND

1799   LMA 1876/MP/06/07b

Hescott SS 288246

TITLE: 'A Map of West Herscott or Thomas's Park, and Lower Hewdon, in the Parish of Hartland, in the County of Devon belonging to Paul Orchard Esqr held on Lease by Thomas Chop. 1799'

SURVEYOR: not named

SCALE: 'Poles'; scale bar; 1"=16 poles; 1:3168

MATERIAL, SIZE & ORIENTATION: paper, slight colour; 54.2cms EW x 44cms NS; north to top

CONTENT: fields outlined in various colours; old hedges named, indicated by broken lines; 'Hedge new made in 1793' named; alphabetic reference to list giving field names and content; waste, green; roads, fenced and unfenced, buff, directions given; peripheral owners and estates named with some land use indicated

DECORATION: 16 point compass rose, light grey/dark grey; north marked by fleur-de-lys

8/7/12

HARTLAND

1799   LMA 1876/MP/06/07c

Fatacott SS 267269

TITLE: 'A Map of the Estate called Fatacutt in the Parish of Hartland, in the County of Devon, belonging to and in the Occupation of Mr John Way 1799'

SURVEYOR: not named

SCALE: 'Poles'; scale bar; 1"=16 poles; 1:3168

MATERIAL, SIZE & ORIENTATION: paper, slight colour; 55.3cms EW x 42.3cms NS; north to top

CONTENT: 'A Particular Clift, waste Hilly Ground declining towards the Sea'; 'A Bason or Concave part in the Clift, with some Short Wood'; 'A Green Slope, declining towards a Perpendicular Clift'; stream, pond, blue; fields outlined in green with numeric reference to table giving field names, content and Remarks, which include 'Parish Value £28 much above the General or Average Rate of the Parish'; private road, unfenced, buff; buildings in plan, pink; indication of peripheral land use; peripheral owners named

DECORATION: 8 point compass rose, black/grey; north marked by fleur-de-lys

8/7/13

HARTLAND

[1799]   LMA 1876/MP/06/08

Milford SS 233226 Elmscott SS 232217 Hardisworthy SS 230205 Docton SS 245211

TITLE: not given

SURVEYOR: not named

SCALE: no unit of measurement stated; scale bar; 1"=4 ?chains; ?1:3168

MATERIAL, SIZE & ORIENTATION: paper, slight colour; 160.5cms EW x 75.3cms NS; east to top

CONTENT: sea and 'Sea on High Clift' named; river, blue with Mill Pond and Mill Lake named; bridge; fields outlined in various colours, named with content; numeric reference in red or black to lists concerning Milford and Elmscott giving field names and content with information about owners, tenants, land use and condition; Commons outlined with broken line and colour, named; alphabetic reference to Hardisworthy giving details of tenants; general statement regarding Docton; land use in adjoining fields indicated; roads, buff, directions given; buildings in plan, in Milford coloured red or blue, elsewhere

plain but in all use indicated; peripheral owners, tenants and estates named; Fire Beacon

DECORATION: 16 point compass rose, light grey/dark grey; north marked by fleur-de-lys

8/7/14

HARTLAND

1834   621B/AT3

Rosedown Farm SS 274243

TITLE: 'A Plan of Rusdon and Wholestone Hill shewing a proposed New Line in the Parish of Hartland; Bideford Trust'

SURVEYOR: N Cumings

SCALE: 'Chains'; scale bar; 1"=4 chains; 1:3168; vertical scale 1"=80 feet

MATERIAL, SIZE & ORIENTATION: paper, coloured; 79cms EW x 27cms NS; north to top

CONTENT: streams, blue; Wholestone hills named on road; fields outlined in green, washed in shades of green and blue; owners named; roads, buff, outlined in green; bridges named; proposed line of new road in ink; buildings in plan, hatched in black and named; courtlage and garden in brown

Vertical section showing proposed cuttings and fillings with detailed measurements

DECORATION: 8 point compass rose, buff/black; north marked by fleur-de-lys

HARTLAND see also C80

8/8/1

HATHERLEIGH

1775/6   NDRO B170/134

Hatherleigh Church SS 541046

See entry under Jacobstowe, 10/1/1

8/8/2

HATHERLEIGH
1789   NDRO 2239B add/P7

Hatherleigh Church SS 541046

TITLE: 'The Manor of Hatherleigh in the County of Devon the property of Sr Wm Molesworth Bart Survey'd & Delineated by David Palmer in 1789'

SURVEYOR: David Palmer

SCALE: 'A Scale of Statute Chains'; divided scale; 1"=3 chains; 1:2376

MATERIAL, SIZE & ORIENTATION: parchment, coloured; 137cmsEW x 223.5cms NS; east to top

CONTENT: river, old river course named, grey stream lines; fields outlined in various colours and with hedge symbols; old strips shown by pecked lines; numeric reference [to Survey Book]; other owners' fields named; asterisks indicating hedge ownership; tree symbols showing orchards, coppices and isolated trees; stippled areas with green bush-like symbols; roads, buff; buildings in plan, grey; peripheral owners, estates and parishes named

DECORATION: title cartouche: separated by tree and fence; scale: rectangular frame with dividers above in yellow and black; 8 point compass rose, pink/grey; NSEW marked by letter

8/8/3

HATHERLEIGH
1807   NDRO 2239B add/P8

Upcott SS 572036

TITLE: 'A Plan of sundry Estates, situate at Upcott within the Parish of Hatherleigh in the County of Devon Property of Mr George Arnold of Iddesleigh Survey'd and Planned in 1807 by William Bear, Land Surveyor, of Bideford, Devon'

SURVEYOR: William Bear

SCALE: 'Scale of Chains, each four Statute Perches'; scale bar; 1"=3 chains; 1:2376

MATERIAL, SIZE & ORIENTATION: parchment, coloured; 98.9cms EW x 74.4cms NS; north to top

CONTENT: rivers, blue, direction of flow indicated; fields outlined in various colours, named with content; alphabetic reference to table distinguishing estates with total content and terms upon which the land is held; asterisks indicating hedge ownership; gates; tree symbols showing copse, coppice and orchard; stippling marking ?waste; roads, yellow, fenced and unfenced; directions given; footpaths, pecked

lines; buildings in plan, hatched black; peripheral parishes and estates named

DECORATION: title cartouche and border: running ribbon pattern; yellow and blue dividers above scale bar; 8 point compass rose, black/plain; north marked by fleur-de-lys

8/8/4

HATHERLEIGH
1813   Private hands

Hatherleigh Church SS 541046

TITLE: 'A Map of the Manor of Hatherleigh situated in the Parishes of Hatherleigh and Monkokehampton Devon Property of the Representatives of Joseph Oldham decd. By Thomas Bradley Launceston 1813'

SURVEYOR: Thomas Bradley

SCALE: 'Scale of Statute Chains'; scale bar; 1"=6 chains; 1:4752

MATERIAL, SIZE & ORIENTATION: copy on oiled silk, coloured; 164.4cms EW x 111cms S; north to top

CONTENT: relief shown by hill shading; quarry; rivers, blue; smaller streams uncoloured; River Torridge, River Lew, 'River Okeham' named; weir; ponds and bridges; fields in various colours and outlined in colour; alpha-numeric reference [to Survey Book]; asterisks indicating hedge ownership; Hatherleigh Moor named; black tree symbols, some on green wash showing orchards and woodland; roads, buff, fenced and unfenced; directions given; footpaths, pecked lines, plain; buildings in plan, black; Hatherleigh Church in elevation with details of churchyard; peripheral owners, estates and parishes named

DECORATION: 8 point compass rose, plain; north marked by fleur-de-lys, east by cross

8/8/5

HATHERLEIGH
1822   3599M/E153

Fishleigh SS 540057   Hele Bridge SS 540064

TITLE: 'Map of West Fishleigh in the Parish of Hatherleigh Property of J.T. Johnson Esqr. taken 1822'

SURVEYOR: not named

SCALE: 'Scale of Chains 4 Poles of 66 ft each'; scale bar; 1"=4 chains; 1:3168

MATERIAL, SIZE & ORIENTATION: paper, coloured; 53.3cms EW x 67.8cms NS; north to top

CONTENT: Looe River named, blue; old river course at 'Heale Bridge' shown; numeric reference to 'Particulars' giving field names, land use and total content; shared ownership of common indicated; asterisks indicating hedge ownership; tree symbols showing orchards; stippling on dark green ?waste; gates; roads, buff; direction given; footpath, pecked line; buildings in plan, black; courtlage, grey; Manor House [not extant] in elevation; peripheral owners named

DECORATION: title cartouche and 'Particulars': running pattern of simple leaf forms; 8 point compass rose; north marked by arrowhead, SEW by letter

8/8/6

HATHERLEIGH
1835   96M Box 65/4

Lewer SS 528056
See entry under Bickington, High, 2/10/2
TITLE: 'Map of Lewer and Bottle Hams'

HATHERLEIGH see also B41, C81

HAWKCHURCH see SUPPLEMENT S4

8/9/1

HEANTON PUNCHARDON
1780   NDRO B534 add3/1

Shankedon (modern Springfield) SS 535360 Horridge SS 530355
TITLE: 'Survey of Shankedon in Heantonpunchardon. the Land of Benjamin Incledon Esqr also of an Estate called Horridge the Land of Lord Courtenay A.D. 1780'
SURVEYOR: not named
SCALE: 'Scale of Chains'; scale bar; 1"=3 chains; 1:2376
MATERIAL, SIZE & ORIENTATION: parchment, slight colour; 69cms EW x 64.4cms NS; north to top

CONTENT: stream, blue; fields outlined in various colours; alpha-numeric reference to list giving field names and content; asterisks indicating estate boundary ownership; gateways, some gates; other owners named; garden; tree symbols black with pink canopies showing orchard and coppice; roads, fenced and unfenced, directions given; buildings in plan; peripheral owners named

DECORATION: 8 point compass rose, plain/red; north marked by fleur-de-lys; scale bar, yellow

8/9/2

HEANTON PUNCHARDON
1797   1262M/E22/43

Heanton Punchardon Church SS 502356
See entry under Braunton, 2/31/3

8/9/3

HEANTON PUNCHARDON
1797–8   1508M/London/M&P/Braunton

Heanton Punchardon Church SS 502356
See entry under Braunton, 2/31/4

8/9/4

HEANTON PUNCHARDON
1812   PRO MPE 673
                                                       Photographic copy

West Ashford SS 533354
TITLE: 'Map of the Manor of West-Ashford in the Parish of Heanton Punchardon in the County of Devon the Property of His Majesty taken in 1812'
SURVEYOR: not named
SCALE: 'A Scale of Chains each 4 Poles or 66 Feet'; scale bar'; 1:3168
MATERIAL, SIZE & ORIENTATION: ?paper, original is coloured; map sheet 50.9cms EW x 58.2cms NS; north to top; key and view sheet, 38.8cms x 53.3cms
CONTENT: 'Barnstaple River or the River Taw' and streams, stream lines; arrows indicating direction of flow; 'fishery', strand, springs, footbridge; fields with alpha-numeric reference to key (on accompanying

sheet) arranged under name of tenement giving field name, land use, content and total content; gates; asterisks indicating hedge ownership; gardens; tree symbols showing orchards and isolated trees; stippling marking furze and coppice; roads, fenced and unfenced; some directions given; footpaths, pecked lines; buildings in plan; lime kiln; peripheral owners and estates named

NOTE: in a later hand that the estate was sold to John Williams Esq. April 1816

DECORATION: title cartouche: ribbons and acanthus leaves surmounted by a crown with leaves; 16 point compass rose; north marked by fleur-de-lys, SEW by letter; magnetic north shown by line with symbol; ribbon pattern over scale bar; view from West Ashford shows river with sailing ships, islands, river banks with houses and bridge

8/9/5

HEANTON PUNCHARDON
1833   NDRO B170/158

Heanton Punchardon Church SS 502356

TITLE: 'A Plan of The Manor of Heanton Punchardon in the County of Devon 1833'

SURVEYOR: 'Surveyed by R. Passmore Braunton'

SCALE: 'Chains'; scale bar; 1"=5.5 chains; 1:4356

MATERIAL, SIZE & ORIENTATION: paper, coloured; 91cms EW x 70.5cms NS; north to top

CONTENT: The River Taw, streams, blue; fields in various colours, some plain with owners' names; numeric reference [to Survey Book]; gates; tree symbols showing orchards, woods and isolated trees; roads, buff, directions given; open space beside river, buff; line of (proposed) new road indicated with content of land lost within each field; buildings in plan, hatched black; peripheral parishes and Wrafton Marsh named

DECORATION: title cartouche: medallion of green leaves and red berries tied with pink ribbon; surveyor's name inscribed on stone plinth with urn above and surrounded by tree trunk, leaves and flowers with Britannia on one side and a sheep on the other; 8 point compass rose, black/plain/grey within circle; north marked by fleur-de-lys

8/10/1

HEMPSTON, LITTLE
1792   DP Q/RUM 8

Little Hempston Church SX 812626
See entry under Ashburton, 1/8/3

8/11/1

HEMYOCK
1709   2547M/SS19/1

Culm Davy Hill ST 124155

TITLE: 'The Mapp of Culme Davy Hill'

SURVEYOR: not named

SCALE: not given

MATERIAL, SIZE & ORIENTATION: parchment, coloured; 65cms x 60cms; no direction

CONTENT: pool; pencil line marking what is now the 800' contour; strips marked with owners' names and figures [indicating shares?]; gates; 3 trees with brown trunks, green canopy and yellow blossom; roads, red pecked lines, named; houses in elevation, red; area boundary shown by blue double cusped design

ENDORSEMENT: 14 October 1709. Inclosure Award of Culme Davy Hill in the Parish of Hemyock

DECORATION: title initials in red embellished by elaborate ink design

8/11/2

HEMYOCK
1709   3137A/PD1

This copy is in the parish deposit and is similar to the above but with the following additions; an orange line edged with double blue cusps marking 'The Brow of the Hill all Round &c' – follows the present 800' contour; tree symbols with red trunks, green canopies, red blossom; roads, red pecked lines but with double blue cusps

HEMYOCK see also C82

8/12/1

HENNOCK

1776   SRO DD/WH h/232

Netton SX 822822

TITLE: 'An Accurate Map and Survey of Nitton Farm in hand situate within the Parish of Hennock in the County of Devon. The Property of William Hilyar of East Coker in the County of Somerset Esqr Taken by Samuel Donne A.D.C. 1776'

SURVEYOR: Samuel Donne

SCALE: not given

MATERIAL, SIZE & ORIENTATION: paper, ink; 49cms x 60cms; no direction

CONTENT: 'Heighna River', streams; bridges; relief shown by hills in profile (crudely drawn); fields with field names and numeric reference to list giving field names, land use and content in customary and statute measure; hedge symbols indicating boundary ownership; gates; tree symbols showing woods and isolated trees; roads, fenced and unfenced; footpaths, broken lines; buildings in elevation; lime kilns; note that 'on this square stood Wittenbury Castle'; peripheral farms and estates named

NOTE: the map appears to be a draft

8/12/2

HENNOCK

1790   1508M/Surveys/V5

Hennock Church SX 831810

See entry under Bovey, North, 2/21/2

8/12/3

HENNOCK

1798   5846Z/E3

Warmhill SX 835804

TITLE: 'Map of Estates called Outer Warmhill situated in the Parish of Hennock in the County of Devon held under the Dean and Chapter of Exeter by Sir Laurence Palk Bart Taken in 98'

SURVEYOR: not named; Alexander Law, see Associated Document below

SCALE: 'Scale of Statute Chains each containing 66 Feet'; scale bar; 1"=4 chains; 1:3168

MATERIAL, SIZE & ORIENTATION: parchment, slight colour; 62.3cms EW x 35.3cms NS; north to top

CONTENT: streams; hill shading; fields outlined in green; alphabetic reference to table giving names of parcels, land use and content; asterisks indicating hedge ownership; gates, red; roads, buff, directions given; buildings on the estates in plan, grey; other houses in elevation

DECORATION: title cartouche: simple rococo; 8 point compass rose, black/plain; north marked by fleur-de-lys, east by cross

ASSOCIATED DOCUMENTS: Exeter D&C 4652 16 May 1797 Bill from Alexander Law To surveying mapping and valuing Outer Warmhill Expenses and Vellum 4:4:0

Exeter D&C 3754 Chapter Act Book p.575

Exeter D&C 7053 Surveyors' Accounts 1803–1860 Account dated 1801, submitted and receipted by Alexander Law

To surveying and mapping your Lands in Hennock Horse and Expenses £4: 4s: 0d

This would appear to refer to other lands held by the Dean and Chapter; there is no map surviving

8/13/1

HIGH BRAY

1802   Gonville and Caius Archive Cambridge Estate Maps

High Bray Church SS 689343

Wallover Barton SS 682384 Fullaford SS 683380

TITLE: 'A Map or Plan of an Estate Called Fullover Situate in the Parish of High Bray in the County of Devon the property of Gonvile [sic] and Caius Colledge Cambridge Survey.d and Mapp.d in the Year 1802 By G. Gould'

SURVEYOR: George Gould

SCALE: 'Scale of Chains Each Containing Four Statute perches'; scale bar; 1"=2.5 chains; 1:1980

MATERIAL, SIZE & ORIENTATION: parchment, slight colour; 80cms EW x 59.3cms NS; north to top

CONTENT: river, blue; arrow indicating direction of flow; fields outlined in yellow with solid and pecked lines; one area described only as 'The Higher Ground' divided by a pecked line; alpha-numeric reference to table giving field names, land use 'Arable And Meadow Pasture; Moory And Bushy Pasture, Hedges and Ditches, Content and Total Content'; asterisks indicating hedge ownership; gates, red; roads, fenced and unfenced; directions given; buildings in plan, outlined in red; peripheral owners, estates and parishes named

DECORATION: title cartouche: delicate scrolls, leaves and flowers with a village scene of trees, cottages and windmills below; 8 point compass rose, plain/black; north marked by fleur-de-lys

NOTE: *Biographical History of Gonville and Caius College, Vol. IV Part II Chronicle of the College Estates* compiled by E.J. Goss (Cambridge, 1819) provides information on the history of the college estates

8/13/2

HIGH BRAY
1803–1804   1148M add/10/3/2

Gratton SS 689373

TITLE: 'A Field Map or Plan of the Manor of Gratton in the Parish of High Bray in the County of Devon the Property of Richard Harding Esq. of Buzzacott House in the Parish of Combmartin in the sd. County. Surveyed and Plann'd by Wm Bear of Buckland Brewer near Bideford in the said County in 1803 and 1804'

SURVEYOR: William Bear

SCALE: not given

MATERIAL, SIZE & ORIENTATION: paper, slight colour; map is in 13 pieces and there are also some small strips; approx. 151cms x 85cms; no direction

CONTENT: fields outlined in yellow, green, blue or pink; field names and content; gates; hedge/fence ownership indicated by 'asterisms'; road, direction given; buildings in plan, hatched black; peripheral owners and estates named

NOTE: construction grid in pencil

8/13/3

HIGH BRAY
19th cent.   1148M add/10/3/1

Kedworthy SS 704370

TITLE: 'Kedworthy in the Parish of High Bray in the County of Devon'

SURVEYOR: not named

SCALE: 'A Scale of 10 Chains'; scale bar; 1"=4 chains; 1:3168

MATERIAL, SIZE & ORIENTATION: paper, coloured; 65cms EW x 45.8cms NS; north to top

CONTENT: river, blue; fields, green yellow or pink wash with numeric reference to table giving field names and content; gates; dotted lines indicating fence ownership; tree symbols showing woods; roads, grey;

footpaths, pecked lines; court[lage], grey; house in elevation; peripheral estates named

DECORATION: 8 point plain compass rose, inner circle, dots; north marked by a symbol

8/13/4

HIGH BRAY
1807   1262M/E4/15

Townhouse SS 683260

TITLE: 'A Rough or eye Sketch of that part of High Bray Estate Rented by Mr Shopland whose Term expires therein at Ladyday 1809'

SURVEYOR: [Robert Ballment]

SCALE: not given

MATERIAL, SIZE & ORIENTATION: paper, ink; 20.1cms x 15.7cms; no direction

CONTENT: river, grey; fields outlined in ink, named with content and numeric reference to table giving field names, computed number of acres, value per acre and amount per annum; gates; gardens; roads; footpaths, pecked lines; peripheral estates and owners named

ENDORSEMENT: 28 Septr. 1807. A Eye Sketch of that Part of High Bray Grounds Rented by Farmer Shopland and Robt Ballment's Valuation of the same

8/14/1

HIGHAMPTON
1831   NDRO B170/23

Highampton Church SS 489046

TITLE: 'Map of the Manor of High Hampton Devon The Property of Sir J Williams Bart'

SURVEYOR: 'Surveyed & Map'd By J Brimacombe Landsurveyor Stoke Climsland Cornwall 1831'

SCALE: 'Scale of Chains 22 Yards each'; scale bar; 1"=6 chains; 1:4752

MATERIAL, SIZE & ORIENTATION: parchment, coloured; *c.*78.5cms EW x *c.*83.5cms NS (badly rolled); north to top

CONTENT: streams, ponds, blue; arrows indicating direction of flow; numeric reference to tables listing by estates field names and content; hedge ownership indicated by 'Black Scrawl'; tree symbols showing orchards, isolated trees and with stippling, copses; stippling alone marking furse; roads, directions given; footpaths, pecked lines; buildings in plan, red or black; peripheral owners and parishes named

DECORATION: title cartouche: elaborate scroll design with flowers and leaves; 8 point compass rose, shaded-line decoration; north marked by fleur-de-lys

8/15/1

HIGHWEEK
1753   1508M/Devon/M&P/Highweek A2

Whitlake Bridge SX 857785

TITLE: 'Field Map of the Hutch Marshes late held of Mr Taylor by Mr Bearne but since purchas'd by Sir William Courtenay Bart Surveyed 20th & 21 June 1753

It lies in the Parish of Highweek, and is call'd in the lease to Christopher Border, by which lease Mr Bearne held it Two marshes view Magers Marsh, and the Common Marsh alias King's Marsh alias Beard's Marsh.

The whole is now divided by ye present currents of ye Rivers and Leat into 7 distinct parcels as appears by the Map'

SURVEYOR: not named

SCALE: no unit of measurement stated; scale bar

MATERIAL, SIZE & ORIENTATION: paper, watermark, ink; 64.1cms EW x 36.8cms NS; south to top; line marked North, South and 'True Meridian'; second line marked 'magnetic meridian'

CONTENT: river with stream lines, 'River Teign, River Lemmon, Whitlake' named; sandbanks; bridges; 'The Hutch Pool, New Salmon Hutch, Old Salmon Hutch' all named; marshes named; peripheral owners named

List describing 7 marsh areas differentiating between land and water areas; includes statement 'Survey'd June 20th & 21st 1753'

8/15/2

HIGHWEEK
1788–89   6107

Greenaway Place SX 853716
See entry under Bridestowe, 2/35/6

8/15/3

HIGHWEEK
1790   3799M add/E1

Staplehill SX 822739

TITLE: 'Map of the Estate called Staplehill situate in the Parishes of Kingsteignton and Highweek in the County of Devon, belonging to the present Fe=ofees (in trust for the Poor of West=Teignmouth). Namely; Sir James Wright Bart. William Mackworth Praed. George Ernest James Wright and William Mackworth Praed Junr, Esqrs. Gilbert Clapp. Richard Brewer. Christopher Towhill. William Tucker. Robert Jordan. William Tapley. Abraham Vicary. John Bartlett. John Margary and Richard Wilkin. Gentlemen. Survey'd and Mapp'd in 1790 by Alexr. Law. Exmouth. Devon'

SURVEYOR: Alexander Law

SCALE: 'Scale of Statute Chains each containing 66 Feet'; scale bar; 1"=3 chains; 1:2376

MATERIAL, SIZE & ORIENTATION: parchment, slight colour; 68cms EW x 95.5cms NS; north to top

CONTENT: stream; relief shown by hill shading; fields outlined in green; alphabetic reference to list giving field names and land use [Arable Meadow and Pasture; Furse Wood and Moorass; Hedges and Ditches] total content; asterisks indicating hedge ownership; gates, red; tree symbols showing orchards and isolated trees; roads, buff, fenced and unfenced; directions given; footpaths, buff, pecked lines; buildings in plan, grey; peripheral owners, estates and parishes named; parish boundary between West Teignmouth and Bovey Heathfield marked by letter and symbol for boundary stones

DECORATION: title cartouche: simple rococo style of leaves and ruched fabric; 8 point compass rose, plain/shaded grey; north marked by fleur-de-lys, east by cross

8/15/4

HIGHWEEK/ILSINGTON
1820   3799M add/E2

Highweek Church SX 851721

TITLE: 'Plan of several Estates known by the names of Ashhill, Titchmoors, Mainbow, Moorlands, Singmore, Rowell's & Archer's Staplehill. Teignmouth Land & Yellowford in the Parish of Highweek Also Lower Gavrick & Lower Staplehill in the Parish of Ilsington Devon'

SURVEYOR: Samuel Elliott of Plymouth

SCALE: 'Scale'; scale bar showing chains and furlongs; 1"=3 chains; 1:2376

MATERIAL, SIZE & ORIENTATION: paper, mounted on cloth, coloured; 31.3cms EW x 75.3cms NS; north to top

CONTENT: river, lakes, ponds, watercourses, leats, blue; fields shown in various colours with alpha-numeric reference [to Survey Book]; different estates in blocks of colour; fences; tree symbols showing plantations [some mixed] and orchards; some gardens in detail; roads, buff; directions given; footpaths, pecked lines; buildings in plan, grey; peripheral owners and estates named

DECORATION: 4 point compass indicator; north marked by fleur-de-lys

HIGHWEEK see also C91–92

HOCKWORTHY see C83

HOLBERTON see C84, C115

8/16/1

HOLCOMBE BURNELL

[early 19th cent.] 1926B/P/E2/7

Culver House SX 845902

TITLE: not given [plan of roads]

SURVEYOR: J. Jones

SCALE: a) 'A Scale of Chains for the Road Mark'd with red Letters'; scale bar; 1"=12.25 chains; 1:9900; b) 'A Scale of Chains'; scale bar; 1"=6.25 chains; 1:4940

MATERIAL, SIZE & ORIENTATION: paper, slight colour; 53.2cms EW x 74.1cms NS; north to top

CONTENT: river, black stream lines, direction of flow indicated; bridge; lands, owners named; tree symbols showing grove and brake; roads, fenced and unfenced, directions given; distances marked from milestones; footpaths, pecked lines; buildings in elevation and in plan

DECORATION: 4 point compass indicator in double circle; north marked by fleur-de-lys

8/17/1

HOLCOMBE ROGUS

1783 1936M/EP1

Fenacre Farm SS 068177

TITLE: not given

SURVEYOR: not named

SCALE: not given

MATERIAL, SIZE & ORIENTATION: paper, ink, slight colour; 38cms EW x 54.4cms NS; north to top

CONTENT: Fenacre water, watercourse and spring head, ancient watercourse all shown; arrow indicating direction of flow; sluices, one on channel from Holcombe Mills and Durley; bays*; fields outlined in grey with hedge symbols placed to indicate ownership; bridge in elevation; table listing points A–D; A = the place in dispute, B = the depth of water, D = a quantity of earth taken away for the making of a bay adjoining 'which Bay turned the water out of its proper course towards B'

DECORATION: 4 point compass indicator; north marked by fleur-de-lys, east by cross

ENDORSEMENT: The Within Watercourse Was Tried at the Castle of Exeter before Mr Barron Eyere at Lammas Assizes in the year 1783. Between Mr B: Nutcombe Bluett and Mr Lethbridge. Given on Mr Bluetts right. Watercourse

* bay = embankment or dam to store water [OED]

8/17/2

HOLCOMBE ROGUS

*c.*1820 74B/MP160 (6)

Holcombe Rogus Church ST 056190

TITLE: 'Plan of the Manor of Holcombe Rogus in the County of Devon Property of Peter Bluett Esqr.'

SURVEYOR: not named

SCALE: 'Chains'; scale bar; 1"=1 chain; 1:792

MATERIAL, SIZE & ORIENTATION: paper, ink; 73.2cms EW x 64cms NS; north to top

CONTENT: streams; fields outlined in ink with alpha-numeric reference [to Survey Book]; roads; footpaths, pecked lines; buildings in plan; peripheral owners and parishes named

DECORATION: 8 point compass rose, black/grey; north marked by fleur-de-lys

8/17/3

HOLCOMBE ROGUS

1821   SRO DD/WY (Devon Maps)

Moorstone Barton ST 016099
See entry under Burlescombe, 2/51/4

HOLCOMBE ROGUS see also C85

8/18/1

HOLLACOMBE

1799   4448Z/Z1

Hollacombe Church SS 378030
See entry under Cookbury, 3/30/3

8/19/1

HOLSWORTHY

1780   1508M/Devon/Surveys/V4

Holsworthy Church SS 342037
See entry under Combe Raleigh, 3/29/1

8/19/2

HOLSWORTHY

1794–5/1824   NDRO B170/186

Holsworthy Church SS 342037
TITLE: 'Map of the Manor of Holsworthy Devon the Property of Sir
    John Davie Bart. Taken in the Years 1794 and 1795: by Robert Ball-
    ment: and Mapp'd in 1824 by Ethelred Still'
SURVEYORS:: Robert Ballment and Ethelred Still
SCALE: 'Scale'; scale bar; 1"=8 chains; 1:6336
MATERIAL, SIZE & ORIENTATION: paper, mounted on linen, repaired, slight
    colour; 122.1cms EW x 76.6cms NS; (assumed) north to top
CONTENT: rivers, blue, direction of flow indicated; fields outlined in
    various colours with alpha-numeric reference to table giving field
    names, content of arable and pasture, moor and waste, hedges and

ditches and total content; 'asterisms' indicating fence ownership;
    gates; tree symbols showing orchards; roads, buff, fenced and un-
    fenced; footpaths, pecked lines; buildings in plan, red; church in
    elevation, red; peripheral owners and estates named
DECORATION: title cartouche: view of town with church, presumably
    Holsworthy; 8 point compass rose, black lines/ plain; symbol,
    presumably indicating north

8/19/3

HOLSWORTHY

[1800]   1508M/Devon/M&P/Holsworthy 1

Holsworthy Church SS 342037
TITLE: 'A Map of Lands lying within the Parishes of North Lee, and
    Holsworthy in the County of Devon Belonging to The Right Honble
    Lord Visct Courtenay'
SURVEYOR: not named [same hand as 1508M/Devon/M&P/Milton
    Damerel 1]
SCALE: 'Eighty Poles five and a half yds each'; scale bar; 1"=16 poles;
    1:3168
MATERIAL, SIZE & ORIENTATION: parchment, slight colour; 60.3cms EW
    x 28.9cms NS; north to top
CONTENT: river marked by stream lines; fields outlined in colour, named;
    numeric reference [to Survey Book]; boundary fences placed to
    indicate ownership; gates; green tree symbols; roads; 'Explanation'
    lists symbols distinguishing High Roads, Driving Roads, Footpaths;
    buildings, some in plan, some in elevation; peripheral owners named
DECORATION: title cartouche: simple scroll design; 16 point compass rose,
    plain/black; centre circle segmented; secondary outer circle; north
    marked by fleur-de-lys, SEW by letter

8/19/4

HOLSWORTHY

1808   2569B/Estate/4/4b

South Arscott SS 353057
TITLE: 'A Plan of Arscott Farm in the Parish of Holsworthy in the County
    of Devon Belonging to Arscott Bickford Esqr 1808'
SURVEYOR: 'Jno Hiles Surveyor'
SCALE: no unit of measurement stated; scale bar shows chains and
    furlongs; 1"=4 chains; 1:3168

MATERIAL, SIZE & ORIENTATION: paper, coloured; 52cms EW x 60.8cms NS; north to top

CONTENT: stream; relief shown by hill shading; fields coloured various shades of green according to land use; plain green, meadow or pasture; green with parallel lines, arable; green with stippling and symbols, 'Fursey Pasture'; hedge symbols used to indicate fence ownership; asterisks used where river forms field boundaries; numeric reference to list on separate sheet giving field names, land use, content, annual value and 'Remarks'; gates; tree symbols showing orchards; roads, fenced and unfenced; directions given; gates across some roads; buildings in plan, hatched black; peripheral owners named

DECORATION: title cartouche: trees and plants; 8 point compass rose, black shading; north marked by fleur-de-lys, east by cross, south by feathers and other directions by letter

8/19/5

HOLSWORTHY
[1825]   2569B/Estate/4/4a,c

Staddon SS 355032

TITLE: 'Map of Staddon in the Parish of Holsworthy in the County of Devon, belonging to the Reverend Wm Holland Coham'

'Crambury in the Parish of Holsworthy'

Cranbury SS 362064

SURVEYOR: not named

SCALE: 'Scale of Chains'; scale bar; 1"=4 chains; 1:3168

MATERIAL, SIZE & ORIENTATION: paper, slight colour; 65.5cms x 96cms; north-west to top

CONTENT: stream, blue; fields outlined in various colours; alpha-numeric reference to separate list giving 'Names of Inclosures', land use and content grouped according to landholders; hedges marked by dotted red lines belong to the 'adjoining Premises'; gardens; green tree symbols showing orchards and coppices; roads, fenced and unfenced; directions given; buildings in plan, outlined in pink; cottages and gardens taken in from waste shown; peripheral owners named

NOTE: Langdon Estate claims right of Common on Common Moor

DECORATION: title embellished with flourishes; 8 point compass rose, plain/grey; north marked by fleur-de-lys

8/19/6

HOLSWORTHY
1825   2569B/Estate/4/13

Chilsworthy SS 327063

TITLE: 'Chilsworthy in the Parish of Holsworthy'; annotation 'The Property of Holland Coham Esqr'

SCALE: 1"=4 chains; 1:3168

See entry under Black Torrington, 2/19/4

8/19/7

HOLSWORTHY
early 19th cent.   NDRO 178B/M/E29

Staddon SS 355032

TITLE: 'Map of a Tenement in Staddon in the Parish of Holsworthy belonging to the Rt Honble Earl Stanhope'

SURVEYOR: not named

SCALE: 'Scale of Chains'; scale bar; 1"=4 chains; !:3168

MATERIAL, SIZE & ORIENTATION: paper, slight colour; 33.4cms EW x 36.6cms NS; north to top

CONTENT: fields, pink wash with numeric reference to table giving field names, content of arable, hedge and waste and total content; common; roads, grey; directions given; peripheral owners and estates named

DECORATION: 8 point compass rose, grey/plain; north marked by fleur-de-lys

ENDORSEMENT: Staddon & Rawrey Meadow

8/20/1

HONEYCHURCH
1775/6   NDRO B170/134

Honeychurch Church SS 629028

See entry under Jacobstowe, 10/1/1

8/21/1

HONITON
1748/9   DD 70384

ST 162004

TITLE: 'A Map of the whole Ground belonging to the abovementioned Tenements in which the Plan of the said intended Buildings is again laid down, in its proper Situation; and the Boundaries of the whole, with the Incroachments made thereon, particularly distinguished'

SURVEYOR: 'Survey'd Janry 11th 1748 by Wm Chapple'

SCALE: 'A Scale of Feet'; scale bar; 1"=20 feet; 1:240

MATERIAL, SIZE & ORIENTATION: paper, watermark, ink and slight grey colour; 27.8cms EW x 45.4cms NS; east to top; directions spelt out on margins

CONTENT: hedge symbols, grey; gates to garden; plan of buildings and wall, grey; details of owners of adjoining tenements and houses; considerable information concerning areas in dispute

Plan of proposed houses above map; similar in size on a scale of 1:180

8/21/2

HONITON
1750   DD 70385

Honiton Church ST 163007

TITLE: 'A Map shewing the several Incroachments made by Mr Thomas Clarke, on the Lands of Sir William Courtenay Bart in the Borough and Manor of Honiton 1750'

SURVEYOR: not named [William Chapple]

SCALE: 'A Scale of Feet'; scale bar; 1"=6.75 feet; 1:78.7

MATERIAL, SIZE & ORIENTATION: paper, watermark, ink, slight colour; east to top; directions spelt out on margins

CONTENT: hedge symbols, gooseberry hedge named; grey tree symbols; new wall grey, others pink; detailed notes on boundaries and structures in dispute; owners named

NOTE: plan prepared for evidence in law suit

8/21/3

HONITON
1754   DD 70386

ST 162004

TITLE: 'A Plan of Two Tenements in the Borough of Honiton the Lands of John Tuckfield Esq; & Mrs E Hillson heretofore in undivided Moieties; now held by Geo. Humphry as Tenant to the sd Mr Tuckfield and Mr Jno Clarke Apothecary as Tenant to the sd Mrs Hillson; distinguishing the sd tenemts as rebuilt since the Fire according to ye Partition or Division thereof made by Agreement between the sd Mrs Hillson and the sd Mr Humphrey. Survey'd & Mapp'd in 1754'

SURVEYOR: not named [William Chapple]

SCALE: 'A Scale of Feet'; scale bar; 1"=40 feet; 1:480

MATERIAL, SIZE & ORIENTATION: paper, watermark, ink and slight colour; 19.8cms EW x 31.5cms NS; north to top; directions on margins

CONTENT: garden with hedge symbols marking boundaries; houses and outhouse in plan; owners named

two copies; identical except one only includes date

8/21/4

HONITON
1780   Private hands

Honiton Church ST 163007

TITLE: 'A Map of Lands within the Borough & Parish of Honiton with[in] the Boundary of the Parish and also of Lands within the Parish of Gittisham, all within the County of Devon. ['Formerly' added later] Belonging to The Rt: Honble Ld: Vsct: Courtenay. By Geoe. Lang 1780'

SURVEYOR: George Lang

SCALE: unit of measurement illegible; scale bar; 1"=16 ?poles; 1:?3168

MATERIAL, SIZE & ORIENTATION: parchment, slight colour, very dirty and most of the colour has been rubbed off; 90cms EW x 211cms NS (edges torn and piece missing at the top); west to top

CONTENT: river, now plain, possible stream lines visible; bridges; fields outlined in various colours, some now feint; fields, mostly named, with alpha-numeric reference [to Survey Book] and keyed to list of owners; some fields outlined in green appear to have been added later and have no references; Green tree symbols showing orchards; stippling marking coppice; roads, plain; footpaths, pecked lines; buildings (outside town) in elevation; Honiton town buildings in plan, red and grey, including chapel and workhouse; peripheral parishes and lands of Sir George Yonge named

    Construction grid, red, lettered a–e on left hand-side

DECORATION: title cartouche: ribbon pattern; border: running figured design; 32 point compass rose (only 16 points now visible) grey/plain; north marked by fleur-de-lys

NOTE: ½ scale version of this map in sections at 1508M/Devon/Surveys/V4 but no town plan present

8/21/5

HONITON
1780   1508M/Devon/Surveys/V4

Honiton Church ST 163007
See entry under Combe Raleigh, 3/29/1

8/21/6

HONITON
1783   281M/E8

Honiton Church ST 163007
See entry under Beer, 2/5/2

8/21/7

HONITON
*c.*1800   337B add3/3/3/10

High Street ST 161006
TITLE: not given; 2 plans showing land in High Street
SURVEYOR: not named
SCALE: not given
MATERIAL, SIZE & ORIENTATION: parchment, slight colour; 16.3cms x 32cms and 16cms x 33.3cms; no direction
CONTENT: 2 plans, originally part of legal documents showing boundary changes [following sale of land with proposed development]; measured plots outlined in blue or red; roads named; some points identified by letter

HONITON see also B33, B91, B110, B120, B122, C86–88

8/22/1

HORWOOD
1783/8   NDRO 2239 add 6/19

Horwood Church SS 502276
TITLE: 'Survey of the Bartons of East and West Horwood lying in the Parish of Horwood in the County of Devon belonging to Thomas Hogg Esqr Coppied 178[3 or 8 illegible]'
SURVEYOR: not named
SCALE: 'A Scale of Chains'; scale bar; 1"=3 chains; 1:2376
MATERIAL, SIZE & ORIENTATION: parchment, slight colour; 90.8cms EW x 70.5cms NS; north to top
CONTENT: pond; fields outlined in green or grey, named with content; asterisks indicating hedge ownership; coppice named, orchards named some with content; furze named with content; brown tree symbols showing woods with content; garden indicated; roads outlined in green; directions given; buildings in plan, outlined in green; Horwood Church in elevation

    2 tables listing field names and content

    'Explanation of the Houses'; listed and planned on a larger scale of 1" to 70 feet; scale bar

DECORATION: 16 point compass rose, plain; north marked by fleur-de-lys

HUISH see C89

8/23/1

HUISH, NORTH
1786/7/9–1808   Z17/3/20–21

North Huish Church SX 711565
See entry under Ashburton, 1/8/2

8/24/1

HUISH, SOUTH
1777   1508M/Devon/M&P/V3

Court Barton SX 694412 Galmpton Church SX 686405
See entry under Alvington, West, 1/6/1

8/24/2

HUISH, SOUTH
1777   1508 Maps/Malborough 1

Court Barton SX 694412 Malborough church SX 706398
TITLE: 'A Map of Lands lying within the Manors of Saltcombe, Collaton-Prawle, Portlemouth, East-Sewer, Bolberry-Beacham and Bolberry-Allen, in the Parish of Malborough; Galmeton, and South-Huish in the Parish of South-Huish; all within the County of Devon; Belonging to The Rt. Hon. W. Ld. Visct: Courtenay By George Lang of Leyland Lancashire 1777'
SURVEYOR: George Lang
SCALE: 'A Scale of 120 Poles five and a half Yards each'; scale bar; 1"=16 poles; 1:12672
MATERIAL, SIZE & ORIENTATION: parchment, coloured; 233cms x 128cms; north-east to top
CONTENT: rivers; cliffs, vertical shading indicating direction of slope and gradient; principal features, coves, rocks and off-shore rocks named and shaded; relief shown by shading, Little Torr named; fields outlined in various colours, named with numeric reference to Survey Book (see note below); 'boundary fences belonging' indicated; symbols indicating ownership of other fields keyed to Explanation; gates; dotted line 'supposed to divided the arable from the cliff'; gardens; green tree symbols showing orchards and, on a green wash, groves; High Roads, Driving roads, some directions given; buildings in elevation, including Old Castle off North Sands; those buildings 'not belonging' in plan; villages named; peripheral owners named; Manor boundaries indicated
     Upper and lower case grid
DECORATION: title cartouche: rococo with coastal, fishing and shipping scenes; 32 point compass rose, plain/black superimposed on 3 circles; north marked by fleur-de-lys; border: elaborate running pattern
NOTE: See letter referred to in 1508 Devon Surveys V3 under Alvington, West

8/25/1

HUNTSHAM
1817   Ex. D&C Ch. Comm. 98/8791

Norwood Farm SS 985188 Three Gates Farm SS 988194 Huntsham Church ST 001204
See entry under Aylesbeare, 1/18/2

HUNTSHAM see also C90

8/26/1

HUNTSHAW
1796 [early 19th cent.]   NDRO 2594A/PZ1

Huntshaw Church SS 507229
TITLE: 'Manor of Huntshaw, Devon, belonging to The Right Honble Lord Clinton'
SURVEYOR: 'Surveyed by Wm White in 1796. Reduced by C. Dean'
SCALE: 'Scale of Chains'; scale bar; 1"= approx. 8 chains; 1:6336
MATERIAL, SIZE & ORIENTATION: paper, repaired, coloured; 61cms x 48cms; north-east to top
CONTENT: streams, 'Stafford Lake'; fields, some coloured, some numbered, some with owners' names; tree symbols showing woods and coppice; Darracot Moor [Lord Clinton's part sold to Lord Rolle in exchange for lands in Merton]; roads, directions given; footpaths pecked lines; buildings in plan, black; peripheral owners and parishes named; parish boundary between Huntshaw and Torrington shown
DECORATION: 16 point compass rose. black lines/ plain; north marked by fleur-de-lys
NOTE: small sections of document missing. Charles Dean was working in Heavitree, Exeter, in 1814

8/27//1

HUXHAM
1840   2547M/E46

Huxham Church SX 947948
TITLE: 'South Hayne Peak & Coppice'
SURVEYOR: not named

SCALE: not given

MATERIAL, SIZE & ORIENTATION: parchment, ink; 29.4cms x 70cms; north-east to top

CONTENT: river, stream lines; bridge; fields outlined in ink; numeric reference to table giving field names and content; roads; buildings in plan, black and hatched black

DECORATION: 4 point compass indicator; north-south line marked by fletched arrow

ENDORSEMENT: 1840 Map of South Hayne Peak & Coppice

9/1/1

IDE
1798   Z17/3/7

See entry under Dunsford, 4/13/5

9/1/2

IDE
1803/1805   Ex. D&C Ch. Comm. 41/75968C/2

Ide Church SX 898903

TITLE: 'Map of the Manor of Ide Taken in 1803'

SURVEYORS:: Survey Book (see note below) states 'Survey'd in 1803 and Mapp'd in 1805 by Alexr Law & Thos Bradley'

SCALE: 'Scale of Statute Chains each containing 66 Feet'; scale bar; 1"=7 chains; 1:5544

MATERIAL, SIZE & ORIENTATION: parchment, coloured; 62.3cms EW X 47cms NS; north to top

CONTENT: streams, black lines; relief shown by hill shading; fields outlined in various colours with alpha-numeric reference to Survey Book giving field names, arable and pasture, furze and waste, hedges and ditches, content and total content; asterisks indicating hedge ownership; gates, red; tree symbols showing orchards; stippling marking ?waste; roads, buff, directions given; most buildings in plan but some houses and church in elevation, grey; peripheral owners, estates and parishes named

DECORATION: title cartouche: leaves and scrolls; 8 point compass rose, plain/black; north marked by fleur-de-lys

ASSOCIATED DOCUMENTS: Ex. D&C Ch. Comm. 41/759688C 'A Survey and Valuation of the Manor of Ide Situated in the Parish of Ide. in the County of Devon Property of the Dean and Chapter of Exeter.

Survey'd in 1803 and Mapp'd in 1805 by Alexr Law & Thos Bradley' (finely-decorated title page)

Exeter D&C 7053 Surveyors' Accounts 1803–1860 To surveying mapping and valuing the Manor of Ide and ascertaining the value of the Tithes £60:0s:0d

Paid for carrying the Chain and other Expences £8:9s:2d

9/2/1

ILFRACOMBE
1797   1262M/E22/43

Ilfracombe Church SS 522478
See entry under Braunton, 2/31/3

9/2/2

ILFRACOMBE
1797–8   1508M/M&P/Braunton

Ilfracombe Church SS 522478
See entry under Braunton, 2/31/4

9/2/3

ILFRACOMBE
1802   Z17/3/2

Ettiford SS 546442
See entry under Berrynarbor, 2/8/2

ILFRACOMBE see also B49

9/3/1

ILSINGTON
1784   1164B/7/22

Sigford Bethel Cross SX 782743

TITLE: 'A Plan of Sigford Farm &c Situate in the Parish of Ilsington and

County of Devon The Property of Wm Jno Hale Esqr Survey'd by Jas Foster Ashburton 1784'

SURVEYOR: James Foster

SCALE: 'A Scale of Chains'; scale bar; 1"=4.25 chains; 1:3366

MATERIAL, SIZE & ORIENTATION: parchment, coloured; 40.7cms EW x 51cms NS; north to top

CONTENT: fields, pale yellow wash outlined in yellow and red; field names; numeric reference to 'Contents' table giving field names and content; crosses indicating hedge ownership; gates; green tree symbols showing orchards; roads, buff; directions given; footpaths pecked lines; buildings in plan, grey; peripheral owners named

DECORATION: title cartouche: delicate acanthus-leaf design with garlands of vine-leaf forms coloured green and yellow surmounted by an urn [identical to photocopy 2959Z/E1]; scale bar, yellow; 17 point compass rose [E through to N to W], striped red/white and striped black/white; concentric circles in centre, black/white, green/white; 'Contents' and 'A Scale of Chains' embellished with ink flourishes

---

9/3/2

ILSINGTON

1805   SRO DD/AH/Box 14

Ilsington Church SX 785761
See entry under Ashburton, 1/8/6

9/3/3

ILSINGTON

1808   1311M/3/4

Owlacombe Cross SX 764727
See entry under Ashburton, 1/8/7

9/3/4

ILSINGTON

1820   3799M add/E2

Gavrick Copse SX 754748
See entry under Highweek, 8/15/4

9/3/5

ILSINGTON

1821   1164B/7/20

Higher Sigford SX 782744

TITLE: 'A Plan of Cockslen Farm situate in the Parish of Ilsington and in the County of Devon the Property of J.Woodley esq. 1821'

SURVEYOR: not named

SCALE: 'Scale of Chains'; scale bar; 1"=2 chains; 1:1584

MATERIAL, SIZE & ORIENTATION: paper, ink and slight colour; 61.7cms EW x 89.1cms NS; north to top

CONTENT: river, direction of flow marked, pond; fields outlined with hedge symbols indicating ownership; numeric reference to table giving field names and content; gates; tree symbols marking orchards and brushwood; roads, direction given; footpaths, pecked lines; buildings in plan, hatched black; peripheral owners named

DECORATION: 8 point compass rose, black/plain; north marked by an arrowhead

ENDORSEMENT: Sigford & Coxland

ASSOCIATED DOCUMENTS: 3 sheets of photocopy, faded and incomplete, are to be found at 2194Z/Z3. See also 1164B/7/2/23 for what appears to be an undated but contemporary copy

---

9/3/6

ILSINGTON

[1821]   1164B/7/2/23

Higher Sigford SX 782744

TITLE: 'A Plan of Cockslen Farm Situate in the parish of Ilsington and County of Devon the property of J[or I] Woodley Esqr.'

SURVEYOR: not named

SCALE: 'Scale of Chains'; scale bar; 1"=2 chains; 1:1584

MATERIAL, SIZE & ORIENTATION: paper, ink and slight colour; 41.9cms EW x 53.7cms NS; north to top

CONTENT: river; fields outlined in yellow; numeric reference to table giving field names and content; 'asterisms' indicating hedge ownership; gates; tree symbols showing orchards and coppice; roads, brown, some named; buildings in plan, grey; peripheral owners named

DECORATION: 4 point compass indicator; north marked by a symbol

9/3/7

ILSINGTON

1822   1311M/3/6

Owlacombe Cross SX 764727
See entry under Ashburton, 1/8/9

9/3/8

ILSINGTON

1840   1508M/London/M&P/Ilsington 1

Haytor Old Quarries SX 755774

TITLE: ['Plan of Haytor Down & quarries belonging to His Grace The Duke of Somerset']*

SURVEYOR: 'Teigngrace, Sept. 16th 1840. E S Bearne'

SCALE: '16 chains to an Inch'; 1:12672

MATERIAL, SIZE & ORIENTATION: paper, slight colour; 31.9cms EW x 35cms NS; north to top

CONTENT: Haytor Rocks, grey; Haytor Down partially outlined in yellow; bound stones; bridge; quarries, buff; rail road leading to the Duke of Somerset's quarries; peripheral parishes named

DECORATION: 4 point compass indicator; north marked by an arrowhead

ASSOCIATED DOCUMENT: letter from E.S. Bearne to Charles Brutton explaining the red lines on the map. The red line on the plan denotes the portion of the Common which the Duke proposes to take and the red dotted line is the portion claimed by the People of Bovey as the property of the Earl of Devon

* taken from associated document

9/3/9

ILSINGTON

19th cent.   1164B/7/21

Owlacombe Cross SX 764727

TITLE: not given

SURVEYOR: not named

SCALE: not given

MATERIAL, SIZE & ORIENTATION: paper, repaired, ink; 54cms x 56.5cms; no direction

CONTENT: spring, brook; relief shown by feint pencil shading; fields outlined in ink; roads, fenced and unfenced; directions given; foot-

paths, broken lines; buildings in plan, hatched; mines indicated by 'ladder' symbols; later annotations

ILSINGTON see also C91–92

9/4/1

INSTOW

[1649–1654]   KAO u269/P11/2

Worlington SS 481306

TITLE: 'Wormbington in Instowe'

SURVEYOR: not named [Thomas Berry]

SCALE: 'A Scale of 16 pches in an inch'; scale bar; 1"=16 perches; 1:3168

MATERIAL, SIZE & ORIENTATION: parchment, coloured; irregular in shape [sheepskin] 88.5cms EW x 65.5cms NS; north to top

CONTENT: stream, green; fields washed in blue, green and buff with deeper colours on margins: some fields with tenants' names, content and land use; pecked lines mark limit of holdings; green tree symbols showing orchards; roads, buff; footpaths, broken lines; buildings in elevation, blue roofs, red chimneys, smoke; farm buildings without chimneys and smoke; peripheral owners named; total content of principal tenants' holdings included randomly around the map

DECORATION: 8 point compass rose, red/blue; NSEW by letter; north also by a cross, south by arrowhead

PUBLICATION: Todd Gray, ed., *Devon Household Accounts 1627–59* DCRS New Series', Vol. 39 (Exeter, 1996), Plate 10

9/4/2

INSTOW

1798   4163M/E1

Instow Church SS 480310
See entry under Alverdiscott, 1/5/2

INSTOW see also C93

9/5/1

INWARDLEIGH
1779   BL Althorp Estate Plans P3&P7

Inwardleigh Church SX 560995
See entries under Okehampton, 15/5/2

9/5/2

INWARDLEIGH
1780   1508M/Devon/Surveys/V4

Inwardleigh Church SX 560995
See entry under Combe Raleigh, 3/29/1

9/5/3

INWARDLEIGH
1817   4974B/E1/1

Curworthy Farm SX 560979
TITLE: 'Plan of the Manor of Curworthy in the Parish of Inwardleigh
    Devon'
SURVEYOR: 'Surveyed by S. Elliott 1817'
SCALE: no unit of measurement stated; scale bar shows chains and
    furlongs; 1"=4 chains; 1:3168
MATERIAL, SIZE & ORIENTATION: paper, mounted on linen, segmented,
    coloured; 113cms x 112.5cms; north-west to top; magnetic north
    indicated
CONTENT: streams, blue; relief shown by hill shading; fields in various
    colours with alpha-numeric reference [to Field Book]; note states
    'The Letters referring to the Respective Estates is explained in the
    preceding part of the Field Book'; boundaries in deeper colour than
    that used on the fields indicates ownership; 'Outboundaries' not
    belonging to the estate, red; tree symbols showing woods, plantations,
    orchards; deciduous and coniferous trees distinguished; roads, buff,
    fenced and unfenced; directions given; footpaths, pecked lines;
    buildings in plan, grey; peripheral owners and parishes named
DECORATION: 4 point compass indicator, shaded line decoration; north
    marked by fleur-de-lys

9/5/4

INWARDLEIGH
1832   Pearse 1948/Maps

Inwardleigh Church SX 560995
TITLE: 'Map of the Glebe of Inwardleigh in the County of Devon The
    Property of the Revd. R Holland Survey'd by T. Jenn and Delineated
    by G Gould in the year 1832 Okehampton'
SURVEYORS:: T. Jenn and G. Gould
SCALE: no unit of measurement stated; scale bar; 1"=4 ?chains; 1:?3168
MATERIAL, SIZE & ORIENTATION: parchment, ink amd slight colour;
    45.2cms EW x 60.3cms NS; north to top
CONTENT: river, blue; bridges; fields outlined in green with numeric
    reference to table giving field names and content; tree symbols show-
    ing orchards and isolated trees; roads, buff; directions given; buildings
    in plan, red and black, church in elevation; peripheral owners and
    estates named
DECORATION: title cartouche: acanthus leaves and flowers; 8 point compass
    rose; north marked by fleur-de-lys with scale bar, yellow and hatched
    grey, superimposed so only 6 points are visible

INWARDLEIGH see also C94

9/6/1

IPPLEPEN
11 July 1794   312M/EH121

Dornafield SX 837682
TITLE: 'An Eye Sketch of the Piece of Land called Stallage, part of
    Dornafield Barton, situate in ye parish of Ipplepen and County of
    Devon, the Lands of Mr Wm Hole, taken on the Spot, ye 11th Day of
    July 1794 by the said Wm Hole'
SURVEYOR: William Hole
SCALE: not given but some road measurements in chains
MATERIAL, SIZE & ORIENTATION: paper, ink; 22.5cms EW x 18.7cms NS;
    north to top
CONTENT: fields; gates; roads, some distances given; Ipplepen Cross and
    Ellacombe Pool marked
ASSOCIATED DOCUMENT: map is endorsed on letter from Thomas Taylor
    of Denbury to William Hole, dated 10 July 1794

9/6/2

IPPLEPEN

1809   Pearse 1948/Maps

Dainton SX 852667

TITLE: 'Daignton In the Parish of Ipplepen and County of Devon. Property of B. Babbage Esquire 1809'

SURVEYOR: C. Tozer

SCALE: 'A Scale of Chains'; scale bar; 1"=4 chains; 1:3168

MATERIAL, SIZE & ORIENTATION: parchment, coloured; 57cms EW x 72.7cms NS; north to top

CONTENT: stream, grey; direction of flow marked; fields, plain and different shades of green or yellow; alpha-numeric reference to tables giving field names and content; hedge symbols indicating ownership; tree symbols showing orchards; roads, plain, directions given; footpaths, pecked lines; buildings in plan, red and black; peripheral owners and estates named

DECORATION: compass indicator, line with fleur-de-lys marking north

10/1/1

JACOBSTOWE

1775/6   NDRO B170/134

Jacobstowe Church SS 586016 Broomford Manor SS 575018

TITLE: 'A Map or Plan of the Manor of Broomford lying within the Parishes of Jacobstow Honychurch & Hatherleigh in the County of Devon the Property of John Burton Esqr Survey'd in 1775 and mapp'd in 1776 by Wm Hole & A Law'

SURVEYORS: William Hole and Alexander Law

SCALE: 'A Scale of Chains each containing Four Statute Perches'; scale bar; 1"=3 chains; 1:2376

MATERIAL, SIZE & ORIENTATION: parchment, coloured; 223cms EW x 206cms NS; north to top

CONTENT: rivers, black margins; streams, grey, named; arrows marking direction of flow; bridges, some in elevation; fields outlined in various colours; alpha-numeric reference [to Survey Book]; 'asterisms' indicating hedge ownership; gates, red; glebe land named; tree symbols showing woods, orchards and isolated trees; stippling, sometimes with trees, marking waste; roads; footpaths, pecked lines; buildings in plan; Jacobstowe Church in elevation; peripheral owners and parishes named

Principal map shows area around Jacobstowe, others as insets

DECORATION: title cartouche: rococo, delicate in style with scrolls, stylised acanthus leaves; flowers, leaves and seed heads above a rural scene showing moorland, houses etc; 8 point compass rose; north marked by fleur-de-lys, east by cross

11/1/1

KELLY

1744   Private hands

Kelly House SX 395815

TITLE: 'A Plan of the Estate of Arthur Kelly Esqr: within the Parish of Kelly in the County of Devon taken by Will Wapshare October 1744'

SURVEYOR: William Wapshare

SCALE: 'A Scale of Perches'; scale bar; 1"=15 chains; 1:11880

MATERIAL, SIZE & ORIENTATION: parchment, mounted on linen, coloured; 144cms EW x 112cms Ns, mounted on rollers; north to top

CONTENT: river, ponds; fields outlined in various colours, some with plough lines (denoting arable) and with alpha-numeric reference [to Survey Book]; hedge symbols indicating boundary ownership; gates, gateways; gardens in detail; black tree symbols marking orchards, woods, coppices and isolated trees; roads, plain, directions given; footpaths, pecked lined, buildings in plan, red; peripheral estates and manors named

Legend with references listing symbols and use of colour

DECORATION: title cartouche, reference list and scale bar decorated with acanthus, scrolls, and ruched fabric (title cartouche also has flowers); 4 point compass indicator; north marked by fleur-de-lys, south by cross, E and W by letter

11/1/2

KELLY

early 19th cent.   Private hands

Kelly House SX 395815

Cloth-bound volume with leather spine, 31cms x 37.4cms. Index listing 15 plans with content.

GENERAL TITLE: 'Plan of the Estates of Arthur Kelly Esquire in the Parishes of Kelly, Dunterton, Broadstone, and Milton Abbot, in the County of Devon and Lezant in the County of Cornwall'

SURVEYOR: not named

SCALE: not given

MATERIAL, SIZE & ORIENTATION: parchment, slight colour; except for Map 1, maps have compass indicators, mostly with north to top

CONTENT: lake and streams, blue; fields, some coloured, outlined with hedge symbols; numeric reference to list on opposite page giving field name and content; green tree symbols of different shapes marking orchards, coniferous trees, woods, plantations and isolated trees; roads, plain; footpaths, pecked lines; buildings in plan, red or grey; peripheral estates named

DECORATION: 4 point compass indicators on all maps except no. 1, some with leaves; map 7 has NS line in the form of a snake

TITLES:

1 Kelly Barton in the Parish of Kelly
2 Kelly Glebe Winbrook and Kelly Mill in the Parish of Kelly
   Winbrook SX 392825
3 Kelly Beare Yoemans and Yoemans Mill in the Parish of Kelly
   Yoemans SX 385825 Kellybeare SX 393833
4 Meadwell in the Parish of Kelly
   Meadwell SX 405817
5 Hole Cleave and Hornibrooks in the Parish of Kelly
   Cleave SX 409827
6 Shute and Halmeadon
   Shute SX 409812
7 Billycomb and Smithson in the Parish of Kelly
   Billacombe SX 421823
8 Dunterton Barton Dunterne and Palmers Cleave Woods in the Parish
   of Dunterton
   Dunterton Church SX376793 Dunterne Wood SX 382782
9 Wrixhill and part of Harestone in the Parish of Dunterton
   Wrixhill SX 375800
10 Eastacott and Shirrill in the Parish of Dunterton
   Eastacott SX390797 Sherrill SX 385796
11 Harestone in the Parish of Dunterton
   Hardstone Farm SX 368794
12 Woodtown Carthamartha and Pilistrey (Pillistreet in Index) in the
   Parishes of Dunterton and Broadstone
   Carthamartha SX 367778 Pallastreet SX 374806
13 Holand Sariton and Tredown in the Parish of Broadstone
   Holland SX 395808 Tredown SX 400805
14 Borough and Beckwell in the Parish of Milton Abbot (later annotations, 1847)
   Borough SX 417814
15 Timbleham in the Parish of Lezant

11/2/1

KENN
1765   63/2/2/1/56a

Kenn Church SX 922857

TITLE: not given but endorsed 'Aug. 1765 Plan of Fields to be exchanged between Mr Ley & Mr Short'

SURVEYOR: not named

SCALE: no unit of measurement stated; scale bar shows chains; 1"=2 chains; 1:1584

MATERIAL, SIZE & ORIENTATION: paper, watermark, ink; 33.2cms x 41.3cms; no direction

CONTENT: river, diagrammatic only; flood hatch named in pencil; spring; fields named distinguishing Mr Ley's or Mr Short's ownership; one area marked off by pricked line; content; asterisks in pencil; gates; tree symbol; short length of road, gated; peripheral owners named

ASSOCIATED DOCUMENT: 62/2/2/1/56b Memorandum by Mr Ley left with Thos Northmore Esq dated Nov 9. 1765 suggesting an exchange of land following the exchange between himself and Mr Short

---

11/2/2

KENN
1787   63/2/1/1/318

Trehill SX 918850

TITLE: 'A Sketch of Westes & part of Bowdens Estates in Kenn Late Mr John Harrisons ... March 18th 1787'

SURVEYOR: not named

SCALE: not given

MATERIAL, SIZE & ORIENTATION: paper, ink; 50.6cms EW x 38.4cms NS; east to top

CONTENT: fields, some named; others with alphabetical reference to table giving; roads; buildings in plan; church, parsonage house and Trehill in elevation

DECORATION: compass indicator; north only marked by a symbol

11/2/3

KENN
1787   Powderham Archive

Kenn Church SX 922857

See entry under Powderham – Estate Atlas, 16/12/7

11/2/4

KENN

early 19th cent.   63/2/2/1/56k

Area unidentified

Rough sketch on the dorse of a letter from Robert Cartwright to Mr Rawling of Taylor's Hall Goldsmiths Street Exeter concerning fields and Common Plots in the area owned by Mr Ley. Cartwright mentions his brother participating in the survey

11/2/5

KENN

19th cent.   2741M/E2/5

Trehill SX 918850

TITLE: not given

SURVEYOR: not named

SCALE: not given

MATERIAL, SIZE & ORIENTATION: paper, ink; 30.7cms EW x 19cms NS; south to top

CONTENT: sketch showing route of proposed new road; fields adjoining and their use indicated; wood, quarry, deep ditch, old and new roads named; spring and watercourse marked by letter and line of crosses

DECORATION: 4 point compass indicator; NSEW marked by letter

ASSOCIATED DOCUMENT: 2741M/E2/4 describes in detail proposed changes

11/2/6

KENN

1805   SRO DD/AH/Box 14

Kenn Church SX 922857

See entry under Ashburton, 1/8/6

11/2/7

KENN

1810   63/2/2/1/56c–g

Kenn Church SX 922857   1 not numbered

TITLE: 'Field Map of Randles in Kenn Property of George Short Esq Survey'd in 1810'

SURVEYOR: not named

SCALE: no unit of measurement stated; scale bar; 1"=3 ?chains

MATERIAL, SIZE & ORIENTATION: paper, damaged, ink; 6 irregularly-shaped pieces *c.*66.5cms x 54cms; no direction

CONTENT: river; relief shown by hill shading; fields named with numeric reference to table giving field names, land use, content and total content; fields arranged in 4 Lots; asterisks indicating hedge ownership; other owners named; gates; tree symbols showing isolated trees; roads, fenced and unfenced, gated; directions given; buildings in plan; peripheral owners and parishes named

11/2/8

KENN

1819   63/2/2/1/56h

Kenn Church SX 922857

TITLE: 'A Map of Lands in the Parish of Kenn, Devon: belonging to Henry Ley Esq'

SURVEYOR: 'Surveyed in Feby 1819, by John Pascoe'

SCALE: 'Scale of Chains'; scale bar; 1"=1.5 chains' 1:1188

MATERIAL, SIZE & ORIENTATION: paper, slight colour; 29.5cms x 36.6cms; north-east to top

CONTENT: stream, blue; fields and gardens outlined in various colours; alpha-numeric reference to list giving area and buildings' names, content and from whom purchased; roads, directions given; buildings in plan; relevant buildings coloured, others hatched black; peripheral owners named

DECORATION: 4 point compass indicator; north marked by symbol

ENDORSEMENT: Aclands Brimages Cottages &c

11/2/9

KENN

1823   Private hands

Race Stand SX 897835

TITLE: not given; printed note on map 'A.D.1823 John Pascoe and Edward Osmond commissioned to allot the commonable land of Haldon Common'

SURVEYORS:: John Pascoe and Edward Osmond

SCALE: 'Scale of Chains'; scale bar; 1"=9 chains; 1:7128

MATERIAL, SIZE & ORIENTATION: parchment, coloured; 79cms x 68cms (attached to document); south-west to top

CONTENT: stream shown in Harcombe Vale; Harcombe and Rushy Coombe shown by shading; Dead Man's Coombe also named; allotments outlined in ink, some coloured with content and owners' names; alphabetic reference to list giving total content of land allotted to each new owner; reference to areas providing sand and gravel for repair of highways with their content; list of colours keyed to turnpike roads, public roads and private roads; some roads named, directions given; race course, green; race stand named; 4 ancient enclosures named, outlined in grey; Kenn Beacon Plantation named; Telegraph Hill in plan and named; peripheral owners named

DECORATION: 4 point compass indicator; north marked by fleur-de-lys, SEW by letter

ASSOCIATED DOCUMENT: 'official' copy filed with the Devon Clerk of the Peace exists at DRO, Enclosure Award 38.

11/2/10

KENN
1825   63/2/2/1/58a–d

Trehill SX 918850

TITLE: 'A Map of Trehill and other Estates in the Parish of Kenn in the County of Devon; the Property of John Henry Ley, Esqr; Surveyed and Copied from former maps, by John Pascoe'

SURVEYOR: John Pascoe

SCALE: no unit of measurement stated; scale bar shows chains; 1"=4 chains; 1:3168

MATERIAL, SIZE & ORIENTATION: parchment, coloured; 4 separate pieces each c.73.7cms x 69.2cms; north-west to top

CONTENT: streams, blue; bridge, named; relief shown by hill shading; fields, green some with parallel lines indicating arable; some with stippling and/or tree symbols superimposed; numeric reference [to Survey Book]; hedge ownership indicated 'The Boundary fences are distinguished by a Scrawl'; gardens; tree symbols showing orchards, coppices and woods; roads, buff, fenced and unfenced; directions given; milestones and distances from Exeter indicated; buildings in plan, red; those not belonging to the estate, hatched black; peripheral owners and parishes named

DECORATION: title embellished with ink flourishes; 8 point compass rose, shaded-line decoration; north marked by symbol

11/2/11

KENN
1828   63/2/2/1/59

Trehill SX 918850

TITLE: 'Plan of Proposed Road at Trehill in Kenn 1828'

SURVEYOR: 'Jno. Pascoe May 1828'

SCALE: 'Chains'; scale bar; 1"=4 chains; 1:3168

MATERIAL, SIZE & ORIENTATION: paper, slight colour; 70.1cms x 32.1cms; no direction

CONTENT: stream, blue; fields outlined in ink, named; quarry, black lines; roads, buff, directions given; new road, red and distances given between points A–D; buildings in plan, red, hatched

INSET: longitudinal section between letters A–C; longitudinal scale 1"= 4 chains; vertical scale 1"=80 feet

11/2/12

KENN
1839   1508M Devon/M&P/Kenton Maps 6

Mellands SX 948848

TITLE: 'A Vale of Land Called Millands Bottom lying in the Parishes of Kenn, Kenton and Powderham Devon 1839'

SURVEYOR: 'Surveyed, November 1839, by Jno Grant'

SCALE: 'Scale of Imperial chains'; scale bar; 1"=2 chains; 1:1584

MATERIAL, SIZE & ORIENTATION: paper, mounted on linen, coloured; 122cms x 56.3cms; north-east to top

CONTENT: river and mill stream, blue with stream lines; arrow indicating direction of flow; Beavis Bridge named; some hill shading; fields outlined with hedge symbols, coloured with content; numeric reference to list giving names of owners, lessees and occupiers, colour used and content; tree symbols showing ?orchards, ?copses and isolated trees; roads, buff, directions given; buildings in plan, grey; Willsworthy Mill and Kenton Mill named

DECORATION: 8 point compass rose, shaded grey; north marked by fleur-de-lys

NOTE: map considerably altered at a later date – hedge banks removed, new roads indicated and new field numbers in red

---

KENN see also C63, C95–99

11/3/1

KENTISBEARE

*c.*1650   SRO DD/WY Acc. No. c/306

Kentisbeare Church ST 068081

TITLE: not given [shows area from Kentisbeare Church to Newland village]

SURVEYOR: not named

SCALE: not given

MATERIAL, SIZE & ORIENTATION: paper, coloured; 69.5cms EW x 35.6cms NS; south to top; directions spelt out on margins

CONTENT: river, grey with buff margins; named 'Kent's Brooke' with 'old streme' marked, now replaced by meander; leats named; fields, outlined in brown, dark green; fields close to river named, 'mead' or 'meade' with their owners; orchard named; 'Higher Common' and 'Common Allers' named, latter with one tree; 'Kents Moore', dark green; roads, reddish brown, named; 'Kentisbeare Town' named; houses and church in detailed elevation; churchyard with one tree outlined in brown; Lych Gate; houses outside the town named; 2 mills, one drawn in great detail with 2 mill wheels, named 'The Mill called Goodiford Mill'; Waldron Water taken across 'Kents Moore' to Newland Farm, in dark brown circular enclosure, and Newland village

Very dark green straight line 0.5cms wide running across the map; not a later addition because where it crosses road and pathways their ink outlines are broken

PUBLICATION: E.S. Chalk, *Kentisbeare* (1934), wrote 'Watercourse. It leaves the little river called Kentelesbroke just below the Domesday Mill [Goodiford Mill ?] and flows westward to Newland to Upton where it goes into the Culm'

11/3/2

KENTISBEARE

1769   3223A add2/PS4

Kentisbeare Church ST 068081

TITLE: 'A Map of the Roads in the Parish of Kentisbeer By Thos Bristow 1769'

SURVEYOR: Thomas Bristow

SCALE: 'A Scale of Chains of 66 Feet'; scale bar; 1"=13 chains: 1:10296

MATERIAL, SIZE & ORIENTATION: paper, slight colour; 66.8cms EW x 49cms NS; south to top

CONTENT: river, blue with pecked lines indicating river banks; fords; Black Down marked by hill shading; The Beacon named, shown by verical strokes in circular form; tree symbols showing hedgerow trees; hedge symbols; moor and common indicated by name; roads, brown; Turnpike Road, yellow; 'Explanation' lists 'The Private Lanes, The Close and Publick Roads, The Open Roads' with their relevant symbols; roads and lanes, named; footpaths, pecked lines; direction posts shown in elevation; new road 'made this year to join the Turnpike' indicated; buildings, including the church, in elevation; named with numeric reference to list giving distance from the church in miles, furlongs and poles; peripheral parishes and parish boundaries marked; gate on 'Cullumpton' parish boundary

DECORATION: title cartouche: 2 columns with ribbon and leaf decoration; 8 point compass rose, plain/grey, superimposed on small yellow and red circles; red centre; NSEW marked by letter; titles to lists decorated with ink flourishes

NOTE: at 3223A/P27 is a rough copy of this map made by E.S. Chalk Rector 1908

11/3/3

KENTISBEARE

*c.*1810   SRO DD/WY

Kentisbeare Church ST 068081

TITLE: 'Map of the Manor of Kentisbeer in The County of Devon'

SURVEYOR: not named

SCALE: 'Chains'; scale bar; 1"=6 chains; 1:4752; inset 1"=11 chains; 1:8712

MATERIAL, SIZE & ORIENTATION: parchment, slight colour; 91.5cms EW (cropped) x 58.5cms NS; north to top

CONTENT: streams; fields outlined in green with numeric reference [to Survey Book]; strips, numbered, separated by pecked lines; tree symbols showing woods, copses and orchards; Aller Wood named, tree symbols with stippling; roads, buff, directions given; buildings in plan, red or grey; peripheral owners named

DECORATION: 8 point compass rose, stippled/shaded grey; north marked by fleur-de-lys

11/3/4

KENTISBEARE
1820   51/3/10/4

Kingsford ST 047089

TITLE: 'Lower Kingsford in the Parish of Kentisbeer Devon'

SURVEYOR: not named

SCALE: 'A Scale of Statute Chains'; scale bar; 1"=3 chains; 1:2376

MATERIAL, SIZE & ORIENTATION: paper, ink; 38cms EW x 47.2cms NS; north to top

CONTENT: fields outlined in ink; numeric reference to list giving field names and content; asterisks indicating hedge ownership; roads; buildings in plan; peripheral owners and estates named

DECORATION: 8 point crude compass indicator; north marked by fleur-de-lys

11/3/5

KENTISBEARE
1825   3223A/PZ4

Kentisbeare Church ST 068081

TITLE: 2 maps 'Part of Kentisbeer Devon 1825'

SURVEYOR: not named

SCALE: 'Scale of 6 Chains to an Inch'; no scale bar; 1:4572; inset on map A has a scale of 12 chains to an inch

MATERIAL, SIZE & ORIENTATION: paper, slight colour; 51.5cms x 40.3cms; directions indicated, west or north to top

CONTENT: fields outlined in blue with numeric reference in black [to Survey Book] and also in red [referring to tithe]; roads, directions given; buildings in plan, red; peripheral owners and parishes named

DECORATION: 8 point plain compass indicator; north marked by fleur-de-lys

NOTE: annotations and additional fields in red

11/3/6

KENTISBEARE
1826   50/3/1/4

Goodiford Mill ST 057083 Aller Farm ST 053067

TITLE: 'Plan of Kentismoor in the County of Devon'

SURVEYOR: not named

SCALE: 'Scale of Perches'; 1"=25 perches; 1:4950

MATERIAL, SIZE & ORIENTATION: paper, slight colour; 65.5cms EW x 71cms NS; north to top

CONTENT: stream, blue, arrow marking direction of flow; fields outlined in yellow with owners' names and content; numeric reference [to Survey Book]; some asterisks indicating fence ownership; evidence of strip cultivation; roads, buff, directions given; buildings in plan, red; Goodiford Mills and Aller Farm House named; peripheral owners named

DECORATION: 8 point compass rose, shaded-line decoration; north marked by fleur-de-lys

11/3/7

KENTISBEARE
c.1826   SRO DD/WY/Box 121

Kentisbeare Church ST 068081

TITLE: 'Map of the Manor of Kentisbeer in the County of Devon'

SURVEYOR: not named [Thomas Hawkes]

SCALE: 'Scale of half a Mile', annotated '6 Chains to an Inch'; statement only; 1:4752

MATERIAL, SIZE & ORIENTATION: paper, mounted on linen; slight colour; 92.8cms EW x 45.4cms NS; north to top

CONTENT: streams, blue; fields outlined in blue or pink (Glebe lands); numeric reference [to Survey Book]; asterisks on manor boundaries indicating fence ownership; strips indicated; Aller Wood (no trees); roads, buff; buildings in plan, red or black. peripheral owners and parishes named

DECORATION: 8 point compass rose, shaded-line decoration; north marked by fleur-de-lys

Later annotations in ink

11/3/8

KENTISBEARE
1827   SRO DD/WY/Box121

Kentismoor ST 062065

TITLE: 'Plan of Kentismoor in the County of Devon 1827'

SURVEYOR: not named [Thomas Hawkes]

SCALE: 'Scale of Perches'; scale bar; 1"=24 perches; 1:4752

MATERIAL, SIZE & ORIENTATION: paper, mounted on linen, slight colour; 51.5cms EW x 67cms NS; north to top

CONTENT: streams, blue; fields outlined in ink with hedge symbols and asterisks indicating hedge ownership; tenants and owners named; content; numeric reference [to Survey Book]; roads, some named, directions given; Turnpike road named; buildings in plan, red; peripheral parishes named

DECORATION: 8 point compass rose, shaded-line decoration; north marked by fleur-de-lys

11/3/9

KENTISBEARE
1827   1926B/W/E2/9

Kentismoor ST 062065

TITLE: 'Plan of Kentismoor in the County of Devon 1827'

SURVEYOR: not named

SCALE: 'Scale of Perches'; scale bar; 1"=17 perches; 1:3360

MATERIAL, SIZE & ORIENTATION: oiled silk, ink; 53.2cms EW x 74cms NS; north to top

CONTENT: river; fields with owners' names and content; numeric reference [to Survey Book]; vestigial strips with content; roads, directions given; buildings in plan, black; peripheral parishes named

DECORATION: 4 point compass indicator; north marked by fleur-de-lys

NOTE: this map is probably a copy of the original 1827 map

11/3/10

KENTISBEARE
1827   SRO DD/WY/Box 121

Blackborough ST 093092

TITLE: 'Plan of Blackborough in the County of Devon 1827'

SURVEYOR: not named [Thomas Hawkes]

SCALE: 'Scale 6 chains to an Inch', statement only; 1:4752

MATERIAL, SIZE & ORIENTATION: paper, mounted on linen, slight colour; 51.8cms EW x 76.5cms NS; north to top

CONTENT: fields outlined in various colours with numeric reference [to Survey Book]; hedge symbols indicating hedge ownership; roads; buildings in plan, red or black, some named; peripheral owners and parishes named

DECORATION: 8 point plain compass indicator; north marked by fleur-de-lys

11/4/1

KENTON
1723   Powderham Archive

Estate Atlas
See entry under Powderham, 16/12/1

11/4/2

KENTON
1747–1759   1508M/Maps/Powderham 2

Estate atlas of 11 maps

TITLE: 'Map of the Manors of Powderham & Kenton' On the last page – 'An Enlargement of Whittlesea's Book-Map of the Manors of Powderham and Kenton'

SURVEYOR: not named; [William Chapple]

SCALES: indicated on each map by statements only, all maps except Maps 1 and 3 'By a Scale of Forty Perches to an Inch'; no scale bars; 1:7920

MATERIAL, SIZE & ORIENTATION: paper, coloured; 30.3cms x 39cms [sheets guarded]; directions indicated

GENERAL CONTENT: river, grey; fields outlined in colour; alphabetic reference to table on facing page giving content of 'each Field or Parcel of Ground, Content of each Tenant's Holdings; Orchard &c in the Same'; formal gardens in plan; tree symbols marking orchards, woods, avenues; lanes, fenced, named; buildings in elevation, some named; apart from Map 1 peripheral owners and parishes named

DECORATION: 8 point compass roses; north marked by fleur-de-lys, east by cross

NOTE: for Whittlesey's Estate Atlas 1723 see entry under Powderham

MAP 1 Powderham Castle SX 966836
   TITLE: 'A Map of the Demesne of Powderham Castle with the Marsh adjoining the same'
   SCALE: not given

MAP 2
   TITLE: 'A Map of the South Part of Powderham Manor'

MAP 3 Exwell Barton SX 957854
   TITLE: 'A Map of Exwell Barton &c'
   SCALE: 'By a Scale of Thirty Two Perches to an Inch'; 1:6336
   CONTENT: right bank only of river Exe, grey; some indication of relief, hills in profile, lit from the west; described in reference table as 'Ye Hill'

MAP 4
TITLE: 'A Map of the North Part of Powderham Manor'

MAP 5 Kenton Church SX 957833
TITLE: 'A Map of the North East Part of Kenton Manor'
CONTENT: additional details: strip field system shown; complete illustration of the Church and on south-west boundary 'Furze Breaks in Hand'

MAP 6
TITLE: 'A Map of the South East Part of Kenton Manor'
CONTENT: additional details: River Exe, right bank only shown, grey; stream bounding Cockwood Lake which is shown as strip of land outlined in yellow; strip field system; 'Salt works by ye Riverside'

MAP 7
TITLE: 'A Map of the South and Middle Part of Kenton Manor'

MAP 8
TITLE: 'A Map of the North and Middle Part of Kenton Manor'
CONTENT: additonal details: Kenton Church in elevation

MAP 9
TITLE: 'A Map of the South West Part of Kenton Manor'

MAP 10
TITLE: 'A Map of the North West Part of Kenton Manor'

MAP 11 Langstone Rock SX 980780
There are 2 maps on this page and the Reference Table is also divided
TITLE: 'A Map of Bond's Estate near Halldown and Wieke'
CONTENT: additional details: upper map shows house surrounded by trees on north and east enclosed by a dotted line and a large area coloured yellow; described as '3 Fields of Course Pasture formerly inclosed but now lie open to Halldown'
Lower map shows part of the river Exe and the Warren; the sea shown with blue brush strokes; Langstone Rock in profile

ASSOCIATED DOCUMENT: 'The General Result of all the foregoing Rentals' in the handwriting of William Chapple gives the total value of all the Courtenay's Devonshire lands including the Manors of Powderham and Kenton, n.d. (1508M Devon add 11/E1)

11/4/3

KENTON
*c.*1760   1508M Devon/M&P/Kenton Maps 13

Maps numbered 1508M Devon/M&P/Kenton Maps 13–17 are incomplete and are probably the work of William Hole.
Cockwood SX 976807
TITLE: not given
SURVEYOR: not named but probably William Hole on stylistic grounds
SCALE: not given
MATERIAL, SIZE & ORIENTATION: parchment , ink; 81.9cms x 66.8cms; no direction
CONTENT: sea, rivers, streams, grey; fields outlined in ink; a few tenements have owners' names; roads; footpaths, pecked lines; buildings in elevation; peripheral parish and owners named

11/4/4

KENTON
*c.*1760   1508M Devon/M&P/Kenton Maps 14

Kenton Church SX 957833
TITLE: not given; map covers whole parish
SURVEYOR: not named but probably William Hole on stylistic grounds
MATERIAL, SIZE & ORIENTATION: parchment, ink; 81.7cms x 66.5cms; no direction
CONTENT: streams; fields outlined in ink, some with owners' names and some with alphabetic reference [to Survey Book]; tree symbols showing orchards; roads; buildings, including the church, in elevation; peripheral estates named
DECORATION: title cartouche: trees, scrolls, plants, flowers, fruit and rural scene with cow, deer being chased by hound, windmill and farmhouse; title not inscribed

11/4/5

KENTON
*c.*1760   1508M Devon/M&P/Kenton Maps 17

Kenton Church SX957833
TITLE: not given
SURVEYOR: not named but probably William Hole on stylistic grounds
SCALE: not given

MATERIAL, SIZE & ORIENTATION: parchment, ink; 108.7cms x 67.1cms; no direction

CONTENT: rivers; fields outlined in ink; some named with numeric reference [to Survey Book] and some with alpha-numeric reference [to Survey Book]; tree symbols showing orchards; roads; buildings, including church and rectory in elevation; peripheral owners and estates named

DECORATION: title cartouche: scrolls, acanthus leaves and cow; title not inscribed

---

11/4/6

[KENTON]
*c.*1760   1508M Devon/M&P/Kenton Maps 17

3 maps with fields, roads and buildings in outline only; 2 identical copies each with cartouche. No titles, no surveyors, no scales and no direction. All on parchment, *c.*56cms x *c.*66cms.

DECORATION: 2 with eagle holding ribbon and fabric in its beak and claws with space for title to be inscribed; this cartouche used by John Richards and William Hole. The latter used it on a map of Luscombe in Bovey Tracey in 1757; he was mapping in Powderham in 1759.

11/4/7

KENTON
*c.*1760   1508M Devon/M&P/Kenton Maps 17a

East Town SX 960836
TITLE: not given
SURVEYOR: not named but probably William Hole on stylistic grounds
SCALE: not given
MATERIAL, SIZE & ORIENTATION: parchment, ink; 81.6cms x 66.3cms; no direction
CONTENT: streams; fields outlined in ink, some with owners' named and numeric reference [to Survey book] and some with alpha-numeric reference [to Survey Book]; tree symbols showing orchards and isolated trees; roads; footpaths, pecked lines; buildings in elevation; peripheral owners and estates named
DECORATION: title cartouche: scrolls, acanthus leaves, pediment at top and rural scene with sheep at bottom; title not inscribed

---

11/4/8

KENTON
1783   1508M Devon/M&P/Kenton Maps 1

Kenton Church SX 957833

TITLE: 'Map of lands lying within the several Manors or Districts of Kenton-Courtenay, Chiverstone, Kenton, West-Town, Hayton, Wilsworthy including Pits-Moor, Hall Down and the Kenwoods, Lyston (alias Lyson)&c, South Town, Staplake, Starcross, Southbrook, Cofford, Week and Week Pitt, all within the Parish of Kenton, in the County of Devon Belonging to The Right Honourable William Lord Viscount Courtenay By G. Lang 1783'

SURVEYOR: George Lang

SCALE: not given

MATERIAL, SIZE & ORIENTATION: 7 pieces of parchment joined, coloured; 295cms x 179cms; north-east to top

CONTENT: English Channel, Cheekstone, Longstone and River Exe named; form lines, shaded pale ochre marking coast and river banks; arrows indicating tidal flow; Exmouth Passage named; brooks, ink stream lines; cliffs in profile, shaded grey; fields outlined in various colours, named; numeric reference, black, [to Survey Book]; 2nd numeric reference, red; areas of strip cultivation; gates; gardens in plan; ownership of boundary fences indicated; green tree symbols showing orchards and isolated trees and on a green wash woods, copses, brakes and plantations; marsh, green; 'Rabbit Warren' (Dawlish Warren), stippled; roads and footpaths, fenced and unfenced; buildings in elevation; 'those not belonging' in plan; salt ponds and salt works; quay; peripheral owners, township, manors and parishes named; Exmouth Church in elevation

Reference list of symbols used

DECORATION: title cartouche: delicate design of acanthus leaves, sprays of flowers and leaves with hanging vine-leaf forms above a view of river with island, trees and cottages on river banks; ships at sea and on river; 32 point compass rose, plain/grey, superimposed on 3 concentric circles; north marked by fleur-de-lys; border running leaf pattern

---

11/4/9

KENTON
1787   Powderham Archive

Kenton Church SX 957833
See entry under Powderham – Estate Atlas, 16/12/7

11/4/10

KENTON
1805   SRO DD/AH/Box 14

Kenton Church SX 957833
See entry under Ashburton, 1/8/6

11/4/11

KENTON
1808   1508M Devon/M&P/Kenton Maps 3

Cockwood SX 976807
See entry under Dawlish, 4/5/5

11/4/12

KENTON
1810   1508M Devon/M&P/Kenton Maps 4

Shutterton Bridge SX 966786
See entry under Dawlish, 4/5/6

11/4/13

KENTON
[1820]   1508M Devon/M&P/Starcross A 4

Junction Turnpike road and Sea-side Road SX 975824
TITLE: 'The Castle Grounds'
SURVEYOR: not named
SCALE: not given
MATERIAL, SIZE & ORIENTATION: paper, slight colour; 55cms x 44.8cms;
no direction
CONTENT: River Exe; fields outlined in ink, named with tenants' names;
1 area outlined in green, hatched in ink with 5 parts named – fields,
garden, yard and barn; roads, named, 'Turnpike Road leading from
Starcross to Exeter, Sea-side Road to Powderham Church, Road to
Staplake House, Ridge Field Lane, to Painters Farm', all shaded with
broken lines; barriers indicated across Staplake Road; Staplake Estate
named

11/4/14

KENTON
19th cent.   1508M Devon/M&P/Rivers/Maps 4

Powderham Church SX 972844
TITLE: not given
SURVEYOR: not named
SCALE: not given
MATERIAL, SIZE & ORIENTATION: paper (torn), coloured; 65.4cms x
52.7cms; no direction
CONTENT: River Exe coloured various shades of blue; River Kenn, blue;
roads, buff, named; buildings in plan, grey and stylised at population
centres (Lympstone, Starcross, Southtown, Kenton and Powderham);
Powderham Castle in plan, grey; Powderham Church in elevation,
grey
ENDORSEMENT: Map Part of Southtown Powderham

11/4/15

KENTON
19th cent.   1508M Devon/M&P/Powderham A5

Exwell Barton SX 957854
TITLE: endorsed 'Old Tracing of part of Exwell'
SURVEYOR: not named
SCALE: not given
MATERIAL, SIZE & ORIENTATION: paper, slight colour; 42cns x 44.6cms
(torn); no direction
CONTENT: fields outlined in pink and named; reference table on the map
arranged under names of fields gives reference [to Survey Book]
and content; building in plan, pink

11/4/16

KENTON
19th cent.   1508M Devon/M&P/Kenton Maps 19

Painters Farm SX 974825
TITLE: 'Plan of Painters Farm'
SURVEYOR: not named
SCALE: not given
MATERIAL, SIZE & ORIENTATION: paper, slight colour; 70.5cms x 58.5cms;
north-west to top

CONTENT: rivers, blue; fields outlined in ink with content; numeric reference [to list]; tree symbols showing mixed woodland; roads, buff; footpaths, broken lines; buildings in plan, red or hatched black

DECORATION: 4 point compass indicator, plain/black; north marked by fleur-de-lys

11/4/17

KENTON
| 19th cent. | 1508M Devon/M&P/Kenton Maps 22 |

Cockwood SX 976807

TITLE: 'A Plan of Cockwood Marshes As Formed by their first Draining by Matthew Rowse Exclusive of * see References'

SURVEYOR: Matthew Rowse

SCALE: 'A Scale of half an Inch to a Chain'; 1"=2 chains; 1:1584

MATERIAL, SIZE & ORIENTATION: paper, slight colour; 89cms EW x 38.3cms NS; north to top

CONTENT: canal and drains, blue/grey; stream, grey, with sluice gate; new drain, yellow, broken lines; marshes outlined in colour, named; banks, brown; alphabetic reference to 'References and Propositions' detailing proposed improvements; roads, buff, directions given; buildings in plan, grey, Lime Kilns, grey

DECORATION: title cartouche: grey abstract design; 4 point compass indicator, shaded grey; north marked by fleur-de-lys, SEW by letter

11/4/18

KENTON
| 1827 | 484M/T3/20 |

Kenton Church SX 957833
See entry under Ashcombe, 1/9/1

11/4/19

KENTON
| 1836 | 484M/T4/37 |

Mowlish SX 951811

TITLE: 'The Schedule referred to by the above written indenture'

SURVEYOR: not named

SCALE: 'Scale of Chains'; scale bar; 1"=5 chains;1:3960

MATERIAL, SIZE & ORIENTATION: parchment, coloured; 97.4cms EW x 70cms NS; north to top

CONTENT: streams, pond, blue; fields coloured with boundaries of estates in deeper colour; numeric reference to lists giving field names, land use and content, grouped by estates; asterisks indicating fence ownership; tree symbols showing orchards, brakes and avenues; roads, buff; buildings in plan, red; parish boundary between Kenton and Mamhead shown; peripheral owners named

DECORATION: 8 point compass rose, shaded-line decoration; north marked by fleur-de-lys

ASSOCIATED DOCUMENT: map is bound in with Conveyance dated 23 March 1836 of a mansion house and farm called Newhouse in Mamhead and Brickhouse, Mowlishes and Cofford Mill in Kenton to the use of Sir Robert William Newman

11/4/20

KENTON
| 1837 | 1508M Devon/M&P/Kenton Maps 5 |

Cofford Farm SX 966806

TITLE: 'A Map of Cofford Mill Estate'

SURVEYOR: J. Brinsden

SCALE: not given

MATERIAL, SIZE & ORIENTATION: paper, coloured; 54.8cms EW x 72cms NS; north to top

CONTENT: stream, blue; fields coloured according to land use, outlined in deeper tones; 'Reference' lists use of colour; content; tree symbols showing orchard; symbols for brakes; road; building in plan, red; peripheral owners and estates named

DECORATION: 16 point compass rose, grey/black with elaborate centre; north marked by fleur-de-lys

11/4/21

KENTON
| post 1837 | 1508M/Estate/M&P/Kenton 3 |

Mamhead Obelisk SX 925807

TITLE: 'Map or Plan referred to'

SURVEYOR: not named

SCALE: 'Scale of Chains'; scale bar; 1"=8 chains; 1:6336

MATERIAL, SIZE & ORIENTATION: paper, watermark, coloured; 87cms EW x 29cms NS; east to top

CONTENT: streams and springs; fields in various colours outlined in deeper shades; alpha-numeric reference [to document]; 'The Obelisk Plant-ation', buff; roads, buff, fenced and unfenced; directions given; 'New Turnpike Road from Chudleigh to Starcross', named; obelisk named, hatched black; peripheral owners and plantations named

DECORATION: 4 point compass indicator; north marked by an arrow

NOTE: map dated by the watermark

11/4/22

KENTON
1839   484M/T4/45

Mamhead Obelisk SX 925807

TITLE: not given

SURVEYORS:: Thomas Michelmore and Robert Dymond

SCALE: 'Scale of Chains'; scale bar; 1"=8 chains; 1:6336

MATERIAL, SIZE & ORIENTATION: parchment, coloured; 73.8cms EW x 28cms NS, bound with Conveyance; north to top

CONTENT: stream; fields outlined in various colours with alpha-numeric references which are described in the Conveyance; 'The Obelisk Plantation', buff [no tree symbols]; roads, buff including new turnpike road; footpaths, pecked lines; obelisk in plan, red; peripheral owners named

DECORATION: 4 point compass indicator; north marked by arrowhead

ASSOCIATED DOCUMENT: map is part of Conveyance dated 29 June 1839 by John Henry Ley of Trehill and others, trustees of the Will of the late Earl of Devon to Sir Robert William Newman

NOTE: there is a second map endorsed on the second membrane of this document but all the details are crossed through

11/4/23

KENTON
1839   1508M Devon/M&P/Kenton Maps 6

Mellands SX 948848

See entry under Kenn, 11/2/12

11/5/1

KILMINGTON
1739   123M/E75

Kilmington Church SY 273980

See entry under Axminster, 1/17/3

11/5/2

KILMINGTON
1776–1778   4377M/E2

Dulshayes SY 267996

See entry under Axminster, 1/17/4

11/5/3

KILMINGTON
1797   50M/E75

Shute Hill SY 258982

See entry under Dalwood, 4/1/5

KILMINGTON see also C100–102

11/6/1

KINGSBRIDGE
1796   PWDRO 74/61/19

Kingsbridge Church SX 733444

See entry under Alvington, West, 1/6/4

11/6/2

KINGSBRIDGE

1799   *Gent. Mag.*, May 1799

Copy of 1586 map   Original not extant

Kingsbridge Church SX 733444

TITLE: 'The trewe Platt of the newe byldying, upon fyve pyllers of stonn betwixt the Church Styles of Kyngsbrydge 1586'

SURVEYOR: original surveyor not named; the map was redrawn in 1796 by G.P. Harris from the original and 'Longmate sc.'

MATERIAL, SIZE & ORIENTATION: paper (material and size of original not known), redrawn version as reproduced in the *Gentleman's Magazine* is 16.9cms EW x 14.1cms NS; north to top

CONTENT: mill leat, stream lines; land holdings, some owners' names given; gardens shown as strips; George French's partially-walled garden shown in detail; hedge symbols showing boundaries (but not ownership); tree symbols showing ?orchards and isolated tree; buildings shown in elevation and in some detail, especially the church, 'the Cheaphouse of Kyngsbridge' and 'the newe Byldyng'; 'the pellery'

NOTE: the accompanying piece in the *Gentleman's Magazine* is contributed by 'AH'

KINGSBRIDGE see also B54, B81

11/7/1

KING'S NYMPTON

1757   1148M add/6/11

Hummacotts SS 703194

See entry under Chulmleigh, 3/15/2

11/8/1

KINGSTEIGNTON

1740   Private Hands

Winstow Cottages SX 864779

See entry under Chudleigh, 3/14/1

11/8/2

KINGSTEIGNTON

1790   3799M add/E1

Staplehill SX 824738

See entry under Highweek, 8/15/3

KINGSTEIGNTON see also SUPPLEMENT S5

KINGSTEIGNTON see also B86

11/9/1

KINGSWEAR

*c.*1800   Northants RO Box X.7243, 102

Photocopies 2788Z/Z1

Kingswear Church SX 882510

See entry under Dartmouth, 4/4/4

11/9/2

KINGSWEAR

1839   1891B/P1

Lower Greenway SX 878553

See entry under Churston Ferrers, 3/17/1

12/1/1

LAMERTON

1744–1758   T1258M/E16c

Lamerton Church SX 451771

Maiden Gore Wood See entry under Tavistock, 19/3/1

12/1/2

LAMERTON
1760–1770   T1258M/E6

Ottery SX 445752
See entry under Tavistock, 19/3/22

12/1/3

LAMERTON
1788–1789   6107

Lamerton Church SX 451771
See entry under Bridestowe, 2/35/6

12/1/4

LAMERTON
18th cent.   L1258M/Maps Lamerton 2

Mill Hill SX 453747
TITLE: 'An Eye Draft of Ottery Mills and part of Mill Hill in the Parish
    of Lamerton'
SURVEYOR: not named
SCALE: not given
MATERIAL, SIZE & ORIENTATION: paper, ink and slight colour; 16cms EW
    x 20.5cms NS; west to top
CONTENT: 'Lumburn River', Mill leat, blue margins, ink shading; west
    banks of river and leat outlined with hedge symbols; Mill Hill named;
    2 fields outlined, with details of tenants and terms of their leases;
    hedge boundaries; alphabetic reference to explanation of closure of
    the way to the Common from the meadow following enclosure of
    the meadow; Ottery Mills and mill wheel in elevation
DECORATION: 4 point compass indicator; NSEW marked by letter

12/1/5

LAMERTON
1825   1262M/E22/45

Lamerton Church SX 451771
See entry under Brentor, 2/33/2

12/1/6

LAMERTON
1836   L1258/M&P/Tavistock 2

Ottery [Park] SX 445752
TITLE: 'Plan of Ottery Park in the Parish of Lamerton Devon the property
    of Mr Maurice Doidge. J Perer 1836'
SURVEYOR: J. Perer
SCALE: 'A Scale of Chains'; scale bar; 1"=4 chains; 1:3168
MATERIAL, SIZE & ORIENTATION: paper, slight colour; 60.6cms EW x
    48.5cms NS; north to top
CONTENT: rivulets and mill stream, blue; arrows indicating direction of
    flow; fields outlined in ink, light blue; numeric reference to list giving
    field names and content in statute and customary measure; fences
    claimed by adjoining proprietors, red; gateways; gardens, green; blue
    tree symbols on blue ground showing orchards, and in a park coloured
    green; isolated trees; roads, fenced and unfenced, some named;
    directions given; buildings in plan; those belonging to the estate,
    red; slate quarries; peripheral owners, Downs and estate named
DECORATION: 4 point compass indicator, blue/yellow; north marked by
    fleur-de-lys

LAMERTON see also C162

12/2/1

LANDKEY
[1649–1654]   KAO U269/P11/1

Harford SS 602318 Newland SS 597313
TITLE: 'Harford cum Newland'
SURVEYOR: not named [Thomas Berry]
SCALE: 'A Scale of 16s in an Inch'; scale bar; 1:3168
MATERIAL, SIZE & ORIENTATION: parchment, coloured; irregular shape
    [sheepskin] c.84.5cms EW x 72.5cms NS; north to top
CONTENT: stream, 'Harford Water', leat leading to pond, blue; fields,
    green, outlined in ink and green and buff; some named with content;
    some with land use indicated; some with tenants' names; green tree
    symbols showing orchards and woods; some indication of formal
    gardens; roads, buff; directions given; paths, broken lines; buildings
    in elevation; principal house has red facade, smoking chimneys; mill;
    stable; peripheral owners named; Table listing landholders and land

use, total content of 'Tillage meadow and wood'; statement that totals are inclusive of orchards, gardens, hopyards and town place

DECORATION: 8 point compass rose, blue/red; north marked by cross, south by arrowhead, NSEW by letter

PUBLICATION: Todd Gray, ed., *Devon Household Accounts 1627–59* DCRS New Series Vol. 39 (Exeter, 1996), Plate 4

12/2/2

LANDKEY
1757   1148M add/6/1

Acland Barton SS 595325 Rivaton SS 638300 Westacott SS 585328 Newland SS 597313

Bableigh [Bathey?] SS 591300

See entry under Chulmleigh, 3/15/2

12/3/1

LEW, NORTH
mid 16th cent.   4088M/

Rutleigh Ball SS 510018

TITLE: not given

SURVEYOR: not named

SCALE: not given

MATERIAL, SIZE & ORIENTATION: paper, coloured; 31.6cms EW x 42cms NS, ragged edges; directions spelt out on margins, south to top

CONTENT: river, 'Kevlake' rising in 3 springs, white; fields coloured in 3 shades of green; some named including 'Redclyff Ball'; landholders named; roads, white; directions given, 'The waye from redcliff to hatherley; The bond between cove aclond and ascott; The bond between cove the duke and cary; Rendon lane'

ASSOCIATED DOCUMENTS: documents relating to the bounds of the Moor which possibly accompanied the map included a 'View taken April 3 Edward VI on Holwaye Moor bounds'. Holwaye, possibly now Hollow Moor; Redcliffe (Rutleigh) is mentioned in other earlier extracts from Court Rolls in the same bundle but there is nothing to indicate that a map was drawn. Handwriting and style of the map appear to be consistent with a mid-16th-century date.

PUBLICATION: Mary R Ravenhill and Margery M Rowe, eds, *Early Devon Maps* (Exeter, 2000), 8

12/3/2

LEW, NORTH
1780   1508M/Devon/Surveys/V4

North Lew Church SX 505991

See entry under Combe Raleigh, 3/29/1

12/3/3

LEW, NORTH
[1800]   1508M/Devon/M&P/Holsworthy 1

North Lew Church SX 505991

See entry under Holsworthy, 8/19/3

12/3/4

LEW, NORTH
1825   1262M/E22/45

North Lew Church SX 505991

See entry under Brentor, 2/33/3

12/4/1

LEW TRENCHARD
1834/36   TD 166 (unlisted)

Lew Trenchard Church SX 457861

TITLE: 'The Estates of Holdstrong Waddlestrong 1834'

SURVEYOR: 'EBG' [?E. Baring Gould]

SCALE: 'Scale of Links'; scale bar; 1"=4.5 chains; 1:3564

MATERIAL, SIZE & ORIENTATION: paper, ink; 63cms x 49.3cms; no direction

CONTENT: fields outlined in ink with field name and content; numerical references [to Survey Book] added later; roads, one with direction 'to Coriton'; buildings in plan, hatched grey; one peripheral owner named

ENDORSEMENT: 1836. EBG

LEW TRENCHARD see also C24

12/5/1

LIFTON
1758   Private hands

Tinhay SX 397852

TITLE: 'A Plan of Whiteley with the Tenements of Gordon, Cross-town,
Cross-parks and Tinny. in the Parish of Lifton, in the County of Devon
Being the Lands of Phillip Welsh of Launceston in Cornwall Surgeon
Survey'd and Plan'd by Richard Martyn 1758'

SURVEYOR: Richard Martyn

SCALE: 'A Scale of Statute Chains, 66 feet to ye Chain'; divided scale;
1"=3 chains; 1:2376

MATERIAL, SIZE & ORIENTATION: parchment, coloured; 64.5cms EW x
79.3cms NS; north to top

CONTENT: 'River Leed', grey, stream lines; arrows indicating direction
of flow; fields outlined in various colours, named and with content;
tables listing field names and content in customary and statute measure, and indicating the colours used to identify the various tenements;
ownership of boundary hedges identified; gates; garden; green tree
symbols marking orchards and isolated trees; roads, plain, directions
given; footpaths, pricked lines; buildings in plan, brown; peripheral
estates named

DECORATION: scale and title enclosed in crude multi-coloured 'pediments';
16 point compass rose, multi-coloured compass points superimposed
upon a yellow circle; compass points indicated by letter

12/5/2

LIFTON
1769   Private hands

Colemans SX 400848

TITLE: 'A Map or Plan of the Estate called Coleman's in the Parish of
Lifton and County of Devon; the Lands of Philip Welsh Esqr Survey'd
and mapp'd in 1769 by Thomas Call'

SURVEYOR: Thomas Call

SCALE: 'A Scale of Chains each containing Four Statute Parches'; 1"=3.5
chains; 1:2772

MATERIAL, SIZE & ORIENTATION: parchment, coloured; 58.3cms EW x
55cms NS; north to top

CONTENT: 'The River Leed', grey; bridge; fields outlined in turquoise
with hedge symbols and 'asterisms' indicating hedge ownership;
numeric reference to table giving field names, content of arable and
pasture, of timber and coppice, of hedges and ditches, and total content

in statute and customary measure; gates; garden; tree symbols
showing orchards, timber and coppice, isolated trees; roads, plain,
directions given; footpaths, broken lines; buildings in plan, red;
peripheral owners named

DECORATION: title on wide ribbon held by an eagle in its beak and claws
(different from the eagle cartouche used by W Hole and J Richards);
8 point compass rose, plain/shaded grey; north marked by fleur-de-
lys, east by cross

12/6/1

LITTLEHAM (Bideford)
1839   NDRO B 138/2

Littleham Church SS 444234

TITLE: 'A Map or Plan of the Parish of Littleham Three Miles from
Bideford in the County of Devon Surveyed & Plan'd by William
Bear, Landsurveyor, Bideford in the year 1839'

SURVEYOR: William Bear

SCALE: 'Scale of Statute Chains Three to One Inch. One fourth of a
Mile'; scale bar; 1"=3 chains; 1:2376

MATERIAL, SIZE & ORIENTATION: paper, mounted on linen, damaged, slight
colour; 151.5cms EW x 132cms NS; north to top

CONTENT: rivers; river banks, pecked lines; leat; bridge; fields outlined
in ink; Hole estate outlined in green; some gates; alpha-numeric
reference – fields numbered, estates distinguished by letter – to lists
giving content of estates; crosses indicating fence ownership; roads,
directions indicated; mile post; footpaths, pecked lines; buildings in
plan, hatched black; peripheral parishes named

DECORATION: 8 point compass rose, shaded-line decoration; north marked
by fleur-de-lys; dividers above scale bar

12/7/1

LITTLEHAM (Exmouth)
late 18th cent.   96M add/E14

Littleham Church SY 029813

TITLE: 'A Map of an estate in the parish of Littleham (late Mr Mundays)
belonging to Denys Rolle Esqr'

SURVEYOR: not named [same hand as 96M add/E13 &15]

SCALE: 'A Scale of Chains'; scale bar; 1"=2.5 chains; 1:1980

MATERIAL, SIZE & ORIENTATION: paper, slight colour; 55.5cms EW x
42.8cms NS; east to top

CONTENT: ponds; fields outlined in red or blue; alpha-numeric reference to table giving field names, land use and content; tree symbols showing orchards, isolated trees; roads, directions given; buildings in plan, red; peripheral owners named; land belonging to Denys Rolle marked by a pricked line

DECORATION: title cartouche: simple scrolls with pendant leaves and urn with leaves at top; 16 point compass rose, red/blue; north marked by fleur-de-lys, crudely drawn, red/blue; outer circle, yellow

12/7/2

LITTLEHAM (Exmouth)

1817	Ex. D&C Ch. Comm. 98/8791

Littleham Church SY 029813
See entry under Aylesbeare, 1/18/2

12/8/1

LODDISWELL

1808	MFM 35

See entry under Haccombe, 8/1/3

12/9/1

LOXBEARE

1756	1148M add 23/E1

Loxbeare Barton SS 913159 Leigh Barton SS 909148 Leigh Town SS 914149 Leigh Mill SS 907149 Churchill SS 904165 Pantacrudge SS 905158 Perry SS 920152
See entry under Broadclyst, 2/39/2

LUNDY

A list of maps and plans of the Island of Lundy, both manuscript and printed will appear in the *Lundy Field Society Annual Report*, No.52, 2001, to be published in 2002. We are most grateful to its compiler, Dr Myrtle Ternstrom, for her help concerning the maps of Lundy. There are two manuscript items which fall within the scope of this present volume and the listing made from photocopies kindly supplied by Dr Ternstrom, is as follows:-

12/10/1

LUNDY ISLAND

1804	PRO, MPH 54 (Photocopy)

Lundy Island Quay SS 143438
TITLE: 'The Island of Lundy proposed as a depot for Prisoners of War'
SURVEYOR: 'Geo. J. Parkyns delin'
SCALE: not given
MATERIAL, SIZE & ORIENTATION: ?paper, watercolour; approx 27.5cms x 17.6cms; no direction
CONTENT: water colour showing the Island of Lundy, mostly green and brown around the harbour area; offshore rocks; pier to harbour; shore-profile drawn at one mile distant

12/10/2

LUNDY ISLAND

1820	Trinity House 1319

Lundy Island Quay SS 143438 (Reduced Photocopy)
TITLE: 'Plan of the Island of Lundy 1820'
SURVEYOR: not named
SCALE: scale bar showing yards and chains; 1"=200 yards according to Dr Ternstrom's list
MATERIAL, SIZE & ORIENTATION: paper; size not known; north to top
CONTENT: bays, named, offshore rocks; cliffs in profile; fields, some with parallel lines indicating ?arable; remaining fields and other areas stippled, ?common, furze; roads; footpaths; lighthouse in plan with symbol, other buildings in plan
DECORATION: 16 point compass indicator; north marked by fleur-de-lys, other points by letter

12/11/1

LYDFORD

1788–1789	6107

Lydford Church SX 509847
See entry under Bridestowe, 2/35/6

12/11/2

LYDFORD
1794/1796   NDRO B170/102

Fernworthy Reservoir SX 665843

TITLE: 'A Map or Plan of the Estates called Fernworthy, Higher and Lower Lowton, Silkhouse and Assercombe Situate in the Parish of Lydford and County of Devon the Lands of Sir John Davie Bart Plann'd in the Year 1794 and Mapp'd in the Year 1796 by Robt Ballment'

SURVEYOR: Robert Ballment

SCALE: 'A Scale of Chains each containing Four Statute Perches'; scale bar; 1"=3 chains; 1:2376

MATERIAL, SIZE & ORIENTATION: parchment, coloured; 127.8cms EW x 142cms NS; north to top

CONTENT: rivers and streams, stream lines; river 'Tvng' and 'River Teing als South Teing' named; headwaters of 'South Teing, Holelake, Lowton Water' named and indicated by symbol; arrows marking direction of flow; well; fields outlined in colour; alpha-numeric reference [to Survey Book]; roads, buff, fenced and unfenced; directions given; information on the open Moor; barrow; stone rows; 'reve' of stones; earth bank; where these divided commons the fact is indicated; boundary stones; survey lines shown; buildings in plan, red; peripheral commons and owners named

DECORATION: title cartouche: swag of drapery; 8 point compass rose, plain/shaded grey; north marked by fleur-de-lys, east by cross

ENDORSEMENT: A Plan and Map of the Estates called Fernworthy Higher and Lower Lowton and Arscombe, situated within the Parish of Lydford & County of Devon; the Lands of Sir John Davie Bart Measured in the year 1794, and map'd in the Year 1796 by Mr Robt Ballment

12/12/1

LYMPSTONE
1743   96 addM/E11

Lympstone Church SX 993842
See entry under Exmouth, 5/11/1

12/12/2

LYMPSTONE
1839   1508 London/M&P/River Exe 1

Exmouth Church SY 002806
See entry under Exmouth, river Exe, 5/11/7

12/12/3

LYMPSTONE
19th cent.   1508M Devon/M&P/Rivers/Maps 4

Lympstone Church SX 993842
See entry under Kenton, 11/4/14

LYMPSTONE see also B73, C103–104

12/13/1

LYNTON
1824   5846Z/E4

Lynmouth SS 722497

TITLE: 'Plan of the Port of Lynmouth in the County of Devon'

SURVEYOR: 'Surveyed and drawn by William Bright Nov, 1824'

SCALE: 'Scale of Chains'; scale bar; 1"=1.5 chains; 1:1188

MATERIAL, SIZE & ORIENTATION: paper, mounted on cloth, slight colour; 52cms x 41.7cms; north-west to top

CONTENT: 'The Lyn River' shaded with horizontal shading; rocks; 'The Beach', stippled; fields; tree symbols showing plantations, isolated trees, and, with additional symbols, woodland; roads, buff, fenced and unfenced; directions given; bridge over river; footpaths, pecked lines; footbridge; buildings in plan, grey; lime kiln

DECORATION: scale bar decorated with shells, flowers and leaves; 8 point compass rose, grey/plain; acanthus leaves between compass points; north marked by acorn and leaf ornament; border: running pattern of stylised flower petals

13/1/1

MAKER (now in Cornwall)

[before 1780]   Antony Muniments CB/FB/3

Maker Church SX 447520

TITLE: 'Lands at West Maker in the Parish of Maker in the County of Devon'

SURVEYOR: not named

SCALE: 'Scale of Chains'; scale bar; 1"=4 chains; 1:3168

MATERIAL, SIZE & ORIENTATION: parchment, coloured; 28cms x 37cms; north-west to top

CONTENT: Cawsand Bay shoreline, green; cliff indicated; spring flowing into pond, blue; relief suggested by hachures; fields outlined in yellow, named with content and numeric reference [to Survey Book]; gardens outlined; tree symbols showing orchard; roads and paths, buff, named; buildings in plan, red; milestone in profile; Lord Edgcumbe's land to east and west indicated

DECORATION: 4 point compass indicator; north marked by fleur-de-lys, SEW by letter

NOTE: in addition to this map, there are maps of Monkton and Dalwood on this sheet of parchment; one square cut out from the top probably contained another map.

13/2/1

MALBOROUGH

1777   1508M/Devon/M&P/V3

Malborough Church SX 706398
See entry under Alvington, West, 1/6/1

13/2/2

MALBOROUGH

1777   1508 Maps/Malborough1

Malborough Church SX 706398
See entry under Huish, South, 8/24/2

13/2/3

MALBOROUGH

1813   Z2/6

Gerston Farm SX 733420 Batson SX 733396
See entry under Alvington, West, 1/6/5

13/2/4

MALBOROUGH

1833   D1508/Deeds/Malborough 6

Moult House SX 729379

TITLE: not given [shows planned route of new road between Malborough and Salcombe Harbour]

SURVEYOR: not named

SCALE: 'Scale of Chains'; scale bar; 1"=4 chains; 1:3168

MATERIAL, SIZE & ORIENTATION: parchment, coloured; 22.3cms x 36.5cms; north-west to top

CONTENT: Salcombe harbour, blue; cliffs in profile; sandy beaches named, North and South Sands, buff and stippled; fields in various colours, outlined with hedge symbols; some named with alpha-numeric reference to Conveyance, with content; owners named; existing roads, buff, named; directions given; proposed new road, red; Moult House in plan, red

DECORATION: 8 point compass rose, shaded-line decoration; north marked by fleur-de-lys, SEW by letter

ASSOCIATED DOCUMENT: plan part of Conveyance from the Earl of Devon to William Jackson of The Moult in Salcombe dated 14 December 1833

Second copy endorsed Lord Devon & Wm Jackson Esq Plan of Land Conveyed & Right of Way

MALBOROUGH see also C105

13/3/1

MAMHEAD

1767   1508/Devon/M&P/Haldon 1

Road junction shown on map SX 903813
See entry under Chudleigh, 3/14/5

13/3/2

MAMHEAD
1805   SRO DD/AH/Box 14

Mamhead Church SX 931807
See entry under Ashburton, 1/8/6

13/3/3

MAMHEAD
1827   484M/T3/20

Mamhead House SX 930811
See entry under Ashcombe, 1/9/1

13/3/4

MAMHEAD
1836   484M/T4/37

New House Park SX 945801
See entry under Kenton, 11/4/19

13/4/1

MANATON
1787   Powderham Archive

Manaton Church SX 749813
See entry under Powderham – Estate Atlas, 16/12/7

13/4/2

MANATON
1790   1508M/Surveys/V5

Manaton Church SX 749813
See entry under Bovey, North, 2/21/2

13/4/3

MANATON
1805   SRO DD/AH/Box 14

Manaton Church SX 749813
See entry under Ashburton, 1/8/6

13/5/1

MARIANSLEIGH
1794   NDRO B170/17

Trittencott SS 759213
TITLE: 'A Map or Plan of the Estate called Trittoncott situate within the
    Parish and Manor of Mareleigh, in the County of Devon: the lands
    of Sir John Davie Bart – And now in the tenure of Melior Rock,
    Widow. Taken in July 1794. By Robt Ballment'
SURVEYOR: Robert Ballment
SCALE: 'A Scale of Chains each containing Four Statute Perches'; scale
    bar; 1"=3 chains; 1:2376
MATERIAL, SIZE & ORIENTATION: parchment, coloured; 59.7cms EW x
    31.3cms NS; north to top
CONTENT: fields outlined in green, numeric reference to table giving
    field names, land use and content; 'asterisms' indicating hedge
    ownership; gates; tree symbols in courtlage; footpaths; buildings in
    plan, red; peripheral owners named
DECORATION: title cartouche: leaf design; 8 point compass rose, black/
    plain; north marked by fleur-de-lys, east by cross
ENDORSEMENT: Map of Trittencott Estate in the Parish of Mareley, the
    Property of Sir John Davie Bart.

13/6/1

MARLDON
1801   Ex. D&C Ch. Comm. 98

Marldon Church SX 866636
TITLE: 'Exeter Precentorship Plan of Lands in the Parishes of Paignton
    and Marldon in the County of Devon'
SURVEYOR: not named
SCALE: 'Scale of Chains'; scale bar; 1"=3 chains; 1:2376
MATERIAL, SIZE & ORIENTATION: paper, mounted and segmented, slight
    colour; c.163cms x c.128cms; no direction

CONTENT: sea, pale green; beach shaded buff/grey; fields, pale pink or green; alpha-numeric reference [to Survey Book]; some fields plain with owners' names; tree symbols showing orchards; with stippling ?waste; roads, buff, directions given; footpaths, dotted lines; buildings in plan, red; those not belonging hatched in ink; terrace, National School and church named, cross hatched; peripheral owners and parishes named

13/7/1

MARWOOD
[1649–1654]   KAO P269/P11/3

Marwood Church SS 544376
See entry under Berrynarbor, 2/8/1
PUBLICATION: Todd Gray, ed., *Devon Household Accounts 1627–59* DCRS New Series Vol. 39 (Exeter, 1996), Plate 9

13/7/2

MARWOOD
1797   1262M/E22/43

Marwood Church SS 544376
See entry under Braunton, 2/31/3

13/7/3

MARWOOD
1797–8   1508M/London/M&P/Braunton

Marwood Church SS 544376
See entry under Braunton, 2/31/4

MARWOOD see also C106

13/8/1

MARYSTOW
1727   158M/E217

Marystow Church SX 434828
TITLE: 'A map, and terrier; of the Vicaridge of marystow'
SURVEYOR: not named
SCALE: not given
MATERIAL, SIZE & ORIENTATION: parchment, coloured; 57cms EW x 41.2cms NS; east to top
CONTENT: 'River Lid', 'Lo', brown; fields, orange, named with land use and content; gates; tree symbols; roads, reddish-brown, some named; paths, pecked lines; buildings in elevation; boundary hatched in brown; peripheral lands named; list of fields and content belonging to the vicarage

13/8/2

MARYSTOW
1727   Diocesan Glebe Terriers Marystow

Marystow Church SX 434828
As above with the following additions:-
SCALE: 'A Scale of Perches 18 foot'; scale bar; 1"=12 perches; 1:2592
CONTENT: below the map: statement of tithes due, list of church furniture, fees and salary for the vicar. Description of Vicarage House and outbuildings; this statement signed by vicar and overseer. Further note by the vicar: 'I have used all fair & honest means to incline my Parishioners to Sign this Terrier but they are so jealous that they refuse to do it. John Teasdale. vica'
ENDORSEMENT: 4th May 1727
NOTE: In August 1726 the Bishop of Exeter ordered terriers to be made in each parish and submitted to the Archdeacon's Visitation Courts to be held in the Spring of 1727

13/8/3

MARYSTOW
1788–89   6107

Sydenham House SX 426837
See entry under Bridestowe, 2/35/6

13/8/4

MARYSTOW

1810   6099

Atlas, leather bound, tooled in gold, 32.5cms x 49cms

TITLE: 'Maps of the Manor of Sydenham and Canon Barn in the County
of Devon the fee of which is in The Revd. H.H. Tremayne Survey'd
and delineated in 1810 By David Palmer'

9 pages of 'Reference to the Maps' listing the maps, tenements. ref. no.,
names of 'Plotts', content in statute and customary measure. 12 maps
on parchment with slight colour, of various sizes but folded to fit the
volume. Some only include a scale bar of statute chains with 1"=4
chains; 1:3168. All maps indicate direction

GENERAL CONTENT: streams, grey with black shading; bridges; quarry
marked with stippling; fields outlined in various colours; numeric
reference; gates; walled garden with ornamental lake; black tree
symbols; roads, straw colour; path, broken line, named; buildings in
plan, outlined in colour; peripheral estates named

TITLES:

1 'Part of the Barton of Sydenham'
       Sydenham House SX 425838

2 'Lee Lee Down Rundles Cott and Northys Cot'
       Lee Farm SX 443837

a2 'Raddon Down'

3 'Blatchfords Cholwell, Bickles Cholwell, Trehill and Thorn the property of the Poor of Maristow'
       Cholwell SX 428857 Thorn SX 438850

4 'Maristow Glebe' with cartouche of a garland of lotus flowers.
        Marystow Church SX434829
      'Shutwell' with dividers above title

5 'Crebers, Dunns, Lang's Dipford Town, Bickles do., Bickles Moiety
of Mills, Tapsons, Bickles (deaf) Gerrys, Warren, Corrys Allerford,
Dodges Allerford'
       Allerford SX 423854

6 'West Raddon, East Raddon, Tibridge, Mill Tenement, Bickles
Tenemt &c., Raddon Chapel'
       Raddon SX 453855 Tibridge SX 448847

7 'Warracott'
       SX 425827

8 'Markstone, Bullhill and Routter in Marystow'
       Router SX 416833

10 [sic] '[Holster Yard]'

9 'Higher Mill and Thruselball' and 'East Musehill'
       Musehill SX 450873

11 'Yeoham, Old Wreys and the Barton of Wreys'
       with simple cartouche
       Wreys Barton SX 438870

12 'New Inn and Canon Barn in Thruselton'
       Canon Barn SX 444871

13/9/1

MARY TAVY

1825   1262M/E22/45

Mary Tavy Church SX 504794
See entry under Brentor, 2/33/3

13/10/1

MEAVY

1793   346M/P1

Meavy Church SX 540672
See entry under Bere Ferrers, 2/6/3

MEETH see C89

13/11/1

MERTON

c.1765   NDRO B230/1

Speccott Barton SS 503141

TITLE: 'To Richard Stevens of Winscott This Map of his Barton of
Speccott is humbly Inscribed by his most obedient Servant Malachy
Hitchins'
        'This Plan of Speccott is reduced from one of a much larger Size,
in which the Fields were measured with great exactness'

SURVEYOR: Malachy Hitchins

SCALE: 'A Scale of Chains 66 feet to the Chain'; scale bar; 1"=3 chains;
1:2376

MATERIAL, SIZE & ORIENTATION: parchment, coloured; 73cms EW x
61.3cms NS; north to top

CONTENT: streams marked by stream lines; fields outlined in various colours; named with content; letters keyed to 'Explanation' indicating land use [M meadow, A arable, C coarse]; gates; gardens in plan, named; green tree symbols showing orchards, coppice and isolated trees; roads, directions given; footpaths, pecked lines; buildings in plan, black; keyed by letter to 'Explanation',[d dwelling, b barn, s stables]; peripheral parishes and owner named

Front elevation of the 'Barton House standing on Pincombe's part of Speccott'

Table giving 'A Summary of all the Tenements contained in this plan'

DECORATION: title cartouche: simple scrolls; 16 point compass rose, buff/ green, buff/yellow, wide yellow outer circle; north marked by fleur-de-lys, SEW by letter

13/11/2

MERTON
18th cent.   96M Box 59/10

Speccott Barton SS 503141
TITLE: not given [appears to be Great Speccott i.e. Speccott Barton with Little Speccott to the east]
SURVEYOR: not named
SCALE: not given
MATERIAL, SIZE & ORIENTATION: paper, damaged, slight colour; approx. 70cms x 63.5cms; no direction
CONTENT: river, streams, pond, well, ink; groups of fields outlined in various colours, named with content; alphabetic reference [to Survey Book]; gates; tree symbols showing orchards, coppice, hedgerow and isolated trees; furze, dotted parallel lines; gardens; roads, some named; footpaths pecked lines; buildings in plan, hatched in ink; pencil construction grid
NOTE: This map is on the same scale and contains the same information as 13/11/1. It would appear to be a preliminary draft and the pencil construction grid suggests the means by which reduction from the map 'of much larger Size' was made.

MERTON see also C89

13/12/1

MESHAW
18th cent.   NDRO B398/1

Meshaw Church SS 758197 Beara, Roseash SS 777202
TITLE: 'A Map of the Parish of Meshaw in the County of Devon' [Also covers Beara in Roseash Parish]
SURVEYOR: not named
SCALE: 'Scale of Chains'; scale bar; 1"=10 chains; 1:7920
MATERIAL, SIZE & ORIENTATION: paper, coloured; 80.3cms EW x 60.9cms NS; north to top
CONTENT: streams, blue, arrows indicating direction of flow; fields named; farms and estates named; Prescot estate outlined in blue; Parsonage estate outlined in red; content of Meshaw Parish; roads, buff, fenced and unfenced; footpaths, pecked lines; houses in Meshaw Town and elsewhere in plan, black; parish boundaries, brown; peripheral parishes named
DECORATION: 8 point compass rose, plain/black; north marked by fleur-de-lys

13/13/1

MILTON ABBOT
1744–1758   T1258M/E16c

Leigh Barton Farm SX 395773
See entry under Tavistock, 19/3/1

13/13/2

MILTON ABBOT
1770   T1258M/E18

Milton Abbot Church SX 406793
TITLE: not given
SURVEYOR: Geo [sic] Aislabie
SCALE: '3 Chains to an Inch' [this statement probably the work of restoration]
MATERIAL, SIZE & ORIENTATION: paper, coloured; 167.4cms EW x 318.4cms NS; north to top
CONTENT: River Tamar named, blue, arrow indicating direction of flow; fields outlined in colour, named with content; tree symbols showing orchards, and with green wash, woods; brake [brushwood], stippled; gardens, named; roads, buff, directions given; buildings in plan, red

on the estates, those outside, grey; mill and Sydenham Church in
elevation; peripheral owners and parishes named

DECORATION: 8 point compass rose, plain; north marked by fleur-de-lys
[?part of the restoration]

NOTE: This map was restored by Leane & Bakewell April 1874

13/13/5

MILTON ABBOT
early 19th cent.   Private hands

Borough SX 417814
See entry under Kelly, 11/1/2

13/13/3

MILTON ABBOT
1770   T1258M/E19

Liddaton SX 457826 Burnshall SX 443826

TITLE: 'A Plan of Several Estates in the Manor of West Liddaton and
Parish of Milton Abbot in the County of Devon belonging to His
Grace the Duke of Bedford. Taken in Augt & Septemr 1770 by Gt
Aislabie'

SURVEYOR: Gilbert Aislabie

SCALE: 'Scale 3 Chains to an Inch' [this statement probably the work of
restoration]

MATERIAL, SIZE & ORIENTATION: paper, coloured; 197cms EW x 90.7cms
NS; west to top

CONTENT: River Lyd named, blue, arrow indicating direction of flow;
fields outlined in colour, named with content; tree symbols showing
orchards; stippling marking moors; gardens named; roads, buff;
directions given; buildings in plan, red on the estates, those outside,
grey; peripheral owners and parishes named

Lists of various estates headed 'Particulars' giving details of
houses, barns, pig-houses, stables etc and fields by name with content
in Statute and Customary measure

NOTE BELOW SCALE: Restored by Leane & Bakewell April 1874

DECORATION: 4 point compass indicator; north marked by fleur-de-lys,
WE by letter

MILTON ABBOT see also C107, C162

13/14/1

MILTON DAMEREL
1694   National Library of Scotland
                                                     Minto Collection MS 13421
                                                     Photocopy at 2536Z/Z1

Milton Damerel Church SS 384107

TITLE: 'An exact Plott of the Barton and Mannor of Thornbury scittuate
within the Parishes of Thornbury and Milton Damerel in ye County
of Deavon John Tanner Esqr Ld of ye same'

SURVEYOR: 'Teste George Withiell who measured & plotted it Anno Dom
1694'

SCALE: 'This scale containeth 39 four pole chains'; scale bar; photocopy
makes accurate measurement difficult

MATERIAL, SIZE & ORIENTATION: parchment, coloured [photocopy only
inspected, Withiell's maps usually coloured]; 70cms EW x 52.4cms
NS; north to top

CONTENT: rivers, stream lines; ford; bridges; fields named with content
and information about some owners; alphabetic reference to table
giving 'An Account of the quantity of Acres in ye Barton and Mannor
of Thornbury' including 'Names of Vilages The Tenants Names'
and content; tree symbols showing woods, orchards, isolated trees;
roads and lanes, some named; buildings in elevation, some in detail;
Cookbury and Milton Damerel Churches with the Parsonage House
well drawn; Milton Mill; deer in park

DECORATION: 2 4 point compass indicators; north marked by fleur-de-
lys, SEW by letter; 32 point compass rose; stylised daisy in centre;
north marked by fleur-de-lys, all other directions by letter; scale bar
decorated by a plaque supported by 2 mermaids with 2 eagles above;
acanthus leaves, strawberry leaves and fruits, coloured

PUBLICATION: J.B. Harley and E.A. Stuart, 'George Withiell – a West

---

13/13/4

MILTON ABBOT
1825   1262M/E22/45

Milton Abbot Church SX 406793
See entry under Brentor, 3/33/3

Country Surveyor of the late seventeenth century' *DCNQ* XXV Part II (Autumn, 1982), 45–58, and Part III (Spring, 1983), 95–115

13/14/2

MILTON DAMEREL

| 1780 | 1508M Devon/M&P/Milton Damerel 1 |

Milton Damerel Church SS 384107
See entry under Cookbury, 3/30/1

13/14/3

MILTON DAMEREL

| 1780 | 1508M Devon/Surveys/V4 |

Milton Damerel Church SS 384107
See entry under Combe Raleigh, 3/29/1

13/14/4

MILTON DAMEREL

| 18th cent. | 1508M/M&P/M&P/Milton Damerel A1 |

Worden Cross SS 381116
TITLE: not given; Endorsed 'An Eye Sketch of Waste Ground in Dispute between Lord Courtenay & Mr Stephens'
SURVEYOR: not named
SCALE: not given
MATERIAL, SIZE & ORIENTATION: paper, ink; 41/4cms x 32.9cms; no direction
CONTENT: river marked by stream lines; arrows indicating direction of flow; road, pecked lines, bounded by hedge and tree symbols; area of furze named; gate; peripheral owners named; 'Spot in dispute' is marked in pencil

---

13/14/5

MILTON DAMEREL

| 1827 | 1508 Devon/M&P/Milton Damerel A2 |

Milton House [formerly Rectory] SS 383119
TITLE: 'A Map of Lord Viscount Courtenay's Wastes in and about the

roads near the Rectory of Milton Damerel in the County of Devon done from memory after a residence of 12 years and subsequent non residence of 15 years. The Wastes are correct but I cannot answer for the correctness of about two thirds of the fields as to the marks of the Hedges. That part of the Map towards Buttermoor & Grattan is rather compressed for the sake of bringing it into the view'
SURVEYOR: Thomas Clack
SCALE: not given
MATERIAL, SIZE & ORIENTATION: paper, coloured; 68.8cms x 48.6cms; south-east to top
CONTENT: streams, pond, blue; fields crudely outlined, some areas turquoise [presumably the areas in dispute]; numbered points refer to accompanying letter and explanation; roads, buff; directions given; buildings in elevation, red; Abbots Bickington Church with blue spire; Milton Church; some farmhouses enclosed by walls; considerable information about landholders and their rights
DECORATION: 8 point compass rose, black; north marked by fleur-de-lys
ACCOMPANYING DOCUMENTS:
1. 'Explanation of a map of sundry wastes adjoining divers persons Lands in the Parish of Milton Damerel in the County of Devon belonging to Lord Viscount Courtenay. 1827'
   'Concerning lands in the possession of the Rector' [not signed]
2. Letter from Thomas Clack to John Wilkinson Esq at Lincoln's Inn. 16 March 1827
NOTE: Rev. Thomas Clack d. 1852 aged 78 at Milton Damerel; Rector, therefore for 58 years; resided at Larkbear in Talaton

---

13/14/6

MILTON DAMEREL

| 1831 | NDRO B170/85 |

Wonford SS 371097 South Wonford SS 381088
TITLE: 'Map of the Village of West Wanford in the Parish of Milton Damerel Devon belonging to Earl Stanhope, The Revd Richd Walter, The Revd Thos H. Kingdon & Mr Philip Veale'
SURVEYOR: not named
SCALE: 'Scale of Statute Chains' scale bar; 12=3 chains; 1:2376
MATERIAL, SIZE & ORIENTATION: paper, torn, mounted, coloured; 75cms x *c.*122cms; north-east to top
CONTENT: river and stream, grey; fields outlined in various colours; alphabetic reference to explanation giving owners' names and note about allotment of the waste to those owners; numeric reference in addition to lands of Mr Philip Veale referring to list prepared in pencil

but not completed; roads, yellow, fenced and unfenced; directions indicated; buildings in plan, outlined in red; peripheral owners named
NOTE: endorsing accuracy of the map witnessed by representatives or tenants of the owners
DECORATION: 8 point compass rose, plain/grey; north marked by fleur-de-lys

13/14/7

MILTON DAMEREL
| 19th cent. | 1508 Devon/M&P/Milton Damerel A3 |

Worden Cross SS 381116 or Whitebear SS 393112
TITLE: not given
SURVEYOR: not named
SCALE: not given
MATERIAL, SIZE & ORIENTATION: paper, ink; 31.5cms x 19cms; no direction
CONTENT: shows road Woodford bridge to Holsworthy, Whidbour Cross and side road to Rectory; trees and furze bordering road; area where new houses are to bebuilt; 2 cottages and their gardens outlined; peripheral owners and glebe land named

13/15/1

MILTON, SOUTH
| 1777 | 1508M Devon/M&P/V3 |

South Milton Church SX 697429
See entry under Alvington, West, 1/6/1

13/15/2

MILTON, SOUTH
| 1836 | 316M/S2A |

Horswell House SX 690422
TITLE: 'Plan of the present and also the proposed new Road near Horswell in the Parish of South Milton Devon 1836'
SURVEYOR: not named
SCALE: 'Scale of Chains'; scale bar; 1"=2 chains; 1:1584
MATERIAL, SIZE & ORIENTATION: paper, slight colour; 49cms x 30.5cms; north-west to top
CONTENT: ponds, blue with grey margins; fields, orchards, gardens, lawn

outlined in ink and named; tree symbols, blue showing isolated trees; old road, fenced and unfenced portions; directions given; proposed new road, red; buildings in plan, grey
DECORATION: 4 point compass indicator; north marked by fleur-de-lys, south by series of triangles
NOTE: map accompanied by diagrams of sections of present and proposed new roads in relation to ground level and named points. Horizontal scale of 1" to 2 chains and vertical scale of 1" to 50 feet
ASSOCIATED DOCUMENTS: details of Vestry meetings to consider proposals

MILTON SOUTH see also C108

13/16/1

MODBURY
| 1740 | 51/7/2/1 |

Sheepham Mill SX 657528
TITLE: none given but note top left 'Some Resemblance of a plan of an Estate in the Parish of Modbury commonly called the park 1740'
'Suppose this is an Eye Draught'
SURVEYOR: not named
SCALE: not given
MATERIAL, SIZE & ORIENTATION: paper, watermark, ink; 38.3cms EW x 47.5cms NS; north to top
CONTENT: brook to 'Shipham Bridge' and 'New Mill Leat'; fields with numeric reference to table giving field names and content according to customary measure; boundary roads named but in a later hand; Shipham Farm and Barracks [endorsed 'sold to Crown 1795'] drawn in plan in the later hand
ENDORSEMENT: Map Modbury Park 1740. A rough plan of Mr Legassickes Park in Modbury

13/16/2

MODBURY
| 1830 | 1601M/T21 |

Higher Ludbrook SX 660538
See entry under Ermington, 5/2/4

13/16/3

MODBURY

| 1832 | 1601M/T32 |

Higher Ludbrook SX 660538
See entry under Ermington, 5/2/6

13/16/4

MODBURY

| 1836 | 1699M/T3 |

Higher Ludbrook SX 660538
See entry under Ermington, 5/2/8

13/16/5

MODBURY

| 1836 | 1601M/T33 |

Higher Ludbrook SX 660538
See entry under Ermington, 5/2/5

MODBURY see also B60

13/17/1

MOLTON, NORTH

| 1757 | 1148M add/6/1 |

Bere SS 706351
See entry under Chulmleigh, 3/15/2

MOLTON, NORTH see also C109

13/18/1

MOLTON, SOUTH

| 1672 | 1262M/E4/1 |

Bremridge Wood SS 688287
TITLE: 'Bremble ridge woode'
SURVEYOR: not named
SCALE: 'This is according to the Statute Measure vizt 16 Foot and halfe to the Pole wch is the Custome of South Moulton for Wood'; no scale bar
MATERIAL, SIZE & ORIENTATION: paper, ink; 38.5cms EW x 52.5cms NS; east to top
CONTENT: watercourses, double dotted lines; note 'A considerable Spring about Embecome Cliffe that will water 8 or 9 Acres & may be carryed towards the House': woods named; meadow, orchards, 'copps', 'fold downe', 'hopp yard', garden named; all demarcated by dotted lines; gates; lanes, fenced and unfenced; directions given; houses in elevation, drawn on opposing horizons, named
List giving contents of various woods and quantities cut; statement giving total area or content of wood in Acres, Quarters, Poles
DECORATION: 8 point compass rose, plain/hatched; directions spelt out
ENDORSEMENT: The exact mapp & measure of Bremeridge Woods taken Novemb 20th & 21th 1672
In a more exact mapp wch was taken upon a second Measuring itt was thus found

The North Wood	33	Acres	1	Pole	10	Perches
Old Wood	11		3		4	
Wood Cutt Down	23		3		18	
South Wood & West wood	72		2		20	
	14	Acres	1		12	

160 Perches to the Acre
Itt was observed by my Son Blundel Mr Boen Mr Blessington & Martin Johns That there were 9 Ricks of Wood standing then in the greate wood, when they tooke a view of itt. Also greate quantitys of broken wood wch then did lye on the ground perishing
There is more 40 Acres wch will tourne to excellent Meddow lying so as the water will rise uppon itt.
There are 4 considerable springs besides that wch goes to the watergate north side of the house

13/18/2

MOLTON, SOUTH

[1757]   1262M/E22/44

Hacche Barton SS 714277 Snurridge SS 703283
See entry under Buckland, East, 2/46/1

13/18/3

MOLTON, SOUTH

1757   1148M add/6/11

Hacche Barton SS 714277
See entry under Chulmleigh, 3/15/2

13/18/4

MOLTON, SOUTH

1769   211M/P4

South Molton Church SS 714259 Clapworthy SS 676239
TITLE: 'A Map or Plan of the Barton of Clotworthy and the Estates
    called West-Ford and Hockell=Down with the Cottage called new-
    Ground, in the Parish of Southmolton and County of Devon, the
    Lands of the Revd Henry Hawkins Tremayne Survey'd and Mapp'd
    in 1769 By Wm Hole & Thomas Call'
SURVEYORS:: William Hole and Thomas Call
SCALE: 'A Scale of Chains, each containing Four Statute Perches'; scale
    bar; 1"=3.6 chains; 1:2851
MATERIAL, SIZE & ORIENTATION: parchment, on rollers, coloured; 95.8cms
    EW x 86cms NS; north to top
CONTENT: River Bray named, pale grey with ink margins; Filleigh Bridge
    in elevation with 2 arches; 'Quarry Pitt', grey margin; 'Rubble Hill',
    dark grey-green; fields outlined with hedge symbols, green; where
    Lord Fortescue's land, blue; alpha-numeric reference to table giving
    names of parcels of ground, field names and land use; 'asterisms'
    indicating hedge ownership; courtlages and gardens shown; gates,
    red; tree symbols showing orchards and with stippling woods and
    coppice; roads, buff; footpaths, pecked lines; directions given;
    buildings in plan, red, some in elevation; peripheral owners named
        Earl Fortescue's land included because some fields were
    exchanged and these are noted in the table
DECORATION: title cartouche: scrolls with acanthus, flowers and leaves
    enclosing a view of a house at the base; on either side 2 mythical

creatures – an odd duck and sheepdog; 8 point compass rose, plain/
shaded grey; north marked by fleur-de-lys, east by cross

13/18/5

MOLTON, SOUTH

c.1775   NDRO B229/5

Kingsland Barton SS 699258
TITLE: 'A Map of Kingsland and Nadderwater Ground Lying in
    Southmolton Parish in the County of Devon Being the Lands of
    William Karslake Gent: Surveyed by me Simon Woolcott'
SURVEYOR: Simon Woolcott
SCALE: 'A Scale of Eighty Poles'; scale bar; 1"=20 chains; 1:15840
MATERIAL, SIZE & ORIENTATION: parchment; coloured; 72.2cms x 52.2cms;
    north-west to top
CONTENT: river, bridge; fields outlined with pricked lines, yellow or red;
    alpha-numeric reference to table giving field names and external and
    internal content of each field; gates; tree symbols showing orchards;
    roads, directions given; buildings in elevation including house and
    Turnpike House; list of fences belonging to the estate
DECORATION: title cartouche: rococo style with scrolls, acanthus and
    ruched fabric; 2 putti, both with writing pads and quills; border round
    scale; 16 point compass rose; north marked by fleur-de-lys, east by
    cross
ENDORSEMENT: Kingsland &c So Molton

13/18/6

MOLTON, SOUTH

1815   1262M/E4/15

South Cockerham SS 709281
TITLE: 'A Plan of part of a Hedge between East and West Cockram in
    the Parish of South Molton. Devon. the Property of the Right Honble
    Earl Fortescue, taken in March 1815, by Robt Ballment'
SURVEYOR: Robert Ballment
SCALE: 'A Scale of Chains each containing Four Statute Perches'; scale
    bar; 1"=.5 chain; 1:396
MATERIAL, SIZE & ORIENTATION: paper, slight colour; 20.2cms EW x 32cms
    NS; north to top
CONTENT: hedge, green; boundary stone; tree symbols; brick wall abutting
    on hedge

ENDORSEMENT: Agreement with Thomas Palmer Acland concerning the hedge, 2 October 1821

DECORATION: 4 point compass indicator; north marked by fleur-de-lys, east by cross

NOTE: 2 copies

13/18/7

MOLTON, SOUTH
[1824]   1262M/E4/23

Clotworthy SS 682282

TITLE: 'A Sketch of the Map and Plan of West Clotworthy belonging to the Right Honble Lord Fortescue'

SURVEYOR: not named

SCALE: not given

MATERIAL, SIZE & ORIENTATION: paper, ink; 45.3cms x 37cms; no direction

CONTENT: river shown by wavy lines; direction of flow indicated; Filleigh Bridge; fields outlined in ink with field names; lands of Lord Fortescue and lands of Tremayne differentiated by letters F and T; roads, directions given; footpaths, pecked lines; buildings in plan; peripheral owners named

NOTE: the date 1824 is assigned by the Devon Record Office

13/18/8

MOLTON, SOUTH
1836   1262M/E22/17

Townhouse SS 683260

TITLE: 'A Map of an Estate called Townhouse in the Parish of South Molton Devon The property of the Right Honbl Earl Fortescue Surveyed & Mapped by Hugh Ballment 1836'

SURVEYOR: Hugh Ballment

SCALE: no unit of measurement stated; scale bar; 1"=3 ?chains; 1:2376

MATERIAL, SIZE & ORIENTATION: paper, mounted on linen, coloured; 131.3cms EW x 75.8cms NS; north to top

CONTENT: rivers, streams, ponds, blue with stream lines; relief shown by hill shading; fields outlined with hedge symbols and coloured green or buff; numeric reference to list giving field names, land use – 'Arable Pasture etc, Hedges Waste and Buildings – total content; some fields with stippled grey parallel lines, others with a variety of small symbols all indicating marsh or moor; asterisks indicating hedge ownership;

gates; gardens; green tree symbols showing isolated trees, wood, orchards and ornamental avenues; roads, buff; directions given; private road and footpath named, buff, marked by pecked lines; Bray Bridge named with 4 arches indicated; buildings in plan, house, red others hatched black

DECORATION: title cartouche and border: plain frame with concave corners; scale bar superimposed on medallion of leaves with dividers, set square and quill pen; 8 point compass rose, shaded line decoration; north marked by fleur-de-lys

NOTE: map signed 'Hugh Ballment Barnstaple 1836'. Road designated 'to Chittlehampton' incorrectly named and pencil annotation 'Black-pool' inserted

MOLTON, SOUTH see also B44, B96, B106

13/19/1

MONKLEIGH
1769   NDRO 2239 add/6/26

Monkleigh Wood SS 467202   Weare Giffard Church SS 478221

TITLE: 'A Map or Plan of Monkley Wood, Pitt Wood & Red Wood in the Parish of Monkley and County of Devon The Lands of Richard Coffin Esqr Survey'd & mapp'd in 1769 By Wm Hole & Thos Call'

SURVEYORS:: William Hole and Thomas Call

SCALE: 'A Scale of Chains, each containing 4 Statute Perches'; scale bar; 1"=3.5 chains; 1:2772

MATERIAL, SIZE & ORIENTATION: parchment, on rollers, coloured; 72cms EW x c.52cms NS; north to top

CONTENT: River Torridge and 'Barehayne Lake' named, light grey; arrows marking direction of flow; woods outlined by hedge symbols in green or yellow with tree symbols and stippling; alphabetic reference to table giving details of dates woods were felled and price per acre for the wood; note stating 'Cliff Wood alias Cleave Wood in the Parish of Little Torrington delineated on the back of this map'; roads outlined in brown, directions given; buildings in elevation drawn in detail, especially Weare Giffard Church and Beam House [SS 473206]; peripheral owners named; Pitt Wood shown in inset with Weare Giffard mansion and Church

DECORATION: title cartouche: rococo with scrolls and acanthus; rural view below with a tree and a cow

TORRINGTON, LITTLE (continued on back)
Cleave Wood SS 472187
SCALE: 'A Scale of Chains each containing 4 Statute perches'; scale bar;
    1"=3.3 chains; 1:2614
CONTENT: as on principal map
ENDORSEMENT: Monkley Woods

13/19/2

MONKLEIGH
1827   NDRO 2239B add/P22

Monkleigh Church SS 458207
TITLE: 'A Plan of the New Road & Canal from Bideford to Torrington
    The property of Richard Pine Coffin Esqr'
SURVEYOR: 'W. Bear Schoolmaster Monkleigh'
SCALE: 'Scale of 100 Poles'; scale bar; 1"=20 poles; 1:3960
MATERIAL, SIZE & ORIENTATION: paper, coloured; 68.5cms x 48.2cms;
    south-west to top
CONTENT: River Torridge, blue with green margins; new canal, pale blue
    with brown towpath; 'Dry Aqueduct', pink; aqueduct carrying canal
    over river indicated; various features and estates named and listed
    with content, 'without fence', and 'one fence'; green tree symbols
    showing wood and orchard; roads, brown, directions given; 'Wood
    Bridge' over canal named; Monkleigh village houses and church,
    coloured, in elevation; Yeo Farm in elevation; peripheral owners and
    estates named
NOTE: 'From Rudd to Stone stile 658 Poles or 2 Miles 18 Poles' i.e.
    length of proposed new road and canal
DECORATION: 32 point compass rose coloured shades of grey, pink and
    yellow; border: yellow and black

MONKLEIGH see also C110–11

13/20/1

MONKOKEHAMPTON
1813   Private hands

Monkokehampton Church SS 581055
See entry under Hatherleigh, 8/8/4

13/21/1

MONKTON
[before 1780]   Antony Muniments CP/FB/3

Monkton Church ST 187031
TITLE: 'Hedgend Farm in the Parish of Monkton: & County of Devon'
SURVEYOR: not named
SCALE: 'Scale of Chains'; scale bar; 1"=4 chains; 1:3168
MATERIAL, SIZE & ORIENTATION: parchment, coloured; 50.5cms x 40.1cms;
    north-west to top
CONTENT: pond, blue; fields outlined in green, named with content;
    numeric reference [to Survey Book]; tree symbols showing orchard,
    copse and avenue; roads, buff, named; buildings in plan, red; Monkton
    Church in elevation; peripheral owners named

13/21/2

MONKTON
1797   54/2/2/6

Monkton Church ST 187031
TITLE: 'A Map and Terrier of the Manor of Monkton in the County of
    Devon the property of Edwd Hall Esqr'
SURVEYOR: James Sherriff
SCALE: 'Scale of Chains'; scale bar; 1"=12 chains; 1:9504
MATERIAL, SIZE & ORIENTATION: parchment, slight clolour; 29.5cms x
    25.7cms; south-east to top
TERRIER: paper; 17cms x 25.7cms
CONTENT: river; fields outlined with hedge symbols and various densities
    of stippling; farms outlined in colour; alpha-numeric reference to
    Terrier giving field names and content; roads and lanes differentiated;
    peripheral owners and parishes named
DECORATION: title cartouche: simple design of scrolls and leaves; 8 point
    compass rose; arrowheads marking north and east, NSEW indicated
    by letter

13/22/1

MORCHARD BISHOP
1830s   Diocesan Glebe Terriers

Morchard Bishop Church SS 773074   Morchard Bishop
TITLE: 'Map of Morchard Glebe. In the County of Devon the property
    of The Revd. J. Bartholomew'

SURVEYOR: not named

SCALE: 'A Scale of Gunter's Chains'; scale bar; 1"=4.5 chains; 1:3564

MATERIAL, SIZE & ORIENTATION: paper, mounted on linen, coloured; 61.1cms EW x 89.1cms NS; east to top

CONTENT: rivers, grey; streams, black; fields, green with numeric and alpha-numeric reference to table giving field names and content; gates; tree symbols showing orchards, woods and isolated trees; roads outlined in red; directions given; footpaths, pecked lines; some buildings, including church in elevation, others in plan, black

DECORATION: 8 point compass rose, plain/black; double outer circle; north marked by fleur-de-lys; scale bar is on a scroll

NOTE: tithe map numbers, red, in a later hand

Revd J.Bartholomew was Vicar of Morchard Bishop from 1831 to 1866 but the map was presumably made before the Tithe Map

MORCHARD BISHOP see also C112

MORELEIGH see C39, C113, C139

13/23/1

MORETONHAMPSTEAD
1790   1508M/Surveys/V5

Moretonhampstead Church SX 755861
See entry under Bovey, North, 2/21/2

13/23/2

MORETONHAMPSTEAD
1840   50/23/3/12

Moor Barton SX 818834

TITLE: 'A Map of Moor Barton in the Parish of Moretonhampstead in the County of Devon The Property of Thomas Cousins Esq 1840'

SURVEYOR: not named [possibly WPD, see below]

SCALE: 'A Scale of Chains'; scale bar; 1"=4 chains; 1:3168

MATERIAL, SIZE & ORIENTATION: paper, ink; 60cms EW x 48.4cms NS: north to top

CONTENT: stream, wavy lines; fields outlined in ink with numeric reference to table giving field names and content; hedge ownership indicated by dotted lines; garden, parterre; roads, directions given; footpaths, pecked lines; buildings in plan; peripheral owners and estates named

DECORATION: 16 point compass rose; north marked by fleur-de-lys

ENDORSEMENT: This Map is a Copy of A Map in the Possession of the Owner especially made for Lawrence Palk Esqre WPD May 1840

13/24/1

MORTEHOE
Late 17th cent.   NDRO 3704M/E2/1

Mortehoe Church
See entry under Georgeham, 7/1/1

13/24/2

MORTEHOE
Late 17th cent.   NDRO 3704M/E2/2

Mortehoe Church
See entry under Georgeham, 7/1/2

13/25/1

MUSBURY
1781   Antony Muniments PP/FX/23

Musbury Church ST 275945
See entry under Colyton, 3/27/5

13/25/2

MUSBURY
1800   Antony Muniments PP/FX25

Musbury Church ST 275945
See entry under Colyton, 3/27/8

14/1/1

NEWTON ABBOT

1756   ECA Book 58

Newton Abbot SX 858713
See entry under Exeter Chamber Map Book, 5/3/49

14/1/2

NEWTON ABBOT

1788–1789   6107

Newton Abbot Church SX 858713
See entry under Bridestowe, 2/35/6

14/1/3

NEWTON ABBOT

18th cent.   1508M London/M&P/Newton Abbot 1

Keyberry Mill SX 873698
TITLE: not given [shows river Teign and Keyberry Mill]
SURVEYOR: not named
SCALE: not given
MATERIAL, SIZE & ORIENTATION: paper, ink; 32cms x 21cms; no direction
CONTENT: River Teign, stream lines; arrows indicating direction of flow;
    Keyberry Bridge; Keyberry Mill [shown with 2 mill wheels]; leat;
    some relief shown by shading; fields named and land use indicated;
    some content shown; gate; tree symbols, 'Plantation of Oaks' named;
    roads named; direction given; footpaths, pecked lines

14/1/4

NEWTON ABBOT

[post 1803]   1508M Devon/M&P/Newton Abbot

Wolborough Street SX 858712 Maps 1
TITLE: not given
SURVEYOR: not named
SCALE: 'Scale 2 chains to an Inch'; 1:1584
MATERIAL, SIZE & ORIENTATION: paper, repaired and mounted on linen;
    c.139cms x c.103cms; no direction
CONTENT: River Teign, River Lemmon, Mr Templer's Canal and streams,

stream lines; ponds; mill leat; salmon weir, bridges and fords; fields,
some named, some with owners' names; alphabetic reference, red,
[to list]; crosses marking fence ownership in some areas; fences in
profile; gates; tree symbols; roads and footpaths, fenced and unfenced,
named in Newton Abbot town with Shambles and Chapel in
Wolborough Street named; directions given; Penn Inn Turnpike Gate
named; buildings in plan, hatched; some drawn in detail, others
generalised and described as 'belongg (sic) to sundry persons'; Ford
House, Golden Lion Inn, Globe Inn, Keyberry Mill, Sherborne Mill
and Paper Mill named; peripheral owners named

NEWTON ABBOT see also B30, B50, B55, B79, B84, B86, B99

14/2/1

NEWTON FERRERS

c.1600   PRO MFC 1/208
                                                      Photocopy, PWDRO 1798/1

Village SX 542481
TITLE: not given 'Pictorial map'
SURVEYOR: not named
SCALE: not given
MATERIAL, SIZE & ORIENTATION: paper, ink; 84cms x 61.6cms (as repaired);
    no direction
CONTENT: river, plain; quay; undergrowth and trees trailing over river
    banks; relief shown by shading in pencil; fields outlined; gates; stile;
    tree symbols showing isolated trees; roads, plain; houses in elevation;
    some burgage plots; church in elevation; cross
DECORATION: horse with accoutrements in field, possibly pinpointing
    the site where the militia trained

14/2/2

NEWTON FERRERS

1756   ECA Book 58

Newton Ferrers Church SX 550478
See entry under Exeter Chamber Map Book, 5/3/48

14/2/3

NEWTON FERRERS

18th cent.   PWDRO 457/B17/327

Brownstone SX 597495 Preston Farm SX 580487

TITLE: 'Brownstone'

SURVEYOR: not named

MATERIAL, SIZE & ORIENTATION: paper, coloured; 67.4cms EW x 48.4cms NS; north to top

CONTENT: fields, green, some named; numeric reference to table giving field names and content; asterisks indicating hedge ownership; hedge symbols; tree symbols showing orchards; footpaths, yellow; buildings in plan, red; peripheral owners named

INSET: 'Map of Little Preston' shows fields with a table, giving field names and content; footpaths and hedge boundaries

DECORATION: 8 point compass rose; north marked by fleur-de-lys, SEW by letter

NEWTON FERRERS see also C84, C114–15

14/3/1

NEWTON ST CYRES

1782   64/12/21/2

Newton St Cyres Church SX 879980

A volume entitled 'Survey of Newton St Cyres 1782' which contains various information on the parish (including a list as far as 1785), evidently compiled by Richard Couch. He also describes himself as 'Dick the plowman'. The two maps in the volume are listed as follows:-

Folio 16

    TITLE: 'A representation of Newton St Cyres Parish with all its ways and waters'

    SURVEYOR: Richard Couch (At back of vol. 'Lands survyd by Dick, the Plowman, and the 10 Eminent Circles On the Terrestrial Globe, Exhibited by the method of the late Mr Bion, a frenchman'

    SCALE: not given

    MATERIAL, SIZE & ORIENTATION: paper, coloured; 50.7cms EW x 39.6cms NS; north to top; no compass rose but NSE in the margins

    CONTENT: River Creedy and streams, black wavy lines; direction of flow indicated; mill leat; weirs; bridges; tithings outlined in various

colours; tree symbols showing woods and isolated trees; roads, with note as to which parish repairs them; directions given; footpaths, pecked lines; church, vicarage (much detail) and houses in elevation; tin mine and adit water; peripheral owners, estates and parishes named; note of acreage, latitude and longitude of parish

Folio 19

    Scrawthorne Plantation SX 879966

    TITLE: not given but description under the plan of Newton St Cyres tin mines reads as follows:- 'This plan, by the 29th Theorem of Kersleys Algebra, is Drawn from and Information Taken from Late Roger Herring decd. Some years ago who occupied ye Estate where, now Mr Ponsfords Family do & Let out Lodgings to Several of the Miners when the Fraternity of Exeter Gentlemen worked Newton mines, at very great Expence, Till their Captain died of the small-pox, whose name was James Prince, a very Faithfull undertaker, which soon obliged the company to vacate the work, having expended about £6000 and during the Interval took up an Immense quantity of very rich Load which they sent to Calis in France for Extraction, Leaving this Brance of Load, here in this plan represented and Large as the bulge of a hogshead.

    The mean Shaft wch is the centre of this plan was when used a great many Fathoms deeper than the Level of ye adit, so that the pumps were kept at work, day and Night to pump up the water to the adit, then in use, to the intent yt the water might not obstruct the Mners work. If what I have hereby Recited is not enough for information, am ready if required, to go in person, and Show the place where underneath the Surface of ye earth, this Load is, as it has been in all my remembrance done Though Not a person of antediluvian this 6th of December 1782'

    SURVEYOR: Richard Couch

    SCALE: not given

    MATERIAL, SIZE & ORIENTATION: paper, cloured; 50.7cms EW x 39.6cms NS; north to top

    CONTENT: adit water, grey; areas of mine, black; shafts, plain, vertical and horizontal planes on same map; gates; some fields and owners named; Load house in elevation

    DECORATION: north marked by fleur-de-lys but no compass rose; indication of direction on border of map

    NOTE: Richard, son of William and Catherine Couch was baptised at Newton St Cyres on 29 December 1715

    PUBLICATIONS: John Pamment and Bill Slater, 'An Eighteenth-century lead and silver mine near Newton St Cyres', *DAS* No. 46, (1988), 149–53. The authors argue that although the plan states it portrays a tin mine, there are good reasons for believing that lead and ore had previously been extracted rather than tin; Todd Gray, ed., *Travels in Georgian Devon. The Illustrated Journals of the Reverend John Swete, 1789–1800* III, (Tiverton, 1999), 129. Sub 1796 'Somewhere in this parish of Newton St Cyres, perhaps among these hills, I remember to have heard some years ago a report of a lead mine having been discover'd, rich impregnated with Silver'.

14/3/2

NEWTON ST CYRES
[1787]   2065M/E3/9

Newton St Cyres Church SX 879980
See entry under Crediton, 3/33/4

14/3/3

NEWTON ST CYRES
1792   Ex. D&C Ch. Comm. 98/8788

Newton St Cyres Church SX 879980
TITLE: 'A Map of the Manor of Norton in the Parish of Newton St Cyres and County of Devon Lands of the Venerable the Dean and Chapter of St Peter in Exeter. Surveyed A.D. 1792 by J. Darch'
SURVEYOR: J. Darch
SCALE: 'Chains 80 to a mile'; scale bar; 1"=4.5 chains; 1:3564; 'Poles 329 to a mile'; scale bar; 1"=17.5 poles; 1:3564
MATERIAL, SIZE & ORIENTATION: parchment, coloured; 103.2cms EW x 70.2cms NS; north to top
CONTENT: River Creedy named with tributaries; black margins with stream lines; arrows marking direction of flow; fields outlined with hedge symbols; coloured; alphabetic reference to table giving 'names of Tenements, Occupiers; No. of Acres and Value'; some owners' names entered on map; tree symbols indicating orchards; roads and lanes; buildings in plan, blue; peripheral owners and parishes named
    Some areas not in proper spatial relation to principal area mapped and this fact explained in notes
    Subsequent annotations give field names and content
DECORATION: title cartouche: rural scene showing river, trees and manor house; table: draped ribbon with delicate plants, leaves and flowers; 16 point compass rose, shaded grey; north marked by fleur-de-lys, east by cross; other directions by letters; lower right copy of seal of Dean and Chapter in red

14/3/4

NEWTON ST CYRES
19th cent.   51/24/8/4

Hayne Barton SX 891994
TITLE: 'Hayne Barton in the parish of Newton St Cyres with Page's and Clampit's tenements in the parish of Upton Pyne the property of Sir Stafford Henry Northcote Bart Pynes House Devon'
SURVEYOR: not named [same hand as 51/24/8/1–3]
SCALE: divided scale; no unit of measurement stated
MATERIAL, SIZE & ORIENTATION: paper, buff coloured, mounted on cloth, ink and slight colour; 62.5cms EW x 91.5cms NS [as repaired]; north to top
CONTENT: fields outlined in blue or yellow, with content and alphabetic reference to table giving field names; tree symbols marking orchards and isolated trees; roads, direction given; buildings in plan, grey; peripheral estates named
DECORATION: 16 point compass rose, plain/black; north shown by fleur-de-lys

14/4/1

NORTHAM
1745   NDRO 4274 add/1

Northam Church SS 448291
See entry under Bideford, 2/14/3

14/4/2

NORTHAM
1779   NDRO 4087M/E12

Burrough SS 454286
TITLE: 'Survey of Burrough and Burroughwell in the Parish of Northam in the County of Devon. The Property of Henry Downe Esqr 1779'
SURVEYOR: not named
SCALE: 'Scale of Chains'; scale bar; 1"=3 chains; 1:2376
MATERIAL, SIZE & ORIENTATION: parchment, coloured; 65.4cms EW x 55.2cms NS; north to top
CONTENT: river Torridge named, green with stream lines; fields outlined in green or yellow, named with content; total content of 2 areas listed at bottom; asterisks indicating hedge ownership; gates; tree symbols;

roads, some with hatched margins; directions given; houses in plan, keyed by letter to Explanation; church and parsonage in elevation; peripheral owners named

DECORATION: 16 point compass rose, red/plain, pink/plain, yellow outer circle; north marked by fleur-de-lys, east, west and south spelt out

14/4/3

NORTHAM
19th cent.   NDRO 1843A/PZ17

Northam Church SS 448291

TITLE: not given but catalogue in NDRO describes it as a draft plan of Cory's Ground

SURVEYOR: not named

SCALE: not given

MATERIAL, SIZE & ORIENTATION: paper, ink; 26.3cms EW x 43.4cms NS; north to top

CONTENT: fields outlined in ink with alphabetical reference to table giving content of each field making up Cory's Ground and total content; ownership of fences indicated; roads, named

NOTE ON DOCUMENT: 'Above I send you Copy of map as promised Wm. ?Callow Jnr'

DECORATION: 4 point compass indicator; north marked by arrow, SEW by letter

NORTHAM see also C116

14/5/1

NORTHLEIGH
1781   281M/E7

Northleigh Church SY 196959

TITLE: 'Plan of Estates in the Parish of Northleigh Devonshire belonging to J.T.B. Marwood Esqr by J Sturge 1781'

SURVEYOR: Jacob Sturge

SCALE: no unit of measurement stated; scale bar shows furlongs, chains and perches; 1"=6 chains; 1:4752

MATERIAL, SIZE & ORIENTATION: parchment, ink and slight colour; 60.5cms x 70cms; south-west to top

CONTENT: rivers, double black lines; relief features shown by hill shading, named; fields outlined with hedge and tree symbols; numeric reference [to Survey Book]; other owners named; tree symbols showing orchards and coppices; roads, fenced and unfenced; buildings in plan, hatched; church named; peripheral owners and parishes named

Explanation identifying symbols used and the distinction between freehold and leasehold lands; 'The Numbers refer to a Survey Book'

Grid lines in red with upper and lower case letter reference system

DECORATION: title cartouche: rural scene, river with tree-lined banks and path leading to river margin; 4 point compass indicator; north marked by fleur-de-lys

14/5/2

NORTHLEIGH
1826   5556Z/ME1

Northleigh Church SY 196959
See entry under Farway, 6/2/4

15/1/1

OAKFORD
1745   1936M/EP7

Oakford Church SS 910212

TITLE: 'A Rough Draught of Forsaken, or Saken Down in the Parish of Oakford in the County of Devon, part of the Mannor of Holcombe Rogus. By Farmer White – one of ye nearest Neighbours of ye Same. Containg about 40 Acres Valu'd at upwards of £10 p. Annum. Now in the possession of Geo. Tarr for his Life about – years of Age'

SURVEYOR: Farmer White

SCALE: not given

MATERIAL, SIZE & ORIENTATION: paper, ink; 36.5cms EW x 48cms NS; north to top; directions spelt out on margins of map

CONTENT: diagrammatic map; all field boundaries straight parallel lines with cross hatching between; fields named with content and additional information regarding ownership; highway running SW and NE; road shown also as parallel lines with cross hatching between

ASSOCIATED DOCUMENT: area referred to in lease of 1768 as Zeacon Down 1936M/L/156

15/2/1

OFFWELL

1781   281M/E6

Offwell Church SY 195996

TITLE: 'A Plan of Estates in the Parish of Ofwell Devonshire belonging to James Benedictus Marwood Esqr and Mrs Sarah Marwood by Jacob Sturge 1781'

SURVEYOR: Jacob Sturge

SCALE: no unit of measurement stated; scale bar shows furlongs, chains and perches; 1"=6 chains; 1:4752

MATERIAL, SIZE & ORIENTATION: parchment, ink, slight colour; 72.2cms x 88.5cms; south-west to top

CONTENT: streams, double black lines; relief shown by hill shading; fields outlined with hedge and tree symbols and coloured as in 'Explanation'; numeric reference to Survey Book; tree symbols marking orchards and coppices; Glebe and owners named; roads, directions given; buildings in plan, black

'Explanation' lists symbols used and identifies colour used to designate properties; 'The Numbers refer to a Survey Book'

Grid lines in red with upper and lower case reference system

DECORATION: title cartouche: rural scene, pond, cottages, ruined ecclesiastical building, village in background; 4 point compass indicator; north marked by fleur-de-lys, south by feathers

15/2/2

OFFWELL

1826   5556Z/ME1

Offwell Church SY 195996
See entry under Farway, 6/2/4

OFFWELL see also C117

15/3/1

OGWELL, EAST

temp. Eliz. I   PRO MPB 47 (E 178/7200)
                                       Photocopy, v faded, of 2 sheets

Holbeam SX 822712

TITLE: not given

SURVEYOR: not named

SCALE: no unit of measurement stated; scale bar

MATERIAL, SIZE & ORIENTATION: paper, ?ink; 2 fragments:- 54.6cms x 21.6cms, no direction and 57.2cms EW x 39.4cms NS; north to top

CONTENT: some fields named; some roads named including 'the way leading from East Ogwell to the myll'; East Ogwell church, the mill, and other buildings including Morley and Wotheridge in elevation

DECORATION: rabbit marking ?the warren; 'Northe' in frame with running pattern

NOTE: the map appears to relate to a right of way dispute but written explanation almost illegible on the photocopy

15/4/1

OGWELL, WEST

1821   Diocesan Glebe Terriers
                                                         West Ogwell

West Ogwell Church SX 818701

TITLE: 'A true Note, and Terrier of the Glebe belonging to the Rectory and the Parish Church of West Ogwell in the County of Devon, and Diocese of Exeter'

SURVEYOR: not named

SCALE: not given

MATERIAL, SIZE & ORIENTATION: parchment, coloured; 25.2cms x 15.5cms; no direction

CONTENT: fields outlined in ink, yellow; numeric reference to list giving field names and content; note below stating 'All the Fences which surround the Glebe, belong to it'; green tree symbols showing orchard and coppice; roads; footpaths, pecked lines; buildings in plan, red; peripheral owners named

15/5/1

OKEHAMPTON

1756/1773   BL Althorp Estate Plans P3

Market Cross SX 587952

TITLE: 'A Plan of the Borough of Okehampton in the County of Devon
  Surveyed by I Wynne, and G. Aislabie, in the Year 1756. and copied
  by T. Richardson Surveyor in 1773'

SURVEYORS: John Wynne and G. Aislabie

SCALE: 'A Scale of Feet' and 'A Scale of Chains and Links'; 2 scale
  bars; 1"=2 chains; 1:1584

MATERIAL, SIZE & ORIENTATION: 4 separate pieces of parchment, coloured;
  when joined approx 112cms EW x 113cms NS; north west to top

CONTENT: rivers, blue; Ockment River and tributaries named; spring and
  well; bridges; fields outlined with green hedge and tree symbols,
  named with content; alpha-numeric reference to the Survey Book;
  green tree symbols showing hedges, woods and orchards; lanes,
  named; buildings, including church, in plan, various colours,
  numbered

LEGEND: 'The Borough of Okehampton as appears by the Charter, is a
  Circle of one Statute Mile Diameter, whose Center is the Market
  Cross, and is distinguish'd by a bright green Circle, whose Circum-
  ference is the Bounds of the Borough.

      The Plan is divided into sixteen districts, each district being
  distinguish'd by a Letter of the Alphabet in a regular Series from A
  to Q both inclusive, which letters are subdivided into Numbers &
  Correspond with the like letters and Numbers in the Field book, where
  each Tenement is discrib'd with the Land Owner and Occupiers
  Names

      Those who have any considerable number of Freeholds are
  distinguish'd by different Colours as undermention'd and all the
  others are Colour'd black with Indian Ink.'

DECORATION: title cartouche: leaf, flower and scroll design; 8 point compass rose, grey/plain; north marked by fleur-de-lys, SEW by letter

ASSOCIATED DOCUMENT: Okehampton Borough Archives, John Wynne
  Field Book and Survey of Okehampton 1759?6; microfiche TD317

NOTE: photocopy of what would appear to be central portion of original
  map in the Okehampton Museum of Dartmoor Life

15/5/2

OKEHAMPTON

1779   BL Althorp Estate Plans P3

Market Cross SX 587952

10 large estate maps covering Okehampton and its immediate
  surrounding area. Two titles could be deciphered but some parts were
  lost when the maps were cut and mounted to fit the bound estate
  volumes

TITLE: 'A Plan of Okehampton Manor in the Parishes of Okehampton
  and Inwardleigh (exclusive of Paddiston & Stureson Farms in
  Inwardleigh) and of other Lands in sd Okehampton Parish not
  belonging to the Manor in the County of Devon Surveyed in the
  Year 1779 by John Corris' [8 maps]

      'A Plan of Paddiston & Stureson Farms being Part of Okehampton
  Manor in the Parish of Inwardleigh & County of Devon Surveyed
  by John Corris 1779' [2 maps]

SURVEYOR: John Corris

SCALE: 8 maps 'A Scale of Chains'; scale bar' 1"=3 chains; 1:2376
       2 maps 'A Scale of Chains'; scale bar; 1"=3 chains; 1:2376

MATERIAL, SIZE & ORIENTATION: paper, coloured; the 10 maps cover a
  very large area, since they are in an atlas total size cannot be assessed

CONTENT: River Ockment and other streams, stream lines; arrows
  indicating direction of flow; fields named with content; numeric
  reference [to Survey Book]; some owners' named; tree symbols
  showing orchards, woods, coppices and moorland; roads, fenced and
  unfenced, some named; buildings in plan, including castle, blue or
  red; market cross; peripheral owners and parishes named; pencil
  construction/survey lines

      'Explanation' identifying use of colour

15/5/3

OKEHAMPTON

1779   BL Althorp Estate Plans P7

Market Cross SX 587952

TITLE: 'A Plan and Survey of Okehampton Manor in the Parishes of
  Okehampton & Inwardleigh and of other Lands in the sd Parish of
  Okehampton not belonging to the Manor in the County of Devon. ...
  Taken by John Corris In the Year 1779'

SURVEYOR: John Corris

SCALE: 'Scale of Chains'; scale bar; 1"=c.10 chains; 1:7920

MATERIAL, SIZE & ORIENTATION: parchment, coloured

CONTENT: similar in style and details to the paper maps in P3; fields are numbered in similar way but colouring of the estates is different; detail about size and shape of the borough seems to have been taken from the 1773 copy of Wynne and Aislabie's map of 1756; turnpike roads, fenced and unfenced, directions given

    'Explanation'; identfying use of colour

DECORATION: title cartouche: rococo, with shell, flowers and lozenge pattern with implements below; view of Okehampton Castle on mound with curtain walls and gatehouse drawn lower left

ASSOCIATED DOCUMENTS: BL Althorp Papers F 181 4 relate to the purchase of Okehampton 1778–1779

15/5/4

OKEHAMPTON

    1780   1508M Devon/Surveys/V4

Okehampton Castle SX 583942
See entry under Combe Raleigh, 3/29/1

15/5/5

OKEHAMPTON

    1795   1508M Devon/M&P/Okehampton A2

Lower Halstock SX 602936
TITLE: 'A Map and measure of Four Lots of Wood in Okehampton Park the property of Lord Visct. Courtenay sold in 1795 made by W. Parr Measured 15th 16th & 17th April 1795 – Customary measure 18 feet to the Perch'

SURVEYOR: W. Parr

SCALE: 'A Scale of Chains, each four Statute Perch'; scale bar; 1"=2.5 chains; 1:1980

MATERIAL, SIZE & ORIENTATION: paper, ink; 48.9cms EW x 37.4cms NS; north to top

CONTENT: East Ockment River, direction of flow indicated; Binham Pool; rocks in profile; fields [four lots] outlined with pecked lines with owners named; peripheral field names

DECORATION: direction marked by single line with north marked by fleur-de-lys

15/5/6

OKEHAMPTON

    [1795]   1508M Devon/M&P/Okehampton A3

Lower Halstock SX 602936
TITLE: not given [shows part of Okehampton park adjoining Halstock Common and Halstock Wood]

SURVEYOR: not named

SCALE: 'A Scale of Chains'; scale bar; 1"=4 chains; 1:3168

MATERIAL, SIZE & ORIENTATION: paper, ink; 31.8cms EW x 39.5cms NS; north to top

CONTENT: East Ockment River, arrow indicating direction of flow; relief shown by hill shading; tree symbols showing part of Okehampton Park; gate; footpaths, pecked lines

15/5/7

OKEHAMPTON

    1798   D1508M add/E34/1

Okehampton Castle SX 583942
TITLE: 'A Map of Okehampton Park, Kennel-Field and Park-Kempleys in the Parish of Okehampton, in the County of Devon, the boundaries of which are laid down agreeable to the best information that could be obtained. F.J. 1798'

SURVEYOR: F.J.

SCALE: '200 Statute Poles'; scale bar; 1"=55 poles; 1:10890

MATERIAL, SIZE & ORIENTATION: parchment, coloured; 55cms x 32.7cms; north-west to top

CONTENT: The River Okement, ink stream lines; tributaries draining Okehampton Park; bridges; some shading suggesting relief; park outlined in red with note stating 'The Park fences itself all round, except against Sweetcombe's'; and 'Park-Kempleys fences itself against Fallowfield-Ball'; table giving contents of 3 areas named; gates into Park named; Castle Ham Stile; Park part plain, part green with green tree symbols; Okehampton Castle in profile; Dartmoor and Fallowfield Ball named

DECORATION: 4 point compass indicator; north marked by fleur-de-lys

15/5/8

OKEHAMPTON

   *c.*1800   1508M Devon/M&P/Okehampton A1

Okehampton Castle SX 583942

TITLE: 'A Plan of Okehampton Park, Kennel Field and Park-Kemplys in the Parish of Okehampton leas'd to Henry Holland Esqr.'

SURVEYOR: not named

SCALE: '200 Statute Poles'; scale bar; 1"=50 poles; 1:9900

MATERIAL, SIZE & ORIENTATION: parchment, coloured; 52.9cms x 32.3cms; north-west to top

CONTENT: River Ockment, black lines; Okehampton Park, Kennel Field and Park-Kemplys outlined in red with references to a table giving content and a note concerning fences; gates; stile; tree symbols on areas coloured green; footpaths, pecked lines

DECORATION: 4 point compass indicator within circle of 2 black lines; north marked by fleur-de-lys

15/5/9

OKEHAMPTON

   1836   867B/P16

East Bridge SX 593963

Copies of 3 maps of tenements in Okehampton Borough drawn on both sides of the paper

Map 1

   TITLE: 'Copy of Map of Houses and Lands in North Lane in Okehampton Borough Devon late the property of John Eastabrooke Esqr decd by Wm Thomas in April 1836'

   SURVEYOR: William Thomas

   SCALE: not given

   MATERIAL, SIZE & ORIENTATION: paper, slight colour; 41cms x 51.5cms; no direction

   CONTENT: 'East Okemont River', blue; East Bridge; arrow indicating direction of flow; 'mill stream to Lake's Mill' named; spring; lands referred to in title, green; owners of other outlined areas named; road, North Lane, named, fenced and unfenced; Postlades House named (no plan); peripheral owner named

Map 2

   TITLE: 'Copy of Map of The Stretch Close and Jopes Meadow in Okehampton Borough Devon by Wm Thomas in April 1836'

   SURVEYOR: William Thomas

SCALE: not given

MATERIAL, SIZE & ORIENTATION: as above; south to top

CONTENT: 2 fields, green, named with numeric reference [to list]; road, grey, fenced and unfenced; directions given; peripheral owners named

Map 3

   TITLE: 'Copy of Map of Serjeants als Rattenbury's als Pring's Plot in Okehampton Borough Devon by Wm Thomas April 1836'

   SURVEYOR: William Thomas

   SCALE: not given

   MATERIAL, SIZE & ORIENTATION: as above; south-east to top

   CONTENT: one field, green, named; road, named; peripheral owners named

   ENDORSEMENT: Sundry Tenements in the Borough of Okehampton No. 2

OKEHAMPTON see also B41, C118

15/6/1

OTTERTON

   1802   96M add/E17

Pinn Beacon Plantation SY 099874

TITLE: 'Map of Otterton Common property of The Right Honble Lord Rolle September 1802'

SURVEYOR: P. Warren

SCALE: 'Scale of Statute Chains'; scale bar; 1"=3.5 chains; 1:2772

MATERIAL, SIZE & ORIENTATION: paper, slight colour; 118.5cms x 52.5cms; north-west to top

CONTENT: sea, form lines along coast; cliffs in profile; ponds, streams; relief shown by hill shading; field boundaries adjoining the Common, green with hedge symbols; content of Common; boundary between Otterton Common and Sidmouth Common, red with ink line of dots and dashes; stones, heaps of stones and old boundary stone shown; green tree symbols marking 'Pinn Beacon alias New Plantation' with content; footpaths across Common unfenced, buff; Race Path named; lanes leading to farms and settlements named and gated; building on cliff top in plan; Reference List giving content of Otterton Common, Roads and 'Plot enclosed by G. Sprague'

DECORATION: title cartouche: title inscribed on stones with tree either side; 4 point compass indicator; north marked by fleur-de-lys; scale inscribed on ribbon with dividers above scale bar coloured yellow; border: twisted ribbon coloured pink and yellow

15/6/2

OTTERTON
1821   96M add/E16

Bulverton Hill SY 107891
TITLE: 'Plan of the Lands belonging to the Manor of Otterton Situate on Peak and Bulverton Hills, in the County of Devon Property of the Right Honble Lord Rolle Surveyed 1821'
SURVEYOR: 'Wm Jn(?) Wallace Sworn Surveyor'
SCALE: 'A Scale of Chains, containing Six to an Inch'; scale bar; 1"=6 chains; 1:4752
MATERIAL, SIZE & ORIENTATION: paper, coloured; 46.4cms EW x 58.5cms NS; east to top
CONTENT: fields, green, outlined in deeper colours, with alphabetical reference to table giving content; gates; asterisks marking trench dividing manor of Otterton from the manor of Sidmouth; roads, buff, directions indicated; peripheral owners and estates named
DECORATION: title cartouche: medallion of flower forms, pink/blue/yellow, with shield and ribbon at the top; 16 point compass rose, pink/plain, blue/plain, yellow/plain; north marked by fleur-de-lys; pediment above reference table

OTTERTON see also C17

15/7/1

OTTERY ST MARY
1773   4712M/E1

Little Woodford SY 103968
See entry under Upottery, 20/5/1

15/7/2

OTTERY ST MARY
1775   337B add 2/M&P 6

Ottery St Mary Church SY 098955
TITLE: 'A Plan of the Demesne & Manor of Ottery St Mary in the County of Devon the Property of Sir George Yonge and Sir John Duntze Bart'
SURVEYOR: not named
SCALE: 'A Scale of Chains each 66 Feet long'; scale bar; 1"=5 chains; 1:3960
MATERIAL, SIZE & ORIENTATION: parchment, mounted on linen and segmented, slight colour; c.60cms EW x 129cms NS; north to top
CONTENT: River Otter; fields outlined in green or yellow, some in ink alone; alpha-numeric reference to Survey Book (see below) giving tenants' names, field names and remarks; other owners named; asterisks indicating hedge ownership; tree symbols showing orchards and isolated trees; some areas stippled; roads and lanes named; buildings, some individually in plan, some which face the streets treated together; church and churchyard in detail; upper and lower case reference grid
INSET TITLE: 'The Town on a larger Scale'
SCALE: 'A Scale of Chains each Sixty Six Feet long'; 1"=2 chains; 1:1584
SIZE: c.34cms EW x 31.5cms NS; north to top
DECORATION: 16 point compass rose; north marked by fleur-de-lys, east by arrowhead; inset: 8 point compass rose; north marked by fleur-de-lys, east by arrowhead
ASSOCIATED DOCUMENT: 337B add 2/Misc Estate 4

15/7/3

OTTERY ST MARY
18th cent.   337 add 3B/3/3/8

Fairmile SY 087971
TITLE: not given [shows fields north and west of Fairmile]
SURVEYOR: not named
SCALE: not given
MATERIAL, SIZE & ORIENTATION: paper, watermark, ink; 32.7cms x 36cms; no direction
CONTENT: 'Tail Water River'; fields named, numeric reference [to Survey Book]; gateways; roads, directions given; footpaths, pecked lines; buildings in elevation [crudely drawn]; peripheral owners named
NOTE: map incomplete, torn across the top

15/7/4

OTTERY ST MARY
1802   5292F/A53 (Map 1)

Higher Rill SY 119945

TITLE: 'Map of the Estate called Higher Rull (Part of Potter's Charity) situate in the Parish of Ottery St Mary. Devon'

SURVEYOR: 'J. Coldridge. Exon 1802'

SCALE: 'Scale of Statute Chains containing 66 Feet each'; scale bar; 1"=2.5 chains; 1:1980

MATERIAL, SIZE & ORIENTATION: parchment, coloured; approx. 62cms EW x 49.1cms NS, [bound into volume and folded]; north to top

CONTENT: pond, grey; relief shown by hill shading; fields named with alpha-numeric reference to table giving field names, land use with content and total content; asterisks indicating hedge ownership; whole estate outlined in blue; furze/waste, grey shading; garden; roads, buff; directions given; footpaths, buff between pecked lines; buildings in plan, grey; peripheral owners and estates named

DECORATION: title cartouche: framed by intertwined leaves and ferns, view of sea and 3 sailing ships to the right; 8 point compass rose, black shaded lines; north marked by fleur-de-lys

ASSOCIATED DOCUMENT: in the accounts section of the same volume is the record of the payment to J Coldridge for mapping and surveying Higher Rull, £1.18s.4½d, 7 July 1802

15/7/5

OTTERY ST MARY
1823/5   961M add/M/E2

Ottery St Mary Church SY 098955
See entry under Feniton, 6/3/3

15/7/6

OTTERY ST MARY
1834   56/4/6/9

Wiggaton SY 101936

TITLE: 'Wiggaton an Estate in the Parish of Ottery St Mary Devon the Property of Mr. Edward Richards 1834'

SURVEYOR: 'By George Dowling Landsurveyor &c Andover Hants'

SCALE: 'Scale of Chains'; scale bar; 1"=3 chains; 1:2376

MATERIAL, SIZE & ORIENTATION: paper, slight colour; 42.3cms EW x 71.3cms NS; north to top

CONTENT: fields outlined in ink with hedge symbols; numeric reference to separate list (56/4/3/2b) giving field name and content with note correcting inaccurate entry; gates; roads, light brown; directions indicated; buildings in plan, red or grey; peripheral owners named

DECORATION: 8 point compass rose, plain/shaded grey; north marked by arrowhead

OTTERY ST MARY see also C119

16/1/1

PAIGNTON
1566/7 [see note]   Wilts RO 2057/S3/3

Paignton Church SX 886608

TITLE: not given [shows area immediately surrounding the church]

SURVEYOR: not named

SCALE: not given

MATERIAL, SIZE & ORIENTATION: [parchment]; 22cms x 23.8cms; no direction

CONTENT: the whole is a bird's flight view of the centre of Paignton; cultivated plots at the rear of houses; trees and hedges in gardens and 8 ridges of 'Lekebeds'; trees, hedges. roads, paths; houses and church in elevation with semblance of reality; walled area surrounding buildings of the Bishop's Palace; position of church would suggest north to top; sea with ships of various sizes but out of scale with the rest of the map

ASSOCIATED PUBLICATION: Charles R. Straton, *Survey of the Lands of William First Earl of Pembroke* (Oxford, 1909) Introduction to Vol. II states illustrations preceding each roll of the survey were drawn by the scribe.

p.lx mentions where leeks were grown as a vegetable they were grown on these 8 ridges

p.lxx mentions a common bakehouse

p.xl states Commissioners began work on the survey in 1566 and reached Paignton some time after March 1567

p.xlviii Palace of the Bishop of Exeter had become a ruin before passing into the Earl's hands

16/1/2

PAIGNTON
1801   Ex. D&C Ch. Comm. 98

Preston SX 888619
See entry under Marldon, 13/6/1

16/1/3

PAIGNTON
[1839]   70/6/6

Paington Church SX 886608

TITLE: 'Plan of Luscombe and Millers Plots situate in the Parish of
    Paignton'

SURVEYOR: [Thomas Hunt]

SCALE: not given

MATERIAL, SIZE & ORIENTATION: paper, coloured; 60.6cms x 37.9cms; no
    direction

CONTENT: fields, pink or green with alpha-numeric reference to 70/6/5;
    roads, buff, directions given; footpaths, pecked lines; buildings in
    plan, red or plain

ASSOCIATED DOCUMENT: 70/6/5 – letter from Tho. Hunt of Matthews
    House, Paignton, dated 24 Jan. 1839 to Ralph Barnes, 'Procter and
    Sollisiter'. Note on this letter by Ralph Barnes, 'steward', that he
    has viewed the spot and has consented to hedges being taken down.

PAIGNTON see also B100, C120, C173

16/2/1

PANCRASWEEK
1788–1789   6107

Blatchborough SS286141 Pancrasweek Church SS 296058
Kimworthy SS 311127
See entry under Bridestowe, 2/35/6

PARKHAM see C121

16/3/1

PAYHEMBURY
1823/5   961M add/M/E2

Payhembury Church ST 088018
See entry under Feniton, 6/3/3

16/4/1

PETERS MARLAND
c.1790   NDRO 2239 B add/P10

Twigbeare SS 478123

TITLE: 'A Map of the Manor of Twiggbear in the County of Devon The
    property of Sr Wm Molesworth Bart Surveyed & delineated by David
    Palmer'

SURVEYOR: David Palmer

SCALE: 'Statute Chains'; scale bar; 1"=3 chains; 1:2376

MATERIAL, SIZE & ORIENTATION: parchment, coloured; c.99.6cms x
    91.5cms; north-west to top

CONTENT: streams suggested by sinuous field boundaries; fields outlined
    in colour with suggestion only of hedges; numeric reference [to
    Survey Book]; 'asterisms' indicating hedge ownership; tree symbols
    showing orchards and avenues; stippling, marking ?moorland or
    furze; roads; buildings in plan, red; peripheral owners named

DECORATION: title cartouche: rococo, scrolls with acanthus, flowers and
    ruched fabric superimposed on trees with rural and coastal scene
    below; 8 point compass rose, black lines/plain; north marked by fleur-
    de-lys

16/4/2

PETERS MARLAND
c.1820   NDRO 2239B add/P11

Stone SS 478116

TITLE: 'Map of Stone Estate in the Parish of Peters Marland'

SURVEYOR: not named

SCALE: not given

MATERIAL, SIZE & ORIENTATION: paper, mounted on cloth, coloured;
    75.8cms EW x 51.4cms NS; north to top

CONTENT: river, streams, blue; relief shown by hill shading; fields outlined
    in green with numeric reference to table giving field names, land use

and content; gates; garden; tree symbols showing orchards and isolated trees; stippling marking ?waste; roads, buff, some directions given; buildings in plan, red

DECORATION: 8 point compass rose, grey/plain; north and east marked by letter

NOTE: later additions in pencil

PETERS MARLAND see also B52

16/5/1

PETER TAVY
[1663 x 1686]   Diocesan Glebe Terriers Peter Tavy

Peter Tavy Church SX 513778

TITLE: 'Terrarium justum ac verum omnium fundorum, pratorum, hortorum … Parrochiam Taviae Sancti Petri quae ad Rectoriam eandem noscuntr sp … memoriam' (A fair and true terrier of all the estates, meadows, gardens … parish of St Peter Tavy which are known [to belong] to the same rectory of ?special memory)

SURVEYOR: not named

SCALE: not given

MATERIAL, SIZE & ORIENTATION: paper, ink; 44.1cms EW x 38.9cms NS [as repaired]; east to top

CONTENT: fields with numeric reference to table giving field names; roads; footpaths, pecked lines; Bowling alley; church marked by symbol

DECORATION: 32 point compass rose; NSEW marked by letter

ASSOCIATED DOCUMENT: this is part of a written document signed by Andrewe Gove, Rector, and John King, Churchwarden; it also gives a description of rooms in the Rectory

NOTE: Andrew Gove was Rector of Peter Tavy from 1663 to 1686. The document is much damaged

16/5/2

PETER TAVY
1727   Diocesan Glebe Terriers Peter Tavy

Peter Tavy Church SX 513778

TITLE: 'A Description of the Situation of the Parsonage House and Glebe Lands belonging to the Rectory of Peter Tavy'

SURVEYOR: not named

SCALE: not given

MATERIAL, SIZE & ORIENTATION: parchment, ink; 34cms EW x 37.1cms NS; east to top

CONTENT: fields with numeric reference to table giving field names and content; roads; footpaths, pecked lines

ASSOCIATED DOCUMENT: this is part of a written terrier which is signed by the Rector, Curate, and Churchwardens; see also Parish copy of Glebe Terrier at 1427 add 2/PB6

ENDORSEMENT: Peter Tavey Exhibit' 4to Maij 1727

16/5/3

PETER TAVY
16 April 1727   1427 add 2/PB6

Peter Tavy Church SX 513778

TITLE: 'A Description of the Situation of the Parsonage House and the Glebe Lands belonging to the Rectory of Peter Tavy'

SURVEYOR: not named

SCALE: not given

MATERIAL, SIZE & ORIENTATION: parchment, ink; 31.3cms EW x 36.6cms NS; east to top

CONTENT: fields with numeric reference to list giving field names and content; roads; footpaths, pecked lines

NOTE AT SIDE OF MAP: 'Nov ye 14th 1735 Planted ye Carrion Garden with 56 Apple-trees'

ASSOCIATED DOCUMENT: Dioc. Glebe Terrier/Peter Tavy

16/5/4

PETER TAVY
26 May 1764   Diocesan Glebe Terriers Peter Tavy

Peter Tavy Church SX 513778

TITLE: 'A Terrier of the Rectory of Peter Tavy'

SURVEYOR: not named

SCALE: not given

MATERIAL, SIZE & ORIENTATION: parchment, ink; 19cms EW x 31.6cms NS; east to top

CONTENT: fields with numeric reference to table giving field names and content; roads; footpaths, pecked lines; buildings in plan

DECORATION: 4 point compass indicator, black/plain; NSEW marked by letter

ASSOCIATED DOCUMENT: this is part of a written terrier which is signed by the church officers

16/5/5

PETER TAVY

1765   L1258M/L/E6/48

Cudlip Town SX 520790

TITLE: 'The Plan refer'd to by the Indenture Annexed'

SURVEYOR: Gilbert Aislabie

SCALE: 'Plotted by a Scale of 3 Statute Chains in an Inch in 1765 by G. Aislabie'; no scale bar; 1:2376

MATERIAL, SIZE & ORIENTATION: parchment, coloured; 60.5cms x 49cms (attached to document)' north-west to top; 4 point plain compass indicator

CONTENT: River Tavy, grey; arrows indicating direction of flow; fields outlined in yellow, named with content; numeric reference to list repeating field names and content in statute and customary measure; green tree symbols showing woods, named with content; roads, buff, directions given; buildings in plan, red or grey; peripheral owners named (including Dr Cudlip)

ASSOCIATED DOCUMENT: map attached to lease dated 29th September 1771 between the Duchess of Bedford and Mr Peter Oxenham

16/6/1

PILTON

1776   NDRO 1239F/MP1

Pilton Quay SS 556340

TITLE: 'Plan Shewing the Situation of the Quay at Pilton'

SURVEYOR: '2d May 1776 Survey'd by John Tamlyn'

SCALE: 'Scale of Feet'; scale bar; 1"=25 feet; 1:300

MATERIAL, SIZE & ORIENTATION: paper, ink; 46.5cms EW x 30.5cms NS; north to top

CONTENT: 'Rawleigh River', showing land covered only at Spring Tides or floods; alphabetic reference to list identifying principal features; Quay and Cut; peripheral owners named

Later annotations indicating buildings, garden, lime kiln, Hospital land and below the title: 'This plan was drawn in order to be produced at the assizes on an action brought by the feofees of the poor Land against William Hole for not paying on unloading a Brig or Bark – he submitted and paid Cost'

DECORATION: 16 point compass rose, lightly shaded; north marked by crescents and diamonds, east by symbols; title embellished by flourishes

ENDORSEMENT: Pilton Quay 1776. The Limekiln is introduced at random and not by scale – no time to do it. A Plan of Pilton Quay very proper to be kept.

16/6/2

PILTON

1779/1822   NDRO TD 146/E1

Pilton Quay SS 556340

See entry under Barnstaple, 2/2/4

16/6/3

PILTON

1823   NDRO 1239/MP1(c)

Pilton Quay SS 556340

See entry under Barnstaple, 2/2/8

16/6/4

PILTON

19th cent.   DD 36473

Pilton Church SS 556341

TITLE: 'A Sketch of certain Lands in the Parish of Pilton Devon belonging to James Whyte, Esqr'

SURVEYOR: not named

SCALE: 'Scale of chains'; scale bar; 1"=8 chains; 1:6336

MATERIAL, SIZE & ORIENTATION: paper, ink; 38.4cms EW x 32.4cms NS; north to top

CONTENT: river Yeo, pecked lines; arrows indicating direction of flow; fields outlined in ink, fence in profile; alpha-numeric reference to list giving field and area names, land use – 'Gardens and Orchards; Arable, Meadow and Pasture; Plantations and Woods; Hedges and Woods' – content and total content; gate; gardens; tree symbols showing isolated trees; stippling marking gardens, lawns, plantations; roads, named, directions given; Pilton Bridge named; footpaths, pecked lines; buildings, some in plan, some, including church, in elevation; peripheral owners and estates named

DECORATION: 4 point compass indicator; north-south line marked by an arrow

16/6/5

PILTON
1834   96M Box 84/1

Pilton Church SS 556341
TITLE: not given
SURVEYOR: not named
SCALE: not given
MATERIAL, SIZE & ORIENTATION: parchment, slight colour; 39.5cms x 21cms; no direction
CONTENT: river, black stream lines, arrows indicating direction of flow; Pilton Bridge; fields outlined with broken lines and pink numeric reference to table in the attached document giving field names and content; waste, plain; roads, directions given; peripheral owners named
ASSOCIATED DOCUMENT: map is part of a Deed of Exchange of 30 April 1834 of lands in Pilton between James White and Lord Rolle

PILTON see also C122–23

PLYMOUTH see B2, B18, B20, B27–28, B31, B38–39, B60–61, B64, B74, B78, B111, B116, C124–28; see Introduction, 1

16/7/1

PLYMPTON ST MARY
1788–89   6107

Colnebrook SX 536573
See entry under Bridestowe, 2/35/6

16/7/2

PLYMPTON ST MARY
1811   PWDRO 370

Newnham SX 554579
TITLE: 'A Map of Newnham and other lands in the Parishes of Plympton St Mary and Shaugh belonging to Richard Strode Esq. 1811'
SURVEYOR: not named
SCALE: 'Scale of Chains'; scale bar; 1"=4 chains' 1:3168
MATERIAL, SIZE & ORIENTATION: paper, ink; 100.8cms x 130.8cms; north-east to top
CONTENT: river; bridges; ford; fields with numeric reference to tables giving field names and content; gateways; roads, fenced and unfenced; directions given; footpaths, pecked lines; buildings in plan, black; parish boundary, red; surrounding heath, common and downland named
DECORATION: 8 point compass rose; north marked by letter N
NOTE: this is a copy of an original; traced in 1967

16/7/3

PLYMPTON ST MARY
1840   PWDRO 655/1

Plympton St Mary Church SX 537563
See entry under Cornwood, 3/31/2

PLYMPTON ST MARY see also B21, C129–36

16/8/1

PLYMSTOCK
1743   L1258/M&P/Plymstock 9

Turnchapel SX 495532
TITLE: not given
SURVEYOR: 'Survey'd July ye 20th; 1743: By William Doidge Surveyor'
SCALE: 'A Scale of 500 Feet'; divided scale; 1"=130 feet; 1:1560
MATERIAL, SIZE & ORIENTATION: paper, ink, slight grey colour; 54.4cms EW x 42.8cms NS; north to top
CONTENT: cliffs in profile; shoreline indicated by grey form lines; Cat Water and Hooe Lake named; road to Plymouth and to Plymstock

named; houses and gardens indicated in words; quays, shipyards etc keyed by letter to reference list; Tan Chapel, Island House and Capt. Graves's House in elevation

DECORATION: 4 point compass indicator shaded white, grey and black; north marked by fleur-de-lys

16/8/2

PLYMSTOCK

1755   T1258M/E24

Plymstock Church SX 517530

TITLE: 'A Survey of the Mannor of Plymstock in the County of Devon Belonging to The Most Noble John Duke of Bedford Taken by Thos Heath 1755'

SURVEYOR: Thomas Heath

SCALE: 'A Scale of Statute Perches'; scale bar; 1"=10 perches; 1:1980

MATERIAL, SIZE & ORIENTATION: parchment, mounted on linen, coloured; 145cms x 130cms; north-north-west to top

CONTENT: 'Radford Lake, Part of Cat Water, Pomphlet Creek, Part of the Lary [Laira]' named; estuary margins blue with blue stream lines; streams, blue; some green or grey shading showing relief; fields outlined in various colours according to the separate tenements; fields named with content; alpha-numeric reference to list giving names of Premises, Tenants' Names, colours used and content all of which are repeated in the Survey Book; gardens; green tree symbols showing orchards and isolated trees; roads, buff, some named including 'Narrow Causeway'; directions given; turnpike gate on London Road; greens and waste named; footpaths buff, pecked lines; buildings in plan, red; church, hatched black; houses and courtlages in Plymstock and Oreston shown in detail; 'A Lime Stone Quarry, Two Limestone Quarrys, A Black Marble Quarry' indicated by grey shading; Pomphlet Mills, red; pier named; peripheral owners and estates named

DECORATION: title cartouche: elaborate rococo design repeated in border; 16 point compass rose, principal points and centre with rococo decorations; north marked by fleur-de-lys, other directions indicated by letter

ROLLED WITH THE MAP:- 'A Survey of the Mannor of Plymstock by Thomas Heath 1755'

This is listed under tenement, owner and with reference to alphabetical sections A–T with arabic numerals, giving field names, customary and statute content

Separate sections for Oreston tenements; roman numerals used for reference with Oreston Cottages using arabic references. Index.

16/8/3

PLYMSTOCK

c.1770   2729Z/E11

Plymstock Church SX 517530
See entry under Brixton, 2/38/2

16/8/4

PLYMSTOCK

18th cent.   L1258/M&P/Plymstock 1–8

Plymstock Church SX 517530

Plan 1

TITLE: not given [shows land north of Radford Lake]

SURVEYOR: not named

SCALE: 'A Scale of Chains and links of Customary Measure'; scale bar; 1"=2 chains; 1:1728

MATERIAL, SIZE & ORIENTATION: paper, coloured; 40.6cms EW x 46.2cms NS; east to top

CONTENT: Radford Lake; fields outlined in yellow, named with content; tree symbols showing orchard; Park Lane; buildings in plan, red; peripheral owners named

DECORATION: ships on lake; 4 point compass indicator; north marked by fleur-de-lys, SEW by letter

Plan 2

TITLE: 'Plan No2' [shows Rowley Close and Longlands Orchard]

SURVEYOR: not named

SCALE: not given [possibly the same as Plan 1]

MATERIAL, SIZE & ORIENTATION: paper, coloured; 47.8cms EW x 38.4cms NS; north to top

CONTENT: pond; fields outlined in yellow; tree symbols showing orchard; peripheral owners named

Plan 3

TITLE: 'A Map or Plan of Home Tenement and a Moiety of Meaders Tenement in the Parish and Mannor of Plymstock in the County of Devon Sold in Fee Farm to John Jeffery'

SURVEYOR: not named

SCALE: 'A Scale of Chains and Links of Customary Measure'; scale bar; 1"=1 chain; 1:864 [each chain contains 4 perches of 18 feet each]

MATERIAL, SIZE & ORIENTATION: paper, coloured; 59.4cms EW x 59.5cms NS; north to top

CONTENT: fields of Home Tenement outlined in red; fields of Meaders outlined in green both with field names and content; roads, named; Mill Lane named; footpaths, pecked lines

INSET: plan of the house, barn, stable, orchard and garden belonging to Home Tenement; 4 point compass indicator; north marked by fleur-de-lys; south-west to top

DECORATION: title cartouche: free-hand pen and ink design enclosed in double red line; 4 point compass indicator; north marked by fleur-de-lys, east by cross

ENDORSEMENT: John Jeffery

Plans 4 and 5 show separate fields, presumably part of number 3
SCALE: same as Plan 3

Plan 6 endorsed Plan No 3

Plan 7 fields same scale as Plan 3

Plan 8
TITLE: 'A Plan of Pomphlet Mills'; SX 507539
SURVEYOR: not named
SCALE: 'A Scale of feet 48 to an inch'; scale bar; 1:576
MATERIAL, SIZE & ORIENTATION: paper, watermark, coloured; 20.3cms EW x 32cms NS; east to top
CONTENT: mill pool and Pomphlet Lake, grey; land, yellow; buildings in plan, red; peripheral owners named

16/8/5

PLYMSTOCK
1823   L1258M/SS/C(DL)E98

Laira bridge SX 502543
TITLE: endorsed 'Lairy bridge'
SURVEYOR: not named
SCALE: 'Scale of Chains'; scale bar; 1"=2.5 chains; 1:1980
MATERIAL, SIZE & ORIENTATION: paper, ink; 77.3cms EW x 46.2cms NS; north to top
CONTENT: Pomphlet Creek, Billacombe Brook, stream lines; fields outlined in ink with field names and content; owners' names of estates given; garden; lines in red ink marking land to be acquired to build the bridge; roads, directions given; buildings in plan, hatched grey
DECORATION: 4 point compass indicator; north marked by fleur-de-lys
ASSOCIATED DOCUMENT: papers re 'Bill for erecting an bridge over the Water of Lary from Pomphlet Point, in the Parish of Plymstock … to Great Prince Rock in the Parish of Charles … 4 Geo IV (Session 1823)'

16/8/6

PLYMSTOCK
1828   PWDRO 1957/12

Gore unidentified
See entry under Brixton, 2/38/11

16/8/7

PLYMSTOCK
1831   PWDRO 1957/16

Stoddiscombe SX 513513
TITLE: 'Rough Map of the Manor of Stoddiscombe in Plymstock'
SURVEYOR: Henry Andrews
SCALE: 'Scale of 4 Chains to an Inch'; 1"=4 chains; 1:3168
MATERIAL, SIZE & ORIENTATION: paper, slight colour; 120.3cms EW x 67cms NS; north to top
CONTENT: 'Bovey-Sand' Bay marked and cliffs on coast indicated by black lines; river, blue; arrows indicating direction of flow; resevoir, blue; fields outlined in black, some field names given; numeric reference to list giving field names and content; asterisks indicating boundary ownership; gateways; tree symbols, black showing woods; stippling marking commons; roads, plain, directions given; footpaths, pecked lines; buildings in plan, red or hatched black; battery marked; peripheral owners named
DECORATION: 4 point compass indicator; NS marked by fletched arrow

16/8/8

PLYMSTOCK
*c.*1840   T1258M/E21a

Oreston Quay SX 500533
TITLE: 'Plan of the Village of Oreston in the Parish of Plymstock in the County of Devon'
SURVEYOR: not named; endorsement states 'Compiled by J Hitchens'
SCALE: 'Scale of Feet'; scale bar; 1"=36 feet; 1:432
MATERIAL, SIZE & ORIENTATION: paper, mounted on linen, coloured; 167cms x 97cms; north-east to top
CONTENT: Catwater named; hill slopes in profile, shaded grey; grey tree symbols showing copse; roads, 'Thornover Lane, Rock Lane' named; buildings in plan, grey; some courtlages blue, some grey; various

areas outlined in colour; steps to waterside; Dock, Pier-head and 'Cemetry' named

DECORATION: 8 point compass rose, grey/shaded grey; north marked by fleur-de-lys

ENDORSEMENT: Oreston Village 36ft to 1in. Compiled by J Hitchens

NOTE: later annotations in pencil

PLYMSTOCK see also C137–38

PLYMTREE see SUPPLEMENT S6

16/9/1

POLTIMORE
1832   50/3/1/5

Ratsloe SX 958977

TITLE: 'Map of Estates in the Parish of Poltimore in the County of Devon The Property of the Rt Honble Lord Poltimore 1832'

SURVEYOR: not named

SCALE: not given

MATERIAL, SIZE & ORIENTATION: paper, slight colour; c.102cms x 115cms (damaged and torn); north-west to top

CONTENT: fields, some outlined in feint colour, named with land use and numeric reference [to Survey Book]; symbols indicating hedge ownership; gates; orchards, named; roads, one named, some gated; lanes and footpaths, broken lines; buildings in plan, blue, pink or hatched black; peripheral owners named

POLTIMORE see also C139

16/10/1

POOL, SOUTH
1777   1508 Devon/M&P/V3

South Pool Church SX 776404
See entry under Alvington, West, 1/6/1

16/10/2

POOL, SOUTH
1777   1508M/M&P/South Pool Maps 1

North Pool SX 776413 Ham point SX 756414

TITLE: 'A Map of Lands lying within the Manor of North Pool in the County of Devon Belonging to The Right Honble Wm: Ld: Visct: Courtenay By George Lang of Leyland' [1777 in pencil]

SURVEYOR: George Lang

SCALE: 'A Scale of Eighty Poles 5½ Yards each'; scale bar; 1"=16 poles; 1:3168

MATERIAL, SIZE & ORIENTATION: parchment, coloured; 77cms EW x 64.2cms NS; north to top

CONTENT: Frogmoor Creek, Fleet Bay, named, form lines with one bank shaded suggesting a steep river bank; tidal flow indicated; red line ?indicating riparian rights; quarry shown by stippling and hill shading; fields outlined in colour, named with numeric reference [to Survey Book]; gates; green tree symbols showing orchards and on green wash a grove and a wood; isolated trees; roads, directions given; footpaths, dotted lines; buildings in detailed elevation; Frogmoor named; key to symbols used for High Roads, Driving Roads, Ownership of Boundary Fences, Footpaths and Brooks and the symbol showing John Parker's land; lime kiln

DECORATION: title cartouche: rural scene with rocks, trees, ruins beside river with rowing boats and small sailing vessels; horses/donkeys on river bank with male figure; 32 point compass rose, plain/black superimposed on 3 concentric circles; north marked by fleur-de-lys; SEW by letter; border: running pattern repeated below scale

16/11/1

PORTLEMOUTH, EAST
1764   Blundell's School

Portlemouth Barton SX 711391

TITLE: 'A Mapp of the Lands belonging to Blundell's School in Tiverton in the Parish of East Portlemouth in the County of Devon survey'd in 1764 by T: Hodge of Silverton'

SURVEYOR: Thomas Hodge

SCALE: 'Scale of Chains'; scale bar; 1"=3.5 chains; 1:2772

MATERIAL, SIZE & ORIENTATION: parchment, coloured; 95cms EW x 96cms NS (on rollers); north to top

CONTENT: streams, grey; fields outlined in grey, with hedge symbols; alpha-numeric reference [to Survey Book]; green tree symbols showing orchards and woods; roads, buff, fenced and unfenced; gated; directions given; buildings in plan, black; peripheral owners named

DECORATION: title cartouche: scrolls with garlands of flowers and leaves; 4 point compass indicator, plain/shaded grey; north marked by fleur-de-lys

16/11/2

PORTLEMOUTH, EAST
1777   1508M/Devon/M&P/V3

Portlemouth Barton SX 711391
See entry under Alvington, West, 1/6/1

16/12/1

POWDERHAM
1723   Powderham Archive

Powderham Castle SX 968836

Estate Atlas. Leather-bound volume tooled in gold, 13cms x 19.5cms, with 'A Book of Maps' on the spine

TITLE: 'A Book of Maps of the Mannors and part of the Parishes of Powderham and Kenton being part of the Estate of the Honble Sr Wm Courtenay Bart. in the County of Devon Survey'd in the Year 1723 By Robert Whittlesey'. This is the original volume for the estate atlas at 1508M/Maps/Powderham 2. The titles of all individual maps are as in the later volume and the map references will be found under that description

SURVEYOR: Robert Whittlesey

SCALE: The scale differs from the later atlas as in the 1723 volume all 11 maps are drawn at a scale of 80 perches to an inch with the exception of Map 3 which is 64 perches to an inch. The scales are given as statements only and there are no scale bars. No scale is indicated for Map 1.

MATERIAL, SIZE & ORIENTATION: parchment, coloured; 13cms x 19.5cms; directions indicated

GENERAL CONTENT: streams, grey, River Exe, grey; relief shown by hill drawn in profile; fields outlined in various colours according to tenants' holding; alpha-numeric reference to lists on facing page giving tenants' names, land use, content of each parcel, content of each tenants' holding, orchards etc; formal garden and 'pit garden'; tree symbols showing avenues, woodlands, orchards and isolated

trees; roads, directions given; buildings in elevation; peripheral owners and parishes named

DECORATION: principal title cartouche: swag of cloth held by cherubs seated on a plinth with coat-of-arms above; title cartouches to individual maps: fish scales, acanthus leaves and shells; scale statements inscribed on a ribbon; 8 point compass rose on all maps; north marked by fleur-de-lys, SEW by letter

NOTE: each manor is followed by an Abstract giving the names of the tenants, map references and the total content in each map

16/12/2

POWDERHAM
1747–1759   1508M/Maps Powderham 2

Powderham Castle SX 968836
See entry under Kenton, 11/4/2

16/12/3

POWDERHAM
1759   Powderham Archive (in Tithe
                                     Apportionment Book)

Powderham Church SX 973844

TITLE: 'A Map of the Glebe belonging to ye Rectory of Powderham in the County of Devon taken for the Revd. Mr. Richard Harrington in September 1759 by Wm. Hole. Junr.'

SURVEYOR: William Hole, Junior

SCALE: 'A Scale of Chains each containing 4 Statute Perches'; scale bar; 1"=4 chains; 1:3168

MATERIAL, SIZE & ORIENTATION: parchment, coloured; 35cms EW x 41cms NS; west to top

CONTENT: 'Part of the River Exe', river bank, dark blue; fields outlined in green with hedge symbols and alphabetic reference to table giving field names and content; tree symbols showing orchards and isolated trees; roads; buildings in elevation; peripheral owners named

INSET: 'The Lands of Mr Robert Moal'

DECORATION: title cartouche: stylised acanthus leaves; reference table and scale bar, both on plinth with pediment; ships and boats on River Exe

NOTE: 3 annotations:-

a) 'Paid for this map 2l 8s 0d R.H. 1759'

b) note dated 1770 on later change of land use

c) note dated 1835 concerning ownership of the Marsh

16/12/4

POWDERHAM
*c.*1775   Powderham Archive

Powderham Castle SX 968836

TITLE: 'A Plan on intended Alterations for Powderham Castle, the Seat of the Rt. Honorable Lord Visct Courtenay'

SURVEYOR: not named

SCALE: no unit of measurement stated; scale bar

MATERIAL, SIZE & ORIENTATION: paper, coloured; 54.5cms EW x 69.5cms NS; map is framed; north to top

CONTENT: river, grey; park, green with green tree symbols marking deciduous and coniferous plantations and isolated trees; paths, buff, broken lines; buildings in plan, buff, named and keyed by letter to reference list; this includes the Castle, stables, orangery, menagerie, intended pleasure grounds and garden [without detail]

DECORATION: 4 point compass indicator, yellow/buff; north marked by fleur-de-lys

NOTE: the map dates from before the Music Room was built

16/12/5

POWDERHAM
*c.*1775   Powderham Archive

Powderham Castle SX 968836

TITLE: not given [shows intended alterations to the river and park]

SURVEYOR: Thomas Gray

SCALE: not given

MATERIAL, SIZE & ORIENTATION: paper, slight colour; 108.8cms x 32.2cms; map is framed; north-east to top

CONTENT: river, ponds, grey; weir; sandy beach, stippled; relief shown by hill shading; park, plain, boundary marked by hedge symbols; gardens outlined in ink, plain; tree symbols showing deciduous and coniferous plantations; footpaths, buff, pecked lines; buildings in plan, buff

DECORATION: single line compass indicator; north marked by fleur-de-lys; 2 rowing boats and a small sailing boat on the Exe

NOTE: annotations in pencil; the map dates from before the Music Room was built

16/12/6

POWDERHAM
1785   1508M Devon/M&P/Powderham Maps1

Powderham Castle SX 968836 Exwell Hill SX 960852

TITLE: 'A Map of Lands within the Township of Powderham with the Glebe Lands of Powderham the Property of The Right Honourable William = Lord Viscount Courtenay By George Lang 1785'

SURVEYOR: George Lang

SCALE: 'A Scale of Twenty Statute Chains'; scale bar; 1"=4 chains; 1:3168

MATERIAL, SIZE & ORIENTATION: parchment, coloured; 169cms x 69.3cms; north-east to top

CONTENT: 'The River Exe', form lines, 'The River Kenn', stream lines; ponds including 'Decoy'; Exwell Hill with obelisk, and The Belvedere, in profile, shaded grey; fields outlined in various colours, named with numeric reference [to Survey Book]; Glebe land distinguished by red G and Mr Pile's land by red symbol; fence symbols; boundary fences 'belonging' distinguished by broken and dotted line; gates; garden in detailed plan, green; maze; green tree symbols distinguishing deciduous and coniferous trees showing orchards, plantations, woodland, copses, hedgerow trees, avenues and isolated trees; roads, high roads and driving roads distinguished, some gated; directions given; buildings, some in plan, stippled red, others in elevation including Powderham Church; peripheral owners and parishes named; 'supposed' parish boundaries across the river to Darling Point and 'Lymston Town' where buildings shown in plan, hatched black; Reference List to symbols used

DECORATION: title cartouche: rocks, trees, shrubs and figure pointing to script; on right view of Castle seen from the river with trees and deer in foreground and boat on river; 32 point compass rose, plain/shades of grey superimposed on 3 concentric circles; north marked by fleur-de-lys, SEW by letter; 2 sailing boats on Exe; border, running pattern of lozenge and star design

16/12/7

POWDERHAM
1787   Powderham Archive

Estate Atlas. Leather-bound volume, tooled in gold with brass clasps, 21.5cms x 35cms, and with title on cover 'Powderham Kenton and other Estates 1787'

TITLE: 'A Survey with maps of Lands lying within the Manors of Powderham, Kenton-Courtenay, Chiverstone, Kenton, Exminster,

Alphington, Whitestone, and East Teignmouth alias Teignmouth-Courtenay; also of the Glebe Lands of Powderham, Kenn and Whitestone all within the County of Devon belonging to The Right Honble Wm Lord Visct. Courtenay'

SURVEYOR: George Lang

SCALE: 'A Scale of 30 Statute Chains'; scale bar; 1"=8 chains; 1:6336

MATERIAL, SIZE & ORIENTATION: all 40 maps are on parchment, some with fold-in areas, some coloured; for size of volume see above; direction is indicated on all maps

GENERAL CONTENT: River Exe and streams, grey; 'The New River' named; relief shown by hill shading; Powderham Park bounded by fence symbol; fields either outlined or washed in various colours, named and with numeric reference to list on facing page; formal gardens; gates; green tree symbols showing woods, orchards, avenues and isolated trees; roads, directions given; buildings in elevation; those 'not belonging' in plan; peripheral owners and parishes named

MAP I 'A Plan of Powderham Castle with the offices, Courts, Stables, Gardens, Park & Plantations'. The Belvedere and the 'sunk fence' are marked
          Powderham Castle SX 968836

MAPS II–IV are of Lands in the Manor of Powderham

MAP V 'The Manor of Kenton-Courtenay and other lands in the Parish of Kenton'
          Kenton Church SX 957833

MAP VI 'Manor of Chiverstone & Parish of Kenton'
          Chiverstone Farm SX 947839
          Un-numbered plan 'Map of Channon's otherwise Lower Marshrow in the parish of Exminster & manor of Chiverstone in the County of Devon, the property of Lord Visct Courtenay'

MAPS VII–XXII relate to property in the parish of Kenton:- East Town, West Town, Hayton, Wilsworthy, 'Hal Down', manor of Kenwoods, Lyston, Kenton Heathfields, Little Mowlish, Southtown, Cofford, Starcross, Week, Week-Pit, 'Rabbit=Warren'
          Wilsworthy Farm SX 941846   North Kenwood SX 920820
          Mowlish Farm SX 951810   Southtown SX 963836   Cofford
          Farm SX 966806   Starcross SX 976817

MAP XXIII 'Cuttridge Estate in the Parish of Kenton with a tenemt. in St Thomas'

MAP XXIV 'A Map of Lands within the Manor of Kenton, in the Parish of Mannaton'
          Manaton Church SX 749813

MAP XXV 'Part of the Manor of Kenton in the Parishes of E. Teignmouth and West Teignmouth with Lands in the Manor of E. Teignmouth alias Teignmouth Courtenay'
          East Teignmouth Church SX 943732   West Teignmouth Church
          SX 939731

MAP XXVI 'A Plan of the Rectory of Kenn in the Parish of Kenn'
          Kenn Church SX 922857

MAPS XXVII–XXIX Lands in the parish of Exminster
          Exminster Church 946877

MAPS XXX–XXXVII Lands in the parish of Alphington
          Alphington Church SX 918899

MAPS XXXVIII–XXXIX Lands within the manor and parish of Whitestone
          Whitestone Church SX 868943

MAP XL 'A Map of the Glebe Lands of Whitestone in the Parish of Whitestone'

DECORATION: title cartouches: rococo frames; borders: vine-leaf pattern; 4 point compass indicators; north marked by fleur-de-lys, SEW by letter

NOTE: accompanying abstract [on paper] gives details of tenants' names, content and map number

16/12/8

POWDERHAM

16 October 1787   Powderham Archive (in Tithe
                                                      Apportionment Book)

Powderham Castle SX 968836

TITLE: 'A Plan of Powderham Glebe'

SURVEYOR: William Cartwright

SCALE: 'Scale of Chains'; scale bar' 1"=3 chains; 1:2376

MATERIAL, SIZE & ORIENTATION: paper, mounted on linen, coloured; 58.3cms EW x 48.4cms NS; north to top

CONTENT: River Exe, blue; river bank, stippled; fields, blue outlined in dark blue, named with content; alpha-numeric reference to list on separate sheet repeating field names and content; crosses indicating hedge ownership; gates, red; formal gardens; tree symbols showing orchards, woods and isolated trees; 'sunk fence'; roads, buff, fenced and unfenced; directions given; buildings in plan, hatched red

DECORATION: title cartouche: rural view with cottages, river with boat; 2

insets of views with houses; hand holding dividers above scale bar; ships and boats on river

16/12/9

POWDERHAM

1793   1508 Devon/M&P/Powderham A3

Exwell Hill SX 960852

TITLE: not given [shows land to the north and north-east of Powderham Park]

SURVEYOR: not named

SCALE: 'A Scale of Chains'; scale bar; 1"=4 chains; 1:3168

MATERIAL, SIZE & ORIENTATION: The River Exe, shaded grey; river Kenn light and dark grey margins; Exwell Hill in profile with staff/obelisk on top; fields outlined in various colours with field names and numeric reference to list giving names of tenements, content and colour key; Glebe land, 'Belvidere Hill' and plantation named; tree symbols showing named orchards and copse; roads, directions given; gates across roads and paths, marked by pecked lines; buildings in elevation; Powderham Arch; peripheral estates and tenements named

ENDORSEMENT: 1793 A Rough Map of Melon's Gorse's and other Estates in Powderham

16/12/10

POWDERHAM

1804   1508M Devon/M&P/Powderham/Maps 3

Powderham Castle SX 968836

TITLE: not given; endorsed 'A Map of that part of the Parish of Powderham in Lord Visct. Courtenay's Hands from Ladyday 1804'

SURVEYOR: not named

SCALE: not given

MATERIAL, SIZE & ORIENTATION: paper, coloured; oddly shaped, max. 59cms x 127cms; no direction

CONTENT: River Exe, plain; streams, black stream lines; bridge; mill; fields outlined in ink, pink; some owners' names; gates; tree symbols showing orchards; roads, plain; footpaths, pecked lines; buildings in plan, including the mill and Belvedere; Powderham Castle in elevation – a later addition in pencil

16/12/11

POWDERHAM

1836   1508M Devon/M&P/Powderham/Maps 5

Powderham Castle SX 968836

TITLE: 'Map of the Parish of Powderham in the County of Devon 1836'

SURVEYOR: Robert Dymond 'Surveyor Exeter'

SCALE: 'Scale of Chains'; scale bar; 1"=4 chains; 1:3168

MATERIAL, SIZE & ORIENTATION: paper, mounted on linen, coloured; 74cms x 154cms; north-east to top

CONTENT: rivers, streams and ponds, blue; fields outlined in dark turquoise and coloured light turquoise, with content and numeric reference [to table]; dotted lines on some fields appear to correspond to areas of woodland on tithe map of 1838 by same surveyor; roads, buff, fenced and unfenced; footpaths, pecked lines; buildings in plan, red, including the Belvedere and the Boat House; church in plan, grey; peripheral parishes named

Later additions in red ink relating to proposed roads and railway

DECORATION: 8 point compass rose, black lines; north marked by symbol

16/12/12

POWDERHAM

1836   1508M Devon/M&P/Powderham/Maps 4

Powderham Castle SX 968836

TITLE: 'A Map of Lands belonging to Powderham Castle'

SURVEYOR: John Brinsdon

SCALE: 'Scale of Chains'; scale bar; 1=3 chains; 1:2376

MATERIAL, SIZE & ORIENTATION: paper, coloured; 63.8cms x 152.3cms; north-east to top

CONTENT: Rivers Exe and Kenn, streams and ponds, dark blue; bridge; fields outlined in dark turquoise and coloured light turquoise or plain with content; some fields with stippling marking ?waste; roads, buff, fenced and unfenced; buildings in plan, red

DECORATION: title cartouche: scroll propped against a tree; 8 point compass rose, black line; north marked by symbol

16/12/13

POWDERHAM
1839   1508M Devon/M&P/Kenton/Maps 6

Mellands SX 948848
See entry under Kenn, 11/2/2

16/12/14

POWDERHAM
19th cent.   1508M Devon/M&P/Rivers/Maps 4

Powderham Church SX 972844
See entry under Kenton, 11/4/14

16/12/15

POWDERHAM
later copy of 1828 map   1508M Devon/Harbours 18

Turf Inn SX 964861
TITLE: not given
SURVEYOR: [James Green]
SCALE: 'Chains'; scale bar; 1"=12 chains; 1:9504
MATERIAL, SIZE & ORIENTATION: paper, coloured; 40.6cms x 26.7cms; no direction
CONTENT: river, channels indicated by dotted lines, basin, all blue; fields, light green; roads, buff; footpaths, dotted lines; buildings in plan, hatched black; alterations to basin at Turf, red lines
ASSOCIATED DOCUMENT: copy of part of the book of reference to the map of Exeter Canal and proposed improvements by Jas Green 29 Nov. 1828

PUDDINGTON see C140

16/13/1

PYWORTHY
1786   DCO 1926

Pyworthy Church SS 313029
TITLE: 'A Map of the Manor of Bradford in the Parish of Pyworthy and County of Devon Part of the Duchy of Cornwall surveyed 1786 by Henry Spry'
SURVEYOR: Henry Spry
SCALE: no unit of measurement stated; scale bar; 1"=4 ?chains; 1:? 3168
MATERIAL, SIZE & ORIENTATION: parchment, coloured; 62.2cms EW x 76.5cms NS [map on rollers]; south to top
CONTENT: rivers and streams, grey; bridge; fields outlined in colour; numeric reference [to Survey Book]; tree symbols showing orchards, woods, copses and individual trees; roads, brown; direction to Holsworthy given; buildings in elevation; peripheral owners named
DECORATION: title cartouche: enclosed in elaborated shield form decorated with leaves and flowers; 16 point compass rose, plain/grey; north marked by fleur-de-lys, east by cross
ENDORSEMENT: Bradford

17/1/1

RACKENFORD
1756   1148M/add23/E1

Backstone SS 835191 Laneland SS 851184
See entry under Broadclyst, 2/39/2

17/2/1

RATTERY
1786   Z17/3/20–21

Rattery Church SX 741615 Marley Farm SX 723614 Mill Cross SX 738612
Bulkamore SX 745627 Luscombe SX 748637
See entry under Ashburton, 1/8/2

17/2/2

RATTERY
1811   872A/PZ 147

Velwell SX 763639
TITLE: 'Velwell Estate in the Parish of Rattery, Devon. The Property of the Revd Richard J Luscombe'
SURVEYOR: 'T Richards Surveyor Totnes'
SCALE: 'A Scale of Statute Chains'; scale bar; 1"=4 chains; 1:3168
MATERIAL, SIZE & ORIENTATION: paper, coloured; 55cms x 42.8cms; north-west to top
CONTENT: fields outlined in ink, coloured green or yellow; numeric reference to list giving field names and content; asterisks indicate those hedges not belonging to the estate; gates; tree symbols showing orchards and, with stippling, coppices; roads; buildings in plan, red; peripheral owners named
DECORATION: 8 point plain compass rose, some line decoration; north marked by fleur-de-lys
ENDORSEMENT: Higher Velwell 1811

17/2/3

RATTERY
1818   Z15/38/1/2

Hood SX 772635
See entry under Dartington, 4/2/4

17/2/4

RATTERY
1839   Z15/18/17a–b

Hood SX 772635
See entry under Dartington, 4/2/5

17/3/1

REWE (Upexe)
1823   2547M/E47

Upexe village SS 942024
TITLE: 'A Plan of the Rydes in the Parish of Upex and County of Devon. Property of Wm Clapp Esqr. Taken in March 1823 by Joseph Otton'

SURVEYOR: Joseph Otton
SCALE: 'Scale of Statute Chains 66 Feet each'; scale bar; 1"=2 chains; 1:1584
MATERIAL, SIZE & ORIENTATION: paper, ink, slight colour; 38.2cms EW x 30.9cms NS; north to top
CONTENT: 2 fields outlined in yellow, named; alpha-numeric reference to list repeating field names and content; asterisks indicating hedge ownership; gates, red; roads, buff; peripheral owners named
DECORATION: 4 point compass indicator; north marked by arrowhead, east by cross, south by symbol; NSEW by letter
ENDORSEMENT: Plan of Rydes

17/3/2

REWE
1825   SRO DD/WY/Box121

Rewe Church SX 945992
TITLE: 'Plan of Rewe, Devon, 1825. viz etc so far as the Lands belonging to ye Lord of ye Manor extend'
SURVEYOR: not named [Thomas Hawkes]
SCALE: '40 Chains = ½ a Mile'; 1"=6 chains; 1:4752
MATERIAL, SIZE & ORIENTATION: paper, mounted on linen, slight colour; 51.5cms x 41.5cms; north-east to top
CONTENT: streams, blue with grey margins; fields outlined in green (belonging to the Lord), pink (Glebe land), yellow, (freeholders); numeric reference [to Survey Book]; roads, buff, directions given; Turnpike road named; buildings in plan, red or black; peripheral owners and parishes named; later annotations
DECORATION: 4 point compass indicator; north-south line fletched arrow

17/4/1

ROBOROUGH
1745   NDRO 4274 add/1

Rapson SS 574179 [Roberstone]
See entry under Bideford, 2/14/3

ROBOROUGH see also C141

ROCKBEARE see C142

17/5/1

ROMANSLEIGH
1757   1148M add/6/11

Romansleigh Church SS 727205
See entry under Chulmleigh, 3/15/2

17/6/1

ROSEASH
18th cent.   NDRO B398/1

Beara, Roseash SS 777202
See entry under Meshaw, 13/12/1

17/6/2

ROSEASH
*c.*1820   SRO DD/WY/Box 121

Burcombe SS 785198
TITLE: 'Burcombe Farm in Rose=Ash, Devon. No 1 Wadham'
SURVEYOR: not named
SCALE: 'Scale of Chains'; scale bar; 1"=6 chains; 1:4752
MATERIAL, SIZE & ORIENTATION: paper, mounted on linen, coloured; 22cms
    EW x 35.7cms NS; north to top
CONTENT: pond, blue; fields, yellow with numeric reference [to table];
    hedge symbols indicating ownership; tree symbols and stippling
    showing woods; roads, directions given; buildings in plan, red; periph-
    eral owners named
DECORATION: 4 point compass indicator; north marked by an arrowhead

SALCOMBE see B43

18/1/1

SALCOMBE REGIŚ
1728   1585F/19/1

Radish Plantation SY 181918
See entry under Branscombe, 2/28/1

18/1/2

SALCOMBE REGIS
1756   ECA Book 58

Salcombe Regis Church SY 148888
See entry under Exeter Chamber Map Book, 5/3/51

18/1/3

SALCOMBE REGIS
1802   337 add3/3/3/22

Salcombe Regis Church SY 148888
TITLE: 'A Map of the Manor of Salcombe Regis in the Parish of Salcombe,
    in the County of Devon Property of the Dean and Chapter of Exeter.
    Survey'd and mapp'd in 1802 by Alexr Law and Thomas Bradley'
SURVEYORS: Alexander Law and Thomas Bradley
SCALE: 'Scale of Statute Chains each containing 66 Feet'; scale bar;
    1"=6 chains; 1:4752
MATERIAL, SIZE & ORIENTATION: parchment, slight colour; 120cms EW
    x157.8cms NS; north to top
CONTENT: The English Channel, green with wave lines; cliffs dark grey
    shading; beach, stippled yellow; rivers, black margins, arrows
    indicating direction of flow; bridges; relief shown by hill shading;
    fields outlined in various colours; alpha-numeric reference to lists
    giving field names, land use – 'Arable and Pasture, Furse and Waste,
    Hedges & Ditches', content and total content; entries grouped by
    holding; asterisks indicating hedge ownership; gates, red; Commons
    stippled and listed separately; tree symbols showing orchards and
    isolated trees; roads, buff, fenced and unfenced; directions and miles
    from Exeter and Lyme [Regis] given; milestones in profile; footpaths,
    pecked lines; buildings in plan, black
DECORATION: title cartouche: simple rococo with scrolls, flowers, leaves
    and ruched fabric; 8 point compass rose, plain/shaded grey; north
    marked by fleur-de-lys, east by cross

ASSOCIATED DOCUMENTS: Exeter D&C Chapter Act Book 3574 18 June 1791 They ordered that the Manor of Salcombe shall be surveyed and mapped by Mr. Alexander Law immediately and that the Lessees shall transmit an Account of all estates within the Manor granted by Copy of Court Roll since the last Renewal

    Exeter D&C 7053 Surveyors' Accounts 1803–1860

        1802 To surveying mapping and valuing the Manor of Salcombe 2207 Acres at 8'd 73:11:4

        Paid for assistance for carrying the Chain showing the Premises and property of the out Hedges &c 27:7:9

        To vellum for Salcombe Map 2:2:0

SALCOMBE REGIS see also C143–44

18/2/1

SAMPFORD COURTENAY

1809   Kings College Cambridge Archive SJP 136

Sampford Courtenay Church SS 632013

TITLE: 'A Map of the Manor of Sampford Courtenay In the County of Devon Belonging to The Worshipful the Provost and Scholars of the Kings College of Our Blessed Lady and St Nicholas in Cambridge 1809'

SURVEYOR: [Webb]

SCALE: 'Scale of Chains'; scale bar; 1"=6 chains; 1:4752

MATERIAL, SIZE & ORIENTATION: paper, coloured; 143.5cms EW x 134cms NS; north to top

CONTENT: river, blue; fields, green, outlined with hedge symbols; glebe, pink; alpha-numeric reference [to Survey Book]; alphabetic reference to list giving names of estates; tree symbols showing woods; roads, buff; directions given; buildings in plan, grey or black

INSETS: of detached areas

DECORATION: 8 point compass rose with compass points elaborately decorated; north marked by crown, SEW by letter

18/2/2

SAMPFORD COURTENAY

[1809]   Kings College Cambridge Archive SJP 134

Sampford Courtenay Church SS 632013

Leather-bound volume, 23cms x 42cms, of 4 maps on parchment

TITLE: of volume: 'Manor of Sampford Courtenay Devon'; maps without titles, each shows portion of the map SJP 136

SURVEYOR: not named; style suggest by same hand as map SJP 136, identified in Kings College catalogue as Webb

SCALE: not given

MATERIAL, SIZE & ORIENTATION: parchment, coloured; 39cms x 41.8cms; no direction

CONTENT: streams, some named, blue; fields, green; alpha-numeric reference [to Survey Book]; glebe outlined in red; roads, yellow; directions given; peripheral owners and parishes named

18/3/1

SAMPFORD PEVERELL

1796   1044B/M/E90

Sampford Peverell Church ST 030142

TITLE: 'A Plan of the Manor of Sampford Peverell in the County of Devon the Property of The Right Hon Earl Poulett, Survey'd by F. Charlton 1796'

SURVEYOR: F. Charlton

SCALE: 'Scale Eight Chains in an Inch'; scale bar; 1"=8 chains; 1:6336

MATERIAL, SIZE & ORIENTATION: paper, mounted on linen, segmented, ink, slight colour; 70.5cms EW x 93.2cms NS; north to top

CONTENT: river and pond, blue; fields outlined in ink; alpha-numeric reference [to Survey Book]; one tenement coloured; strips to south of village have tenants named; some areas stippled; moors named; roads fenced and unfenced; directions given; buildings in plan, red for houses, grey for other buildings; Uplowman Church in elevation; peripheral owners and parishes named

NOTE: annotations of a later date, 1840; tenants' names added on some fields

DECORATION: 8 point compass rose, black/plain; north marked by fleur-de-lys, SEW by letter

18/4/1

SAMPFORD SPINEY
1788–1789   6107

Sampford Spiney Church SX 534725
See entry under Bridestowe, 2/35/6

18/4/2

SAMPFORD SPINEY
1793   346M/P1

Sampford Spiney Church SX 534725
See entry under Bere Ferrers, 2/6/3

18/5/1

SANDFORD
1763   NDRO B170/64

Ruxford Barton SS 817024
TITLE: 'A Plan of the Manor of Ruxford and other Estates in the Parish
    of Sandford in the County of Devon Late of Mrs Mary Hooper Descd
    by her Gift of Master Willm Coxe Fourth Son of John Hippisley
    Coxe Esqr'
SURVEYOR: 'Survey'd and Colour'd by James Rice 1763'
SCALE: 'A Scale of 1/3 of an Inch to a Chain or 4 Pole'; scale bar; 1"=3
    chains; 1:2376
MATERIAL, SIZE & ORIENTATION: parchment, coloured; 83.3cms EW x
    98cms NS; north to top
CONTENT: stream, green; some fields outlined in green or yellow, named
    with content; alpha-numeric reference [to Survey Book]; asterisks
    indicating hedge ownership; roads and footpaths including the
    turnpike road to Crediton; buildings in plan, yellow
DECORATION: 8 point compass rose, gold/pink, green/plain; north marked
    by fleur-de-lys, gold
ENDORSEMENT: Ruxford. Survey of Ruxford & Lands lying in the Parish
    of Sandford

18/5/2

SANDFORD
1773 & 1793   NDRO B170/185

Creedy Park SS 833016
See entry under Crediton, 3/33/3

18/5/3

SANDFORD
c. 1775   NDRO B170/107

Sandford Church SS 828025
TITLE: not given; map unfinished
SURVEYOR: not named; probably William Hole with Alexander Law
SCALE: not given
MATERIAL, SIZE & ORIENTATION: parchment, coloured; 183.5cms EW x
    157cms NS; north to top
CONTENT: rivers, grey margins; arrows indicating direction of flow; ponds;
    bridges; fields outlined in colour; alpha-numeric reference [to Survey
    Book]; asterisks indicating hedge ownership; gates; tree symbols
    showing orchards and with stippling, waste and woods; roads and
    lanes; footpaths, pecked lines; buildings in plan and elevation
DECORATION: title cartouche: delicate rococo design of scrolls, acanthus
    leaves, flowers and leaves, shell at top, above a rural scene of trees,
    vegetation, hills and farmhouse; 8 point compass rose, plain/shaded
    grey; north marked by fleur-de-lys, east by cross
ENDORSEMENT: Lands in Sandford Shobrooke &c

18/5/4

SANDFORD
late 18th cent.   1238A/PX68

Sandford Church SS 828025
TITLE: not given [shows lands of H.R.F. Davie Bart. and proposed and
    original paths to church gate]
SURVEYOR: not named
SCALE: not given
MATERIAL, SIZE & ORIENTATION: paper, ink, slight colour; 61.2cms x
    44cms; no direction
CONTENT: fields outlined, some with cottages and gardens; tree symbols;
    roads, directions given; footpaths, pecked lines; buildings in plan
    including the church, the school and Park House; latter, red
ENDORSEMENT: Alteration of footpath before Park House

18/5/5

SANDFORD
early 19th cent.   2380C/417(1)

Sandford Church SS 828025

TITLE: 'Frostland in Sandford. Mr. J. Skinner's'

SURVEYOR: R. Gilbert

SCALE: no unit of measurement stated; scale bar

MATERIAL, SIZE & ORIENTATION: parchment, slight colour; 54cms EW x
48cms NS; north to top

CONTENT: fields outlined in various colours; numeric reference to list
giving field names and content; roads, yellow; direction from Crediton
indicated; footpaths, pecked lines, brown; buildings in plan, grey

DECORATION: title cartouche and border: running pattern of stylised leaf
forms; 4 point compass indicator, red/yellow; north marked by
modified form of fleur-de-lys

18/5/6

SANDFORD
1819   NDRO B170/61

Sandford Church SS 828025

TITLE: 'A Plan of The Several Tenements Lake's alias Withewind,
Cobley's, Northlakes, Venn, Moor Acre, Lanes, alias Collins's, Claces
and the Crofts. Situated in the Parish of Sandford in the County of
Devon. The Land of Sir John Davie Bart, 1819'

SURVEYOR: 'By Thomas Shearm, Landsurveyor, Stratton, Cornwall'

SCALE: 'Scale of Chains, 22 Yards each'; scale bar; 1"=3 chains; 1:2376

MATERIAL, SIZE & ORIENTATION: parchment, coloured; 76cms EW x
c.80cms NS (map on rollers); north to top

CONTENT: river, grey; fields outlined with 'scrawl' (hedge symbols)
indicating fence ownership; various colours indicating individual
tenements with names of tenements, field names and content; numeric
reference to lists repeating field names, content and total content of
each tenement; fields belonging to others named; roads, brown,
directions given; turnpike gate; buildings in plan; dwelling houses,
red; outbuildings, black; houses in Sandford village generalised, red;
church in elevation; peripheral owners named
    Explanation of colours used

DECORATION: 8 point compass rose, pink/red; north marked by fleur-de-
lys

18/5/7

SANDFORD
1819   NDRO B170/181

Pidsley SS 811051

TITLE: 'A Map of East Pidsley in the Parish of Sandford in the County
of Devon The Land of Sir John Davie Bart 1819'

SURVEYOR: 'By Thomas Shearm, Landsurveyor, Stratton, Cornwall'

SCALE: 'Scale of chains, 22 Yards each'; scale bar; 1"=3 chains; 1:2376

MATERIAL, SIZE & ORIENTATION: parchment, coloured; 58.2cms EW x
51.8cms NS; north to top

CONTENT: rivers, blue; fields outlined in yellow or green with field name
and content; numeric reference to table giving field names, content
and total content; hedge symbols indicating fence ownership; gates,
garden; tree symbols showing orchards; stippling marking coppice;
roads, buff, directions given; footpaths, buff; buildings in plan, red
or grey; peripheral owners named

DECORATION: 8 point compass rose, red and pink

18/5/8

SANDFORD
1831   DRO Unlisted

Dira SS 849056 Chilton SS 864041 Perry Green SS 866053
See entry under Cheriton Fitzpaine, 3/10/2

SANDFORD see also C145

18/6/1

SEATON
1783   281M/E8

Seaton Church SY 247906
See entry under Beer, 2/5/2

SEATON see also B4, B93, C146–47

SHALDON see B47, B99, C157

18/7/1

SHAUGH PRIOR
temp. Chas. II   PRO E 178/7037, S9129

Shaugh Prior Church SX 543631
TITLE: 'Mapp of Godwin's Croft'
SURVEYOR: not named
SCALE: not given (diagrammatic map)
MATERIAL, SIZE & ORIENTATION: paper, ink; 22.9cms EW x 27.8cms NS; north to top; directions spelt out on margins
CONTENT: tenements shown as strips divided by straight lines, some dotted; names of tenants/owners given; roads, directions given – 'The Lane leading to Lee', 'The 4 Lans leading to Shaw Bridge'; peripheral owners named
NOTE: 'The Lane leading to Lee' = west, and 'The 4 Lans leading to Shaw Bridge' = south

18/7/2

SHAUGH PRIOR
1811   PWDRO 370

Shaugh Prior Church SX 543631
See entry under Plympton St Mary, 16/7/1

18/7/3

SHAUGH PRIOR
1840   PWDRO 655/1

Shaugh Prior Church SX 543631
See entry under Cornwood, 3/31/2

SHAUGH PRIOR see also C131

18/8/1

SHEBBEAR
post 1830   2569B/Estate/4/5b

Lovacott SS 459081
TITLE: not given
SURVEYOR: not named
SCALE: not given
MATERIAL, SIZE & ORIENTATION: paper, watermark [1830], ink, slight colour; 41cms x 32.2cms; no direction
CONTENT: streams, blue; fields outlined in ink and various colours; areas named and owners' names also present; gates; information regarding former position of gates which are no longer present; Beara Wood named; roads and footpaths, fenced and unfenced, buff; some named; gates across some roads; quarry, grey; buildings in plan, outlined in pink; peripheral owners and estates named

SHEBBEAR see also SUPPLEMENT S7

18/9/1

SHEEPSTOR
1775   PWDRO 874/75/1

Longstone SX 556685
TITLE: 'A Plan of the Barton of Longstone in the Parish of Shipstone in the County of Devon Property of Mr Willm Smith'
SURVEYOR: 'Mw Blackamore Surveyed Augt 1775'
SCALE: 'A Scale of Chains'; scale bar; 1"=3 chains; 1:2376
MATERIAL, SIZE & ORIENTATION: paper, mounted on linen, coloured; 53.5cms EW x 66.7cms NS; north to top
CONTENT: river Shipstone named, mill stream, Plymouth leat and sluice, stream lines; bridge; fields outlined in green, named; alpha-numeric reference to tables giving field names and content; red crosses indicating hedge ownership; gates, red; garden and 'tatoe' garden; tree symbols showing orchards; roads, brown; buildings in plan, hatched in red; peripheral owners named
PUBLICATION: Todd Gray, *The Garden History of Devon* (Exeter, 1995), 22. Detail of map of Longstone
NOTE: premises now under Burrator Reservoir

18/9/2

SHEEPSTOR

1814*   PWDRO 1503 (formerly WW21)

Eylesbarrow Tin Mine (disused) SX 601684

TITLE: 'Plan of Ellisborough Tin Mine in the Parish of Sheepstor Devon
    Land of Sir M Lopes Bart'

SURVEYOR: not named

SCALE: 'Chains each 11 Fathoms'; scale bar; 1"=5 chains; 1:3960

MATERIAL, SIZE & ORIENTATION: paper, torn, mounted on linen, coloured;
    88.8cms EW x 72.5cms NS; north to top

CONTENT: river and brooks including Stamping Mill Leat, blue; Great
    Harter Torr, Little Harter Torr named; Ellisborough shafts, lodes indic-
    ated by black lines; mine buildings in plan, some named – stamping
    house, blowing house etc; reference table note that Ellisborough Tin
    Set is coloured green and has numeric reference to shafts and alpha-
    betic reference to lodes

DECORATION: 16 point compass rose; north marked by fleur-de-lys, all
    other points by letter

NOTE: later annotations mark part of Wheal Katherine Tin Set or Grant
    of 1817, part of South Ellisborough Tin Set or Grant of 1823 and
    West Ellisborough Tin Set or Grant of 1823

*   from endorsement

18/10/1

SHEEPWASH

1829   2569B/Estate/4/6a

Upcott SS 476075

TITLE: 'Manor of Upcott [Avenel, in a later hand] in Sheepwash Devon
    1829'

SCALE: 1"=12 chains; 1:9504

For detailed analysis see entry under Black Torrington

18/11/1

SHELDON

1831   2729Z/E3

Sheldon Church ST 120086

TITLE: 'Plan of Sheldon Common'

SURVEYOR: 'Thos. Wright Comms' [Commissioner]

SCALE: 'Scale of Chains'; scale bar; 1"=7 chains; 1:5544

MATERIAL, SIZE & ORIENTATION: parchment, slight colour; 63.3cms EW
    x 77.6cms NS; north to top

CONTENT: stream, blue; fields outlined in blue with hedge symbols;
    numeric reference to Indenture to which map formerly attached; some
    owners named; roads, pink or buff, fenced and unfenced; directions
    given; buildings in plan, red; peripheral parishes named

DECORATION: 16 point compass rose, line decoration; north marked by
    series of shaded diamond shapes

18/12/1

SHERFORD

1777   215M/ZF14

Sherford Church SX 779443

TITLE: 'A Map or Plan of Duncombe's Tenement, in the Parish of Sher-
    ford, and County of Devon, Taken in June 1777, by E. Reed, and J.
    Paddon'

SURVEYORS:: E. Reed and J. Paddon

SCALE: 'A Scale of Chains'; scale bar; 1"=2 chains; 1:1584

MATERIAL, SIZE & ORIENTATION: parchment, coloured; 44.7cms EW x
    29.6cms; north to top

CONTENT: fields outlined in ink and 4 areas distinguished in dark green;
    individual fields within each area outlined in lighter green; alpha-
    numeric reference to table giving names of 4 areas, total content and
    content of individual fields; asterisks indicating hedge ownership;
    gates; roads, sludge green, fenced and unfenced; directions given;
    buildings in plan; peripheral owners named

INSET: 'Plan of some Tenements in the Town of Kingsbridge belonging
    to Mr Duncombe's Trustees'

DECORATION: title cartouche: swag of cloth; 8 point compass rose, grey/
    plain; north marked by fleur-de-lys

18/12/2

SHERFORD

1786   2595Z/E1(Photocopy)

Sherford Church SX 779443

5 Maps with accompanying tables, probably from an atlas

MAP 1

TITLE: 'A Plan of the Manor of Sherford Situate in the Parish of

Sherford and County of Devon Survey'd by J Foster Ashburton 1786'

SURVEYOR: James Foster

SCALE: not given

MATERIAL, SIZE: not known; ORIENTATION: east to top

CONTENT: streams, arrows indicating direction of flow; fields outlined ?in colour; alphabetic reference to page listing 'Contents of the Manor of Sherford'; tree symbols; roads, directions given; footpaths, pecked lines; buildings in plan; church in elevation; peripheral owners named

DECORATION: title cartouche: delicate acanthus leaf design with garlands of vine-leaf forms surmounted by an urn; 8 point compass rose, two colours/plain with ink rays; north marked by fleur-de-lys, SEW by letter

MAP 2

Bowden SX 759441

TITLE: 'A Plan of Several Farms Situate at Bowden in the Manor of Sherford'

SCALE: 'A Scale of Chains'; scale bar

ORIENTATION: north to top

CONTENT: fields as in Map 1 but include alpha-numeric reference to list of tenements on separate page giving field names and contents; crosses indicate hedge ownership; gates

MAP 3

TITLE: 'A Plan of Several Farms &c in the Manor of Sherford'

MAP 4

TITLE: 'A Plan of Several Farms in the Manor of Sherford Devon'

MAP 5

TITLE: 'A Plan of Several Tenements & Cots in the Manor of Sherford'

NOTE: the owner has withdrawn the original maps from the Devon Record Office

18/13/1

SHILLINGFORD ST GEORGE

*c.*1837   58/9 Box 122/26

Shillingford St George Church SX 904878

TITLE: 'A Plan of the present and intended Glebe of Shillingford in exchange for the Glebe of Dunchideock in the County of Devon'

SURVEYOR: not named [Alexander Law and Edward Osmond]

SCALE: not given

MATERIAL, SIZE & ORIENTATION: paper, coloured; 32.4cms EW x 39cms NS; north to top

CONTENT: stream, arrows indicating direction of flow; relief shown by hill shading; fields, green with numeric reference to table giving field names and content; tree symbols indicating orchard; stippling marking moor; roads, directions indicated; buildings in plan, red; church in elevation

DECORATION: 4 point compass indicator; north marked by fleur-de-lys, E by letter

ASSOCIATED DOCUMENTS:

a) a written Particular of lands allotted for Shillingford Glebe in exchange for Dunchideock Glebe

b) 'A Particular and Valuation of Lands in the parish of Shillingford St George in Exchange for Dunchideock Glebe, taken by Messrs. Law and Osmond 18th march 1806', extracted from the Principal Registry of the Lord Bishop of Exeter, 15 September 1837

18/13/2

SHILLINGFORD ST GEORGE

1838   58/9 Box 122/28

Shillingford St George Church SX 904878

TITLE: 'Plan of part of the Glebe in Shillingford Parish' 'For the Revd. R.P. Welland Shillingford'

SURVEYOR: 'Murray Vicars, Surveyor, Saint Paul Street, Exeter, Feby. 28 1838'

SCALE: 'Scale of Chains'; scale bar; 1"=1.5 chains; 1:1188

MATERIAL, SIZE & ORIENTATION: paper, slight colour; 40.5cms x 26.1cms; no direction indicated

CONTENT: field, green, with content; hedge symbols indicating ownership; gate; peripheral owners named

SHILLINGFORD ST GEORGE see also C98

18/14/1

SHIRWELL

1601   Diocesan Glebe Terriers Shirwell

Shirwell Church SS 598374

TITLE: 'Sherwell The nomber of the Acers of the glebe land belonging to the Personage of Sherwell are 77 acres and an half

Ano Dm 1601 The 28 of Septeb'

SURVEYOR: not named

SCALE: 'Perches'; scale bar; 1"=20 perches; 1:3960

MATERIAL, SIZE & ORIENTATION: paper, damaged, ink; 30.2cms EW x 59.5cms NS; directions indicated on margins, north to top

CONTENT: streams; fields, named, content in words and figures; 2 separate strips shown; gates; tree symbols showing individual trees; 'Sherwell Grene'; roads, directions given; 'The waye to Upcote, The waye to Wolley, The waye to Yulson, The waye fro Barnestable to Ilfercom, The waye to Arlington, The waye to forde'; gates shown across some roads; 'The Quarie'; buildings in elevation; 'Sherwel Church' and 'The personage house' in some detail

PUBLICATION: Mary R Ravenhill and Margery M Rowe, eds, *Early Devon Maps* (Exeter, 2000), 24

18/14/2

SHIRWELL

18th cent.   NDRO 50/11/38/13

North Woolley SS 601394

See entry under Down, East, 4/7/2

SHIRWELL see also C148–49

18/15/1

SHOBROOKE

c.1775   NDRO B170/107

Shobrooke Church SS 863011

See entry under Sandford, 18/5/3

18/15/2

SHOBROOKE

1813   5242 Box 19/7

Shobrooke Church SS 863011

See entry under Cadbury, 3/1/6

18/15/3

SHOBROOKE

1831   DRO Unlisted

Dira SS 849056 Chilton SS 864041 Perry Green SS 866053

See entry under Cheriton Fitzpaine, 3/10/2

18/16/1

SHUTE

1780   281M/E4

Moorcox SY 229997

See entry under Dalwood, 4/1/4

18/16/2

SHUTE

1781   Antony Muniments PP/FX/23

Shute House SY 252974

See entry under Colyton, 3/27/5

PUBLICATION: Todd Gray, *The Garden History of Devon* (Exeter, 1995), 205. Detail from map of garden front, 1781; detail from map, 1781

18/16/3

SHUTE

1797   50M/E75

Shute Hill SY 258982

See entry under Dalwood, 4/1/5

18/16/4

SHUTE

1800   Antony Muniments PP/FX25

Shute House SY 252974
See entry under Colyton, 3/27/8

SHUTE see also C150

18/17/1

SIDBURY

1756   ECA Book 58

Sidbury Church SY 140918
See entry under Exeter Chamber Map Book, 5/3/51

18/17/2

SIDBURY

mid 18th cent.   337B add2/M&P/7

Sidbury Church SY 140918
TITLE: 'Map Broadway … Parishes of Sidmouth and Sidbury in Devon … and distances from each other and from the … the one fences belonging therefore …'
SURVEYOR: not named [John Richards, on stylistic grounds]
SCALE: 'A Scale of Chains each containing 4 Statue Perch[es]'; scale bar; 1"=3.7chains; 1:2930
MATERIAL, SIZE & ORIENTATION: parchment, damaged, part missing, coloured; 77.5cms x 66.5cms; north-west to top
CONTENT: river 'Syd' and Mill leat named; arrows indicating direction of flow; fields, green, and outlined in green; lengths of some hedgerows indicated; Roman numerals referring to table [missing]; crosses indicating hedge ownership; gates; green tree symbols showing orchards and isolated trees; roads, buff, some named; footpaths, pecked lines, named; 'This Lane from A to B is laid down by guess'; buildings in plan; Sidmouth Church in elevation; peripheral owners named
NOTE: lower right, almost illegible, giving information about timber

DECORATION: title cartouche: on shredded ribon held in beak and claws of an eagle [see Z1/50/11, under Crediton]; coat of arms [unidentified] suspended by ribbons, red, gold, black and blue; scale: in scroll with dividers above held by hand in brown coat sleeve and frilled shirt; 8 point compass indicator; north marked by fleur-de-lys, east by cross; wide red border

18/17/3

SIDBURY

*c.*1800   Exeter D&C M5

Sidbury Church SY 140918
TITLE: not given
SURVEYOR: not named
SCALE: not given
MATERIAL, SIZE & ORIENTATION: parchment, slight colour; 136.8cms x 160.2cms; no direction
CONTENT: rivers and streams, grey; fields outlined in various colours; alpha-numeric reference to table giving names of tenants, tenements and measured content; tree symbols; roads; buildings in plan, grey; peripheral owners named
NOTE: the details suggest a Survey Book was needed in addition to the Reference Table
Exeter D&C Chapter Act Book 3574 The following entry may or may not refer to the above map 18 August 1792 They ordered Mr Alexander Law's Bill of one hundred and eight pounds, nineteen shillings and three pence for surveying and mapping the Manor of Sidbury, and for a Copy of his Valuation of the Manor of Dawlish to be paid

18/17/4

SIDBURY

1829/34/37   906M/T73–75, 76–77

Sidbury Church SY 140918
Detailed particulars of sales by auction dated 1829, 1834 and 1837 with sketch plans identifying the various Lots

SIDBURY see also C151–52

18/18/1

SIDMOUTH

mid 18th cent.   337B add2/M&P/7

Sidmouth Church SY 125873
See entry under Sidbury, 18/17/2

18/18/2

SIDMOUTH

1789   52/5 UFP

Sidmouth Promenade SY 125872
TITLE: 'Manor of Sidmouth The property of Thomas Jenkins Esqr.
    Surveyed by William Day 1789'
SURVEYOR: William Day
SCALE: no unit of measurement stated; scale bar shows chains; 1"=4
    chains; 1:3168
MATERIAL, SIZE & ORIENTATION: coloured photographic facsimile on paper;
    124cms EW x 115.3cms NS; north to top
CONTENT: rivers, sea, blue with black stream lines; high-water mark,
    hachured; beach, stippled; (course of rivers broken where they are
    outside the manor); cliff shown by stylised symbols; hill slopes shown
    by black stippling; 'Pick' Hill, with 'Seven Stones', Bulverton Hill
    and Core Hill named; also Bulverton Bottom; fields outlined with
    hedge symbols; alpha-numeric reference [to Survey Book]; strips
    indicated; gardens; tree symbols showing ?orchards, ?woods; roads,
    buff, fenced and unfenced; 'walk' beside the beach named (modern
    promenade); buildings in plan, grey; Church Yard named; Sidford
    Village named
DECORATION: title cartouche: medallion of bead design with wreath of
    flowers surrounding title, garlands of flowers and leaves above and
    below; 16 point compass rose, centre circular design within diamond;
    north marked by fleur-de-lys, east and west by symbol; border:
    running lozenge pattern

18/18/3

SIDMOUTH

1823–1825   961M add/M/E2

Sidmouth Church SY 125873
See entry under Feniton, 6/3/3

18/18/4

SIDMOUTH

1835   382 add/P13

Sidmouth Promenade SY 125872
TITLE: 'Plan of the Parish of Sidmouth and of the Parish of Salcombe
    Regis in the County of Devon. The Proposed site for the Chapel is
    coloured Light Red'
SURVEYOR: 'Enlarged from the Ordnance Map of Devonshire, by Murray
    Vicars, Surveyor: St Paul Street, Exeter, Decr 29 1835'
SCALE: 'Scale of Eight Furlongs or One Mile'; scale bar; 1"=2 furlongs;
    1:15840
MATERIAL, SIZE & ORIENTATION: paper, coloured; 38cms EW x 34.4cms
    NS; north to top
CONTENT: sea, blue; sea wall; site of proposed harbour; cliffs, shaded
    grey; streams, black; relief shown by hill shading, grey; Peak Hill,
    Beacon Hill, Corr Hill, Salcombe Hill, named; gardens of principal
    houses, green; roads, buff, fenced and unfenced; directions given;
    buildings in plan, black; principal houses, named; hamlets named;
    churches marked by crosses; parishes outlined in various colours
    and washed in lighter shades
DECORATION: 8 point compass rose, shaded-line decoration; north marked
    by fleur-de-lys

18/18/5

SIDMOUTH

19th cent.   906M/Z7

Weston Mouth SY 164880
TITLE: 'The Manors of Sidbury Sidmouth Salcombe & Weston'
SURVEYOR: not named
SCALE: 'Scale an inch to a mile'; no scale bar
MATERIAL, SIZE & ORIENTATION: paper, watermark 1838, ink; 18cms x
    22.4cms; no direction
CONTENT: streams; Weston Mouth named; some attempt to show relief;
    Peak Hill and Beacon Hill named; roads, directions given; manors
    named and boundaries indicated by broken lines; total acreage and
    value listed

SIDMOUTH see also B13, B24, B33, C153–55

18/19/1

SILVERTON
1752   3359A &add/PB1

Silverton Rectory [now Prispen House] SS 959033
TITLE:'A True map of Parsonage or Glebe of Silverton 1752'
SURVEYOR: 'T Hodge Fecit'
SCALE: 'Scale of Chains or 66 Feet to an Inch'; 1:792
MATERIAL, SIZE & ORIENTATION: parchment, coloured; 57.7cms EW x 69.8cms NS; east to top
CONTENT: fields outlined with hatched green or yellow lines; field names and content; tree symbols indicating hedge boundaries and orchards; gateways; terrace/garden; willow bed; roads, some named including Roach Lane and Butts; buildings in plan, black; Church and Rectory named

18/19/2

SILVERTON
1798   Z17/3/7

Silverton Church SS 957027
See entry under Dunsford, 4/13/5

18/19/3

SILVERTON
1827   SRO DD/WY/Box 121

Silverton Church SS 957027
TITLE: 'Plan of Silverton Devon 1827'
SURVEYOR: not named [Thomas Hawkes]
SCALE: '12 Chains to an Inch'; no scale bar; 1:9504
MATERIAL, SIZE & ORIENTATION: paper, mounted on linen; slight colour; 85.5cms x 39.8cms; south-east to top
CONTENT: stream, grey margins; fields outlined in blue with numeric reference [to Survey Book]; hedge symbols indicating hedge ownership; roads, directions given (later additions); buildings in plan, red; peripheral parishes named
DECORATION: 4 point compass indicator, line decoration; north marked by fleur-de-lys

18/19/4

SILVERTON
1829   SRO DD/WY/Box 121

Hayne House SS 966018
TITLE: 'Hayne Meadow in Silverton Devon'
SURVEYOR: not named
SCALE: not given
MATERIAL, SIZE & ORIENTATION: paper, ink; 25.4cms x 35.8cms; no direction
CONTENT: fields outlined with dotted lines with owners' names and numeric reference [to table];
Note by Thomas Hawkes of Williton that this is a copy (by him?) of a sketch lent to him by Mrs Land who owns Hayne Farm but 'It is not mathematically correct – scale not mentioned'

SILVERTON see also C156

18/20/1

SOURTON
1780   1508M Devon/Surveys/V4

Sourton Church SX 536903
See entry under Combe Raleigh, 3/29/1

18/20/2

SOURTON
1788–1789   6107

Sourton Church SX 536903
See entry under Bridestowe, 2/35/6

18/20/3

SOURTON

1810   1292M/maps/K

Oatnell (Wottneal) SX 513922

TITLE: 'A Map of the Barton of Wottneal with Church Parks & Hams In the Parish of Sourton Devon – the Lands of Calmady Pollexfen Hamlyn Esquire of Leawood 1810'

SURVEYOR: not named

SCALE: not given

MATERIAL, SIZE & ORIENTATION: parchment, ink, slight colour; 62.4cms EW x 40.6cms NS; north to top

CONTENT: Wotneal Brook, blue; arrow indicating direction of flow; fields, named, some with numeric reference [to document]; hedge boundaries, dotted; roads and footpaths; fenced and unfenced; peripheral owners named

DECORATION: 4 point compass indicator within double circle ; north marked by arrow

ENDORSEMENT: part of a Bankruptcy Commission concerning William Salter, 1793

NOTE: additional copy on paper, much damaged with fields coloured green; no scale or orientation

18/21/1

SOUTHLEIGH

1684 x 1706/7   123M/E88

Wiscombe Park SY 187931

TITLE: 'A Description of Six Estates of the Right Honorlb Thomas Lord Petre Baron of Writtle with a Rent Role of the Same beinge Wiscombe Parke in the Parish of South Leigh in the County of Devon; Contayning Six hundred & forty Acres therein Particularly described Except what is Contayned in Wood water &c in all time past Reputed 800 Acres or upwards & yett Thought to be more Acres Admitting Sphaerical Admeasurement'

SURVEYORS:: 'Wee whose Names are hereunto Subscribed have made a Rent Role and year[l]y of the whole Particulars to the best of our Knowledge with Moderation &c Consideration to Quantitie & Quallitie by which it may bee seen how this Estate hath bin Improved & what may hereafter appear to Posteritie in what lyeth yet unimproved Samuel Clode Samuel Clode junior Thomas Cookney and John Coffyn'

SCALE: 2 scales: 'Scale of Perches'; scale bar; 1"=120 perches; 1:23760; 'Scale of Miles'; scale bar; 1"=4 miles; 1:253440; both scales numbered from the right

1st scale applies to map of fields; 2nd scale applies to general map placing Wiscombe Park in relation to the principal towns of south Devon

MATERIAL, SIZE & ORIENTATION: parchment, coloured, on original small wooden roller; 15.5cms EW x 73.3cms NS; north to top

MAP 1: fields outlined in various colours with boundaries defined by black spots; some in full colour; numeric reference, red, to table giving 'Number, Acres, Shillings, [field names], Acres, Roods, Perches, Pounds, Shillings, Pence'; road, named 'The Way from Southleigh'; peripheral Downs and Commons named

MAP 2: sea named 'Pars Maris Britannici'; coastline outlined in green; map extends from 'Lime' to 'Withicomb' and 'Excester' in west, 'Hunnington' and Chard in north and Axminster in east; towns marked by red spots surrounded by 3-towered symbol; church symbols, red, marking North Leigh and South Leigh; 'Wiscomb Parke' named in red, coloured green with red and black ink boundary; Blackberry Castle named, outlined in black by simple scroll design

DECORATION: title cartouche: enclosed in decorative ink cartouche with coat of arms above; 16 point compass rose, blue/red; ½ and ¼ cardinals indicated by blue designs superimposed on double-lined circle drawn in red; outer circle double-blue lines; centre circle blue with concentric circles defined by ink dots; directions spelt out; outside the compass rose, in blue, 'Marle pits how they may bee Improved by planting Timber Trees'

NOTE: top right of coat of arms; 'The Circumference of Wiscomb is 1280 Poles which makes 4 Miles & Contaynes Acres as profitable as other Lands being planted with Wood The Inward fences are also planted with Wood Rivulets of Waters full of Trouts & in the Woods Raspisberries Straberrys … Observations upon this Rentall South Downes & the Moor valued but at 2 shillings the Acre but is thought to bee worth 20 shill. per Acre in respect of the Moor which may make ye … the 3 peices of Downes worth 20 Shills per Acre or 30llper annum and will doe well to be kept & lett together'; at the side of this the statement 'Acres 8 in the Circumference'

ASSOCIATED DOCUMENT: 123M/E611 An account of Samuel Clode for 1705–6 includes 'to bee allowed for drawing the Rentall, Assisting the Reave in his Collecion & receiving & payeing in the Lords Rent this Yeere £2.00.00'

NOTE: Wiscombe (part of the Shute and Southleigh estate) was acquired by Sir William Petre in 1554. Extensive marginal notes give additional information on owners and rents

PUBLICATION: Mary R Ravenhill and Margery M Rowe, eds, *Early Devon Maps* (Exeter, 2000), 50

18/21/2

SOUTHLEIGH
1775   4377M/E1

Southleigh Church SY 204934

TITLE: 'A Plan of the Manor of Southleigh in the County of Devon Belonging to the Right Honble Lord Petre Survey'd by James Haywood Eaton Street London 1775'

SURVEYOR: James Haywood

SCALE: 'Scale of Chains'; scale bar; 1"=*c*.3.2 chains; 1:2354 [paper in poor condition]

MATERIAL, SIZE & ORIENTATION: paper, coloured; 189cms EW x 166.5cms NS; north to top

CONTENT: rivers, blue; relief shown by hill shading in grey; fields outlined in green with hedge and hedgerow-tree symbols; alpha-numeric reference [to Survey Book]; green tree symbols on green wash showing orchards, woodland and coppices; avenue to Borcombe House; gardens, pale green; turnpike road and footpaths, buff; houses and church in plan, red; some houses named; marl pits, grey

Blackberry Castle: ramparts in 2 shades of green; 4 entrances with paths between, buff

ASSOCIATED DOCUMENTS: 123M/E681 John Knight's account for the Petre Estate contains details of payments to 'Mr Haywood' for surveying between 1774 and 1778

    1774–5 Mr Haywood – surveying on account, £150

    1775   Mr Haywood on your Lordship's account, £250

    1775–6 To Mr Haywood in part account for Surveying, £42

    1776–7 Mr Haywood in part of Account for Surveying as per receipts, £75

    1777–8 Messrs Coles & Evens for Vellum, Books, Paper used by Mr Haywood Surveyor about the Devon and Somersett Estates as per Bill, £23. 14. 3

           What he paid Mr Haywood on account, £25

18/21/3

SOUTHLEIGH
1781   281M/E5

Southleigh Church SY 204934
See entry under Colyton, 3/27/7

18/21/4

SOUTHLEIGH
1826   5556/Z/ME1

Southleigh Church SY 204934
See entry under Farway, 6/2/4

18/22/1

SOWTON
1756   ECA Book 58

Middlemoor SX 964923
See entry under Exeter Chamber Map Book, 5/3/50

18/22/2

SOWTON
1775   5308 unlisted

Sowton Church SX 976925

TITLE: 'The Manor and Lands of Sowton, or Clist Fomison, in the Parish of Sowton and County of Devon, the Inheritance of Mrs Ann Salter. 1775'

SURVEYOR: not named

SCALE: 'Chains, each containing four Statute Perches'; scale bar; 1"=3 chains; 1:2376

MATERIAL, SIZE & ORIENTATION: paper, mounted on linen, coloured; 165cms x *c*.74cms; north-west to top

CONTENT: river, streams, buff; arrows indicating direction of flow; pond, buff with grey lines; weir; 'Honiton's Clist Bridge'; fields in various colours outlined in grey with field names and content; alphabetical reference to table giving field names, content and total content arranged under the tenement; crosses indicating hedge ownership; gates; grey tree symbols showing orchards; roads, buff, directions given; footpaths, pecked lines; buildings in plan, grey (including church) and red; parsonage in elevation; peripheral owners named

INSET: 'Whippon Meadows in the Parish of Heavitree the Lands of Mrs Ann Salter'; same scale; north-east to top

DECORATION: 4 point compass indicator, black/white; north marked by fleur-de-lys

18/22/3

SOWTON

c.1800   5308 unlisted

Sowton Church SX 976925

TITLE: 'A Plan of the Manor of Sowton in the County of Devon belonging to the Right Honorable Lord Graves'

SURVEYOR: not named [William Day on stylistic grounds]

SCALE: 'Scale of Chains'; scale bar; 1"=6 chains; 1:4752

MATERIAL, SIZE & ORIENTATION: parchment, coloured; 85cms EW x 90cms NS; north to top

CONTENT: rivers, streams, blue; arrows indicating direction of flow; fishponds; bridges; relief shown by slight hill shading; fields outlined with hedge and tree symbols; those belonging coloured green indicating meadow and orchards, those coloured ochre indicating arable; alphabetic reference to other owners listed in table; 'Horse Park' shown by fenced enclosures; green tree symbols showing orchards and coppice; bog and furze, stippled green; rookery; roads, fenced and unfenced some with green verges, directions given; milestones and boundary stones; Sandygate and turnpike marked; Bishops Clist Bridge; buildings in plan, pink; principal houses named, others, hatched black; peripheral parishes named

   Suggested new roads shown by broken lines crossing fields and other features

DECORATION: title cartouche: medallion of leaf sprays tied with ribbon; 4 point compass indicator, north marked by fleur-de-lys

NOTE: Lord Graves purchased the estate in 1800

The Land of the Dean and Chapter of Exeter Held under them by Sir Martin Folkes Bart in trust for his four sisters. Survey'd 1776 and mapp'd 1777 by Wm Hole and A Law'

SURVEYORS: William Hole and Alexander law

SCALE: 'A Scale of Chains each containing Four Statute Perches'; scale bar; 1"=3 chains; 1:2376

MATERIAL, SIZE & ORIENTATION: parchment on rollers, coloured; 278cms EW x 227cms NS; north to top

CONTENT: River Dart named, tributary streams, black margins; arrows indicating direction of flow; Staverton Bridge in detail; fields outlined in various colours; alpha-numeric reference [to Survey Book]; 'asterisms' indicating hedge ownership; gates, red; tree symbols showing orchards; with stippling, ?woods; stippling alone ?waste; roads; lanes and footpaths, pecked lines; buildings in plan but some large houses and church in elevation; peripheral owners named

DECORATION: title cartouche: rococo embellished with acanthus leaves, fruit, flowers and ruched fabric; rural scene below; 2 large trees, fields, sheep, moorland; 8 point compass rose; north marked by fleur-de-lys, east by cross

ASSOCIATED DOCUMENTS: Exeter D&C 3571 Chapter Act Book p.488 20 December 1776 They ordered, that a Sum not exceeding a Third Part of the Charge of surveying amd Maping the Manor of Staverton, to be paid by the Dean and Chapter, upon Condition that Sr Martin Folkes, Baronet (the Lessee), do defray the Remainder, & do send to the Dean & Chapter for their Use a Copy of the Maps, & Books – And they desired Mr. Dean to transact this Business with the Lessee. This would imply Tothill's participation in the project with Hole and Law.

   Exeter D&C Chapter Act Book 3572 20 Dec 1777 The Dean and Chapter having agreed to defray Sixty four Pounds Eight Shillings, & Eight pence, one Third Part of the Expences lately incurr'd by planing and maping their Manor of Staverton, They ordered, that their Receiver do discount & allow that sum to their Lessee out of the High Rent reserv'd & due to them out of the said Manor.

18/23/1

STAVERTON

1776–1777   Ex. D&C Ch. Comm./98

Staverton Church SX 793639

TITLE: 'A Map or Plan of the Manor of Staverton in the County of Devon

18/23/2

STAVERTON

1786/7/9–1808   Z17/3/20–21

Staverton Church SX 793639

See entry under Ashburton, 1/8/2

18/23/3

STAVERTON
1789   2496B/P1

Staverton Church SX 793639
See entry under Broadhempston, 2/41/1

18/23/4

STAVERTON
1792   DP Q/Rum 8

Staverton Church SX 793639
See entry under Ashburton, 1/8/3

18/23/5

STAVERTON
1805   Ex. D&C Ch. Comm. 6034/6/1a–b

Staverton Church SX 793639
Two survey books with plans, 20.9cms x 33.8cms and 20.7cms x 33.4cms
a) has 62 maps of individual holdings in Staverton and b) has 37 maps
TITLE: not given
SURVEYOR: not named
SCALE: not given
MATERIAL & ORIENTATION: paper, ink; no directions
GENERAL CONTENT: fields in outline with alpha-numeric reference to
    written survey which gives timber (oak, ash and elm), timber not
    fellable, saplings, and comments; asterisks indicating hedge bound-
    aries; roads, directions given; quarries

18/23/6

STAVERTON
1807/9   Exeter D&C 6034/20

Abham SX 772645
TITLE: not given
SURVEYOR: not named
SCALE: 'Scale for the new Road'; no unit of measurement stated; scale
    bar; 1"= 2 ?
MATERIAL, SIZE & ORIENTATION: paper, watermark ?1807; slight colour;
    60.7cms x 48.9cms; north-east to top

CONTENT: River Dart generalised; outlined in blue with ink stream lines
    on grey background; arrow indicating direction of flow; old road,
    light fawn with green margins; directions given; new road, buff shown
    by dotted lines with bridge over river Dart; buildings in Emmett in
    plan, red; 'Mrs Edwards new house', hatched black; small ink sketch
    on smaller scale showing road 'thrown into the Field some Years'
    and site of Mrs Edwards 'good house'
ASSOCIATED DOCUMENTS: dated 1809
NOTE: Higher and Lower Emmett appear on the Tithe Apportionment as
    part of the tenement of Abham

18/23/7

STAVERTON
1826   Ex. D&C Ch. Comm. 6034/5/2/1

Bridge SX 785637
TITLE: not given; endorsement 'Staverton Map of Spots in dispute'
SURVEYOR: not named, John Coldridge, see below
SCALE: not given
MATERIAL, SIZE & ORIENTATION: paper, watermark, slight colour; 40.5cms
    x 32.2cms; no direction
CONTENT: river, with mill leat, blue; arrow indicating direction of flow;
    'Wear' stakes; arched bridge; well built in 1780; butments dated 1768
    and 1824; disputed areas buff and green; claimants named; Staverton
    Woods and meadow named; mills in plan; Staverton and Dartington
    Parishes named
ASSOCIATED DOCUMENTS:
Exeter D&C 3579 Chapter Act Book p.491 21–22 December 1826
Records the dispute with the Lord of the Manor of Dartington about
the boundary between the 2 manors and a decision not to allow him
to take possession of a 'spot of ground' immediately below Staverton
Bridge.
    p.562 28 July 1827 Records perambulation of the bounds of the
Manor of Dartington and the fact that Dartington abandoned all claim
to the land below Staverton bridge. However stakes had been placed
on the Staverton side of the river to mark the claim by Dartington to
the whole of the bed of the river.

Exeter D&C 3580 Chapter Act Book p.44 1st March 1828 The
boundary of the Manor of Staverton to lie in the middle of the river,
and not as claimed by Dartington.
    p. 148 25 April 1829 Arbitration proposed by the Lord of the
Manor of Dartington and the Chapter agreed, desired an 'amicable'
settlement.

p.186 17 October 1829 William Courtenay lately one of the Masters of the High Court in Chancery and now Clerk of the Parliament to arbitrate.

p.218 27 February 1830 Middle of the river to be the boundary as to the soil

Exeter D&C 3581 Chapter Act Book p.23 26,27,28 December 1832 Award by William Courtenay concerning the river boundary (of Staverton) to be copied in the Register Book and the expenses audited

STAVERTON see also B1

18/24/1

ST GILES in the HEATH

1761   T1258M/E27

St Giles in the Heath Church SX 354907

TITLE: 'A Plan of that part of the Manor of Werrington containing the Parishes of St Giles in the Heath and Werrington in the County of Devon belonging to the most Noble John Duke of Bedford as taken in the Year 1761 by Thos Pride'

SURVEYOR: Thomas Pride

SCALE: 'A Scale of a Mile or 40 Chains 4 Poles each'; 1"=6 chains; 1:4752

MATERIAL, SIZE & ORIENTATION: parchment on rollers, coloured; 150cms EW x 177cms NS; north to top

CONTENT: rivers, named, stream lines in ink; bridges named; fields outlined in colour, named with content; numeric reference to list giving colour reference, names of tenants, premises, quantities of timber trees on each farm identified by type – oak, ash or elm; roads, buff; directions given; buildings in plan, red; hamlets named; boundary of the manor, red; peripheral farms, owners and parishes named

DECORATION: title cartouche: elaborate rococo style with ruched fabric, acanthus, flowers, leaves, shaded grey; 8 point compass rose; north marked by fleur-de-lys

18/24/2

ST GILES in the HEATH

1765   1258M/E28

Title as above but in addition, 'Copied by T Richardson Surveyor in 1765'. Also originally on rollers; identical except for the title cartouche which is in similar elaborate rococo style.

18/25/1

ST GILES in the WOOD

1809   1148M add/10/1b

St Giles in the Wood Church SS 533190
See entry under Beaford, 2/3/1

18/25/2

ST GILES in the WOOD

19th cent.   96add M/E18

Woolleigh Barton SS 532168

TITLE: 'A Plan & Admeasurement of 3 Waste Spots on the North side of Woolleigh Park belonging to Sir T. D Ackland in the Parish of St Giles'

SURVEYOR: not named

SCALE: not given

MATERIAL, SIZE & ORIENTATION: paper, watermark 1816, ink; 32.3cms EW x 18.7cms NS; north to top; directions indicated by letter

CONTENT: river, stream lines, arrows indicating direction of flow; former meander shown; numeric reference to 3 areas of waste, listed with content; tree symbols; roads, one gated, directions given; one house in elevation, crudely drawn; peripheral land owner (Lord Rolle) named

ST GILES in the WOOD see also C141

18/26/1

STOCKLAND (now in Devon)
1782   281M/E1

Stockland Church ST 245045

TITLE: 'Survey of Estates in the Parish of Stockland Dorsetshire belonging to James Benedictus Marwood Esqr by Jacob Sturge'

NOTE: no contemporary map exists accompanying this Survey Book, but in the 19th century copies were made and the maps are listed below. In the Survey Book places are identified by a numeric grid reference system. The maps are to be found at DRO 50/3/2

    Colyton and Coliford
    Awlescombe Buckerell Gittisham
    Stockland
    Upottery and Luppit
    Churchstanton Dunkeswell
    Hemyock Payhembury Ottery St Mary
    East Mare [?More] in Tiverton and lands in Uplowman

18/26/2

STOCKLAND (now in Devon)
1795   282M/Legal & Estate/S1

Lower Farm ST 260020

TITLE: 'A Plan of Farm otherwise Petty-Newberry Estate in the Parish of Stockland and County of Dorset belonging to John Follett Esq. Survey'd &c in 1795 by C. Tozer, Broadhempston. Devon'

SURVEYOR: Charles Tozer

SCALE: 'A Scale of Statute Chains'; scale bar; 1"=4 chains; 1:3168

MATERIAL, SIZE & ORIENTATION: paper, mounted on linen, segmented to fit red leather slip case tooled in gold (14cms x 16.5cms), coloured; *c.*63cms x *c.*50.5cms; north-west to top

CONTENT: River Yarty, blue with black stream lines; arrow indicating direction of flow; relief shown by hill shading; Harner Hill named; fields, yellow or green outlined with green hedge symbols; numeric reference to list giving field names and content; gates; garden in plan; green tree symbols showing orchards, avenue and with stippling, coppices; roads, buff, fenced and unfenced; directions given; buildings in plan; farmhouse, pink, barns etc outlined in black; peripheral owners named

DECORATION: 4 point compass indicator; north marked by fleur-de-lys, east by cross

18/27/1

STOCKLEIGH POMEROY
1772   2346M/E59

Stockleigh Pomeroy Church SS 877035

TITLE: 'A Plan of the Parish and Manor of Stockleigh Pomeroy within the County of Devon the property of Sir John Davie Baronet Surveyed by Lewis Thomas Anno 1772'

SURVEYOR: Lewis Thomas

SCALE: 'A Scale of Gunter's Chains'; scale bar; 1"=4 chains; 1:3168

MATERIAL, SIZE & ORIENTATION: parchment, coloured; 121cms EW x 74.3cms NS; north to top

CONTENT: rivers and streams outlined in black, one heavy, one feint line; Harts Well named; fields outlined in various colours indicating tenants' holdings and with hedge and tree symbols; alpha-numeric reference [to Survey Book]; letters on map identifying tenants and their holdings refer to table listing total content; Glebe land identified by Roman numerals; tree symbols, black, showing woods, named; roads, directions given; 'Intended New Road(s)' and 'Intended Turnpike Road' named; lanes, broken lines; buildings in plan, hatched black, some named; Grist Mill, Barn, Parsonage House; church in elevation; peripheral owners named
Later annotations in pencil

DECORATION: title cartouche: frame of scrolls decorated with cornucopia and urn holding leaves flowers and fruit; at top two mythical figures with spears supporting an urn; scale bar inscribed on a scroll; 8 point compass rose, plain/black; north marked by fleur-de-lys, east by symbol

18/27/2

STOCKLEIGH POMEROY
1823   NDRO B170/113

Stockleigh Pomeroy Church SS 877035

TITLE: 'Map of the Manor of Stockley Pomeroy, Devon. The Property of Sir John Davie Baronet'

SURVEYOR: 'Surveyed by John Mallet. Torrington. 1823'

SCALE: 'Scale of Chains'; scale bar; 1"=3 chains; 1:2376

MATERIAL, SIZE & ORIENTATION: parchment, coloured; 147.3cms EW x 99.3cms NS; north to top

CONTENT: river and ponds, blue; fields outlined in various colours with numeric reference [to Survey Book] and alphabetic reference to list giving owners' names and content; hedge/fence boundary ownership marked by asterisks (?added later); gates; tree symbols showing orchards, woods and isolated trees;; stippling marking waste; roads, buff, fenced and unfenced; footpaths, buff, pecked lines; buildings in plan, red, green or grey; peripheral owners and estates named

DECORATION: 8 point compass rose, black lines; north marked by fleur-de-lys, SEW by letter

NOTE: 2346M/E60 parchment Reference Roll endorsed Stockleigh-Pomeroy. Arranged by tenants with alpha-numeric reference to a map giving field names. 'Clear Statute Measure content, Hedges and Waste content'. There is some indication of land use. This seems to belong with this map, although the documents are in different collections.

18/28/1

STOKE CANON

1799   Ex. D&C Ch. Comm. 98/8783

Stoke Canon Church SX 939980

TITLE: 'A Map of the Manor of Stoke Canon and Stoke Woods situated in the Parish of Stoke Canon in the County of Devon Property of the Dean and Chapter of Exeter Surveyed and mapped in 1799 by Alexr Law'

SURVEYOR: Alexander Law

SCALE: 'Scale of Chains each containing Four Perches of [66] Feet'; scale bar; 1"=4 chains; 1:3168

MATERIAL, SIZE & ORIENTATION: parchment, slight colour; 103.7cms EW x 125cms NS; north to top

CONTENT: Rivers Culm and Exe in detail with meanders, islands, tributary streams, weirs, leats and bridges; bridge at Stoke Canon in elevation; relief shown by hill shading; fields outlined in colour, some with fences; alpha-numeric reference to tables giving names of Parcels, land use – Arable and Pasture, Furse Wood and Waste, Hedges and Ditches – content and total content; some landowners' names in fields; gates, red; tree symbols showing orchards and isolated trees; roads, fenced and unfenced; directions given; buildings in plan except for Church and Manor House, in elevation; peripheral parishes named

DECORATION: title cartouche: simple rococo style of scrolls and ruched fabric; 8 point compass rose, plain/grey; north marked by fleur-de-lys, east by cross; wide yellow border

ASSOCIATED DOCUMENT: Exeter D&C 4652 26 Jan 1799 To surveying Mapping and Valuing the Manor of Stoke Canon 42:0:0; Expenses for Board carrying the Chain Vellum &c 15:3:6

NOTE: Exeter D&C 3571 Chapter Act Book p.193 22 Dec. 1772 includes a payment to Mr Tothill, Surveyor' of £30.3.0 for 'planing, & maping Stoke-Canon Manour, & other incidental Expenses'. This map does not survive.

18/28/2

STOKE CANON

1827   Ex. D&C. Ch. Comm. 6034/5/2/1

Cowley Bridge SX 908953 Stoke Canon Bridge SX 938975

TITLE: not given; endorsement 'Stoke Canon New Road Dec 1827'

SURVEYOR: not named, John Coldridge, see below

SCALE: not given

MATERIAL, SIZE & ORIENTATION: paper, watermark, ink; 52cms x 41cms; no direction

CONTENT: river, bridge; fields with numeric reference to separate list naming various areas, parish and county, landowners, leaseholders, quantity, value, Dean and Chapter's interest, leasehold value, terms on which land held; gates; road, solid lines, new road, broken lines

ASSOCIATED DOCUMENTS: many dealing with the details of the acquisition of the land necessary for the construction of the new road; letters suggest that John Coldridge was the surveyor

Exeter D&C 3580 Chapter Act Book p.139 28 March 1829 John Coldridge was ordered to survey the line of the new Turnpike road from Cowley Bridge to Stoke Canon passing through 'Stokewood', to report to the Chapter about the line and the 'terms to be made on behalf of the Chapter'.

p.146 28 April 1829 John Coldridge made his report and the land concerned (5a.1r.5p) valued at £387 and offered to the Commissioners of the Exeter Turnpike for this sum

STOKE CANON
1836

Exeter D&C 3581 Chapter Act Book p.317 16 January 1836 Concerning the Bristol to Exeter railroad passing through Stoke Canon, The Surveyor to report on the effect the Rail Road would have on the 'occupations of the Lands adjoining'

p.322 6 February 1836 A Bill was to be presented to Parliament for making a Railway from Bristol to Exeter through Stoke Canon and the consent of the Dean & Chapter sought. John Coldridge ordered to survey the land in order to see whether 'the line proposed be the best that can be obtained for the property and for the benefit of the

Parish'; other stipulations expressed and in the meantime the answer of the Dean & Chapter was suspended.

No map has been traced

18/29/1

STOKE FLEMING
1798	1659/108

Bugford Farm SX 834511

TITLE: 'A Map of Bugford Estate In the Parish of Stoke Fleming and County of Devon. The Property of Andrew Pinson Esquire'

SURVEYOR: 'C Tozer, Marldon 1798'

SCALE: 'A Scale of Chains'; scale bar; 1"=4 chains; 1:3168

MATERIAL, SIZE & ORIENTATION: paper mounted on linen, coloured; 48.3cms x 37.8cms; no direction

CONTENT: fields, buff or green, outlined with green hedge symbols; numeric reference to table giving field names and content; asterisks indicating hedge ownership; green tree symbols showing orchard; roads, buff, directions given; buildings in plan, red; peripheral owners named

---

18/30/1

STOKE GABRIEL
1748	DD 3725

Sandridge SX 862565

TITLE:' A Plan of the Barton of Sandridge lying in the Parish of Stoake Gabriell in the County of Devon belonging to Pomeroy Gylbert Esqr Survey'd March MDCCXXXXVIII by Willm Doidge Surveyor'

SURVEYOR: William Doidge

SCALE: 'A Scale of Chains Each 66 Feet'; divided scale; 1"=6 chains' 1:4752

MATERIAL, SIZE & ORIENTATION: parchment, ink; 60.8cms EW x 41.1cms NS; north to top

CONTENT: River Dart, feint stream lines; fishing boats; large vessel with guns; boat house; ponds; fields outlined in ink with alphabetic reference to table giving field names and content; also various notes indicating responsibility and ownership of hedges; in 2 areas a note stating 'There is 16½ Feet outside this Hedge belonging to the Barton'; gardens; tree symbols showing orchards, trees along the river bank and isolated trees; smaller tree symbols marking a wood; roads, directions given; footpaths, pecked lines; buildings in plan

TOP LEFT: 'A South Prospect of Sandridge House'; detailed elevation with gardens in front

DECORATION: title on a scroll; table and scale in plain frame, some acanthus decoration at base of table; 4 point compass indicator; north marked by fleur-de-lys

ENDORSEMENT: Map of Sandridge Barton

18/30/2

STOKE GABRIEL
1837	Private Hands

Stoke Gabriel Church SX 848572

TITLE: 'Plan of Stoke Estate in the Parish of Stoke Gabriel Devon'

SURVEYOR: not named

SCALE: 'Scale of Chains'; scale bar; 1"=4 chains; 1:3168

MATERIAL, SIZE & ORIENTATION: paper, coloured; 99.3cms EW x 66.3cms NS; north to top

CONTENT: River Dart, Mill Pond, grey margins, blue with stream lines; fields, green; numeric reference to table giving field names, content within hedges, content of hedges and waste and total content; asterisks indicating hedge ownership; gateways; green tree symbols on green wash showing orchards, wood, coppice and isolated trees; roads, buff, fenced and unfenced; direction given; footpaths, dotted lines; Cart Path named; buildings in plan, red or hatched black; some keyed by letter to Remarks

DECORATION: title cartouche: leaf garlands and scrolls; Remarks in a leaf-decorated panel with urn above; 16 point compass rose, buff/grey; 4 point indicator in centre, buff/grey; north marked by fleur-de-lys

---

18/31/1

STOKEINTEIGNHEAD
1741	563Z/P1

The Ness SX 941719

TITLE: 'A Plan of the Manor of Ringmore lying in the Parish of Stokentinhead & St Nicholas both in the County of Devon belonging to the Rt Honble Ld Clifford Survey'd May MDCCXLI by Willm Doidge Surveyor'

SURVEYOR: William Doidge

SCALE: 'A Scale of Chains each 66 Feet'; divided scale; 1"=4 chains; 1:3168

MATERIAL, SIZE & ORIENTATION: parchment, ink; 159cms EW x 77.7cms NS; north to top

CONTENT: rivers and sea, shot-silk shading; rocks, cliffs and sandbanks marked; hills across the estuary in profile; fields outlined, some with hedge symbols indicating ownership of fences; alphabetic reference to tables giving field names, and content, grouped by holdings; common land stippled; tree symbols showing orchards; road, named, direction given; buildings in plan; in Teignmouth shown in elevation with some houses larger than others; various ships shown in estuary, fishing and rowing boats anchored to stakes, and ocean-going vessels at sea; man with horse on point at Teignmouth; 'Stoke Beckon'; across estuary and north and south in sea, lines drawn marking the 'Limit of your Lorsdhips Royalty'

DECORATION: title cartouche: swag of cloth surrounded by 2 dolphins and nymph seated in shell and holding a paddle, the whole resting on a fretted scroll; tables in plain frames with a semi-circular top decorated with a shell; 4 point compass indicator; north marked by fleur-de-lys

18/31/2

STOKEINTEIGNHEAD
1745/6   ECA Book 58

Stokeinteignhead Church SX 916704
See entry under Exeter Chamber Map Book, 5/3/47

18/31/3

STOKEINTEIGNHEAD
1835   Pearse Box 119

Charlecombe SX 909710

TITLE: 'A Map of an Estate known by the name of Charleycombe situate in the Parish of Stokeinteignhead in the County of Devon the property of Mr Stephen Lang, Yeoman of, (and owner of) Gullum's Well in Combeinteignhead in the said County Reference as to Area Description &c &c as below'

SURVEYOR: 'I Crocker Surveyor'

SCALE: 'Scale of Ten Chains'; scale bar; 1"=2 chains; 1:1584

MATERIAL, SIZE & ORIENTATION: parchment, coloured; 64.5cms EW x 72.5cms NS; north to top

CONTENT: river, ponds, blue; arrows indicating direction of flow; fields,

yellow with parallel pricked lines; numeric reference to list giving field names land use and content [expressed by letter but meaning unclear]; meadows, green; orchards, green with tree symbols; symbols indicating hedge ownership; roads, buff, named, directions given; buildings in plan, grey; peripheral owners named

DECORATION: title cartouche: intertwined scrolls with male and female heads in profile [Stephen Lang and wife ?]; 16 point compass rose, plain/grey; north marked by plumb, EW by letter with scale bar between; surveyor's name on ribbon threaded through compass points

STOKEINTEIGNHEAD see also C157

STOKENHAM see C158

18/32/1

STOODLEIGH
*c.*1636–1637   SRO DD/TB 36/108

Stoodleigh Church SS 923188 East Stoodleigh Barton SS 936197

TITLE: not given

SURVEYOR: not named

SCALE: 'The Scale of Chaynes the Chaine beinge 4 perches'; scale bar; 1"=13 chains; 1:10296

MATERIAL, SIZE & ORIENTATION: parchment, slight colour; 67cms EW x 38.3cms NS; north to top; directions spelt out in margins

CONTENT: Exe Water, blue; Okeford bridge, Cove Bridge; Radninchford; no fields; gates across roads, 'widow Dobles gate, widdow Heardes gate, two gates furslande, Chaves gate'; 'The Crosse' in Bampton named; cross roads in contention coloured and keyed to explanation, others shown by black lines; buildings in elevation including 'Studley Churche' and Cove Church; buildings in Bampton in plan; Sir John Carewe's house in elevation contained within defensive wall with 4 corner towers and 2 gateways, one on the south wall and one on the west wall; 'the kilve' outside Bampton

NOTE: in bottom right-hand corner; 'The wayes in Controversy are in a greene Colour, the wayes allowed are in a yellow Colour, and the waters are in blewe

To the waye from the Widd[ow] heardes gate unto Bampton Crosse by Cove bridge is almoste 48 Chaines moore then the waye by Okeford bridge.

And the waye by Okeford bridge is Nine Chaines and a halfe then the waye by Radninche Forde'

DECORATION: border: running bead pattern, yellow

NOTE: horizontal pencil lines across the map

PUBLICATION: Mary R Ravenhill and Margery M Rowe, eds, *Early Devon Maps* (Exeter, 2000), 56

18/32/2

STOODLEIGH
*c.*1636–1637   SRO DD/TB 36/109

East Stoodleigh Barton SS 936197

TITLE: 'A mappe for a house to be builded at East Studley'

SURVEYOR: not named

SCALE: 'The Scale of feete'; scale bar: 1"=12 feet; 1:144

MATERIAL, SIZE & ORIENTATION: parchment, coloured; 68.5cms EW x 61.8cms NS; north to top

CONTENT: ground plans of 'The firste storie' and 'The seconde storie' [i.e. ground floor and first floor] of a house to be built on the site of Sir John Carewe's house which is shown on SRO DD/TB 36/108. The rooms on the ground floor are described

NOTE: It is probable that both maps are in the same hand. 'Southe' is marked at the bottom of the house plan and seems identical to that on the disputed right-of-way map.

The will of Sir John Carew dated 1636 and proved in 1637 (F. Crisp, *Somerset Wills*, p.25) left instructions to his sons for the building of mansion houses at East Stoodleigh and Camerton in Somerset and for the 're-edifying' of Carew Castle in Pembrokeshire. There is no evidence that any of this building work was carried out and the Carew family suffered great financial loss as a result of the Civil War. East Stoodleigh Barton is listed Grade II, and some of the building dates from the seventeenth century. It is possible that part of the defensive wall shown on SRO DD/TB 36/108 which was then part of Sir John Carew's property, was incorporated into the Barton.

The spelling of Carew[e] varies from document to document.

PUBLICATION: Mary R Ravenhill and Margery M Rowe, eds, *Early Devon Maps* (Exeter, 2000), 57

18/32/3

STOODLEIGH
1770   Balliol College Archives C 18/3A Photocopy

Thorne SS 895194

TITLE: 'A Plan of an Estate, call'd Thorn's lying in the Parish of Stoodley in the County of Devon, belonging to Balliol College Oxford'

SURVEYOR: 'Robert Leave, Exeter. 1770'

SCALE: 'A Scale of Chains'; divided scale; 1"=2.5 chains; 1:1970

MATERIAL, SIZE & ORIENTATION: parchment, slight colour; *c.*66.5cms EW x *c*50.5cms NS; north to top

CONTENT: river, stream lines; fields, named; 'References to the Plan' giving field named and content; gates; hedge symbols indicating ownership; tree symbols showing isolated trees and with stippling marking orchards and coppices; stippling alone marking waste; lanes; buildings in plan; peripheral owners named

DECORATION: 32 point compass rose, black/plain; north marked by fleur-de-lys

ENDORSEMENTS: in three different hands; Stoodley Devon, and Thornes, Stoodley Devon. [one endorsement possibly by Henry Wall, the other, larger and bolder, definitely by Richard Jenkyns, Master 1819–1854.]

18/33/1

SWIMBRIDGE
1788/1823   NDRO B170/25

Accott SS 642325

TITLE: 'Map of the Manor of Accott situate in the Parish of Swimbridge in the County of Devon the property of Charles Chichester Esqr'

SURVEYORS: 'Surveyed in the Year 1788 by Robert Ballment and Plann'd in the Year 1823 by Ethelred Still'

SCALE: 'Scale of Chains'; scale bar; 1"=6 chains; 1:4752

MATERIAL, SIZE & ORIENTATION: paper, much damaged, coloured; *c.*79cms EW x 148.5cms NS; north to top

CONTENT: river, blue; fields various colours with numeric and alpha-numeric references to table giving field names, content of arable and pasture, moor and waste, hedges and ditches and total content; 'asterisms' indicating hedge ownership; gates; tree symbols showing orchards and isolated trees; stippling marking ?waste; roads, buff; buildings in plan, red

DECORATION: 8 point compass rose, black line decoration; north marked by fleur-de-lys

18/33/2

SWIMBRIDGE

1791   NDRO B201/1–2

Swimbridge Church SS 621300

TITLE: 'A Field Map or Plan of the Estate called Gill's in the Parish of Swimbridge and County of Devon the Property of Mrs Jane Hamilton taken in January 1791 by Robt Ballment & James Pitts under the directions of Mr Hole'

SURVEYORS: Robert Ballment and James Pitts

SCALE: no unit of measurement stated; no scale bar as such but 2 lines of figures to be read from opposite sides of the map

MATERIAL, SIZE & ORIENTATION: paper, watermark, ink; 51.7cms EW x 70cms NS; east to top; line marking magnetic north

CONTENT: river, arrow indicating direction of flow; fields, named and with content; alpha-numeric reference to table giving names of fields or parcels of ground, land use – 'Arable and Pasture, Moory Pasture, Furse Wood and Waste, Hedges and Ditches, Total Content'; asterisks indicating hedge ownership; gates; roads, fenced and unfenced; footpaths, pecked lines; buildings, including Swimbridge Church in elevation, drawn on opposing horizons; peripheral owners named

DECORATION: 8 point compass rose; north marked by fleur-de-lys

ENDORSEMENT: Field Map of an Estate in the Parish of Swimbridge, in the County of Devon the Property of Mrs Jane Hamilton Taken by Mr Robert Ballment & Mr James Pitts in Jany 1791

2ND ENDORSEMENT: Field Map of an Estate in the Parish of Swimbridge near Barnstaple, in the County of Devon Taken by Mr Robert Ballment & Mr James Pitts, under the Direction of Mr Wm Hole in the Month of Jany 1791 for the use, and by the Direction of Mrs Jane Hamilton the Owner

18/33/3

SWIMBRIDGE

1802   NDRO 1308Z/E5

Cobbaton SS 614268   ?Woodland SS 619262

TITLE: 'Plan of two Farms called Cobbaton & Wolland in the Parish of Swimbridge Devon The Property of James Nott Esqr 1802'

SURVEYOR: 'Surveyd by W. Isaac'

SCALE: 'Scale of Chains'; scale bar; 1"=2 chains; 1:1584

MATERIAL, SIZE & ORIENTATION: paper, coloured; 33.5cms EW x 44.2cms NS; north to top

CONTENT: river, blue, stream lines; direction of flow indicated; fields outlined in green with field names and content; symbols, probably to indicate land use, but not explained; reference key giving total and individual content of two farms; hedge/fence ownership indicated; gates; roads, buff, directions given; buildings in plan, grey; peripheral owners named

DECORATION: 8 point compass rose, black lines emanating from grey/ plain centre; north marked by fleur-de-lys, SEW by letter

18/33/4

SWIMBRIDGE

1806   NDRO 186M/P1

Swimbridge Church SS 621300

TITLE: 'Plan of an Overland called the Parish Ground in the Parish of Swimbridge Devon Survey'd by W Isaac 1806 The Property of the Poor of Swimbridge afors'd'

SURVEYOR: William Isaac

SCALE: 'Scale of Chains'; scale bar; 1"=2 chains; 1:1584

MATERIAL, SIZE & ORIENTATION: paper, slight colour; 26.5cms x 45.5cms; north east to top

CONTENT: fields outlined with hedge symbols, coloured yellow or blue; named, with content; hedges with lines outside do not belong to the estate; gates; roads, yellow, directions given; 'Rivaton Mill' and barn in plan, hatched black; peripheral owners named

DECORATION: title cartouche; medallion; 8 point compass rose, plain/ blue line decoration; north marked by blue fleur-de-lys, other compass directions by letter

18/33/5

SWIMBRIDGE

1832   NDRO B 170/179 a–b

East Stowford SS 632267

TITLE: 'Map of East Stowford Estate and Nott's Tenement situate in the Parish of Swimbridge in the County of Devon the Property of The Revd. Thos Hooper Morrison Surveyed and Plan'd in the Year 1832 by Ethelred Still'

SURVEYOR: Ethelred Still

SCALE: 'Scale of Chains'; scale bar; 1"=5 chains; 1:3960

MATERIAL, SIZE & ORIENTATION: paper, mounted on linen, damaged with part missing, slight colour; 79.5cms x 65cms; north-east to top

CONTENT: stream, pond, blue; arrow indicating direction of flow; fields outlined in yellow, green or blue with hedge symbols which also indicate ownership; alpha-numeric reference to table (largely missing) giving field names, land use, content and total content; gates; tree symbols showing orchard, isolated trees, and with stippling woods/ copses; roads, buff, directions given; buildings in plan, red; peripheral owners named

DECORATION: 8 point compass rose, shaded-line decoration; north marked by fleur-de-lys

    2nd copy showing same area at a scale of 2.5chains to one inch; 1:1980. Very badly torn and fragile

18/34/1

SYDENHAM DAMEREL
1825   1262M/E22/45

Sydenham Damerel Church SX 409760
See entry under Brentor, 2/33/3

19/1/1

TALATON
1795   961M/E25 and 26

Escot House SY 082981
See entry under Feniton, 6/3/2

19/1/2

TALATON
1800–1808   961M/E28

Escot House SY 082981
TITLE: endorsed 'Plan of Intended Peice[sic] of Water at Escot The Seate of Sir John Kenaway Bart'
SURVEYOR: not named
SCALE: not given
MATERIAL, SIZE & ORIENTATION: paper, ink and slight colour; 45.7cms x 72.8cms; no direction
CONTENT: mill leats and streams, grey; relief shown by hill shading; coniferous and deciduous tree symbols showing isolated and groups of trees; footpaths, dotted lines; buildings in plan, pink

19/1/3

TALATON
1823/5   961M add/M/E2

Escot House SY 082981
See entry under Feniton, 6/3/3

19/1/4

TALATON
19th cent.   4421A/PB8

Talaton Church SY 067997
TITLE: 'Plan of the Glebe Lands Belonging to the Parish of Talaton Devon Robert Palk Welland Rector' [Rector 1833–1879]
SURVEYOR: 'Edmund Yeakell Surveyor Alphington'
SCALE: 'Scale of Chains; scale bar; 1"=4.5 chains; 1:3564
MATERIAL, SIZE & ORIENTATION: paper, coloured; 55.3cms EW x 59cms NS; east to top
CONTENT: fields outlined with tree and hedgerow symbols; coloured brown with plough lines, or green wash; numeric reference to list giving field names and content; areas referred by letter to note describing exchange of land; Talaton Common named; house, drive, formal garden; 'Lawn' and 'Cow Park' described separately; tree symbols showing isolated trees, orchard and en masse coloured light green indicating wood and copse; buildings in plan, red; principal buildings named; peripheral owners named
DECORATION: title cartouche inscribed on swag of cloth; 4 point compass indicator, N-S lines superimposed on scythe, sickle, pitchfork and sheaf of corn; north marked by fleur-de-lys, SEW by letter; wide grey border

TALATON see also C159

19/2/1

TAMERTON FOLIOT
1676   PWDRO 70/323

Maristow House SX 476646
See entry under Buckland Monachorum, 2/48/1

19/2/2

TAMERTON FOLIOT

1786   PWDRO 2415/1

Warleigh SX 458617

TITLE: 'The Plan of the Barton of Warleigh, with a small part of the Manor of Tamerton, in the Parish of Tamerton-Foliot, and County of Devon. The Property of Walter Radcliffe Esqr.'

SURVEYOR: 'Survey'd, plann'd etc, by Richard Cowl Plymouth 1786'

SCALE: 'A Scale of Chains'; scale bar; 1"=4 chains; 1:3168

MATERIAL, SIZE & ORIENTATION: paper, mounted on fabric, slight colour; 124.5cms EW x 69.4cms NS (framed); south to top

CONTENT: 'Tavey River', 'Tamerton Lake', streams, ponds, marked by stream lines; direction of flow indicated; jetties; belvedere overlooking Tamerton Lake; relief shown by hill shading; rocks in profile; fields outlined by hedge symbols with numeric reference to lists giving field names and content; gateways; garden in detailed plan; bowling green; quarry; black tree symbols showing orchards, woods, isolated trees and hangers; roads, buff, fenced and unfenced; buildings in plan, buff, outlined in brown; boathouse; dovecote; mill; peripheral estates, including 'Borough of Tamerton Foliot', named

    Later annotations include names of peripheral owners

DECORATION: title cartouche: medallion with simple design of leaves and scrolls with pendant foliage; 8 point compass rose, plain/grey; north marked by fleur-de-lys, south, east and west spelt out

19/2/3

TAMERTON FOLIOT

1787   PWDRO 407/12/2[a]

Warleigh Point SX 445610

TITLE: 'The Plan of Part of Point Wood on the Barton of Warlegh the Property of Walter Radcliffe Esqr'

SURVEYOR: 'Surveyed by me Rich. Cowl sworn Surveyor 29th June 1787'

SCALE: scale bar; 1"=2.5 chains' 1:1980

MATERIAL, SIZE & ORIENTATION: paper, watermark, slight colour; 39.9cms x 31.4cms; no direction

CONTENT: river, blue margin; wood outlined in pink; content stated – '27 acres 0 roods 14 Poles Statute Measure 16½ feet to the pole'; '22 acres 3 roods 2 Poles customary Measure 18 feet to the pole'; footpaths peripheral to the wood

On the back of the map, possibly in a different hand:

22	3	2 at 13. 10, 0 pr ACR	
307	1		
		3	8d
307	3	8d	

153	10		
139			
14	10		
His part	0	10.6	
To the Surveyor			
	15	0 6	
Recd			

19/2/4

TAMERTON FOLIOT

1787   PWDRO 407/12/2[b]

Warleigh Point SX 445610

TITLE: 'A Plan of part of Point Wood, on the Barton of Warlegh, the property of Walter Radcliffe Esqr'

SURVEYOR: 'Surveyed by me Rich. Cowl, sworn Surveyor. 29th June 1787'

SCALE: 'Scale 2 Chains & 4 tenths to the Inch'; no scale bar; 1:1901

MATERIAL, SIZE & ORIENTATION: paper, damaged, slight colour, watermark; 40.2cms x 31.5cms; no direction

CONTENT: river, blue; coppice outlined in pink with content in statute and customary measure; footpaths, broken lines; note stating statute measure 16½ feet to the pole and customary measure 18 feet to the pole

ENDORSEMENT: Southpoint Coppice with details of content and value

19/2/5

TAMERTON FOLIOT

1787   PWDRO 407/12/1

Haxter Lodge SX 495630

TITLE: 'Hextor Estate belonging to J.B. Herring Esqr Survey'd by David Palmer 1787'

SURVEYOR: David Palmer

SCALE: 'A Scale of Statute Chains, each Four Yards' 9(sic); scale bar; 1"=3 chains; 1:2376 ?

MATERIAL, SIZE & ORIENTATION: paper, ink; 74.8cms x 43.9cms; north-west to top

CONTENT: fields, named with content; hedge symbols; Roborough Down partly with content; boundstones; footpaths, pecked lines; building in plan; peripheral owners and estates named

DECORATION: 4 point compass indicator, black/plain; north marked by fleur-de-lys

19/2/6

TAMERTON FOLIOT

1790   1508M Surveys/V5

Tamerton Foliot Church SX 471609
See entry under Bovey, North, 2/21/2

19/2/7

TAMERTON FOLIOT

1791   PWDRO 407/12/3

Warleigh Point SX 445610

TITLE: 'A Plan of a Lot of Coppice-wood, on the Barton of Warlegh; Taken Septe 1791 by, Thomas Jope'

SURVEYOR: Thomas Jope

SCALE: 'Scale 30 Statute Chains'; no scale bar

MATERIAL, SIZE & ORIENTATION: paper, slight colour, watermark; 37.5cms x 30.5cms; north-east to top

CONTENT: river, 'Warlegh Lake', blue; arrows indicating direction of flow; coppice in 3 numbered parts outlined in ink and colour; one boundary named 'Hedge Greep'; roads, buff, fenced and unfenced; list of 'Content in Statute Measure'; Deduct for Roads and Hedge Greep in Statute Measure'; 'Content in Customary Measure' to be paid for

ENDORSEMENT: (in a later hand) Buttshead Wood

19/2/8

TAMERTON FOLIOT

1793   346M/P1

Tamerton Foliot Church SX 471609
See entry under Bere Ferrers, 2/6/3

19/2/9

TAMERTON FOLIOT

1793/1803/1814/1834   PWDRO 407/12/10/1–5

Tamerton Foliot Church SX 471609

5 maps covering the same area, showing primarily the alteration in the course of a river and the marking of a new boundary

1793 PWDRO 407/12/10/2 & 3

TITLES: 'A Plan of a Tenement on Tamerton Church-Town, belonging to Walter Radcliffe Esqr. Taken in Septr 1793 by Thomas Jope'

SURVEYOR: Thomas Jope

SCALES: not given

MATERIAL, SIZE & ORIENTATION: paper, coloured; 47.6cms EW x 30cms NS; north to top

CONTENT: river, blue with arrow indicating direction of flow; old course on one map, old and new courses on the other; fields coloured green or yellow; alphabetic reference to list giving details of land ownership and content; some hedge symbols; one map shows hedges removed and sites of new boundary stones; additional land 'taken in' shown on one map; 'Road to Tamerton Church' named, buff; buildings in plan, red

NOTE: dated October 30th 1803 signed by Walter Radcliffe and Jonathan Elford confirming one plan to be 'a true Plan before any alteration was made' and the other 'a true Plan the alteration there hath been made'

DECORATION: 4 point compass indicator; WES marked by letter

407/12/10/4 Copy of the above in a different hand

407/12/10/5 Rough plan of the maps under 2 & 3 with notes dated 1834

407/12/10/1 Plan of 1 field in the Manor of Tamerton Foliot with details of lease dated 25 March 1793; additional details added in 1814 refer to 'Taprill's Plan' and imply disagreement between Tamerton and St Budeaux over rights and responsibilities concerning water

19/2/10

TAMERTON FOLIOT

1805–6   PWDRO 407/12/4

Warleigh SX 458617

TITLE: 'Plan of Part of Warlegh Coppice as bought by Mr Taprell 1805' (endorsed)

SURVEYOR: not named

SCALE: not given

MATERIAL, SIZE & ORIENTATION: paper, ink; 40.3cms x 21.9cms (torn); no direction

CONTENT: outline of South Point Wood as felled in 1805–6, divided into sections giving content and price [of timber] per acre; footpath, pecked line

NOTE: survey and construction lines in pencil

19/2/11

TAMERTON FOLIOT

[1805]   PWDRO 407/12/5

Warleigh SX 458617

TITLE: 'Plan of the Coppice Sold to Taprell & Co 1805'

SURVEYOR: 'W.T. Stentaford, Land Surveyor, Stoke Climsland, Cornwall'

SCALE: not given

MATERIAL, SIZE & ORIENTATION: 29.2cms x 22cms; no direction but Tamerton Lake is at the bottom of the map

CONTENT: 'part of Tamerton Lake'; coppice outlined in ink, with customary measure and sale price for timber; roads, unfenced, dotted lines, directions given; footpath, pecked line

19/2/12

TAMERTON FOLIOT

1817   Ex. D&C Ch. Comm. 98/8791

Tamerton Foliot Church SX 471609

See entry under Aylesbeare, 1/18/2

19/2/13

TAMERTON FOLIOT

1835   PWDRO 407/12/6

Tamerton village SX 472608

TITLE: 'Proposed Plan for Improving mutually the S.E. Entrance into the Village of Tamerton Foliot, and the adjoining property of Mark Grigg Esqr in the County of Devon'

SURVEYOR: 'Geo: Wightwick Archt Plymoh: 1st August 1835'

SCALE: 'Feet'; scale bar; 1"=20 feet; 1:240

MATERIAL, SIZE & ORIENTATION: paper, slight colour; 57.2cms x 22.6cms; no direction

CONTENT: area of land at entrance to village, yellow; divided into 3 plots, to be given up by Mark Stephens Grigg to Rev. Walter Radcliffe as Lord of the Manor of Tamerton Foliot; area, brown, divided into 2 plots to be given up by Walter Radcliffe to Mr Grigg

TAMERTON FOLIOT see also C160

19/3/1

TAVISTOCK

1744–1758   T1258M/E16c

A volume of estate maps, 26.5cms x 42.5cms

TITLE page: 'Plans and Particulars of all the Timber and Coppice woods belonging to His Grace the Duke of Bedford in the County of Devon shewing How the same have been sold from time to time from the year 1686 to the present year 1758 by John Wynne'

'An Index to the Plans and Descriptions of the Woods'

'An Abstract of His Grace the Duke of Bedford's Woods in the County of Devon, the Plans and Particulars of which are contain'd in this Book'

SURVEYOR: John Wynne; other surveyors, Richard Martyn (maps dated 1751, 1752, 1755), Thomas Doidge (map dated 1751), William Doidge (map dated 1750)

SCALE: 'A Scale of Chains and Links Customary Measure each Chain containing 4 perches of 18 feet each'; scales vary between 1"=2.5chains and 1"=5 chains; 1:2160 and 1:4320

MATERIAL, SIZE & ORIENTATION: paper, coloured; most maps on one page; directions indicated but vary

GENERAL CONTENT: rivers, blue with darker blue margins; arrows indicating direction of flow; navigable reaches of rivers indicated, some boats shown; 'wears' including salmon 'wears'; quays; rocks, brown; woods, green with green stippling, outlined with grey-green and hedge symbols; some green tree symbols; lists giving content in statute measure inclusive and exclusive of waste and rocks; roads and footpaths, buff, fenced and unfenced; some directions given; houses in elevation; copper mines and stamping mills named; peripheral owners named

Each map preceded or accompanied by a description and account of various woods and coppices with details and condition of sales and monies received

DECORATION: 4 point compass indicators with points and centres in a variety of colours within coloured circles; north marked by coloured fleur-de-lys

LIST OF MAPS:- all are on a scale of 1"=2.5 chains (customary measure) unless other wise stated

p.11 'A Plan of Higher Blackmoreham Wood Survey'd 1757 by John Wynne'

p.12 'A Plan of Middle Blackmoreham Wood Survey'd in 1757 by John Wynne'

p.14 'A Plan of Lower Black=Moreham Wood Surveyed in 1757 by –' Note states 'survey by John Wynne'

p.16 'A Plan of Maddacleave Wood in the Parish of Tavistock Survey'd in 1744 by John Wynne' 1"=5 chains; 1:4320

p.18 'A Plan of Belkamore Wood Survey'd in 1757 by John Wynne'

p.20 'A Plan of Waterhal Wood Survey'd in 1747 by John Wynne'

p.22 'A Plan of Woodyates Wood Survey'd in 1756 by John Wynne'

p.24 'A Plan of Sheeperidge Wood Survey'd in 1744 by John Wynne'

p.27–28 No actual title but two woods named on the map – Haywood and Impham Plain 'These Woods were Survey'd in 1758 by John Wynne'

p.30 'Impham Ball and Wear Woods Survey'd in 1758 by John Wynne'

p.33–34 'A Plan of Great Hatch Wood & Little Hatch Wood Survey'd in 1746 by John Wynne'
　　Hatch Wood SX 437717

p.36 'A Plan of Heath Wood Collins Woods and Hanging Cleave Wood Survey in 1748 by John Wynne'

p.39–40 'A Plan of Shillacleave Wood in the Parish of Tavistock Survey'd in 1750 and Copied fair into this Book in Novemr 1757 by John Wynne'

p.43–44 'A Plan of South Greenaven Wood in the Parish of Tavistock Survey'd and delineated in 1757 by John Wynne' 1"=3 chains; 1:2592
　　Grenoven Woods SX 416743

p.46 'A Plan of Hartshole Coppice Wood Survey'd in 1757 by John Wynne'
　　Hartshole Farm SX 461708
　　'A Plan of Newton Coppice Wood Survey'd in 1757 by John Wynne' Both maps 1"=2 chains; 1:1728
　　Newton SX 456734

p.48 'A Plan of Taviton Wood Survey'd in 1758 by J. Wynne'
　　Taviton SX 500744

p.50 'A Plan of Bockwell otherwise Bickwell's Grove otherwise Wilminston Wood'
　　Wilminstone SX 494764
　　'A Plan of Davies's Coppice Wood at Wilminston both Woods survey'd in 1757 by John Wynne' 1"=2 chains; 1:1728

p.52 'A Plan of Parswell Wood in the Parish of Tavistock Survey'd in 1755 by Richard Martyn'
　　Parswell SX 463731
　　'A Plan of Crowndale Wood in the Parish of Tavistock Survey'd in 1751 by Richd Martyn' Both maps 1"=2 chains; 1:1728
　　Crowndale SX 473727

p.54 'A Plan of North Greenaven Wood Survey'd in 1751 by Thomas Doidge' 1"=4 chains; 1:3456
　　Grenoven Woods SX 416743

p.56 'A Plan of Frementorr Wood alias Part of Lower Blanch=down Wood Survey'd in 1753 by John Wynne' 1"=4 chains; 1:3456
　　Blanchdown wood SX 423730

p.58 'A Plan of a Wood by Lobscombe Lane called the Woodranger's Piece Survey'd & Delineated in October 1758 by John Wynne' 1"=2 chains; 1:1728
　　Luscombe Down Plantation SX 439715

p.62 'A Plan of Asheltor Wood in the Parish of Brentor Survey'd in 1748 by John Wynne'
　　Asheltor Wood SX 473829

p.64 'A Plan of Exweek alias Wexin Wood adjoyning to the Barton of Leigh in the Parish of Milton Abbot Survey'd in 1752 by Richard Martyn' 1"=2 chains; 1:1728
　　Leigh ?Wood SX 390775

p.66 'A Plan of Higher Artiscombe Wood Survey'd in 1758 by J. Wynne'
　　'A Plan of Lower Artiscombe Wood Survey'd in 1758 by John Wynne' 1"=2 chains; 1:1728
　　Artiscombe SX 449741

p.68 'A Plan of Facy's Ogbear Wood above the Hedge. Facy's Lower Ogb. Wood. Cudlip's Ogbear Wood Survey'd in 1758 by J. Wynne'
　　Ogbear ?Wood SX 451746

p.70 'A Plan of Maiden Gore Wood in the Parish of Lamerton Survey'd & delineated in Augst 1758 by John Wynne' Note by G. Aislabie that he re-measured the wood and 5 fields adjoining and found difference from Wynne's measure; He therefore employed 'young Mr Jope to cast up the same plan'; he agreed with Aislabie's figure

p.74 'A Plan of Stiles Week Wood Survey'd by John Wynne in 1758' 1"=2 chains; 1:1728

p.76 'A Plan of Higher BlanchDown Wood in the Parish of Tavistock Survey'd in 1758 by John Wynne'
　　Blanchdown Wood SX 423730

p.79 'A Plan of Lower Blanch Down Wood Survey'd in 1750 by Willm Doidge and reduced to a smaller scale in 1758 by Jno Wynne' 1"=3 chains; 1:2592

4 maps follow by John Hitchin. These maps are of a later date; probably early 19th cent.

SCALE: 'Scale of Chains'; scale bar; 1"=3 chains; 1:2592

MATERIAL, SIZE & ORIENTATION: small maps each on a single page, coloured; directions indicated but vary

CONTENT: streams, blue; woods, green with darker green shading; numeric reference to list giving content; roads and lanes, fenced and unfenced; peripheral owners named

List of Maps:- (all in Lamerton Parish) Cole's Wood
    Maiden Gore Wood
    Lower Broaderidge Wood
    Higher Broaderidge Wood

19/3/2

TAVISTOCK
1744–1811   T1258M/E16b

Volume of estate maps, largely a copy of T1258M/E16c, but with information concerning the woods up to 1811. Additional maps by Thomas Jope, 1791–1811, and maps by Gilbert Aislabie and John Jope copied into the volume in 1812.

Of the maps copied from John Wynne's atlas there are some differences: the 4 point compass indicators are plain; there are few scales included; the title of the plan of Shillacleave Wood states 'Survey'd in 1750 & Copied fair into this Book in Novembr 1768 by G. Aislabie' Following Wynne's maps are 4 maps by Thomas Jope.

TITLES:
'A Plan of Rubby Town Wood' 'Survey'd in 1791 by Thomas Jope' 'Scale 30'[sic] Rubbytown SX 435741
'West Broadridge and Clayland Wood Tho Jope 1803' 'Scale 30'
'East Broadridge Wood Thomas Jope Land Surveyor Janry 1805' 'Scale 3 Stat. chs to an Inch'; 1:2376
'A Plan of Petertavy Wood in the Parish of Petertavy in the County of Devon, belonging to His Grace the Duke of Bedford Surveyed in June 1811 by Thomas Jope' 'Scale, three Statute Chains to an Inch'; 1:2376 Peter Tavy Church SX 513778

MATERIAL, SIZE & ORIENTATION: maps, coloured, on single page; direction indicated on maps 1 and 2

CONTENT: rivers, blue, arrows indicating direction of flow; rocks, grey; woods, green stippling, some with tree symbols; content, including and excluding waste in statute and customary measure; roads, buff, fenced and unfenced; Wheal Peter Mine; buildings in plan, red
    Details of sales and methods of payment on facing pages

TITLE: 'Plans and Particulars of Coppice Woods In the Parish of Tavistock belonging to His Grace the Duke of Bedford surveyed by Gilbert Aislabie between the Years 1770 & 1773 And also of Woods in the Parish of Milton-Abbott belonging to the sd Duke. Surveyed by John Jope in 1763 and Copied into this Book in the year 1812 by Thomas Jope'
    Index follows to 'Woods in Tavistock' and 'Woods in Milton-Abbott'

SCALE: 'A Scale of Twenty Statute Chains, or ¼ of a Mile'; 'N.B. This Scale serves for all the Plans in this Book unless expressed to the contrary'; scale bar; 1"=3 chains; 1:2376

MATERIAL, SIZE & ORIENTATION: small maps on a single page, coloured; directions indicated on all maps but variable; 4 point compass indicators; north marked by diamond, SEW by letter

GENERAL CONTENT: rivers, blue, named; arrows indicating direction of flow; rocks shaded in ink; woods, green or pink with some tree symbols and content; numeric reference to list giving names and content in statutary and customary measure; roads, some directions given; copper mines; peripheral owners and estates named

MAPS:-

p.1 'Tavistock Parish' 'A Plan of Grammeby Woods, Part of the Barton of Kilworthy'
    Kilworthy SX 482770

p.2 Fitzford Wood

p.5 Little Ogbear Wood'
    Ogbear SX 438749

p.7 'Shellamill Woods'
    Shillamill Mill SX 465721

p.9 'Enoch's Wood and Woodland Coppice Part of Broadwell Farm'
    Broadwell SX 461703

p.11 'Honey's Tor Wood'
    Honey Tor SX 443734

p.13 'Rubbytown Little Wood'
    Rubbytown SX 442740

p.15 'Island Park, part Coppice Wood, and Part pasture Belonging to Blanchdown Farm'
    Blanchdown Wood SX 423730

p.25 'Parish of Milton-Abbott' 'Plans of the Three Long Timber Woods, Part of the Barton of Leigh'
    Leigh Wood SX 390775
    'Plotted by a Scale of Six Devonshire, or Customary Chains, to an Inch. This Scale serves for all the plans of Woods in Milton-Abbott contained in this book'; no scale bar; 1:5184

p.27 'Inglesley Wood'
   ?Endsleigh SX 391786
p.29 'Plans of two Woods, part of Newton, in Milton-Abbott'
p.31 'A Plan of Easthill Wood, part of Beara in Milton-Abbott'
   Beara Farm SX 403759
p.33 'Plans of two Woods, part of Beara in Milton-Abbott'

19/3/3

TAVISTOCK
1746   L1258/M&P/Tavistock 17a

Taviton Village SX 500744

TITLE: 'A Plan of Little Down als Taviton Down with some Grounds adjoyning taken in 1746'

SURVEYOR: not named

SCALE: 'A Scale of chains and Links of Customary Measure each chain containing 4 perches or 72 feet in length'; scale bar; 1"=2.4 chains; 1:2073

MATERIAL, SIZE & ORIENTATION: paper, watermark, coloured; 48.8cms EW x 38.3cms NS; north to top

CONTENT: rivulet marking boundary between Tavistock and Whitchurch parishes; fields outlined with double line, green with hedge symbols; content, customary measure, black; statute measure, red; road, direction given

NOTE: 'NB the red prick'd lines cold with brown thus ::: shews the Horse Road
   The spaces between black prick'd double lines colour'd with a faint yellow thus ::: shew the Banks of the old fences wch are still remaining made by Mr Leere when he tilled up the Down and sow'd it'

NOTE: 'The Down in Mr Smith's Survey is said to be but 33.1.5 but I make it 39.2.6 road included The Turbary at the bottom of the Down is not at all mentd in Mr Smiths Survey'

DECORATION: 4 point compass indicator; north marked by fleur-de-lys, SEW by letter

ENDORSEMENT: A Plan of Little Down als Taviton Down with some Grounde adjoyning taken in 1746

19/3/4

TAVISTOCK
1746   L1258/M&P/Tavistock 1

Hole Farm SX 459649

TITLE: 'A Map or Plan of an Estate called Hole Situate in the Parish of Tavistock Survey'd in July 1746'

SURVEYOR: not named

SCALE: 'A Scale of Devon Chains & Links each Chain containing 4 perches or 72 feet'; scale bar; 1"=2.4 chains; 1:2073

MATERIAL, SIZE & ORIENTATION: paper, watermark, slight colour; 40cms EW x 26.1cms NS; south to top

CONTENT: wells and small stream, blue; fields outlined with double lines and hedge symbols, named with content: alphabetic reference, red, to table giving names of 'Premises' and 'Quantity'; gates; green tree symbols showing orchard and isolated trees; road and lane; peripheral owners named

DECORATION: 4 point compass indicator, yellow/red; north marked by blue fleur-de-lys

19/3/5

TAVISTOCK
1750   L1258M/L/E2/103/8

Tavistock Church SX 481744

TITLE: not given

SURVEYOR: not named

SCALE: 'Scale of Feet'; scale bar; 1"=50 feet; 1:600

MATERIAL, SIZE & ORIENTATION: parchment, coloured; 16.5cms EW x 11.2cms NS; south to top

CONTENT: River Tavy, black wavy lines; 'East bridge'; garden and tanyard, yellow with content; roads, directions given; buildings in plan, red or dotted red; peripheral owners and estates named

DECORATION: 4 point compass indicator, plain/black lines; north marked by fleur-de-lys, SEW by letter

ASSOCIATED DOCUMENT: map is in margin of Lease for 99 years, dated 23 March 1749/50, of the Red Lyon alehouse, granted by the Duke of Bedford to Abraham Craise, cordwainer

19/3/6

TAVISTOCK

*c.*1750   L1258/M&P/Tavistock 15

Horrabridge Church SX 512696

TITLE: 'A Plan of Saint John's Chappell fallen in hand by the Death of John Cunningham Sanders'

SURVEYOR: not named

SCALE: 'A Scale of Feet'; scale bar; 1"=70 feet; 1:840

MATERIAL, SIZE & ORIENTATION: paper, slight colour; 19cms EW x 12cms NS; west to top

CONTENT: blue/grey tree symbols in area noted as being without a fence on 2 sides; hedge symbols on 3rd side and a wall, named, on 4th side; hedge symbols beside a road to 'Harrowbridge' which is coloured red; Summer House belonging to Johns Farm, in plan, red

DECORATION: NS line indicated by letter and fleur-de-lys; red margin

19/3/7

TAVISTOCK

*c.*1750   L1258/M&P/Tavistock16

Hurdwick Farm SX 472759

TITLE: not given; endorsed 'A Plan of Quilletts adj. to Hurdwick Plan of Benn Parks & Quilletts abt. Hurdwick'

SURVEYOR: not named

SCALE: 'A Scale of Perches containing 18ft each Perch'; scale bar; 1"=8 perches; 1:1728

MATERIAL, SIZE & ORIENTATION: paper, ink; 32.2cms x 20.4cms; no direction

CONTENT: fields outlined and shaded in pencil; crop named and content; tree symbols showing avenue leading to Hurdwick House; house in plan, shaded in pencil; road, named and direction indicated; 'Old Quarry' named

19/3/8

TAVISTOCK

*c.*1750   L1258/M&P/Tavistock 17

Taviton Village SX 500744

TITLE: 'A Plan of the Watercourse at Taviton in Dispute between Mr Hornbrook & Mr Roskelly & Mr Hornbrook'

SURVEYOR: not named

SCALE: 'A Scale of Customary Chains & Links each Chain being 4 perches or 72 feet in length'; scale bar; 1"=2.45 chains; 1:2117

MATERIAL, SIZE & ORIENTATION: paper, watermark, slight colour; 29.8cms EW x 24.4cms NS; south to top

CONTENT: fields named according to owners – Mr Hornbrook and Mr Roskelly; tree symbols showing orchards; various points along the watercourse identified in the Explanation which also explains the substance of the dispute

NOTE: 'NB. All the Red is Water The Black double lines shaded with Green are hedges'

DECORATION: 4 point compass indicator, yellow; NSEW indicated by letter, north also marked by fleur-de-lys

19/3/9

TAVISTOCK

1750   L1258M/L/E6/15/15

Tavistock Church SX 481744

TITLE: not given; map part of lease concerning 'Little Field or Meadow late Lavers'

SURVEYOR: not named but John Wynne's signature on the lease

SCALE: not given

MATERIAL, SIZE & ORIENTATION: parchment, ink; small diagram illustrating the field in question, 8.6cms EW x 10.5cms NS; north to top

CONTENT: field with acreage and dimensions on boundaries; named; 'Dry House' in one corner, with its dimensions; lanes; peripheral owners named on west and east

19/3/10

TAVISTOCK

1752   L1258M/E6/10/6/34

Tavistock Church SX481744

TITLE: not given; map part of lease concerning 'A House called Mudges Bakehouse'

SURVEYOR: not named but John Wynne's signature on the lease

SCALE: not given

MATERIAL, SIZE & ORIENTATION: parchment, ink; small diagram illustrating the area in question, 7.8cms EW x 5.4cms NS; north to top

CONTENT: house, outhouse, linney and yard with dimension entered on the plan; peripheral owners named

19/3/11

TAVISTOCK

1752–1753   Part of TD 273

Tavistock Church SX 481744

TITLE: 'A Plan of the Town & Borough of Tavistock In the County of Devon. Belonging to His Grace the Most Noble John Duke of Bedford.'

SURVEYOR: 'Survey'd in 1752 & 1753 by John Wynne'

SCALE: 'A Scale of Feet'; scale bar, divided scale; 1"=70 feet; 1:840

MATERIAL, SIZE & ORIENTATION: parchment, coloured; 159.8cms EW x 140.5cms NS; east to top

CONTENT: The River Tavy, streams and leats, green; islands of Tavy shown by dotted lines; East Bridge in detailed elevation, other bridges; fields outlined in various colours named with numeric reference [to Survey Book]; coloured according to ownership, listed in table; green tree symbols showing orchards/gardens; brown tree symbols showing ?woods; roads, buff, some named especially in town; town area plots of gardens and buildings in plan outlined in various colours according to ownership with alpha-numeric reference [to Survey Book]; some public buildings named; bull post; source of water supply; borough boundary, red dotted lines

  Pencil construction grid

DECORATION: title cartouche: gold rococo outline decorated with acanthus leaves and flowers shaded pink, blue, yellow and mauve, surmounted by Duke of Bedford's coat of arms with supporters and motto ('che sara sara') and with coat of arms of Borough of Tavistock at the bottom; 8 point compass rose, blue/yellow; north marked by yellow fleur-de-lys, SEW spelt out

19/3/12

TAVISTOCK

1753   L1258/M&P/Tavistock 20

Higher Edgecombe SX 401796

TITLE: 'A Plan of Part of Higher; otherwise Over Edgcombe and also of several Fields &ca called Edgecombe Leys the Lands of his Grace the Duke of Bedford – Calmady Esqr & Dr Batty. Surveyed January 8th 9th & 10th 1753 Gt Aislabie'

SURVEYOR: Gilbert Aislabie

SCALE: 'A Scale of Devon Chains & Links; Each Chain contg 4 perches and each Perch 18 Feet'; divided scale; 1"=1 chain; 1:864

MATERIAL, SIZE & ORIENTATION: paper, watermark, coloured; 80cms EW x 80cms NS; north to top

CONTENT: fields outlined with double lines and coloured red, green or yellow according to owner; content and numeric reference, red, to table repeating content and owners' names with note below 'NB All the Grounds, or Fields from No 1 to No 17 inclusive were formerly one Common Field & in 1676 were Divided as above'; tree symbols marking orchards and isolated trees, some with a note – 'these trees are above 100 yr Growth', 'The stumps of ye Trees cut down'; roads marked with double lines, named; buildings in plan, coloured according to the fields to which they belong

DECORATION: 8 point compass rose, red/green, within yellow outer circle; north marked by fleur-de-lys, SEW by letter; scale, green

19/3/13

TAVISTOCK

1755   L1258M/L/EC/8/9

Tavistock Church SX 481744

TITLE: not given; part of lease concerning 'House Stable Curtlage & Garden in Barley Market Street & Two Gardens in Exeter Lane'

SURVEYOR: not named

SCALE: 'Plan'd by a Scale of 30 to an Inch'; no other unit of measurement stated

MATERIAL, SIZE & ORIENTATION: parchment; 2 plans one overlaying the other;

  Plan 1: ink; 6.1cms EW x 17.3cms NS; north to top; directions entered on margins of plan

  Plan 2: coloured; 11.3cms EW x 23.3cms NS; north to top; directions entered on margins of plan

CONTENT:

  Plan 1: house, stables and garden; dimensions of house entered; lanes named on north and south; peripheral owners named on east and west

  Plan 2: mill leat, blue; 2 orchards outlined in green with green tree symbols; dimensions entered on boundaries of each orchard; 'Orchard belongg to the House', 'Orchard purchased of Jno Edwards in 1732'

19/3/14

TAVISTOCK
*c.*1757   L1258/M&P/Tavistock 14

Tavistock Church SX 481744

TITLE: 'A Map of the Premises that fell in Hand on Mr Bulteel's Death
& the adjoining Premises'

SURVEYOR: [John Wynne]

SCALE: 'A Scale of Feet, 36 to an Inch'; divided scale; scale bar; 1:432

MATERIAL, SIZE & ORIENTATION: paper, mounted on linen, coloured; 72cms
EW x 71.2cms NS; north to top

CONTENT: River Tavy and 'The Canal' named, blue; meadow, orchard,
gardens named with content; tree symbols marking 'The Walk' and
'The Walk by the River Side'; buildings in plan, owners, tenants
described and coloured according to the Explanation – 'The premises
fallen into Hand on Mr Bulteel's Death are coloured & shaded Red
All the premises adjoiuning that are His Grace's Lands, are coloured
Yellow. Those Premises which are the Lands of other Persons, are
coloured & shaded Black. The same Number repeated shew those
Premises to belong to the same thing. Water is coloured and shaded
blue'

DECORATION: 4 point compass indicator, red/yellow with green centre,
outer circle, ink; north marked by fleur-de-lys, SEW by letter

ENDORSEMENT: A Map of the Premises that fell in Hand on Mr Bulteel's
Death

19/3/15

TAVISTOCK
1758   L1258/M&P/Tavistock 18a

Wapsworthy SX 538801

TITLE: 'A Plan of an Estate in Wapsworthy in the Parish of Tavistock
Situate about 6 mile NE of the Town of Tavistock Purchased by his
Grace the Duke of Bedford of Denys Rolle Esqr. Surveyed in March
1758 by John Wynne'

SURVEYOR: John Wynne

SCALE: 'A Scale of Chains and Links Customary Measure each Chain
containing 4 Perches of 18 feet each; scale bar; 1"=2.4 chains; 1:2074

MATERIAL, SIZE & ORIENTATION: paper, watermark, coloured; 2 irregular
pieces of paper with instructions for joining them; south-east to top

CONTENT: River Tavy, Wapsworthy Water, green; direction of flow
indicated; fields outlined with double ink lines and yellow, named
with content; numeric reference [to Survey Book]; gardens; wood

indicated by rough shading and 'Marsh under'; other woods merely
named; road, buff, direction given; buildings in plan, light brown;
peripheral owners, Commons and parishes named

DECORATION: 4 point compass indicator, green/red with yellow outer
circle; north marked by fleur-de-lys, SEW by letter

19/3/16

TAVISTOCK
1761   L1258M/L/E6/2/7

area unidentified, north-west of Tavistock

TITLE: not given

SURVEYOR: not named

SCALE: 'Customary Chains, each 72 feet'; scale bar; 1"=2 chains; 1:1728

MATERIAL, SIZE & ORIENTATION: parchment, coloured; 27cms EW x
32.5cms NS; north to top

CONTENT: fields outlined in green or yellow indicating fence ownership;
named with content; numeric reference to list repeating field names
and content stating 'Custumy' [measure] used; road, buff, directions
given; roadside hedges yellow or green; footpath, buff line with
direction given; building in plan, pink; small area separate from principal plan with detail as above except for a cottage in elevation and
'Mount Hungry' named

NOTE: lower left 'Replann'd'

DECORATION: north/south line; north marked by green fleur-de-lys, S by
letter

ASSOCIATED DOCUMENT: map part of lease dated 29 September 1761

19/3/17

TAVISTOCK
1762   L1258M/L/E2/118d/4

Tavistock Church SX 481744

TITLE: not given

SURVEYOR: not named

SCALE: 'Scale of Feet'; 1"=132 feet; 1:1584

MATERIAL, SIZE & ORIENTATION: parchment, coloured; 28.4cms EW x
35.4cms NS; south to top

CONTENT: River Tavy, blue; direction of flow indicated; bridge; fields
named; hedge symbols indicating ownership; roads, buff, fenced and
unfenced; some named, some with directions given; buildings in plan,
red

DECORATION: compass, single arrow; north marked by fleur-de-lys, south by letter

ASSOCIATED DOCUMENT: map is part of a Deed dated 29 July 1762 between Trustees of an Act for altering roads in Tavistock and the Duke of Bedford

19/3/18

TAVISTOCK

1762   L1258M/Maps/Roads 4

Tavistock Church SX 481744

TITLE: 'Copy of a Plan and Reference sent by Mr Turner'

SURVEYOR: Richard Turner

SCALE: 'Scale of Feet'; scale (line only); 1"=600 feet; 1:7200

MATERIAL, SIZE & ORIENTATION: paper, slight colour; map (portion of whole sheet) 14.5cms x 26.2cms; no direction

CONTENT: 'Tavy River', blue; direction of flow indicated; bridges; fields adjoining river and roads have alphabetical references to table giving field names, owners'/lessees' names and content; hedge symbols indicating ownership; roads, plain, directions given; buildings in plan, red;

Note stating 'Provided the new intended Road takes Place the following Lands are measured'

ASSOCIATED DOCUMENT: on the same sheet of paper is a copy of The Duke of Bedford's directions to Mr Turner, dated 5 July 1762

19/3/19

TAVISTOCK

1764   L1258M/L/E2/60/7

Newton SX 456734

TITLE: not given; map is attached to lease

SURVEYOR: not named

SCALE: not given

MATERIAL, SIZE & ORIENTATION: parchment, slight colour; 67cms x 54cms; north-west to top

CONTENT: 'Lumburne River', blue; bridge; fields outlined in yellow with hedge symbols; named with content in customary measure; numeric reference to 2 lists headed Newton and 'Lumburne Parks' repeating field names and content in customary and statute measure; vague symbols showing orchard; roads, buff, directions given; Turnpike

road from Callington named; buildings in Newton village in plan, hatched red; 'Lumburne' and Newton mills in elevation; peripheral lessees named

NOTE: map attached to lease dated 1 December 1764 between the Duke of Bedford and John Wilcock, cooper, of Tavistock

DECORATION: 4 point compass indicator; north spelt out

19/3/20

TAVISTOCK

1768   L1258M/L/E2/68/2

Lumburn Bridge SX 460731

TITLE: not given

SURVEYOR: Gilbert Aislabie

SCALE: 'Plotted by a Scale of 3 Chains to an Inch Statute Measure'; no scale bar; 1"=3 chains; 1:3168

MATERIAL, SIZE & ORIENTATION: parchment, coloured; 14.3cms x 41.5cms; north-west to top

CONTENT: river, blue; 'Lumburn Bridge' and 'Clam' bridge named; fields outlined in yellow, named with content; numeric reference to list giving field names and additional information in customary and statute measure; green tree symbols showing orchard; roads, buff, directions given; peripheral land owned by the Duke of Bedford named

DECORATION: 4 point compass indicator; north marked by cross bar, SEW by letter

ASSOCIATED DOCUMENT: map part of lease dated 29 September 1768

19/3/21

TAVISTOCK

1768   1508M/Devon/M&P/Tavistock Map 1

Tavistock Church SX 481744

3 maps joined together

TITLE: 'A Survey of Several Estates in the Parish of Tavistock and County of Devon belonging to the Right Honourable William Lord Viscot Courtenay Taken in 1768 by G Aislabie'

SURVEYOR: Gilbert Aislabie

SCALE: 'A Scale of Chains & Links of three to an Inch Statute Measure each Chain containing 4 Poles or 66 Feet'; 1:2376

MATERIAL, SIZE & ORIENTATION: parchment, coloured; right map: 75.4cms EW x 68.4cms NS; centre map, 80.3cms EW x 68.2cms NS; left map, 66.3cms EW x 89.6cms NS; directions indicated variously on each map

CONTENT: right map: shows Great Crease (SX 463740) and Lumburn River

Lumburn River and Newtown leat, blue; fields outlined in green, named with content; tree symbols, green, showing wood and orchards; furze, stippled green; road, lane, buff, direction given; buildings in plan, green; peripheral owners named

INSET: of Pitts Cleave; River Tavy, blue; fields outlined in green, named with content; tree symbols, green, marking wood; furze, stippled green; road, buff, direction given; buildings in plan, green; peripheral owners named

2 TABLES:

1) 'Particulars of Great Crease in the Tenure of William Bredall' with fields named with content in Statute and Customary Measure

2) 'Particulars of Pitts Cleave in the Tenure of Richard Dobson'

DECORATION: title cartouche: rococo style with elaborate pencil shading; 4 point compass indicator; north marked by fleur-de-lys

CENTRE MAP: shows scattered holdings to the west of Tavistock; rivers and Lumburn River, blue; fields outlined in various colours, named with content; tree symbols showing orchards; roads, buff, named; Turnpike road named; buildings in plan, various colours; peripheral owners named

4 TABLES:

1) Particulars of Higher Crebar in the Tenure of George Cudlipp'

2) 'Particulars of Lower Bucktor in the Tenure of John Rundle' SX 462724

3) 'Particulars of Little Parswell in the Tenure of Nicholas Hyne' SX 463731

4) 'Particulars of Lumburn Tenement in the Tenure of William Crabb' SX 459730

DECORATION: 8 point compass rose; north marked by fleur-de-lys

LEFT MAP: river Tavy, blue; fields outlined in various colours, named with content; green tree symbols showing woods coloured green, orchards with symbols only; furze and timber stippled green; roads and lanes, buff; directions given; footpaths, pecked lines; buildings in plan; village 'Romansleigh als Rumley'; peripheral owners named

2 TABLES:

1) 'Particulars of Romansleigh in the Tenure of John Gill Portacleve Wood N.B. There is some Waste in the above Woods which cannot be truly ascertained untill they are cut down' Portacleve Wood is Particliffe Wood

2) 'Particulars of Ramsham in the Tenure of William Gill'

DECORATION: 8 point compass rose; north marked by fleur-de-lys

19/3/22

TAVISTOCK
1760–1770   T1258M/E6

Hurdwick Farm SX 472759 Ottery SX 445753

TITLE: 'Plan of the West Part or Division in the Parish of Tavistock containing the Manors of Hurdwick, Ogbear, and Morwell Also of the Manor of Ottery, in the Parish of Lamerton belonging to His Grace the most Noble John, Duke of Bedford Taken between the Years 1760, and 1770 By G. Aislabie'

SURVEYOR: Gilbert Aislabie

SCALE: 'A Scale of Chains and Links Statute Measure, each containing 4 poles or 66 feet'; scale bar; 1"=3 chains; 1:2376

MATERIAL, SIZE & ORIENTATION: parchment, coloured; 145cms x 336cms; north-west to top

CONTENT: River Tavy, pond, leat, blue; islands, ford, bridges; fields outlined in various colours, named with content; numeric reference [to Survey Book]; tree symbols showing orchards and woods; roads, buff, some directions given; lanes, light brown; footpaths, pecked lines; buildings in plan, dwelling houses, red; other buildings, hatched black; quarries; peripheral parishes named

'Explanation' that the Duke of Bedford's lands are shaded with different colours showing the method of holding; the lands of other persons are shaded in Indian ink; the letters and numbers in the plan refer to the Survey Book

DECORATION: title cartouche: rococo scrolls, acanthus leaves and flowers with a mythical beast; scale bar: yellow and green; 8 point compass rose, black/plain, segmented centre; north marked by fleur-de-lys

ENDORSEMENT: Middle Division

NOTE: there are later additions, including Tithe Map numbers, and the lines of the railway and new roads. The map was evidently in use in the Estate Office for many years and was part of a map in three sections. The other two sections are as follows:-

T1258M/E7 endorsed Western Division

Shows River Tamar , rocks and mines; Harwood House in elevation

SIZE: 142cms x 358cms

T1258M/E5 endorsed Eastern Division

Settlements are named

SIZE: 145cms x 321cms

19/3/23

TAVISTOCK
1769/70   T1258M/E15

Cudliptown SX 522790

TITLE: 'A Plan, of the East Part or Division, of the Parish of Tavistock, being Part of the Manor of Hurdwick in the County of Devon – belonging to His Grace the most Noble Duke of Bedford Taken in 1769 & 1770 By G. Aislabie'

SURVEYOR: Gilbert Aislabie

SCALE: 'A Scale of Chains and Links Statute Measure each Chain containing 4 Poles or 66 Feet'; scale bar; 1"=3 chains; 1:2376

MATERIAL, SIZE & ORIENTATION: parchment, coloured; 201cms x 236cms; north-east to top

CONTENT: River Tavy, blue with dark blue margins; arrow indicating direction of flow; streams, blue; Horndon Bridge named; rocks grey with dark grey shading, some named, White Tor, Cudliptown (tor), Bremel Tor, Brownstone Tor, Arthur's Hill; some fields outlined in colour, named with content; tree symbols showing woods, copses, orchards and isolated trees; roads, buff, fenced and unfenced; unfenced 'Turf Paths to Dartmoor' named; buildings in plan, red; settlements named; Old Tin Works, Deadlake Well and White Barrow named; peripheral parishes named; red dotted line marking boundary between Tavistock and Forest of Dartmoor

DECORATION: 8 point compass rose, plain/grey, centre circle outlined in grey; north marked by fleur-de-lys, SEW by letter

19/3/24

TAVISTOCK
1779   1508M Devon/M&P/Tavistock A2

Particliffe Wood SX 464713

TITLE: 'A Plan of Higher and Lower Particlift Woods in the Parish of Tavistock in the County of Devon; belonging to the Rt Honourable Lord Viscount Courtenay; taken in April 1779 by Thomas Jope'

SURVEYOR: Thomas Jope

SCALE: 'A Scale of Customary Chains each Seventy two Feet'; scale bar; 1"=1 chain; 1:864

MATERIAL, SIZE & ORIENTATION: paper, watermark, slight colour; 45.8cms EW x 83cms NS; west to top

CONTENT: Tavy River, blue; arrow indicating direction of flow; rocks named but no symbol; woods outlined in yellow with isolated tree

symbols; 'Higher and Lower Particlift Woods' named with content; Lower Particlift Wood divided into 3 named Lots and all listed under Particulars; 'Standing Coppice' named ; roads, buff, named

DECORATION: 4 point compass indicator; directions spelt out

19/3/25

TAVISTOCK
18th cent.   L1258/M&P/Tavistock 6

Tavistock Church SX 481744

TITLE: not given

SURVEYOR: not named

SCALE: not given

MATERIAL, SIZE & ORIENTATION: paper, ink; 19.8cms x 31.7cms; no direction

CONTENT: house plans referred by letter to explanatory list; dimensions of houses and gardens included

ENDORSEMENT: Plan of Some Houses in Tavistock

19/3/26

TAVISTOCK
18th cent.   L1258/M&P/Tavistock 23

Tavistock Church SX 481744

Book of plans showing houses, gardens, and orchards and their relation to various streets, with dimensions. Paper has feint pencilled grid lines to facilitate production of scale plans. Scale appears to be 1" to 40 feet. 6 pages each 25.7cms x 40.2cms.

19/3/27

TAVISTOCK
1790   1508M/Surveys/V5

Tavistock Church SX 481744

See entry under Bovey, North, 2/21/2

19/3/28

TAVISTOCK

late 18th cent.   L1258/Maps/Tavistock 4

Southcombe Farm SX 393765

TITLE: 'An Eye Draft of the two Southcombe's in Lease to Jno Axworthy The yellow is No.22 in Survey and ye black is No.21'

SURVEYOR: not named

SCALE: not given

MATERIAL, SIZE & ORIENTATION: paper, damaged, slight colour; 37.3cms x 30.8cms; north-east to top

CONTENT: River Tamar, banks hatched with stream lines; fields named, with content, some outlined in colour; numeric reference to note in title; tree symbols showing coppice; buildings in plan, grey ; peripheral leaseholders 'under his Grace' named; Barton of Leigh named

DECORATION: 4 point compass indicator; north marked by fleur-de-lys, NSEW by letter

ENDORSEMENT: An Eye Draught of the Two Southcombs in Lease to John Axworthy

19/3/29

TAVISTOCK

18th cent.   L1258M/Maps/Roads 1

West Bridge Tavistock SX 482744   East Bridge Tavistock SX 484746

TITLE: not given; endorsement 'Plan of Roads about Tavistock'

SURVEYOR: not named

SCALE: not given

MATERIAL, SIZE & ORIENTATION: paper, watermark, ink; 69.6cms EW x 48.5cms NS; north to top

CONTENT: River Tavy, West Bridge, East Bridge; roads, fenced and unfenced, named within the town; directions given; some distant settlements named but not true to any scale – topological indication

DECORATION: 4 point plain compass indicator; NSEW marked by letter

19/3/30

TAVISTOCK

18th cent.   L1258M/Maps/Roads 2

Tavistock Church SX 481744 Okehampton Town Cross SX 587952

TITLE: not given; endorsed 'A Plan of Roads between Okehampton & Tavistock and Between Tavistock & Plymouth'

SURVEYOR: not named

SCALE: 'Furlongs'; scale bar; 1"=8 furlongs; 1:63360

MATERIAL, SIZE & ORIENTATION: paper, repaired, coloured; 22.6cms EW x 85.6cms NS; north to top

CONTENT: rivers, blue; Roborough Down, Whitchurch Down, Heathfield and Blackdown outlined in green; roads, plain or buff, directions given; footpaths, dotted lines; buildings in plan, red, giving an indication of larger settlements

19/3/31

TAVISTOCK

18th cent.   L1258M/Maps/Roads 8

Wringworthy Farm SX 500773

TITLE: not given

SURVEYOR: [Richard Turner]

SCALE: 'Chains, each 72 feet'; scale bar; 1"=1.5 chains; 1:1296

MATERIAL, SIZE & ORIENTATION: 2 pieces of paper, joined at one section only, slight colour; 60.2cms EW x 39.4cms NS; north to top; north-south line only, north marked by fleur-de-lys

CONTENT: fields outlined in ink, some named; some lessees named; hedge symbols indicating ownership; tree symbols showing orchards; roads, directions given and distances between two points, lettered A–B noted; buildings in plan, red; North Wringworthy Farm in elevation

19/3/32

TAVISTOCK

19th cent.   L1258 add 8M/E12/2

Wilminstone SX 495763

TITLE: 'Cakes Wilminstone 33a 3r 32p The Property of Mr James Blanchard'

SURVEYOR: not named

SCALE: not given

MATERIAL, SIZE & ORIENTATION: paper, ink; 40.7cms EW x 33.3cms NS; north to top

CONTENT: streams, bridge, mill; fields outlined in ink, named with content; tree symbols showing wood; potato plots; roads, directions given; buildings in plan, hatched grey; peripheral owners named

DECORATION: 4 point compass indicator, north marked by arrow

19/3/33

TAVISTOCK

1804   T1258M/E8

Tavistock Church SX 481744 Mount Tavy House SX 494751 (now Newton House)

Taviton Village SX 500744

TITLE: not given; map endorsed 'Plan of Lands exchanged with Mr Carpenter'

SURVEYOR: 'Tho: Jope Land-surveyor 1804'

SCALE: 'Statute Chains'; scale bar; 1"=3 chains; 1:2376

MATERIAL, SIZE & ORIENTATION: paper, mounted on linen, coloured; 214.4cms EW x 76.7cms NS; north to top

CONTENT: River Tavy, blue, stream lines; direction of flow indicated; streams and leats, blue; islands, yellow; 'Head Wear'; bridges; fields outlined in various colours with content; numeric reference to Explanation giving name of estate, name of occupier, content, name of landowner and how coloured on the map; tree symbols showing woods and 'Intended Plantation'; roads, buff, fenced and unfenced, some named; footpaths, pecked lines; buildings in plan, red or black; Mount Tavy House in elevation; peripheral parishes named

NOTES: that on a field called Jessop Hay the Canal Basin will be made; that there are stone quarries on Deer Park and that it is Mr Carpenter's intention to destroy part of the Turnpike leading to Moorton. Moorton SX 526739

INSET: Smaller inset map shows principal streets of Tavistock and other lands described in the map on the north of the River Tavy; 'Surveyor: Wm. Martin Junr'

DECORATION: 8 point plain compass indicator; north marked by fleur-de-lys, SEW by letter

19/3/34

TAVISTOCK

1825   1262M/E22/45

Tavistock Church SX 481744

See entry under Brentor, 2/33/3

19/3/35

TAVISTOCK

*c.*1827   L1258M/SS/L/14

Morwell Down Plantation SX 456715

TITLE: 'Sketch of Morwell Down Parish of Tavistock'

SURVEYOR: not named

SCALE: not given

MATERIAL, SIZE & ORIENTATION: paper, ink; 53cms x 32.6cms; north east to top

CONTENT: Morwell Down outlined in ink; roads, fenced and unfenced; directions given; peripheral owners named

DECORATION: 4 point compass indicator; north marked by fleur-de-lys

ENDORSEMENT: Plan of Morwell Down

ASSOCIATED DOCUMENTS; letters regarding Inclosure, rights of Commoners; application to Parliament; Inclosure Agreement; Act passed in 1828

19/3/36

TAVISTOCK

1835   L1258 Maps/Tavistock 5

Taviton Village SX 500744 Kingford Farm SX 504752

TITLE: not given; endorsement 'Plan of Taviton Down'

SURVEYOR: not named

SCALE: not given

MATERIAL, SIZE & ORIENTATION: paper, watermark, ink; 32.4cms EW x 40.5cms NS; north to top; north-south line only with north marked by fleur-de-lys

CONTENT: 3 fields outlined in ink, named with content; total content; roads, fenced and unfenced, direction given; building, Kingford, in plan, hatched black; Kingford Farm and Part of Tavyton Barton named

ENDORSEMENT: Plan of Taviton Barton sent up Dec 1835 with a proposal of exchange of this farm with Mr Carpenter at Pellow

19/3/37

TAVISTOCK

| [1835–8] | L1258 add Devon/L & P 16 |

Heathfield SX 464792

TITLE: not given

SURVEYOR: not named

SCALE: 'Scale of Chains'; scale bar; 1"=8 chains; 1:6336

MATERIAL, SIZE & ORIENTATION: paper (torn), slight colour; 59.8cms EW x 48.8cms NS; north to top

CONTENT: rivers, streams, blue; fields outlined in ink with owners' names and some with content; roads, fenced and unfenced; directions given; footpaths, broken lines; mine; 'Battens Steps'; peripheral owners and parishes named

DECORATION: 4 point compass indicator; north marked by fleur-de-lys, EW by letter

19/3/38

TAVISTOCK

| 1836 | L1258 Maps/Tavistock 25 |

Morwell Down Plantation SX 455715 The Rock Crossroads SX 451752

TITLE: 'Morwell Down in the Parish of Tavistock in the County of Devon'

SURVEYOR: 'John King Lethbridge 1836'

SCALE: 'Scale of Lengths'; scale bar shows chains; 1"=10 chains; 1:7920

MATERIAL, SIZE & ORIENTATION: paper, slight colour; 64.5cms EW x 97cms NS; north to top

CONTENT: fields outlined in ink and coloured according to allotments; alphabetic reference to list giving details of allotments and content; asterisks indicate responsibility for repairs of fences; roads, buff, fenced and unfenced; directions given; peripheral owners named

NOTE: at bottom of the map; This is the Map of Morwell Down referred to in the accompanying Award

DECORATION: 8 point compass rose, shaded-line decoration; north marked by decorated arrowhead

TAVISTOCK see also B8, B45, B116, C161-62

19/4/1

TAWSTOCK

| 1765–1770 | Z17/3/42 b/w photograph |

Roundswell SS 541310 Rowden SS 537301 Eastacombe SS 538297 Nottiston SS 530298 Westacomb and Gulliford not identified

Pages 151–152 in the Sturt Estate Atlas

TITLE: 'The leasehold Estates At Roundswell, Rouden, Eastacomb, Westacomb, Gulliford & Nottiston &c in the Manor of Hele Parish of Tawstock And County of Devon'

SURVEYOR: Isaac Taylor

SCALE: 'A Scale of Chains or ½ a Mile'; divided scale; 1"=9 chains; 1:7128

MATERIAL, SIZE & ORIENTATION: map size 41.6cms EW x 31.5cms NS; north to top

CONTENT: rivers; fields outlined with hedge symbols; estates distinguished in ?colour and named; fields named with tenants' names in addition; numeric reference [to list]; freehold fields show content only; gates; tree symbols showing orchards, woods etc; roads, directions given; buildings in plan; peripheral owners and parishes named; alpha-numeric grid-reference system

DECORATION: title cartouche: elaborated design of scrolls, leaves, lion's mask, 2 sieves; 8 point plain compass rose; north marked by letter N

19/4/2

TAWSTOCK

| 1765–1770 | Z17/3/42 b/w photograph |

Rushcott Farm SS 529290 Rooty Cross SS 529286 Charlacot Cross SS 538279 Tennacot SS 534277 Bettiford not identified

Pages 157–158 of the Sturt Estate Atlas

TITLE: 'The Leasehold Estates At Bettiford, Rushcot, Ruty, Charlacot, and Tennacot in the Manor of Hele Parish of Tawstock and County of Devon'

SURVEYOR: Isaac Taylor

SCALE: 'A Scale of Chains ½ a Mile'; divided scale; 1"= 9 chains; 1:7128

MATERIAL, SIZE & ORIENTATION: map size 40cms x 31.2cms; no direction

CONTENT: see previous Tawstock map

DECORATION: title cartouche: drapery drawn back below pediment decorated with acanthus leaves, and in centre globe surrounded by laurel wreath; 8 point plain compass rose with no indication of north

19/4/3

TAWSTOCK
1765–1770   Z17/3/42 b/w photograph

Hele Manor SS 544322

Page 148 of the Sturt Estate Atlas

TITLE: 'The Manor Farm of Hele and Templand in the Parish of Tawstock
   and County of Devon'

SURVEYOR: Isaac Taylor

SCALE: 'A Scale of Chains, 10 to 1 furlong'; scale bar; 1"=9 chains;
   1:7128

MATERIAL, SIZE & ORIENTATION: 22.7cms x 35cms; south-west to top

CONTENT: River Taw, banks shaded; on one bank 'The Tenants of the
   Manor of Hele , used to fetch their sand from hence'; 'Barnstaple
   Bridge 16 Arches'; marsh; fields outlined with hedge symbols and
   some trees, named; numeric reference [to list] gates; tree symbols
   showing orchards, woods and isolated trees; roads, directions given;
   Turnpike House and gate; footpaths, double pricked lines; buildings
   in plan, those in Barnstaple generalised; peripheral owner and parish
   named; alpha-numeric grid-reference system

DECORATION: title cartouche: elaborate rococo; 8 point plain compass
   rose; NS marked by letter

19/4/4

TAWSTOCK
1792   NDRO 2288A add/PF62

Collabear SS 545286

TITLE: 'A Plan of the Poor Lands at Collibear at Tawstock Devon 1798'

SURVEYOR: not named

SCALE: 'Scale of Chains each containing 66 feet'; scale bar; 1"=4 chains;
   1:3168

MATERIAL, SIZE & ORIENTATION: paper, coloured; 50.5cms x 39.1cms; no
   direction

CONTENT: stream, double ink line, arrow marking direction of flow; fields
   outlined in green, alphabetic reference to table giving field names
   and content; crosses indicating hedge ownership; roads outlined in
   light green, directions given; buildings in plan, brown; peripheral
   owners named

TAWSTOCK see also C163

19/5/1

TAWTON, NORTH
1765–1770   Z17/3/42 b/w photograph

Stone Farm SS 684017

Pages 169–170 photographed in an atlas of estate maps belonging to the
Sturt family of Dorset, mapped by Isaac Taylor of Ross-on-Wye

TITLE: 'A General Map of Leasehold Estates in the Manor of Stone,
   alias Crook-Burnel In the Parish of North Tawton & County of Devon'

SURVEYOR: Isaac Taylor

SCALE: 'A Scale of 40 Chains or ½ A Mile'; scale bar; 1"=10 chains;
   1:7920

MATERIAL, SIZE & ORIENTATION: map 40cms x 31cms; north east to top

CONTENT: stream, fields outlined in ink with hedge symbols outlining
   holdings which are named; gates; roads, fenced and unfenced;
   buildings in plan; peripheral owners, commons, moors and parishes
   named; grid but no reference system

DECORATION: title cartouche: architectural-style frame with pediment,
   pendant swags of foliage and flowers; 8 point plain compass rose;
   north marked by letter

19/5/2

TAWTON, NORTH
1756–1770   Z17/3/42 b/w photograph

Crooke Burnell SS 684009

Page 172 from the Sturt estate atlas

TITLE: 'Crook Farm in the Manor of Stone, & Parish of North Tawton in
   the County of Devon'

SURVEYOR: Isaac Taylor

SCALE: no unit of measurement stated; scale bar; 1"=8 ?

MATERIAL, SIZE & ORIENTATION: 22.5cms EW x 35cms NS; south to top

CONTENT: pond, stream; fields outlined with hedge symbols, named;
   numeric reference to list giving field names, fields adjoining, content
   and grid reference; gates; tree symbols showing orchards and isolated
   trees; roads, fenced and unfenced; directions given; buildings in plan;
   peripheral owners, farms and commons named; alpha-numeric grid-
   reference system

DECORATION: title cartouche: scrolls, shells, leaves and flowers; 8 point
   plain compass rose; NS marked by letter

19/5/3

TAWTON, NORTH

1765–1770   Z17/3/42 b/w photograph

Stone Farm SS 684017

Page 174 from the Sturt estate atlas

TITLE: 'Lower Stone Middle Stone Upper Stone, and Crook Down In the Parish of North Tawton and County of Devon'

SURVEYOR: Isaac Taylor

SCALE: 'A Scale of 20 Chaines, or ¼ of A Mile'; scale bar; 1"= 9 chains; 1:7128

MATERIAL, SIZE & ORIENTATION: 22.5cms EW x 35cms NS; south-east to top

CONTENT: stream; fields outlined with hedge and tree symbols, named; numeric reference [to list]; gates; tree symbols showing orchards and isolated trees; roads; buildings in plan; peripheral owners and estates named; alpha-numeric grid-reference system

DECORATION: title cartouche: rococo with scrolls and acanthus leaves; figure entering records in book above; 8 point plain compass rose; north marked by letter

INSET: drawing of cottage and barns

19/5/4

TAWTON, NORTH

c.1780   Private hands Photocopy

North Tawton Church SS 664017

TITLE: not given [map is concerned with lands belonging to the glebe]

SURVEYOR: not named

SCALE: no unit of measurement stated; scale bar; 1"=1?chain; 1:?792

MATERIAL, SIZE & ORIENTATION: ?paper, ?coloured; 29.7cms EW x 40.2cms NS; north to top

CONTENT: ?pond, stippled with depth marked; fields outlined with hedge symbols indicating ownership; tree symbols showing orchard and isolated trees in churchyard; gardens, that in front of the Parsonage in some detail; hopgarden; pound; roads, directions given and measured distances across field and on the road towards Bondleigh; footpath, pecked lines; Town Cross; lych gate; pump; buildings in elevation including the church, parsonage and school

DECORATION: 4 point compass indicator; north marked by symbol, SEW by letter; dividers above scale bar

TAWTON, NORTH see also C164

19/6/1

TAWTON, SOUTH

1811   69/1/3/1

South Tawton Church SX 653944

TITLE: 'Map of Town Barton Situate in the Parish of South-Tawton and County of Devon the Lands of Messrs. F & T Hole, Surveyed in the year 1811. By W. Croote'

SURVEYOR: W. Croote

SCALE: 'Scale of Chains'; scale bar; 1"=3 chains; 1:2376

MATERIAL, SIZE & ORIENTATION: parchment, coloured; 61.5cms EW x 52.5cms NS; north to top

CONTENT: 'The River Taw', blue; fields, green with numeric references [to table]; 'asterisms' indicating hedge ownership; roads, directions given; buildings in plan; church in elevation; peripheral owners named

DECORATION: title cartouche: acanthus leaves, flowers and scrolls intertwined and below, a trowel, set square with dividers and a mason's maul or 'common gavel' implying a connection with Free-masonry; scale bar, yellow; 8 point compass rose; north marked by fleur-de-lys

19/6/2

TAWTON, SOUTH

1811   53/6 Box 51/50

South Tawton Church SX 653944

TITLE: 'Map of Addlehole Situate in the Parish of South-Tawton and County of Devon the lands of Messrs F & T Hole, Surveyed in the year 1811, By W. Croote'

SURVEYOR: W. Croote

SCALE: 'Scale of Chains'; scale bar; 1"=3 chains; 1:2376

MATERIAL, SIZE & ORIENTATION: parchment, coloured; 51.7cms EW x 68.4cms NS; north to top

CONTENT: river and stream, blue; direction of flow indicated; pond, blue; fields, green with numeric reference [to table]; 'asterisms' indicating hedge ownership; gates; roads, buff; footpaths, pecked lines; buildings in plan, red or plain; church and church house in elevation; pumps marked by black lines; kilns, yellow or red; peripheral owners and estates named

INSET: map of 'The State of Lime Quarry and Lime Kilns, now in work, with the Fields that have been did'd up, And the Fields that are covered with the Rubbish'; quarry area, grey

DECORATION: title cartouche: acanthus leaves, flowers and scrolls; below, trowel, set square with dividers and a mason's maul or 'common gavel' implying a connection with Freemasonry; scale: yellow; 8 point compass rose, black/plain; north marked by fleur-de-lys

19/6/3

TAWTON, SOUTH
1837   4210Z/Z74

Powlesland Farm SX 688960 West Nymph SX 668958

TITLE: 'A Map of Nymph and Powlesland Estates in the Parish of South Tawton property of Mr Phillip Cann. A.D. 1837'

SURVEYOR: not named

SCALE: 'Scale of Chains'; scale bar; 1"=4 chains; 1:3168

MATERIAL, SIZE & ORIENTATION: paper, coloured; 53.4cms x 66.2cms; north-west to top

CONTENT: Long Brook, ink stream lines; fields outlined in various colours, named; table listing names of fields, 'Measurement within the fences', 'Gross measurement'; estates of Nymph and Powlesland distinguished; gates; crude tree symbols showing plantations; roads, buff, directions given; footpaths, pecked lines; buildings in plan, red; ownership of estate boundary fences distinguished by colour; peripheral estates named

DECORATION: title cartouche: oval medallion, blue, yellow, red with a running pattern of leaves; blue, red and yellow border to table; scale bar, green, red and yellow with dividers in blue and yellow above; 8 point compass rose, red/yellow, blue/yellow in yellow outer circle; north marked by red and yellow fleur-de-lys; border, red and yellow

19/7/1

TEDBURN ST MARY
1767   2729Z/E1

East Upacott SX 821942

TITLE: 'A Map of East Upacott in Tedburn St Mary. Lands of John Newcombe Esqr'

SURVEYOR: 'William Hayman Surveyor in Exeter'

SCALE: 'a scale of chains'; scale bar; 1"=2 chains; 1:1584

MATERIAL, SIZE & ORIENTATION: paper, coloured; 44.2cms EW x 57.3cms NS; south to top

CONTENT: river, bridge; fields with reference to table giving field names and content; hedge symbols, green, indicating ownership; gates; tree symbols showing coppice; roads, footpaths; buildings in plan, grey; peripheral owners named

DECORATION: title cartouche: two gothic pillars with crocketed spires joined by semi-circular arch; 16 point compass rose, blue/black, blue, black, inner segments blue and gold; north marked by fleur-de-lys, south by arrow

19/7/2

TEDBURN ST MARY
1775   SRO DD/HIc/738(521/3)

Tedburn St Mary Church SX 817942
See entry under Cullompton, 3/35/4

19/7/3

TEDBURN ST MARY
1788–1789   6107

Tedburn St Mary Church SX 817942
See entry under Bridestowe, 2/35/6

19/7/4

TEDBURN ST MARY
1798   Z17/3/7

Oak Farm SX 818931
See entry under Dunsford, 4/13/5

19/7/5

TEDBURN ST MARY
1834   253B/ME9

Rubhay SX 805951
See entry under Colebrooke, 3/26/9

TEIGNMOUTH see B36–37, B40, B69, B83, B89–90, B92, B94

19/8/1

TEIGNMOUTH, EAST

1756   ECA Book 58

East Teignmouth Church SX 943732

See entry under Exeter Chamber Map Book, 5/3/48

19/8/2

TEIGNMOUTH, EAST

1759   D1508M/M&P/Teignmouth Maps 1

East Teignmouth Church SX 943732

TITLE: 'A Map of the Manor of East Teignmouth alias Teignmouth-Courtenay also that part of the Manor of Kenton which lies in the Parishes of East and West Teignmouth in the County of Devon, being the Lands of the Honble Sir Willm Courtenay Bart Survey'd in Septr 1759 by Mr Wm Hole'

SURVEYOR: William Hole

SCALE: 'A Scale of Chains'; scale bar; 1"=2 chains; 1:1584

MATERIAL, SIZE & ORIENTATION: parchment, coloured; 134.8cms EW x 113.5cms NS; north to top

CONTENT: 'Mouth of the River Teign'; present and ancient course of the river Tame marked; cliffs indicated by hill shading; beach stippled; high water mark; 'The Denn' coloured green indicating pasture; considerable information about the use and misuse of this area; marsh, stippled blue; roads, direction given; buildings in plan; East and West Teignmouth churches in elevation; boundaries of manors and parishes indicated verbally and with symbols; table giving details of leaseholders, tenements and content; references to the 'Abstract Book'

DECORATION: 16 point compass rose, plain/black, plain/grey; north marked by fleur-de-lys, SEW by letter

ENDORSEMENT: East Teignmouth and part of Kenton

19/8/3

TEIGNMOUTH, EAST

1767   1919Z/p.67

Holcombe Down SX 937750

TITLE: 'A Plan of an Estate called Southcott's Ground Situate in the Parish of East Teignmouth in the county of Devon; the Property of Mr. Henry Tarrant of the City Christopher Hamlyn; Surveyd et Del 1767'

SURVEYOR: Christopher Hamlyn

SCALE: 'A Scale of Chains and Links'; divided scale; 1"=3 chains; 1:2376

MATERIAL, SIZE & ORIENTATION: paper, mounted in a volume (modern History of Teignmouth), slight colour; 36.8cms EW x 53.2cms NS; north to top

CONTENT: fields outlined with hedge symbols, named; alphabetic reference to table repeating field names with content; 'asterisms' indicating hedge ownership; gates; tree symbols showing hedgerow and isolated trees; roads, brown, marked by double broken lines; Woodway Lane named, directions given; peripheral owners, common land and Holcombe Down named; note that 'This Estate has a Right of Common on Holcome [sic] Down'

DECORATION: title cartouche: view of church and churchyard wall; 32 point compass rose, plain/grey; north marked by fleur-de-lys, NSEW by letter; scale, brown

---

19/8/4

TEIGNMOUTH, EAST

1771   1508M/London/M&P/Teignmouth 1

East Teignmouth Church SX 943732

TITLE: 'A Plan of the Harbour of Teignmouth, Taken in May 1771'

SURVEYOR: not named

SCALE: 'A Scale of Chains, each containing 4 Statute-Perches'; scale bar; 1"=6 chains; 1:4752

MATERIAL, SIZE & ORIENTATION: paper, coloured; 37.7cms EW x 23.7cms NS; north to top

CONTENT: river Teign, yellow and black lines; arrow indicating direction of flow; Lang Pool, The Bite, Shaldown Pool, The Passage Point, mouth of the river, Ness Point, the bar, 'The Main Sea' all named; high and low water marks of the common spring tides; Sprat Sand and the Eastern Pole, yellow; sand bank called Salthay, brook or rivulet called Tame and other brooks, grey; two parts of Lord

Courtenay's manor, yellow and green; 'Place where a wind mill stood'; fort; houses in elevation

DECORATION: 8 point compass rose, black/plain; north marked by fleur-de-lys, east by cross

19/8/5

TEIGNMOUTH, EAST

1787   Powderham Archive

East Teignmouth Church SX 943732

See entry under Powderham, 16/12/7

19/8/6

TEIGNMOUTH, EAST

early 19th cent.   1508M Devon/M&P/Teignmouth 4

East Teignmouth Church SX 943732

TITLE: not given; shows 'Teingmouth Denn'

SURVEYOR: not named

SCALE: no unit of measurement stated; scale bar shows Chains and Feet; 1"=2 chains; 1:1584

MATERIAL, SIZE & ORIENTATION: paper, watermark, ink with slight colour; 74.2cms x 46cms; north-west to top

CONTENT: coast, ink with form lines; Passage Point named; river 'Tame' and 'The River Teing' named; roads, fenced and unfenced, direction given; buildings in plan, hatched black; some buildings plain, outlined in orange; 3 terraces facing the sea outlined in orange with front and back gardens named and outlined in green; some houses indicated with numbers and names inserted; 'East Teingmouth' church in elevation; Fort facing the sea shown by shading

NOTE: this map gives the impression of being drawn for a builder developing the sea front and other areas in the town

DECORATION: 4 point compass indicator; north marked by fleur-de-lys

ENDORSEMENT: Teigno = The Denn

TEIGNMOUTH, EAST see also B46, B56

19/9/1

TEIGNMOUTH, WEST

1727   1508M Devon/Maps/Special Subjects/Rivers M 1

Bishopsteignton SX 911735

West Teignmouth Church SX 939731

TITLE: 'A Draught of The Harbor of Teignmouth, By Richard Prowse, August ye 15th 1727'; shows the river from Teignmouth to Newton Abbot

SURVEYOR: Richard Prowse

SCALE: 'A Scale of English miles'; scale bar; 1"=*c.*15 chains; 1:11880

MATERIAL, SIZE & ORIENTATION: parchment, ink and grey colour; 78cms EW x 36.2cms NS; north to top

CONTENT: river shown with channel marked by dotted lines; sandbanks, stippled and named – Sprat land, Saltey, Ridge, midle sands; features named on river banks – arches brook (south bank); ballace Stone, bittern, broad mead, kithill, red b–, Salton, floor[point], sea mill (north bank); off shore, 'Windmill' and 'the Fort' shown by pictographs; lands adjoining the river, grey with some tree symbols, houses and churches in elevation; following features named – Shaldown, Renmor [Ringmore], Teingharvy, Coom cellers, Metheton [Netherton] (south bank); East Teingmh, West Teingmh, Park, Bishopstenton church, coles barne, p'sons house, [ki]lt house, Lower Ware, uper Ware, cley houses, Kingstenton, milber, highWek, newton, milber, Ford (north bank); rhumb lines with 4 fleur-de-lys indicating north, grey

ENDORSEMENT: Chart of the Harbour of Teignmouth

19/9/2

TEIGNMOUTH, WEST

1756   ECA Book 58

West Teignmouth Church SX 939731

See entry under Exeter Chamber Map Book, 5/3/48

19/9/3

TEIGNMOUTH, WEST

1759   D1508M/M&P/Teignmouth Maps 1

West Teignmouth Church SX 939731

See entry under Teignmouth, East, 19/8/2

19/9/4

TEIGNMOUTH, WEST

1787   Powderham Archive

West Teignmouth Church SX 939731
See entry under Powderham, 16/12/7

19/9/5

TEIGNMOUTH, WEST

1790   5846Z/E6

Bitton House SX 936731
TITLE: 'Map of Bitton Estate situated in the parish of West=Teignmouth in the County of Devon The Property of William Mackworth Praed Esqr Taken in 1790 by Alexr Law'
SURVEYOR: Alexander Law
SCALE: 'Scale of Statute Chains each containing 66 feet'; scale bar; 1"=3 chains 1:2376
MATERIAL, SIZE & ORIENTATION: parchment, slight colour; 34.8cms EW x 28.5cms NS; north to top
CONTENT: streams, river [Teign] stippled; margin thick black line marking 'High Water mark at ordinary Tides'; fields outlined in green, alphabetic reference to table giving names of parcels, land use and content; 'asterisms' indicating hedge ownership; gates, red; tree symbols showing orchard, plantation and isolated trees; roads, buff, fenced and unfenced; directions given; buildings in plan, grey
DECORATION: title cartouche: simple rococo, ruched fabric; 8 point compass rose, black/plain; north marked by fleur-de-lys, east by cross; sailing and rowing boats on river

19/9/6

TEIGNMOUTH, WEST

1829   260M add/P1

West Teignmouth Church SX 939731
TITLE: 'Map of Land in the Parish of West Teignmouth Devon The Property of the late James Coysh Esqr 1829'
SURVEYOR: J. Taperell
SCALE: 'Scale of Chains'; scale bar; 1"=4 chains; 1:3168
MATERIAL, SIZE & ORIENTATION: parchment, coloured; 39.1cms EW x 41.7cms NS; north to top

CONTENT: stream, blue, direction of flow indicated; fields, green with numeric reference to table giving field name, content excluding hedges, content including hedges and total content; 'asterisms' indicating hedge ownership; hedgerow symbols; tree symbols showing orchards; roads, buff, directions given; footpaths, pecked lines; buildings in plan, red or grey
DECORATION: 8 point compass rose, shaded line decoration; north marked by fleur-de-lys; magnetic north indicated

TEIGNMOUTH, WEST see also B56, C165–66

19/10/1

TEMPLETON

early 19th cent.   Diocesan Glebe Terriers Templeton

Templeton Church SS 888140
TITLE: 'A Map of the Glebe of Templeton Parish'
SURVEYOR: not named
SCALE: not given
MATERIAL, SIZE & ORIENTATION: parchment, coloured; 19.7cms EW x 26.5cms NS; north to top
CONTENT: River Dart and tributaries, blue; arrows indicating direction of flow; fields, shades of green or blue; numeric reference to list giving field names, space for content but not entered; fields outside the glebe with owners' names in red; tree symbols; roads, buff, directions given; buildings in plan, named; 'Temple' Church marked by cross
DECORATION: 'GLEBE' in title decorated with terrier (dog) incorporated in capital G; 4 point compass indicator; north marked by arrowhead
ENDORSEMENT: Map and Terrier of the Glebe Lands of Templeton Tempore Edwardi Pole Rectoris huius Ecclesiae

19/11/1

THORNBURY

1694   National Library of Scotland
                      Minto Collection MS 13421 Photocopy at 2536Z/Z1

Thornbury Church SS 401084
See entry under Milton Damerel, 13/14/1

19/11/2

THORNBURY
1825   2569B/Estate/4/13

Little Lashbrook SS 405071

TITLE: 'Little Lashbrook in the Parish of Thornbury' annotation 'The
   Property of M H Coham'

SURVEYOR: not named

SCALE: 'Scale of Chains'; scale bar; 1"=5 chains; 1:3960

MATERIAL, SIZE & ORIENTATION: parchment, coloured; 24.5cms EW x
   38cms NS; north to top

CONTENT: river Torridge, streams and ponds, blue; fields outlined in blue,
   pink or green; numeric reference to lists on separate sheets giving
   field names, content of arable, hedges and total content; note: 'Hedges
   dotted on the outside belong to the adjoining Premises'; green tree
   symbols showing orchards, hedgerow and isolated trees; roads, buff,
   fenced and unfenced; directions given; footpaths, buff, pecked lines;
   buildings in plan, red; peripheral owners named

DECORATION: 8 point compass rose, plain/grey; north marked by fleur-
   de-lys, grey

THORNBURY see also B25

19/12/1

THORNCOMBE (now in Dorset)
1793   Bristol RO 40906/20

Thorncombe Church ST 376033

TITLE: 'Bateman and Westham Park Farms in Thorncoomb Devon. The
   Property of the Honorable James Everard Arundell And his Lady'

SURVEYOR: 'By Wm Bond of Axminster February 28th 1793'

MATERIAL, SIZE & ORIENTATION: parchment, ink; 65.8cms EW x 55.6cms
   NS (framed); north to top

CONTENT: 'Ax River', streams, black stream lines, arrow indicating
   direction of flow; bridge; relief shown by hill shading; fields outlined
   with numeric reference [to Survey Book]; hedge symbols indicating
   ownership; gates; tree symbols showing woods; tree symbols with
   stippling marking ?waste; gardens with some detail; roads, plain;
   footpaths, pecked lines; buildings in plan, hatched black or grey;
   peripheral owners named

DECORATION: 4 point compass indicator; north marked by fleur-de-lys,
   east by symbol and south by fletched arrow

19/13/1

THORVERTON
1770   Private hands

Bowley SS 908042
See entry under Cadbury, 3/1/1

19/13/2

THORVERTON
18th cent.   Private hands

Fursdon SS 925046 Chilton SS 922058 Perry SS 928056
See entry under Cadbury, 3/1/2

19/13/3

THORVERTON
1808   253B/ME8

Raddon Court SS 903026

TITLE: 'Rough Map of Raddon Court and East Raddon Estates in
   Thorverton Parish and County of Devon The Property of Rd Hippisley
   Tuckfield Esqr 1808'

SURVEYOR: not named

SCALE: not given

MATERIAL, SIZE & ORIENTATION: paper, coloured; 92.4cms x 166cms; no
   direction

CONTENT: river, pond, blue; tributary streams, black; fields, various
   colours, outlined in darker shades; field and tenants' names; numeric
   reference [to Survey Book]; gates; tree symbols showing orchards;
   stippling marking brakes [brushwood]; formal gardens in plan; stone
   quarries; roads, buff, some directions given; footpaths, pecked lines;
   buildings in plan, pink or hatched in black; peripheral owners named

PUBLICATION: Todd Gray, *The Garden History of Devon* (Exeter, 1995),
   188

19/13/4

THORVERTON

1812   Ex. D&C Ch. Comm. 6055/12

Thorverton Church SS 924022

TITLE: 'Map of Thorverton by Coldridge 1812'

SURVEYOR: John Coldridge

SCALE: 'Scale of Statute Chains each containing four perches or 66 feet'; scale bar; 1"=6 chains; 1:4752

MATERIAL, SIZE & ORIENTATION: parchment, coloured; 72.4cms EW x 88.3cms NS; north to top

CONTENT: rivers, green; streams, grey; bridges; weir; relief shown by hill shading; fields outlined in various colours with numeric reference [to table]; alphabetic reference to list on map giving field names; asterisks indicating hedge/fence boundaries; tree symbols showing orchards; roads, some directions given; footpaths, dotted lines; buildings in plan, grey; peripheral owners named

DECORATION: 8 point compass rose, black/plain; north marked by fleur-de-lys

ASSOCIATED DOCUMENTS: Exeter D&C 3577 Chapter Act Book p.56 13 March 1811 They directed the Manors of Thorverton Colyton and Bole Aller to be mapped and valued by Mr Coldridge, and the expenses thereof to be paid out of the timber fund.

p. 333 22 Dec 1813 Among bills to be paid – Mr John Coldridge on account towards his bill for the new map of Thorverton 50.0.0

19/13/5

THORVERTON

1813   Pearse Box 141/4/27a–b

Thorverton Church SS 924022

TITLE: 'Plan of Tenements in the Manor of Thorverton held under the Dean and Chapter of Exeter by Martin Sanford – 1 November 1813'

SURVEYOR: John Coldridge

SCALE: not given

MATERIAL, SIZE & ORIENTATION: parchment, coloured; 10cms x 19.4cms; no direction

CONTENT: river, black stream lines; bridge; roads, buff, Milfords Lane named; cottages, hatched black; premises granted, yellow and adjoining plots to these have numeric reference [to Survey Book]

ASSOCIATED DOCUMENT: Lease by the Dean and Chapter of Exeter to Martin Sanford dated 27 August 1818

19/13/6

THORVERTON

1813/1814   Ex. D&C Ch. Comm. 98/8786

Thorverton Church SS 924022

Atlas, 27cms x 35.2cms, of 11 maps with Reference Tables opposite followed by 2 pages of Abstract

TITLE: 'A Survey of the Manor of Thorverton Devon. The Property of The Venerable Dean and Chapter of Exeter Done by John Coldridge in the years 1813 & 1814'

SURVEYOR: John Coldridge

SCALE: 'Scale of Statute Chains each containing 66 Feet'; scale bars; 1"=9 or 6 chains; 1:7128 or 1:4752

MATERIAL, SIZE & ORIENTATION: parchment, coloured; 27cms x 35.2cms; direction indicated on each map

GENERAL CONTENT: River Exe named, blue with stream lines; tributaries; arrows indicating direction of flow; relief shown by hill shading; fields outlined in colour according to holding; alpha-numeric reference to list opposite giving field names, land use, content and total content; asterisks indicating hedge ownership; gateways; tree symbols showing orchards, isolated and hedgerow trees; with stippling marking copses; roads; buildings in plan, grey; peripheral owners named

DECORATION: 8 point plain compass rose; north marked by fleur-de-lys

MAPS:-

Stone & Pitt

Batcombe and Easton

Bidwell. Court Hayes; scale 1:9.5 chains; 1:7524

Thorverton Court Barton; shows Thorverton Bridge and Weir

Channons Ashley

Hole's Barliabin's; scale 1"=6 chains; 1:4752

Glebe. Cleave's. Burt's.; scale 1"=6 chains; 1:4752; shows Thorverton Mill

Home Tenem,t Mills; scale 1"=6 chains; 1:4752; shows Thorverton Mills

Pyne's. Purls and Tickels

Yellowford; scale 1"=9.5 chains; 1:7524

Thorverton; scale 1"=3 chains; 1:2376; house plots with numeric reference to list giving occupiers' names and measured quantity

ASSOCIATED DOCUMENT: Exeter D&C Chapter Act Book p.523 20 & 21 Dec 1815 Among bills to be paid – The same (John Coldridge) for map of Thorverton 27.11.0

THORVERTON see also C167

THROWLEIGH see C36

19/14/1

THRUSHELTON
[1609] 189M add 3/E4/3

Wollocott SX 533925
TITLE: not given; original title in a square, now removed but note nearby 'the litle platt ye lieth at the west end of ye litle mead with this sign + set in it is now of Wollocot as the fermour saye'
SURVEYOR: not named
SCALE: not given
MATERIAL, SIZE & ORIENTATION: paper, watermark, coloured; 30.9cms EW x 61cms NS; directions spelt out on margins of map; east to top
CONTENT: 'Thrushell Ryver', and other streams, blue; fields, green, named; gates; tree symbols showing woods; roads and footpaths, red lines, part following lane, part crossing fields and crossing through houses; houses in elevation, crudely drawn
    Square area marked with wavy lines intended for title but removed and now repaired
ENDORSEMENT: Wollocott

19/14/2

THRUSHELTON
1788–1789 6107

Thrushelton SX 447876
See entry under Bridestowe, 2/35/6

19/14/3

THRUSHELTON
1810 Tremayne Collection, unlisted

Musehill SX 450873 Canon Barn SX 444871
See entry under Marystow, 13/8/3

19/15/1

THURLESTONE
1777 215M/ZF28

Whitley SX 698442
TITLE: 'Map of the Barton of Whiteley in the Parish of Thurlestone and County of Devon Survey'd in May 1777, by E Reed and J Paddon'
SURVEYORS: E Reed and J Paddon
SCALE: 'A Scale of Chains'; scale bar; 1"=3 chains; 1:2376
MATERIAL, SIZE & ORIENTATION: parchment, coloured, damaged; 56.2cms EW x 49.4cms NS; north to top
CONTENT: fields outlined in green; alphabetical reference to table giving field names and content; 'asterisms' indicating hedge ownership; some owners named; tree symbols; road, direction given; buildings in plan, grey
DECORATION: title cartouche: acanthus leaves; 8 point compass rose; north marked by fleur-de-lys

19/15/2

THURLESTONE
1777 1508M Devon/M&P/V3

Thurlestone Church SX 673429
See entry under Alvington, West, 1/6/1

19/16/1

TIVERTON
1724 NDRO 2309B/FS32/2–3

East Barton SS 945087
TITLE: 'East barton in Tiverton divided into two Parts about the Year 1724'
SURVEYOR: not named
SCALE: not given
MATERIAL, SIZE & ORIENTATION: paper, coloured; 24.6cms EW x 38.5cms NS; north to top
CONTENT: River Exe, tributary streams, blue; arrow indicating direction of flow; fields with numeric reference to separate table listing houses, barns etc and fields by name with content; the 'two Parts' outlined in blue and red; gates; crosses indicating hedge ownership; tree symbols showing woods, named; road, buff, named; footpaths, dotted lines; buildings in plan, red or blue

DECORATION: 4 point compass indicator; north marked by fleur-de-lys, SEW by letter

NOTE: the document, separate from the map, is dated 1798

19/16/2

TIVERTON

| 1750 | King's College Cambridge Archive SJP 231 |

Copplestone SS 986126 Manley SS 989118

TITLE: 'Late Coppleston's and Sellick's Farm at Manley in Tiverton Devon 1750'

SURVEYOR: not named

SCALE: not given

MATERIAL, SIZE & ORIENTATION: paper, watermark, ink; 32.3cms EW x 77.3cms NS; east to top

CONTENT: 'A fine spring'; fields outlined in ink with solid and broken lines, named; 2 holdings distinguished by letter and listed giving field names and content, 'Hedges &c included' in statutory and customary measure – under customary list '16 Foot to Perch'; gardens and courtlage; orchard, woodland, waste and furze named; 'Improved Land' named; roads, directions given; buildings in plan; peripheral estates named

DECORATION: 4 point compass indicator; north marked by letter

ENDORSEMENT: St James's Priory Copplestone's & Sellacks Tenements 1750

19/16/3

TIVERTON

| 1756 | 1148M/add23/E1 |

Lurley SS 924148

See entry under Broadclyst, 2/39/2

19/16/4

TIVERTON

| [after 1764] | Knightshayes Estate Office |

Mills SS 950142

TITLE: 'A Plan of Marsh, Haydon, Coydon, Little Marsh and a Set of Dye-stuff Mills in Tiverton Devon'

SURVEYOR: not named

SCALE: 'A Scale of Chains each 4 Poles or 66 Feet long'; scale bar; 1"=4 chains; 1:3168

MATERIAL, SIZE & ORIENTATION: parchment, coloured; map in 2 pieces; 45cms EW x 68.6cms NS; and 45.5cms EW x 38.6cms NS; north-south line

CONTENT: 'River Ex', arrow indicating direction of flow; fields outlined in various colours according to holding and with alpha-numeric reference to table giving field name and content; symbols indicating hedge ownership; gates; green tree symbols showing orchard and isolated trees; roads, buff, directions given; buildings in plan, dye-stuff mills named; peripheral owners named

Key describing symbols for genus of tree

19/16/5

TIVERTON

| 1774 | Knightshayes Estate Office |

Lythecourt SS 949157 Rock Tenement SS 945168

TITLE: 'A Description of the Water Course in Dispute between the Occupiers of Higher Rock Tenement & Lithy Court in the Parish of Tiverton in the County of Devon Taken by Mw Blackamore of Exeter March 2 1774'

SURVEYOR: Matthew Blackamore

SCALE: not given

MATERIAL, SIZE & ORIENTATION: paper, coloured; 75.2cms EW x 52.8cms NS; south to top; directions indicated by letters in the margins

CONTENT: River Exe, grey with arrow indicating direction of flow; watercourse in dispute, blue, with 'gutters' and leat, grey; bridge; peripheral meadows and marsh outlined in green, named; garden; coppice, named; roads, buff, gated; Rock Mill in plan, pink; 2 reference panels giving information on the dispute

19/16/6

TIVERTON

| 18th cent. | Knightshayes Estate Office |

Lythecourt SS 949157 Rock Tenement SS 945168

TITLE: not given

SURVEYOR: not named [Matthew Blackamore]

SCALE: 'Scale of Chains'; scale bar; 1"=1.2 chains; 1:approx 950

MATERIAL, SIZE & ORIENTATION: paper, damaged, in 2 pieces, coloured; 42.5cms x 92cms; south-east to top

CONTENT: River Exe, grey with stream lines; watercourse, leats and drainage; pot water; fields outlined in brown or yellow, some named; gardens, named; orchard, named; gates; roads, directions given; footpath to Tiverton, buff, broken lines; buildings in plan, outlined in colour, named

DECORATION: 4 point compass indicator, plain/grey; north marked by fleur-de-lys, east by cross

19/16/7

TIVERTON

1776   Tiverton Museum

Exe Bridge (Tiverton) SS 953125

TITLE: 'A Plan of Lands in the Parish of Tiverton Given by John Greenway to Trustees for Charitable Uses. also Elevation of the Fronts of the Buildings there to belonging. Trustees the Revd Samuel … [illegible] Peter Blundell Richard … [illegible] Mr Benjamin Dickinson Mr John Davey Mr William Horabin, Mr John Owen … [illegible] Churchwardens'

SURVEYOR: 'Surveyed, plan'd &c by M. Blackamore Exon 1776'

SCALE: 'Scale of Chaines'; scale bar; 1"=3 chains; 1:2376

MATERIAL, SIZE & ORIENTATION: parchment, coloured, framed; *c.*72.5cms EW x 88.5cms NS; north to top

CONTENT: map relates to isolated areas in and close to Tiverton. River Exe, grey stream lines; bridge in plan showing abutments; fields green, outlined in dark green; alphabetic reference to list giving field names and content; symbols indicating hedge ownership; gates; gardens in detailed plan; tree symbols; roads, buff, directions given; buildings in plan, outlined in colour; peripheral owners named

INSETS: 'Greenways Arms'; 'Mr Chilcotts Peter Street'; 'Brick House'; 'South Front of the Hospital-Workhouse in Tiverton 1776'; 'Greenways Almshouse in Gold Street'; 'Mr Bidgood's House St. Peter Street'; 'Mr Cooke's House upon Angel Hill'; Mr Owen's House in Peter Street'; 'Front of three houses in Fore Street'; 'Little Holwell House'

DECORATION: title cartouche: rococo scrolls with acanthus leaves and flowers; 8 point compass rose, plain/grey; north marked by fleur-de-lys, NSEW by letter

19/16/8

TIVERTON

1777   Tiverton Museum

Exe Bridge (Tiverton) SS 953125

TITLE: 'An actual Survey and Plan of the Town of Tiverton in the County of Devon Together with the Town Lake from Coggams Well in the said Town to Buckhayes and Widdon and Norwood Common. M. Blackamore surveyed and delin.d 1777'

SURVEYOR: Matthew Blackamore

SCALE: not given

MATERIAL, SIZE & ORIENTATION: 3 sheets of parchment, heavily repaired and some lost, slight colour; sheet 1 = 75cms[EW] x 67.5cms [NS], sheet 2 = 90.5cms [NS], sheet 3 = 75.5cms[EW] x 65.5cms [NS]; no direction

CONTENT: River Exe and River Loman, mill leat, grey stream lines; arrows indicating direction of flow; bridges; tenements; gardens; Bowling Green; hedge symbols indicating boundaries where fields adjoin the road or river; roads, named, directions given; buildings in plan, outlined in pink and generalised in the town; reference table indicating use of colour

INSETS:

sheet 1. Town Seal – 'Sigillum Oppidi Tiverton' depicting castle, church, woolsack and skeins of wool; 'Greenway Almshouse in Gold Street'; Waldrons Alms House in Wellbrook'; [part only] 'the Castle'

sheet 2. 'South View of the Hospital in the Town of Tiverton 1777' [shows garden in great detail]' 'View of Tiverton from Westex' [shows rackfield]

sheet 3. 'St Georges Chapel in Tiverton'; 'The South West Prospect of St Peters Church in the Town of Tiverton 1777'

DECORATION: title cartouche: rococo with scrolls, leaves and flowers

19/16/9

TIVERTON

*c.*1780   2723M(B10)

East Barton SS 945087

TITLE: 'All that is coloured Yellow, is part of East Barton Estate. One fourth part of which, is the property of Sr. Thomas Carew Bart. The other Colour, is part of an Estate held by Thomas Ewings & is soley[sic], the said Sr. Thos. Carew's'

SURVEYOR: not named

SCALE: not given

MATERIAL, SIZE & ORIENTATION: paper, coloured; 19.8cms EW x 32.1cms NS; north to top

CONTENT: River Exe and stream, grey stream lines; ancient course of the River Exe, plain; fields, outlined with hedge symbols, yellow or grey; one noted as 'lost'; roads, direction given; buildings in plan, red hatched

DECORATION: 8 point compass rose, grey/plain; north marked by fleur-de-lys; view of a tree

19/16/10

TIVERTON

1791   4302B/T3

Heathcoat Factory SS 953126

TITLE: not given

SURVEYOR: not named

SCALE: not given

MATERIAL, SIZE & ORIENTATION: paper, coloured, damaged; 95.3cms EW x 54.3cms NS; north to top

CONTENT: River Exe and 'old leat', blue; arrows indicating direction of flow; weir and 'fender' (sluice gate) named; area between, green; buildings in plan, grey and distinguished 'Factory mills taken down', 'Houses'; 'Site of New Mill' indicated by circle; the 'intended new leats' buff and functions of each described

DECORATION: 32 point compass rose, plain/grey; north marked by symbol; border of one wide pink and 4 ink lines

ASSOCIATED DOCUMENT: 4302B/T1 Contract between Thomas Heathfield and Nicholas Dennys with William Gream of Ottery St Mary to build a mill for the manufacture of cotton, dated 30 Sept. 1791, 'on, across or near the Mill Stream in West Exe Tiverton'. £1. 8s. is to be paid for building every rood of work 'at and after the rate of 272½ft. to the Rood'. It is to be built as is specified in a plan then in the hands of Nicholas Dennys and endorsed by all the parties to the Contract' 4302B/T2 Agreement. Heathfield and Dennys with Gream to dig the foundation of the intended cotton mill, 7 Oct. 1791

NOTE: The premises were acquired by John Heathcote for his lace factory in 1816

19/16/11

TIVERTON

1791   Blundell's School

Exe Bridge (Tiverton) SS 952125

TITLE: 'Plan of the Lands and Houses belonging to the Feoffees of Blundell's School in the Parish of Tiverton Devon'

SURVEYOR: 'Survey'd &c by Thomas Huggins in Novemr. 1791'

SCALE: 'Scale of Chains for Boyes Ham'; scale bar 1"=5 chains; 1:3960; 'Scale of Chains for Dairy House'; scale bar; 1"=2 chains; 1:1584; 'Scale of Chains for the Bowling Green, Horells-Court, Tuckers› Court, Little Silver and Broad Lane'; scale bar; 1"=1 chain; 1:792

MATERIAL, SIZE & ORIENTATION: paper, slight colour; 53cms EW x 75cms NS; north to top

CONTENT: River Exe and River Loman, leats, ink stream lines; arrows indicating direction of flow; bridges, including Exe bridge in elevation; former course of river marked, shown at two different periods; landholdings identified by name with numeric reference to tables giving present occupiers, description of tenement and content; gardens; gates; tree symbols distinguishing deciduous and coniferous trees showing isolated trees; roads, some named, directions given; footpaths pecked lines; buildings in plan including Church and Castle, hatched black, some named; peripheral owners named

DECORATION: 16 point compass rose, grey/black; north marked by fleur-de-lys, SEW by letter

19/16/12

TIVERTON

1792   Blundell's School

Fordlands SS 991157

TITLE: 'Plan of an Estate call'd Fordland in the parish of Tiverton in the County of Devon out of which an Annuity of Twelve Pounds Yearly is Payable for ever to the Feoffees of Blundells Foundation in the said Parish'

SURVEYOR: 'Surveyed by T. Huggins 1792'

SCALE: 'Scale of Chains'; divided scale; 1"=4 chains; 1:3168

MATERIAL, SIZE & ORIENTATION: parchment, ink; 41cms EW x 63.5cms NS; north to top

CONTENT: River Loman, grey with arrows indicating direction of flow; fields outlined in grey with numeric reference to table giving field names and content; gardens; gates; tree symbols distinguishing deciduous and coniferous trees, showing orchards, nursery and isolated trees; roads, directions given; footpath, pricked lines; build-ings in plan, black or hatched black; peripheral owners named

DECORATION: title cartouche: simple scrolls; 16 point compass rose, grey/black; north marked by fleur-de-lys, SEW by letter

19/16/13

TIVERTON

18th cent.   2723M/

Wormsland SS 931108

TITLE: 'Wormsland Estate in Tiverton in the County of Devon The Property of Sir Thos Carew Bart. W Pilkington Surveyor Exeter'

SURVEYOR: William Pilkington [W Wilkington]

SCALE: no unit of measurement stated; scale bar; 1"=3 ?chains; 1:?2376

MATERIAL, SIZE & ORIENTATION: paper, slight colour; 60cms EW x 48.7cms NS; north to top

CONTENT: fields outlined in ink; numeric reference to list giving field names and content; green tree symbols showing orchards and isolated trees; roads; buildings in plan, red or black

DECORATION: title cartouche: title inscribed on shield leaning against a tree; 8 point compass rose, plain/grey; north marked by fleur-de-lys with globe in centre; border running pattern

1916/14

TIVERTON

1796   R4/1/C352

St Peter's Church SS 954128

TITLE: not given

SURVEYOR: not named

SCALE: '½" scale'

MATERIAL, SIZE & ORIENTATION: paper, ink; 49.9cms x 40.5cms; no direction

CONTENT: line of road shown with names of owners of houses contiguous to the road; footway; intended and old wall round the churchyard

ENDORSEMENT: Tiverton Churchyard, new Wall, etc 1796

19/16/15

TIVERTON

*c.*1800   R4/1/C357

Moorhayes SS 962139

TITLE: 'Plan of the Town Leat'

SURVEYOR: not named

SCALE: 'Datum to 00'

MATERIAL, SIZE & ORIENTATION: paper, slight colour; 55.4cms x 22.8cms; no direction

CONTENT: leat, watercourse, blue; ford marked; fields outlined in ink, some with owners' names; roads, buff, directions given; footpath, pecked lines; buildings in plan, black or grey

ENDORSEMENT: draft cross section plan

19/16/16

TIVERTON

1801   R4/1/C352

Tiverton Castle SS 954130

TITLE: not given

SURVEYOR: not named

SCALE: not given

MATERIAL, SIZE & ORIENTATION: paper, watermark, ink; 50cms x 40.5cms; no direction

CONTENT: gardens, courtlage, named; gates; roads, fenced and unfenced; directions given; turnpike gate; buildings in plan, generalised, hatched; castle, its court, garden, courtlage and orchards named

ENDORSEMENT: Sir Thos Carew Ap. 1801 Bartows Cosway &c

19/16/17

TIVERTON

1803   Ex. D&C Ch. Comm. 6027/2

St Peter's Church SS 954128

TITLE: not given; endorsed 'Rock Tenement Tiverton Smale agt Evans'

SURVEYOR: not named; Alexander Law, see Associated Document below

SCALE: 'Scale of Chains'; scale bar; 1"=1 chain; 1:792

MATERIAL, SIZE & ORIENTATION: paper, coloured; 42.7cms x 92.2cms (approx. as document torn and in 2 halves); north-west to top

CONTENT: River Exe, stream, mill leat, grey lines; direction of flow indicated; fields adjoining streams and mill outlined in various

colours, named with owners' names; gardens; orchard; 'deep ditch';
Rock Mill, sluice gate; roads, directions given; footpaths, pecked
lines; buildings in plan

DECORATION: 4 point compass indicator, grey/plain; north marked by
fleur-de-lys, east by cross

ASSOCIATED DOCUMENT: Exeter D&C 7053 Surveyors' Accounts 1803–
1860 To surveying mapping & valuing Rock Estate in Tiverton 5:15:0

19/16/18

TIVERTON

1803   R4/1/C352

St Peter's Church SS 954128

TITLE: 'A Plan of Lugg's Court Path into the Back Way'

SURVEYOR: not named

SCALE: not given

MATERIAL, SIZE & ORIENTATION: paper, watermark, ink; 41.4cms x
17.2cms; no direction

CONTENT: street plan showing present and intended path with the 'Watercourse represented by dotted lines'; 'Waste Spot' marked

ENDORSEMENT: April 1893 Plan of Alteration of Water path to Peter Street

19/16/19

TIVERTON

early 19th cent.   R4/1/C352

Exe Bridge (Tiverton) SS 953125

TITLE: 'Angel Hill'

SURVEYOR: not named

SCALE: 'Scale of Feet'; scale bar; 1"=20 feet; 1:240

MATERIAL, SIZE & ORIENTATION: paper, slight colour; 40.7cms x 24.9cms;
no direction

CONTENT: detailed street plan, yellow; streets named; Exe bridge;
buildings outlined in grey; owners named

ENDORSEMENT: Angel Hill

19/16/20

TIVERTON

1808   MFM 35

See entry under Haccombe, 8/1/3

19/16/21

TIVERTON

1809   R4/1/C352

St Peter's Church SS 954128

A series of 16 large-scale plans of Tiverton (scales vary) forming the
basis of an agreement, dated 24th May 1809, between Edward Boyce
of Tiverton, Builder, and Matthew Marshal of Tiverton, Bricklayer,
with 5 of the Commissioners appointed by Parliament to supervise
the paving and improvement of the town of Tiverton.

19/16/22

TIVERTON

early 19th cent.   Knightshayes Estate Office

Chettiscombe SS 967147

TITLE: 'Manor of Chettiscombe'

SURVEYOR: not named

SCALE: 'A Scale of Quarter a mile'; scale bar; 1"= ?5 chains; 1:?3960

MATERIAL, SIZE & ORIENTATION: parchment, coloured; 67cms EW x 88cms
NS [on rollers]; north to top

CONTENT: river, stream (Town Water), arrow indicating direction of flow;
fields, green, plain or yellow, outlined with hedge symbols; alpha-
numeric reference to tables giving field names, content according to
land use and total content, grouped by holding; gates; tree symbols
showing orchards; roads, directions given; manor houses in elevation,
other buildings in plan; peripheral owners named

DECORATION: 16 point compass rose; shaded line; north marked by fleur-
de-lys

19/16/23

TIVERTON
early 19th cent.   SRO DD/CN 34/7

Chevithorne Barton SS 986158

TITLE: 'A Plan of Chevithorne Barton in the Parish of Tiverton, in the County of Devon belonging to J.F. Gwyn Esqr'

SURVEYOR: not named

SCALE: 'A Scale of Chains'; scale bar; 1"=3 chains; 1:2376

MATERIAL, SIZE & ORIENTATION: parchment, coloured; 68.7cms EW x 83cms NS; north to top

CONTENT: stream, blue, arrows indicating direction of flow; pond, black wavy lines; fields outlined in blue, with numeric reference in red to table giving field names and content; gardens; gates; tree symbols showing orchards; green tree symbols and stippling marking coppice; roads, buff, directions given; buildings in plan, red, some named; estate boundary, blue; peripheral owners named
      Later annotations in pencil

DECORATION: title cartouche: medallion frame; 8 point compass rose, plain/black; north marked by fleur-de-lys; scale bar, yellow

19/16/24

TIVERTON
1813   4210Z/Z83

Bradford Farm SS 994143 Little Gornhay SS 975139 Great Gornhay SS 974133

TITLE: 'Map of Bradford in Tiverton The Property of The Revd Archdeacon Barnes Copied from an old Map of Gornhay by J: Coldridge. Decr 1813'

SURVEYOR: John Coldridge

SCALE: 'Scale of Statute Chains each containing 66 Feet'; 1"= 6 chains; 1:4752

MATERIAL, SIZE & ORIENTATION: parchment, slight colour; 41.2cms EW x 35.3cms NS; north to top

CONTENT: River Loman, King's Leat, blue; fields outlined in buff with numeric reference to list giving field names and content; some fields divided by pecked lines; roads, directions given; buildings in plan, grey; peripheral owner named

DECORATION: 8 point compass rose, yellow/grey; north marked by fleur-de-lys

19/16/25

TIVERTON
1815   Knightshayes Estate Office

Heathcoat Factory SS 953126

TITLE: 'Plan of a mill and other property at Tiverton purchased by Messrs. Heathcoat & Co of Messrs Heathfield & Co in 1815'

SURVEYOR: Charles Dean 'survr'

SCALE: no unit of measurement stated; scale bar shows chains; 1"=2 chains; 1:1584

MATERIAL, SIZE & ORIENTATION: paper, coloured; 57cms EW x 85.5cms NS; north to top

CONTENT: River Exe, black stream lines with arrows indicating direction of flow; sluices; stippled banks of shale; leats and drainage channels; 'Head Wear', and bridge; footbridge; some fields indicated and named, outlined with hedge symbols; some areas identified by letter and areas forming part of purchase, green; tree symbols; roads, buff, directions given; footpaths, broken lines; buildings in plan, some coloured and named; St Peter's Church in elevation

DECORATION: 4 point compass indicator, shaded line; north marked by fleur-de-lys

19/16/26

TIVERTON
1816   4210Z/Z82

Exe Bridge (Tiverton) SS 953125

TITLE: 'Map of Lands in Tiverton, Devon belonging to R.H.Tuckfield Esqr 1816'

SURVEYOR: not named

SCALE: 'Scale of Chains'; scale bar; 1"=3 chains; 1:2376'

MATERIAL, SIZE & ORIENTATION: paper, watermark, slight colour; 44.4cms EW x 58.9cms NS; north to top

CONTENT: River Exe, black stream lines; arrow indicating direction of flow; fields, yellow or buff, named; numeric reference to list giving 'Names of Lessees, Description of Premises', content; asterisks indicating hedge ownership; gates; tree symbols; roads, named, direction given; buildings in plan, some coloured with numeric reference to table, others generalised, hatched black

DECORATION: 4 point compass indicator; north marked by symbol

NOTE: this map drawn at a date later than that suggested in the title – watermark evidence, 1818

19/16/27

TIVERTON
1817   Ex. D&C Ch. Comm. 98/8791

St Peter's Church SS 954128
See entry under Aylesbeare, 1/18/2

19/16/28

TIVERTON
1828   2140B/M/E12

Pool Anthony SS 978128
TITLE: 'Part of Town Tenement No 11 Pool Anthony'
SURVEYOR: 'Surveyed in 1828 by Thomas Hawkes. Williton, Somerset'
SCALE: 'Scale of 40 feet to an Inch'
MATERIAL, SIZE & ORIENTATION: parchment, coloured; 33.2cms x 15.2cms; north-east to top; north-south line marked by arrow
CONTENT: house and building plots fronting Hammas or Hammett's Lane, red or grey; garden, buff; owners named; statement describing the Tenement and the terms on which it is held
NOTE: 49/9/6/30 identical copy of the above on paper with watermark 1839

19/16/29

TIVERTON
1836   1130B/T23

Site of Turnpike Gate SS 959125
TITLE: not given
SURVEYOR: not named
SCALE: 'Scale of Chains'; scale bar; 1"=3 chains; 1:2376
MATERIAL, SIZE & ORIENTATION: parchment, slight colour; 30cms EW x 33cms NS; north to top
CONTENT: River Loman, blue; fields outlined in ink with some areas separated by pecked lines; alpha-numeric reference to list distinguishing lands conveyed giving field names and content, and lands assigned for terms of years; fence symbols; roads, buff, directions given; Turnpike Gate; buildings concerned in Schedule in plan, red; others hatched in ink
DECORATION: 8 point compass rose, shaded-line decoration; north marked by fleur-de-lys

ASSOCIATED DOCUMENT: the map is part of a Conveyance dated 9 Jan 1836 Ralph Barnes and the Rev. Charles Strong to J S Howe of parcels of land
NOTE: 1130B/T25 dated 12 Jan 1836 Mortgage from J S Howe of Tiverton to Ralph Barnes and the Rev. Charles Strong of the same property

19/16/30

TIVERTON
1837   1130B/T27

Site of Turnpike Gate SS 959125
TITLE: not given
SURVEYOR: not named
SCALE: 'Scale of Chains'; scale bar; 1"=6 chains; 1:4752
MATERIAL, SIZE & ORIENTATION: parchment, slight colour; 25cms EW x 17cms NS; north to top
CONTENT: River Loman, blue; fields outlined in grey; 2 fields coloured green and outlined in green, named; some fields with content, some with alpha-numeric reference to list; roads, buff, directions given; buildings in plan, red, named; peripheral owners and estates named
DECORATION: 8 point plain compass indicator; north marked by fleur-de-lys, black
ASSOCIATED DOCUMENT: the map is part of a Conveyance dated 10 Jan 1837 by Ralph Barnes of Exeter gent. and the Rev. Charles Strong late of Tiverton now of Torquay to John Shuckburgh Howe of Tiverton Gent. of Elm Field and part of Home Meadow

19/16/31

TIVERTON
1838   Knightshayes Estate Office

SS 950137
TITLE: 'The River Exe in Mr Talley's Estate Tiverton Devon'
SURVEYOR: Edwin Palmer
SCALE: no unit of measurement stated; scale bar shows chains; 1"=0.5 chain 1:396
MATERIAL, SIZE & ORIENTATION: paper, coloured; approx, 150cms EW x 310cms NS; north to top
CONTENT: rivers, leats, blue; 'The Old Leat' and 'Carriage Gutter' named; groynes to stop erosion; section drawings across river; shading showing river banks; blue areas [?water meadow] with numeric

reference [to table]; 'Plantation destroyed by cattle'; gates; tracks, buff; buildings in plan, grey; peripheral owners named
NOTE: 2 copies, not quite identical, one may be a draft

19/16/32
TIVERTON
*c.*1840   Bristol RO 37959(13)

Fairby SX 943174
TITLE: not given
SURVEYOR: not named
SCALE: not given
MATERIAL, SIZE & ORIENTATION: paper, mounted on linen, ink and some colour; 107cms EW x 138cms NS; north to top
CONTENT: river, lake, streams, blue; relief shown by hill shading; fields, plain, named with content; numeric reference [to Survey]; gateways; roads, plain, some directions given; footpaths, pecked lines; buildings in plan, red or hatched grey; peripheral owners, estates and parish (Washfield) named
DECORATION: 4 point compass indicator; north marked by an arrow
ENDORSEMENT: T. Daniel Esqre 663 L.B. 18
NOTE: Thomas Daniel is known to have occupied Fairby in the 1840s (Harding, *History of Tiverton*). Possibly the map is later than 1840.

TIVERTON see also B11, B15, B66, C168

19/17/1
TOPSHAM
1757   D1508M/M&P/Rivers Maps 2

Topsham Church SX965880
TITLE: 'A Map of Topsham-Harbour within the Port of Exeter, shewing the Coast and distinguishing the Villages and Creeks on each Side from Topsham to Exmouth, and thence to the Bar: Shewing also the present Course of the Channel, and ye several Beds or Banks of Sand as they now appear at Low Water. Survey'd and Map'd in Febry. 1757'
SURVEYOR: [William Chapple]
SCALE: 'A Scale of Miles and Furlongs' and 'A Scale of Chains each

containing 4 Statute Perches or 66 Feet; scale bars; 1"=25 chains; 1:19800
MATERIAL, SIZE & ORIENTATION: paper, coloured; 66.6cms x 33.4cms (as repaired); north-east to top
CONTENT: river and channel, blue with stream lines; detailed survey of the main channel of the Exe with sandbanks named and coloured with brown stippling on buff background; land outlined in green; bridges; various features named – Watch-house, Cockwood Cliff, Salt works, Turf-Reach, Nutwell House, Powderham Castle; churches in elevation; stylised houses in elevation at Topsham, Star-Cross, Exmouth and Lympstone
DECORATION: 8 point compass rose, blue/plain; north marked by fleur-de-lys, east by cross; fishing vessels and ocean-going ships marked in channel

19/17/2
TOPSHAM
1787   3612M/T11

Countess Wear SX 946901
TITLE: not given
SURVEYOR: not named
SCALE: 'Scale of Chains each 4 Stat. perches'; scale bar; 1"=3 chains; 1:2376
MATERIAL, SIZE & ORIENTATION: parchment, slight colour; 13.1cms EW x 17.9cms NS; east to top
CONTENT: river, grey wave lines, direction of flow indicated; bridge; properties granted outlined in yellow; asterisks indicating fence ownership; garden; road; footpath, pecked lines; buildings in plan, hatched grey; peripheral owners named
DECORATION: 4 point compass indicator; north marked by fleur-de-lys, east by cross
ASSOCIATED DOCUMENT: map is part of a Conveyance dated 2 May 1787 from Josias Lee of Wear in Topsham to Thomas Hole and John Codrington of a newly erected dwelling house and parcel of Overdown and Wonford meadow and of a field called The Rag

19/17/3

TOPSHAM
| 19th cent | 1508M/Maps/Rivers/F2 |

Double Locks Inn SX 932900

TITLE: not given; 2 plans showing lands at Double Lock belonging to Lord Devon

SURVEYOR: not named

SCALE: 'Scale of Chains'; scale bar; Plan 1, 1"=4.5 chains; 1:3564; Plan 2, 1"=4 chains; 1:3168

MATERIAL, SIZE & ORIENTATION: paper, coloured; 40.3cms EW x 13cms NS; west to top; north-south line marked by arrow

CONTENT:

Plan 1 'According to the Lease of 1758 granted to John White'
Plan 2 'According to Lang's Map of 1784
River, blue; locks marked by double arrows; field green; in Plan 2 this divided into more plots than in Plan 1; tree symbols separating field from towpath; buildings in plan, some hatched black

TOPSHAM

Exeter D&C 3577 Chapter Act Book p.361 30 &31 March 1814 They ordered the Tenement and Closes of Land at Topsham late Burgess's to be measured and mapped & valued by Mr Coldridge. No map has been traced

19/17/4

TOPSHAM
| 1817 | Ex. D&C Ch. Comm. 98/8791 |

Topsham Quay SX 966878
See entry under Aylesbeare, 1/18/2

19/17/5

TOPSHAM
| c.1820–1824 | ECA (no further ref.) |

Topsham Quay SX 966878

TITLE: 'A Map of Lands in the Town of Topsham, Devon. The Property of the Chamber of Exeter'

SURVEYOR: not named

SCALE: no unit of measurement stated; 2 scale bars showing chains and feet; 1"=.5 chains; 1:396

MATERIAL, SIZE & ORIENTATION: paper, watermark 1820, mounted, coloured; 55cms x 40 cms; north-west to top

CONTENT: Topsham Harbour outlined in blue; The Quay named with Scales, Weighing House and Crane shown in plan; roads, buff, named and directions given; buildings in plan in various colours; alphanumeric reference to list giving names of buildings, their use and content; 3 coal yards named; peripheral owner named

DECORATION: title in elaborate style of lettering; 4 point compass indicator; north marked by arrowhead

NOTE: on back of document, in pencil, 'A F Burnett was Wharfinger of Topsham prior to 1824'

19/17/6

TOPSHAM
| 1827 | Ex. D&C Ch. Comm. 6068/5/3 |

Topsham Church SX 965880

TITLE: 'Plan of Premises in Topsham, shewing that part of the Lands of the Dean & Chapter proposed to be taken for enlarging the Church Yard'

SURVEYOR: 'Saml T: Coldridge Surveyor Exeter Novr 30 1827'

SCALE: 'Scale'; scale bar; 1"=20 feet; 1:240

MATERIAL, SIZE & ORIENTATION: paper, coloured; 54.3cms EW x 45.8cms NS; north to top

CONTENT: river Exe, various shades of blue; relief shown by hill shading; lands and gardens outlined;buildings in plan, grey, including church and burial ground; burial ground enlargement shown by red line; road, 'street leading through Topsham Town'; footpath, dotted line

DECORATION: title cartouche: scroll; 4 point compass indicator, grey shaded lines; north marked by fleur-de-lys

ASSOCIATED DOCUMENT: Exeter D&C 3579 Chapter Act Book p.568 8 Sept. 1827 John Coldridge was ordered to inspect lands at Topsham with a view to enlarging the churchyard

19/17/7

TOPSHAM
| 1836 | 2729/E5 |

Topsham Church SX 965880

TITLE: 'A Map of the Town of Topsham in the County of Devon 1836'

SURVEYOR: 'I. Poole. Landsurveyor, Dorset'

SCALE: '5 chains to an Inch' (sic); scale bar; 1"=3 chains; 1:2376

MATERIAL, SIZE & ORIENTATION: paper, ink; 85.1cms x 65.4cms; no direction

CONTENT: rivers and streams; fields and tenements with numeric reference [to Survey Book]; gates; stippling marking ?waste; roads, named in the town with directions given; footpaths, pecked lines; buildings in plan; peripheral parishes named

NOTE: appears to be a later copy which may account for the discrepancy in the scale

MATERIAL, SIZE & ORIENTATION: paper, watermark, coloured; 20.2cms x 32cms; no direction

CONTENT: 3 fields, green with numeric reference to list; one field divided by dotted line showing where a fence is to be erected; roads, brown, directions given; peripheral owners named

ASSOCIATED DOCUMENT: map is attached to a copy of an Agreement dated 24th June 1840 between 'Sir Lawrence Vaughan Palk Bart and Lawrence Palk Esqre his Eldest Son and Heir Apparent and the Reverend Thomas Kitson of Shiphay' for sale of land

TOPSHAM see also B3, B71, B109, C169–71

TORMOHAM see also C176–78

19/18/1

TORMOHAM
1808   TD 386

Torre Abbey SX 909638

TITLE: not given except for 'Reference to the Manor of Torabbey in the Parish of Tormoham Devon'

SURVEYOR: not named

SCALE: not given

MATERIAL, SIZE & ORIENTATION: paper, mounted on card, slight colour; 83cms x 62.3cms; no direction

CONTENT: coastline, streams, bridges; Livermead Sands and principal headlands named; fields outlined in ink with numeric reference to list giving field names and content; gardens in detailed plan; tree symbols showing avenues and isolated trees; roads, directions given; buildings in plan, red or grey; detailed settlement around harbour; jetty; peripheral owners and parishes named

ENDORSEMENT: Manor of Torre Abbey 1808

TORQUAY
1770

Map on parchment by Matthew Blackamore of Robert Palk's estate. See Appendix A under BLACKAMORE, Matthew. This map has not been traced

TORQUAY (including St Marychurch) see B30, B47, B79, B103, B113, C172–78

19/19/1

TORRINGTON, GREAT
1745   NDRO 4724 add/1

Great Torrington Church SS 495192
See entry under Bideford, 2/14/3

19/18/2

TORMOHAM
1840   58/9 Box 128/44

Junction of Shiphay and Torquay roads SX 897662

TITLE: not given

SURVEYOR: not named

SCALE: not given

TORRINGTON, GREAT
1777

A map by John Jewell is referred to in *DCNQ* XVIII, 151 as being in the possession of the Conservators of Great Torrington Commons. See Appendix A under JEWELL, S. This map has not been traced

TORRINGTON, GREAT see also B67, C179

19/20/1

TORRINGTON, LITTLE
[1649–1654]   KAO U269/P11/2

Worlington SS 481306 Stapparke not identified
See entry under Instow, 9/4/1

19/20/2

TORRINGTON, LITTLE
1769   NDRO 2239 add6/26

Cleave Wood SS 472187
See entry under Monkleigh, 13/19/1

19/20/3

TORRINGTON, LITTLE
18th cent.   3599M/E154

Frizenham SS 478182
TITLE: 'A Plan of several Estates situate in the Manor and Parish of
    Little Torrington [ye] Property of [Charles Roberts Barnstaple]' (later
    insertions)
SURVEYOR: [John Case]
SCALE: 'Scale of Statute Chains containing 66 Feet each'; scale bar;
    1"=4.25 chains; 1:3366
MATERIAL, SIZE & ORIENTATION: parchment, coloured; 67.5cms EW x
    82.5cms NS; north to top
CONTENT: stream and river Torridge, blue with stream lines; relief shown
    by hill shading; fields outlined in brown, named; alpha-numeric
    reference [to Survey Book]; asterisks indicating hedge ownership;
    gates; green tree symbols in areas coloured green; some attempt to
    distinguish deciduous and coniferous trees; roads, buff, directions
    given; buildings in plan, red; peripheral owners named; farm names
    and owners' names inserted in later hand and line of road passing
    Frizenham Farm also inserted, red
DECORATION: title cartouche: view of castle on scarp above river ?Torring-
    ton; 8 point compass rose; directions spelt out

19/20/4

TORRINGTON, LITTLE
19th cent.   NDRO B229/15

Frizenham SS 478182
TITLE: 'A Plan of several estates situate in the Manor & Parish of Little
    Torrington the Property of Messieurs Roberts Barnstaple'
SURVEYOR: not named
SCALE: 'Scale of Statute Chains containing 66 Feet'; scale bar; 1"=4
    chains; 1:3168
MATERIAL, SIZE & ORIENTATION: paper, mounted on linen, coloured;
    66.6cms EW x 84.5cms NS; north to top
CONTENT: The River Torridge and other streams, blue; fields in various
    colours, probably indicating ownership; named with numeric
    reference[to Survey Book]; green tree symbols showing woods,
    coppice and orchard; roads, buff; road through South Frizenham Farm
    inserted later; buildings in plan, red; peripheral owners named
DECORATION: 8 point compass rose, yellow/blue; north marked by fleur-
    de-lys, yellow/blue

19/20/5

TORRINGTON, LITTLE
1809   1148M add/10/1(b)

Wooleigh Barton SS 531168 Little Torrington Church SS 491167
See entry under Beaford, 2/3/1

19/20/6

TORRINGTON, LITTLE
1820   56/10 Box 27/14

Bowden SS 475177
TITLE: 'A Plan of Bowden and Westcott Estate in the Parish of Little
    Torrington Devon 1820'
SURVEYOR: [E.R. Roberts]
SCALE: 'Scale of Statute Chains'; scale bar; 1"=4 chains; 1:3168
MATERIAL, SIZE & ORIENTATION: parchment, coloured; 37.8cms EW x
    31.5cms NS; north to top
CONTENT: river, blue; ford; fields outlined in various colours, named
    with content; numeric reference [to table]; 'mow' plot; gates; tree
    symbols showing orchards and isolated trees; roads, buff, directions
    given; buildings in plan, red; peripheral owners and estates named

DECORATION: 8 point compass rose, black lines, in double circle; north marked by fleur-de-lys, east by cross

10/20/7

TORRINGTON, LITTLE
1820   56/10 Box 27/24

Service SS 480192

TITLE: 'A Plan of Servis Estate in the Parish of Little Torrington Devon 1820'

SURVEYOR: 'E R Roberts Delt'

SCALE: not given

MATERIAL, SIZE & ORIENTATION: parchment, coloured; 30.7cms EW x 35.8cms NS; north to top

CONTENT: 'Torridge River', direction of flow indicated, and tributaries, turquoise; fields outlined in various colours and ink with content and numeric reference [to table]; gates; tree symbols showing woods, copses, orchards and isolated trees; roads, buff; buildings in plan; peripheral owners and estates named

DECORATION: compass is NS line only contained in a circle; north marked by fleur-de-lys, east by cross

19/20/8

TORRINGTON, LITTLE
1820   56/10 Box 27/8

Bowden SS 475177

TITLE: 'A Plan of North Hole Estate in the Parish of Little Torrington Devon 1820'

SURVEYOR: 'E R Roberts Delt'

SCALE: not given

MATERIAL, SIZE & ORIENTATION: parchment, coloured; 35.8cms EW x 31.6cms NS; north to top

CONTENT: streams, plain; fields outlined in various colours, named with content; numeric reference [to table]; gates; tree symbols showing orchards; roads, buff, some directions given; buildings in plan, red; peripheral owners and estates named

DECORATION: 4 point compass indicator in double circle; north marked by fleur-de-lys, SEW by letter

19/20/9

TORRINGTON, LITTLE
1820   56/10 Box 27/19

Frizenham SS 478182

TITLE: 'A Plan of South Frizenham Estate in the Parish of Little Torrington Devon'

SURVEYOR: 'E R Roberts Del 1820'

SCALE: 'A Scale of Statute Chains'; scale bar; 1"=4 chains; 1:3168

MATERIAL, SIZE & ORIENTATION: parchment, coloured; 38cms EW x 31.4cms NS; north to top

CONTENT: River Torridge, direction of flow indicated, stream, blue; fields outlined in various colours, named with content; numeric reference [to table]; additional note giving content of gardens and orchards, arable, pasture and tillage, coppice, furze and waste, and total content; 'mow' plot; gates; tree symbols marking orchards, coppice, wood and isolated trees; roads, buff, directions given; footpaths, pecked lines; buildings in plan, plain or red; peripheral owners and estates named

19/20/10

TORRINGTON, LITTLE
*c.*1820   56/10 Box 27/15

Bowden SS 475177

TITLE: 'Little Bowden Farm contg 11a. 2r. 20p.'

SURVEYOR: [E.R. Roberts]

SCALE: not given

MATERIAL, SIZE & ORIENTATION: parchment, ink; 28cms EW x 36.6cms NS; north to top

CONTENT: fields outlined in ink, named with content; alpha-numeric reference [to table]; gates; tree symbols showing isolated trees; roads, directions given; buildings in plan; peripheral estates named

DECORATION: compass indicator is NS line only with north marked by symbol

19/20/11

TORRINGTON, LITTLE
*c.*1820   56/10 Box 27/18

Frizenham SS 478182

TITLE: 'North Frizenham containing 78a 5r 30p'

SURVEYOR: [E.R. Roberts]

SCALE: not given

MATERIAL, SIZE & ORIENTATION: parchment, ink and slight colour; 42.9cms EW x 29.9cms NS; north to top

CONTENT: stream; fields outlined in ink, named and with content; alphanumeric reference [to table]; North Frizenham outlined in red; roads, directions given; buildings in plan, red; peripheral owners and estates named

DECORATION: compass indicator is NS line only, north marked by symbol, S by letter

TORRINGTON, LITTLE see also B67

19/21/1

TOTNES
1638   1579A/10/31

Totnes Church SX 802605

TITLE: not given

SURVEYOR: not named

SCALE: not given

MATERIAL, SIZE & ORIENTATION: paper, ink; *c.*6.1cms EW x *c.*6.7cms NS; south to top; directions spelt out on margins

CONTENT: small sketch to show area concerned in a legal case of trespass on 'a Garden 1 Sept 14 Charles II [1638] M[ayor] & B[ailiffs] v. John Laskey & Margaret his wife'

19/21/2

TOTNES
[1638]   1579A/10/32

Totnes Church SX 802605

TITLE: not given

SURVEYOR: not named

SCALE: not given

MATERIAL, SIZE & ORIENTATION: paper, ink; 6.5cms EW x 5.9cms NS; south to top

CONTENT: diagram of area in question similar to 1579A/10/31 with an addition on the west side with the words 'the mapp'

NOTE: case for opinion in trespass case; the plan is illustrating the plaintiff's title, based on a counterpart lease of 4 Jan. 20 Henry VI [1442]

19/21/3

TOTNES
1700   3799M/E8/1

Totnes Bridge SX 806603

TITLE: not given

SURVEYOR: 'Surveyed and measured anno 1700 per me Ralph Michell: Philo=mat'

SCALE: 'Scala perticarum'; scale bar; 1"=8 perches; 1:1584; 'Note a Rood is a Quarter of an Acre And 40 Perch one Rood'

MATERIAL, SIZE & ORIENTATION: paper, ink, slight colour; 75cms x 54.2cms; north-east to top

CONTENT: rivers named, stream lines; island in river; arrow indicating direction of flow; 'Hutches' shown by grid symbols; these and other symbols keyed by letter to 'Explanacon'; bridges, including principal river bridge which is shown with arches; rocks and high land shown by shading, grey; landowners named; content of some named areas; gates; tree symbols showing isolated trees; 'Road to Hampston' named; buildings in elevation, on opposing horizons along Totnes Street; 'Mad Wises' house named; The Town Mill named

DECORATION: 4 point compass indicator, grey/plain; NSEW marked by letter; dividers, grey, above scale bar

19/21/4

TOTNES
1792   DP Q/Rum 8

Totnes Church SX 802605

See entry under Ashburton, 1/8/3

19/21/5

TOTNES
1800   118M/F3

Totnes Church SX 802605
See entry under Ashprington, 1/10/3

19/21/6

TOTNES
1824   1352A/PFB20

Peak Cross SX 789591
See entry under Harberton, 8/4/4

TOTNES see also B1, B42, B68, B77, B85, C180

20/1/1

UFFCULME
*c.*1750   Dors RO D/FFO:38/28

Craddock House ST 086121
TITLE: 'An Exact mapp together with the Tenements adjacent belonging to the Honourable Edward Digby Esqr Surveyed by George Smyth'
SURVEYOR: George Smyth
SCALE: no unit of measurement stated; divided scale showing chains with 'The Visuall Point is from the Glebe Lands of' above; 1"=4 chains; 1:3168
MATERIAL, SIZE & ORIENTATION: parchment, coloured; 89cms x 71.2cms; north-west to top
CONTENT: spring, river 'Vaga Flu' pricked lines with pale green margins; fields outlined in various colours, named; numeric reference to tables giving field names and content listed according to land use; holdings of adjacent tenants listed under tenants' names; gardens; green tree symbols showing woods, copse, avenues, orchards and isolated trees; roads, fenced and unfenced; buildings in plan, hatched in sepia
DECORATION: title cartouche: medallion of leaves and flowers; scale, yellow with dividers above; 8 point compass rose, turquoise, red, yellow, plain with applied design in ink; north marked by fleur-de-lys, SEW by letter; border: printed and pasted on to the map showing acanthus, animals and putti with the design arranged horizontally top and bottom and vertically at sides

20/1/2

UFFCULME
1756   ECA Book 58

Uffculme Church ST 068127
See entry under Exeter Chamber Map Book, 5/3/49

20/1/3

UFFCULME
1789   3321 add 3 (uncatalogued)

Bridwell ST 059126
TITLE: 'A Plan of the Intended Alterations For Breadwell The Seat of Richd Hall Clark Esqr'
SURVEYOR: 'By Thos Gray 1789'
SCALE: 'Scale of Chains'; scale bar; 1"=1.5 chains; 1:1188
MATERIAL, SIZE & ORIENTATION: paper, coloured, mounted on paper, damaged; 180cms x 97cms; north-east to top
CONTENT: pond, intended stream with islands, shaded grey margins; kitchen gardens in plan; park, green; green tree symbols, decidous and coniferous trees, showing orchards, plantations and isolated trees; some hedge symbols; roads and footpaths, buff, fenced and unfenced; buildings in plan, light brown; various features keyed by letter to list describing intended alterations
DECORATION: 4 point compass indicator, yellow, buff; north marked by fleur-de-lys

20/1/4

UFFCULME
18th cent.   1926B/W/E2/19

Bradfield House ST 052100
TITLE: 'A Plan of Bradfield Great Meadow'
SURVEYOR: not named
SCALE: not given
MATERIAL, SIZE & ORIENTATION: paper, watermark; 45.7cms EW x 36.7cms NS; north to top
CONTENT: 'The River' named; possible sluice or weir shown across the river; field, green; hedge boundary indicated by dark green symbols; tree symbols, one within the field; content in panel; gates; small building in plan

DECORATION: 4 point compass indicator; north marked by fleur-de-lys, SEW by letter

ENDORSEMENT: A Plan of the great Meadow

DECORATION: 16 point compass rose, shaded-line decoration; north marked by fleur-de-lys, south by feather, EW by letter

ASSOCIATED DOCUMENT: Conveyance of a messuage and lands near Craddock dated 12 April 1834 by Edward Manley Leigh of Cullompton to Daniel Cave and others

20/1/5

UFFCULME

19th cent.   5846Z/E8–9

Gaddon House ST 069116

TITLE: 'Gaddon Estate in the Parish of Uffculme'

SURVEYOR: not named

SCALE: no unit of measurement stated; scale bar shows chains; 1"=3 chains; 1:2376

MATERIAL, SIZE & ORIENTATION: paper, ink; 53.7cms x 48.4cms; north-east to top

CONTENT: ponds, stream lines; fields outlined in ink, named with content; numeric reference to list repeating field names and giving land use and content; gates; asterisks separating land not part of the estate; tree symbols showing orchard; roads, directions given; buildings in plan, hatched; peripheral owners named

DECORATION: 8 point compass rose, shaded in ink; north marked by fleur-de-lys

NOTE: second copy includes statement of scale, '3 Chains to an Inch'; no scale bar, some hill shading; 4 point compass indicator

20/1/6

UFFCULME

1834   4243M/T99(b)

Craddock House ST 086121

TITLE: 'The Map or Plan to which the foregoing Deed refers'; map is attached to a Conveyance

SURVEYOR: not named

SCALE: no unit of measurement stated; scale bar shows chains; 1"=4 chains; 1:3168

MATERIAL, SIZE & ORIENTATION: parchment, slight colour; 47.5cms EW x 68cms NS; west to top

CONTENT: fields, green, and outlined in green with hedge symbols; numeric reference to table giving field names. land use and content; gates; garden; other owners named; tree symbols; roads; footpaths, pecked lines; buildings in plan, dark green

20/1/7

UFFCULME

1834   74B/ME 98

Weir ST 069124

TITLE: 'Brown & Davy (v) Fox Brothers Plaintiffs Map'

SURVEYOR: not named

SCALE: not given

MATERIAL, SIZE & ORIENTATION: paper, coloured; 94cms EW x 47cms NS; north to top

CONTENT: new mill pond; new course of the river and mill leat, blue; ancient course of river and mill leat, pink; direction of flow indicated; bridges, ford, mills; fields, pale green, some named; hedge symbols indicating ownership; roads, pale pink, some directions given; buildings in plan; some numeric reference to buildings and bridges to explain the points in dispute

DECORATION: 4 point compass indicator; north marked by arrow, SEW by letter

ASSOCIATED DOCUMENT: Arbitrator's Award dated 21 November 1834 between Edward Brown, Joseph Davy and Thomas Davy of Cullompton, woollen manufacturers and Edward Fox, Sylvanus Fox, Samuel Fox, Henry Fox and Charles Fox, all of Wellington, Som., woollen manufacturers concerning the weir on the River Culme

UFFCULME see also C78, C181

20/2/1

UGBOROUGH

temp. Eliz. I (1558–1603)   PRO, MPA 86(C.108/414)

Ugborough Church SX 677557

TITLE: not given

SURVEYOR: not named

SCALE: not given; statement that 'Rydinge Waye in Question' = 34 perches; remainder of map topological in form

MATERIAL, SIZE & ORIENTATION: ?paper, coloured; approx. 34cms EW x approx. 30.7cms NS (edges uneven); south to top; directions spelt out on margins (in frames)

CONTENT: fields, various shades of green; 'Lyttle Hokmore, Great Hokmore and Crosspark' named; hedge symbols, dark green/black; isolated trees, dark green/black; gates and stiles in elevation; roads, buff; 'The Waye from Enaton', 'Ugborough Towne' and 'Enaton' named; Ugborough Church, Venn House, Woodes House, Shutmas House, Coles House named and drawn in elevation; other houses also in elevation; white with green roofs

NOTE: 'The Rydinge Waye in Question' points to the map being produced in a right of way dispute. Unfortunately, PRO class C.108/414 consists of Master's exhibits in chancery cases unattributed to any cause, so it is unlikely that any ancillary documentation may be found in that Office. It is possible that the map is contemporary with the sale of Crosspark by Christopher Savery to Walter Hele in 1586 (Devon Deeds Enrolled, nos. 1254 and 1255 calendared by J.C. Tingey as 'Exeter Castle MSS') but there is nothing to substantiate this.

PUBLICATION: Mary R Ravenhill and Margery M Rowe, eds, *Early Devon Maps* (Exeter, 2000), 18

20/2/2

UGBOROUGH
1787/89   Z17/3/20–21

Ugborough Church SX 677557
See entry under Ashburton, 1/8/2

20/2/3

UGBOROUGH
1794   51/7/7/2

Ugborough Church SX 677557
See entry under Dartmoor, 4/3/5

UGBOROUGH see also C182–84

20/3/1

UPEXE
1823   2545M/E47

Upexe village SS 942024
See entry under Rewe, 17/3/1

20/4/1

UPLYME
1775   Photocopy supplied by Mr G. Gosling

Uplyme Church SY 325934

TITLE: 'Borough-shot and Hunters Lodge in the Parish of Uplime in the County of Devon 1775'

SURVEYOR: 'John Thompson fecit'

SCALE: 'A Scale of Chains'; scale bar; 1"=8 chains; 1:6336

MATERIAL, SIZE & ORIENTATION: ?paper, ?ink; 12.6cms x 22.8cms; south-east to top

CONTENT: fields with numeric reference to table giving 'Names of Inclosures', content of each and total content; hedge and tree symbols indicating hedge ownership; gates; tree symbols showing orchards; stippling marking furze; roads, 'Turnpike Road from Axminster to London' shown; footpaths, pecked lines including one to Lyme Regis; buildings in plan; peripheral owner named

DECORATION: title cartouche: rococo style with leaves and scrolls; 4 point compass indicator; north marked by fleur-de-lys

UPLYME see also C185

20/5/1

UPOTTERY
1773   4712M/E1

Upottery Church ST 202075

TITLE: 'A Plan of the lands and Tenements Belonging to the Town of Taunton Lying in Upottery in the County of Devon'

SURVEYOR: 'suvd by I Blackamore in 1773'

SCALE: 'A cale[sic] of 28 Gunters Chains or 112 Statut[sic] Poles'; scale bar; 1"=4.5 chains; 1:3564

MATERIAL, SIZE & ORIENTATION: paper, mounted on card, coloured; 53.3cms EW x 67.5cms NS; west to top

CONTENT: Swankham Brooks, footbridges named; fields outlined in various colours, named; alpha-numeric reference to tables giving owners, field names, contents and kind of trees – oak, ash, elm; asterisks indicating hedge ownership; green tree symbols on field boundaries, within fields and also showing orchards; roads, brown, some named; buildings in plan, hatched in red; church in elevation 'Refferances to the Plan. Roads are Brown. Buildings are Red The Little Astericks stands in the Lands to which the Hedges belong'

DECORATION: title cartouche: elaborate rococo design with acanthus leaves, flowers, bird; scroll with I Blackamore's name and date; detailed view of church and churchyard; 8 point compass rose, plain/shaded grey; double circle superimposed on compass points; north marked by fleur-de-lys

INSET: Woodford SY 103968

TITLE: 'A Plan of Little Woodford in the Parish of Ottery St Mary in the County of Devon; Belonging to Taunton'

SURVEYOR: I Blackamore

SCALE: 'a Scale of 24 Gunters Chains or 96 Statut Poles; scale bar; 1"=4.5 chains; 1:3564

MATERIAL, SIZE & ORIENTATION: paper, as above, slight colour; map irregular in shape, c.21.5cms EW x 34cms NS; west to top

CONTENT: fields outlined in ink with hedge and tree symbols, stippled; alpha-numeric reference to table giving field names and content; tree symbols showing orchard; roads, brown, some named; directions given; footpaths, brown; buildings in plan, hatched in red or black

DECORATION: title cartouche: rococo, acanthus leaves and flowers; detailed elevation of Ottery St Mary Church; compass rose, as above; scale: carrying case of surveyor's instruments with name of John Brown

NOTE: M & I Blackamore owned a writing and drawing school in Exeter where they taught amongst other things land survey, perspective and landscape drawing

20/5/2

UPOTTERY
1817   Ex. D&C Ch. Comm. 98/8791

Upottery Church ST 202075
See entry under Aylesbeare, 1/18/2

20/5/3

UPOTTERY
c.1830   152M/Box 49/Estate 2

Upottery Church ST 202075

TITLE: 'Plan of a Common Situated in the Parish of Upottery the Property of the Right Honorable Viscount Sidmouth'

SURVEYOR: not named

SCALE: 'Scale of Chains'; scale bar; 1"=10 chains; 1:7920

MATERIAL, SIZE & ORIENTATION: paper, coloured; 23.4cms x 36.4cms; north-east to top

CONTENT: relief shown by hill shading; fields, plain or yellow, all outlined in red; gates; hedge symbols indicating ownership; roads, buff, fenced and unfenced; some directions given; buildings in plan, hatched grey; adjoining parish named

DECORATION: 4 point compass indicator, oak-leaf design; north marked by symbol

UPOTTERY see also B19, B23, B93, B108, C186–89

20/6/1

UPTON HELLIONS
1773   2087M/MP7

Merrifield SS 847018

TITLE: 'A Plan of the Estate call'd Merrifield in the Parish of Upton Hellyons in the County of Devon the property of Mr Will Holmes Exeter M: Blackamore Deld Exon 1773'

SURVEYOR: Matthew Blackamore

SCALE: 'A Scale of Chains; scale bar; 1"=3 chains; 1:2376

MATERIAL, SIZE & ORIENTATION: parchment, coloured; 46.6cms EW x 62.3cms NS; north to top

CONTENT: River Creedy, with an ox-bow lake, leat and watercourse to Merrifield House from a spring, blue with one dark blue margin; Creedy Bridge in elevation, red; fields outlined in green with estate boundary having a wider green border; fields named with alpha-numeric reference to list in red giving field names and content; crosses indicating hedge ownership; tree symbols showing orchards and isolated trees along river banks; roads, brown, directions given; buildings in plan, red; peripheral owners named; legend explaining use of colour and some symbols

DECORATION: title cartouche: rococo, shaded grey with acanthus, flowers, leaves and ruched fabric; scale and reference table decorated with ink flourishes; 8 point compass rose, principal points plain/shaded grey, others short red rays; NSEW indicated by letter; margin, black and red

20/7/1

UPTON PYNE
1775   1262M/E22/40

Three Horse Shoes Inn SX 903962

TITLE: 'A Map or Plan of the Estate called North Duryard Wood otherwise the North Part of an Estate so called situate in the Parish of Upton Pyne in the County of Devon; the Property of the Plaintiff, Mr Edmund Roberts. Taken the 16th and 17th of June 1775 by Wm Hole'

SURVEYOR: William Hole

SCALE: 'A Scale of Gunter's Chains, each containing Four Statute Perches'; scale bar; 1"=2.4 chains; 1:1901

MATERIAL, SIZE & ORIENTATION: paper, watermark, coloured; 55 cms EW x 41.2cms NS; north to top

CONTENT: 'rivulet of water', orange; arrows indicating direction of flow; plaintiff's estate outlined in green; area in dispute, yellow; field boundaries on plaintiff's estate outlined in ink; field names; gates, red; orchard, gardens, courtlage distinguished by name; isolated tree symbols; roads, buff; Exeter to Crediton Turnpike named; buildings in plan, outlined in red; peripheral owners and parishes named

EXPLANATORY NOTE: 'The Premises within the colour green are indisputably admitted to be the Property of the Plaintiff. The Premises colour'd Yellow are the Object of the present Suit – Hath now growing upon it Wood of different Kinds, and many Timber Trees and Saplings

The Rivulet or Brook of Water on the West or South-West Side of the above Plan, colour'd orange is that mentioned in the Plaintiff's Title-Deeds, to be there the Boundary of his Estate

The Hedge or Fence represented by the Black line, between the Premises colour'd Green and the Rivulet or Brook of Water, is, all the Way, a Single-Dyke Hedge, and the acknowledged Property of the Plaintiff, with the Ditch or Trough on his Side of it, and the Ground (in dispute) between it and the Brook, forms (for the most Part) a gentle Slope, from the Top of the said Single Dyked or One-Sided Hedge to the Water

At a and b are Rails from the Plaintiff's Hedge to the Brook; which Rails have always been repaired by the Plaintiff'

DECORATION: 8 point compass rose, black/plain; north marked by fleur-de-lys, east by cross

20/7/2

UPTON PYNE
19th cent.   51/24/8/2

Stevenstone SX 910995

TITLE: 'Stevenstone Barton in the Parish of Upton Pyne the property of Sir Stafford H. Northcote Bart'

SURVEYOR: not named

SCALE: 'Scale of Chains'; scale bar; 1"=3 chains; 1:2376

MATERIAL, SIZE & ORIENTATION: paper, buff coloured, mounted on linen, slight colour; 66.2cms EW x 93.8cms NS; north to top

CONTENT: fields, some outlined in blue, some plain, some blue, all with field name and content; repeated in table with total content; asterisks indicating hedge ownership; tree symbols showing orchards, plantations, furze and coppice; stippling showing willow beds; roads, directions given; buildings in plan, grey

DECORATION: 4 point compass indicator; north marked by flower bud

20/7/3

UPTON PYNE
19th cent.   51/24/8/3

Oakford Farm SX 904968

TITLE: 'Oakford Farm with Sewards and Mill-cot tenements in the Parish of Upton-Pyne the Property of Sir Stafford Henry Northcote Bart'

SURVEYOR: not named

SCALE: 'Scale of Chains – three to an inch'; scale bar; 1"=3 chains; 1:2376

MATERIAL, SIZE & ORIENTATION: paper, buff coloured, mounted on linen, slight colour; 65.2cms EW x 96cms NS; north to top

CONTENT: fields, some outlined in blue, all with field name and content; field name and content repeated in table; gardens including walled garden [?at Pynes]; tree symbols showing orchards and plantations; roads, directions given; buildings in plan; peripheral estates named

INSET MAP: Title: 'Jackamoor Tenement Upton Pyne Sir S H Northcote Bart'

Jackamoor SX 904986

Scale and content as above

DECORATION: 4 point compass indicator; north marked by flower bud

20/7/4

UPTON PYNE

19th cent.   51/24/8/4

Upton Pyne Church SX 891994
See entry under Newton St Cyres, 14/3/4

UPTON PYNE see also C190

WARKLEIGH see C191

21/1/1

WASHFIELD

1780   Tiverton Library Portfolio 9

Washfield Church SS 935154   eM/1780/1246
TITLE: 'Survey of the Lands of Mr William Ley lying in the Parish of
    Washfield in the County of Devon called by the Several names of
    North Windbow, Heddon Downe. Claypitt. and Little Moore.. A:D:
    1780'
SURVEYOR: not named
SCALE: 'Scale of Chains'; scale bar; 1"=3 chains; 1:2376
MATERIAL, SIZE & ORIENTATION: parchment, slight colour; 80.5cms EW
    x 70cms NS (tightly folded); north to top
CONTENT: river, double black lines, arrow indicating direction of flow;
    fields outlined in 2 shades of green or yellow indicating areas named
    in title; named, with gardens, orchards and woods also named; all
    listed in tables with content; hedge ownership indicated by crosses
    with explanatory note; total content distinguished with and without
    hedges; content of houses, courtlages and gardens listed; green tree
    symbols showing wood; plain tree symbols marking orchards; roads,
    green margins, one unfenced; directions given; buildings in plan;
    peripheral owners named
DECORATION: 16 point compass rose, cardinals, plain/pink; north marked
    by elaborate fleur-de-lys; scale bar, yellow; some elaborate ink
    flourishes in title

21/1/2

WASHFIELD

1789   NDRO 2309B/E27

Washfield church SS 935154
TITLE: 'A Plan of Badcott situate in the Parish of Washfield in the County
    of Devon the property of Mr Jacob Melhuish Suryed [sic] &c by
    Thos Huggins April 1789'
SURVEYOR: Thomas Huggins
SCALE: 'Scale of Chains'; divided scale; 1"=2 chains; 1:1584
MATERIAL, SIZE & ORIENTATION: parchment, coloured; 31.3cms EW x
    32.2cms NS; north to top
CONTENT: River Exe, Lang Brooke, Mill Stream, ink stream lines; arrow
    indicating direction of flow; Lang Bridge; fields outlined in green,
    with alphabetic reference to table giving field names and content;
    dotted lines indicating fence ownership; gates; garden in plan; tree
    symbols showing isolated trees and woods referred by letter to table,
    others named on map without symbols; roads, buff, fenced and un-
    fenced; directions given; footpaths, pecked lines; buildings in plan,
    hatched in ink; gardens and yard named; peripheral features and
    owners named
        Pencil grid for construction of the map
DECORATION: 16 point compass rose, ink shading/ black or brown; north
    marked by fleur-de-lys

21/1/3

WASHFIELD

1789   NDRO 2309B/E28

Washfield Church SS 935154
TITLE: 'A Plan of Badcot situate in the Parish of Washfield in the County
    of Devon the Property of Mr Jb Melhuish'
SURVEYOR: at bottom 'Surveyed &c by Thos Huggins 1789'
SCALE: 'Scale of Chains'; divided scale; 1"=2 chains; 1:1584
MATERIAL, SIZE & ORIENTATION: paper, coloured; 37cms EW x 44.5cms
    NS; north to top
CONTENT: River Exe, Lang Brooke, Mill Stream, ink stream lines; Lang
    Bridge; fields outlined in yellow and green; alphabetic reference to
    table giving field names and content; dotted lines indicating fence
    ownership; gates; garden in plan; tree symbols showing wood, orchard
    and isolated trees; roads, fenced and unfenced, directions given; foot-
    paths, pecked lines; buildings in plan, hatched black; peripheral
    features and owners named

NOTE: 'Fences belong to the Lands on the side the Lines are dotted'

DECORATION: title cartouche: simple scroll; 32 point compass rose, plain/black, pink/red, light/dark blue; north marked by fleur-de-lys, SEW by letter; border, hatching at right angles to map

21/2/1

WEARE GIFFARD
1721/1726   1262M/E2/1

Weare Giffard Woods SS 478218
4 plans and surveys of woodlands

TITLE: 'A True Plot of Wear Coppes Wood Surveyed by Joseph Phillips'
SURVEYOR: Joseph Phillips
SCALE: no unit of measurement stated; scale bar
MATERIAL, SIZE & ORIENTATION: paper, ink; 24.4cms EW x 15.7cms NS; north to top; [inserted later]
CONTENT: wood outlined in ink
ENDORSEMENT: A Plan of Ware Wood 14ac. 00r. 19per. in 1721. Jos. Phillips

TITLE: 'The Plot of Road Cleave Wood more exact then the former'
SURVEYOR: Joseph Phillips
SCALE: 'The Scale by which it was plotted and cast up'; no unit of measurement stated; scale bar
MATERIAL, SIZE & ORIENTATION: paper, ink; 20.1cms x 16.2cms; no direction
CONTENT: outline of wood in ink
ENDORSEMENT: A Plan of Road Cliff Wood 7ac. 3rod. 8per. in 1721 Jos. Phillips

TITLE: 'The Figure of Road Cleave Wood plotted and cast up by a Scale of Ten Pole in an Inch by me Jos. Phillips Land Meter'
SURVEYOR: Joseph Phillips
SCALE: 'Ten Pole in an Inch'; 1:1980
MATERIAL, SIZE & ORIENTATION: paper, ink; 15.4cms EW x 19cms NS; north to top
CONTENT: dotted line outlining wood
DECORATION: 16 point compass rose; north marked by fleur-de-lys, SEW by letter
ENDORSEMENT: Cleave Wood

TITLE: 'A True Plan of Clift Easter Wood. Taken by Jos Phillips May the 13th 1726. For the Right Honble Hugh Lord Clinton'
SURVEYOR: Joseph Phillips

SCALE: 'Scale of Perches'; scale bar; 1"=1980
MATERIAL, SIZE & ORIENTATION: paper, ink; 7.7cms EW x 8.4cms NS; north to top
CONTENT: wood outlined in ink
DECORATION: 16 point compass rose; north marked by fleur-de-lys, SEW by letter
ENDORSEMENT: Map of Clift Easter Wood 2A. 1R. 36P

21/2/2

WEARE GIFFORD
1810   1262M/E22/73

Weare Gifford Church SS 476221
TITLE: 'Plan of part of the Proposed Torrington Canal'
SURVEYOR: 'F.G. Novr 1810'
SCALE: 'Scale of Chains'; scale bar; 1"=5 chains; 1:3960
MATERIAL, SIZE & ORIENTATION: paper, coloured; 43.1cms EW x 71.4cms NS; east to top
CONTENT: River Torridge, blue, direction of flow indicated; streams, blue; relief shown by hill shading; proposed canal indicated by red line; fields outlined in ink; roads, fenced and unfenced, buff; footpaths, pecked lines; buildings in plan, hatched grey; Wear Mill, lime kilns and Wear Dock named
DECORATION: 4 point compass indicator; (meridian) north marked by an arrow, S by letter

21/2/3

WEARE GIFFORD
c.1837   1262M/E2/32

Weare Gifford Church SS 476221
TITLE: not given
SURVEYOR: not named
SCALE: not given
MATERIAL, SIZE & ORIENTATION: paper, ink; 33.6cms x 33,5cms; no direction
CONTENT: tree symbols indicating Wear Wood; roads showing intended new road and old road with measurements; roads named as from Wear Dock to Torrington and 'Road to Rising Sun'
ASSOCIATED DOCUMENTS: accounts, specification for building a tollhouse, in same bundle with map

21/3/1

WEMBURY

1788–1789   6107

Langdon SX 515498 Down Thomas SX 503503
See entry under Bridestowe, 2/35/6

21/3/2

WEMBURY

1791   PWDRO 74/153/33

Down Thomas SX 503503
Leather-bound volume tooled in gold, 15cms x 22cms
TITLE: 'A Survey and Valuation of the Manor of Down=Thomas situated in the Parish of Wembury, in the County of Devon. Property of John Spurrell Pode Esqr Survey'd and mapp'd in 1791 by Alexr. Law Exmouth. Devon
4 pages giving alpha-numeric references, 'Names of Parcels' with content of 'Gardens & Orchards', Arable and Pasture', Furse Coppice & Waste', Hedges and Ditches' and 'Total Content' arranged by holding.
2 pages, 'An Abstract of the Manor of Down Thomas' giving names of tenants, tenements, terms on which land held and value.
TITLE: of map bound in volume; 'Map of the Manor of Down-Thomas Taken in 1791'
SURVEYOR: Alexander Law
SCALE: 'Scale of Statute Chains each containing Four Perches of 16½ Feet'; scale bar; 1"=8 chains; 1:6336
MATERIAL, SIZE & ORIENTATION: parchment, coloured; 46.7cms EW x 38.5cms NS; north to top
CONTENT: English Channel named, slight ink shading; cliffs and off-shore rocks shaded; relief indicated by hill shading; fields outlined in various colours; alpha-numeric reference to details listed on previous pages; other owners named; asterisks indicating hedge ownership; gates, red; black tree symbols showing orchards and with stippling, woods; roads, buff, fenced and unfenced; footpaths, pecked lines; buildings in plan, grey; peripheral owners and estates named
    Note explaining use of asterisks
DECORATION: title cartouche: simple medallion of ruched fabric and acanthus leaves; 8 point compass rose, plain/shaded grey; north marked by fleur-de-lys, east by cross; fishing boats and rowing boat in the Channel
    Title page decorated in style common to all Alexander Law's surveys with delicate flower and leaf tendrils

LATER NOTE: in pencil that Down Thomas was purchased by James Calmady

21/4/1

WEMBWORTHY

1769   211M/P5

Rashleigh Barton SS 672128
TITLE: 'A Map or Plan of the Manor of Rashleigh in the Parish of Wembworthy and County of Devon the Lands of the Revd Mr Henry Hawkins Tremayne. Survey'd & mapp'd in 1769 by Wm Hole and Thos Call'
SURVEYORS: William Hole and Thomas Call
SCALE: 'A Scale of Chains, each containing 4 Statute perches'; scale bar; 1"=3.5 chains; 1:2772
MATERIAL, SIZE & ORIENTATION: parchment on rollers, coloured; 103cms EW x 86cms NS; north to top
CONTENT: rivers Taw, Dart and the Mill 'Leet' named, grey; streams, ink; bridges, red; fields outlined in various colours and with hedge symbols; alpha-numeric reference to table giving field names and parcels of ground with land use content and total content [some additions made in 1811]; tree symbols showing orchards and with stippling woods and coppices; roads, buff, fenced and unfenced; directions given; buildings in plan, red; courtlages and gardens indicated; peripheral owners named and some peripheral buildings in elevation
DECORATION: title cartouche: scroll with acanthus leaves, flowers and ruched fabric superimposed on rural scene with cottages and a cow; 8 point compass rose, shaded grey; north marked by fleur-de-lys, east by cross

21/5/1

WERRINGTON (Cornwall)

1761   T1258M/E27

See entry under St Giles in the Heath. Map includes part of the Manor of Werrington which is in Devon. 18/24/1

21/5/2

WERRINGTON
1765   T1258M/E28

See entry as above

21/6/1

WESTLEIGH
1745   NDRO 4724 add/1

Westleigh Church SS 472286
See entry under Bideford, 2/14/3

21/6/2

WESTLEIGH
1798   4163M/E1

Westleigh Church SS 472286
See entry under Alverdiscott, 1/5/2

21/7/1

WHIMPLE
1823/5   961M add/E2

Whimple Church SY 044972
See entry under Feniton, 6/3/3

WHIMPLE see also C192

21/8/1

WHITCHURCH
early 18th cent.   1508M/M&P/Whitchurch A2

Moortown SX 527639 Grimstone SX 515707
2 maps, which are almost identical, with a copy of each making 4 maps
   in all, for use in a legal dispute concerning a watercourse
TITLE: not given

SURVEYOR: not named
SCALE: not given
MATERIAL, SIZE & ORIENTATION: paper, watermark, slight colour; 79.5cms
   x 31.6cms; no direction
CONTENT: detail around Plasterdown but less in surrounding area; rivers
   Tavy and Walkham, blue; leats supplying water to large houses, blue
   (Grimston, Sortridge, Tuddebrooke, Moortown, Okeley, Easton
   Towne); controls on leats called Gutterholes, named; mills and mill
   pools; Plaster Down outlined in yellow; gates to Down; on one copy
   area to one side of Plasterdown shown in elevation with hills and
   tors of Dartmoor; roads, buff, named; houses, church and mill in
   elevation; explanatory note on each map but with different information

21/8/2

WHITCHURCH
mid 18th cent.   1508M/M&P/Whitchurch A4

Plasterdown SX 515725
TITLE: not given
SURVEYOR: not named
SCALE: not given
MATERIAL, SIZE & ORIENTATION: paper, ink; 32.2cms x 41cms; no direction
CONTENT: 2 sketch maps showing Plaster Down and water supplies to
   Taviton, Brooke and Grimston Mills

21/8/3

WHITCHURCH
1788–1789   6107

Whitchurch Church SX 493727
See entry under Bridestowe, 2/35/6

21/8/4

WHITCHURCH
1781   RIC HS/2/89

Longford SX 520748
TITLE: 'A Plan of Longford in the Parish of Whitchurch & County of
   Devon J. Ridout's Property 1781'

SURVEYOR: 'Surveyed. Plan'd &c by R Cowl; Plym'o in 1781'

SCALE: not given

MATERIAL, SIZE & ORIENTATION: paper, (torn at edges), slight colour; 73.4cms EW x 52.3cms NS; north to top

CONTENT: rivers and streams, blue, arrow indicating direction of flow; relief shown by hill shading; fields outlined by black symbols indicating hedge ownership; alphabetic reference to list giving field names, content and total content; black tree symbols showing orchards; garden in detail; stippling marking marsh; roads, buff, some named; buildings in plan, red

DECORATION: title cartouche: view of church and tree enclosed in yellow circle; 4 point compass indicator, yellow/grey with 8 lettered segments; north marked by fleur-de-lys

ENDORSEMENT: Great Brake Lode

LATER ADDITIONS: (in ink) shafts, copper lodes, waterwheel, line of rods, engine house, court house for ?mine; (in ink) symbols showing lands belonging to – Donn and 'to neighbours'; (in pencil) line of lodes, etc

21/8/5

WHITCHURCH
1786   1508M/M&P/Whitchurch A3

Whitchurch Down SX 507737

TITLE: 'A Sketch of the Watercourse from Whitchurch Down, to Brooke Mills part of and belonging to the Manor of Walreddon, in the County of Devon, taken from Whitchurch taken from Whitworth Common and Conveyed through the old and ancient Channel, 'till it empties itself into the River Tavy July 6th 1786'

SURVEYOR: not named

SCALE: not given

MATERIAL, SIZE & ORIENTATION: paper, damaged, slight colour; c.119cms x 31.8cms; no direction indicated

CONTENT: River Tavy, leats amd mill pools, blue; where leat crosses field boundaries, ochre; arrows indicating direction of flow; fields and landholders named; roads, buff; where they pass over leats marked and named; bridges; some buildings in plan

Reference 'a Here the accident happened'; no indication as to what this was

Additional information in a later hand

NOTE: map may have originally been larger – some names appear truncated

ENDORSEMENT: Plan of Brook Mill leat

21/8/6

WHITCHURCH
1793   346M/P1

Whitchurch Church SX493727

See entry under Bere Ferrers, 2/6/3

21/8/7

WHITCHURCH
1804   T1258M/E8

Taviton Barton SX 501744

See entry under Tavistock, 19/3/33

21/8/8

WHITCHURCH
19th cent.   D1508M/M&P/Whitchurch Maps 3

Caseytown SX 505732

TITLE: 'The Lands of His Grace the Duke of Bedford adjoining' (sic)

SURVEYOR: not named

SCALE: 'Statute Chains'; scale bar; 1"=3 chains; 1:2376

MATERIAL, SIZE & ORIENTATION: paper, slight colour; 131cms EW x 76.2cms NS; north to top

CONTENT: streams, blue; arrows indicating direction of flow; estates outlined in various colours; gates; mine ramparts shown by clusters of rocks; roads, buff, directions given; footpaths, pecked lines; peripheral owners and estates named

DECORATION: 4 point compass indicator; north marked by a symbol, SEW by letter

21/8/9

WHITCHURCH
1813   1508M/M&P/Whitchurch Maps 4

Walreddon SX 477712

TITLE: [in pencil] 'A Plan of Walreddon Down, Buckton Down & West Down belonging to the Manor of Walreddon, in the Parish of Whitchurch, in the County of Devon'

SURVEYOR: not named; 'Survd July 1813'

SCALE: 'Statute Chains'; scale bar; 1"=3 chains; 1:2376

MATERIAL, SIZE & ORIENTATION: paper, coloured; 107.3cms x 63.6cms; north-east to top

CONTENT: River Tavy and River Walkham, blue; arrows indicating direction of flow; Wash ford named; adit to 'Old Mine', blue; Walreddown Down, Buckton Down, West Down outlined in yellow, pink and blue respectively; furze, waste and coppice distinguished and outlined in colour with ink symbols; Pasture land and Hams (meadows) named; gates; roads, single broken lines; directions given; quarries, including slate quarry; peripheral owners and estates named

Pencil construction grid

DECORATION: 4 point compass indicator; north marked by diamond, SEW by letter

21/8/10

WHITCHURCH

1813   D1508M/M&P/Whitchurch Maps 5

Caseytown SX 505742

TITLE: 'Plan of Whitchurch Down alias Wherry Down, Caseytown, Buechey and Budgehill, belonging to the Manor of Walreddon in the Parish of Whitchurch in the County of Devon'

SURVEYOR: 'T.H.Lakeman surveyor Milton Abbot 1813'

SCALE: 'Scale of Statute Chains'; scale bar; 1"=6 chains; 1:4752

MATERIAL, SIZE & ORIENTATION: paper, slight colour; 72.5cms EW x 46.8cms NS; north to top

CONTENT: streams, blue, dotted lines; estates outlined in various colours which also denote fence ownership, owners' named; mine ramparts shown by clusters of rocks; roads, buff; directions given; footpaths, dotted lines; peripheral owners named

Reference key

DECORATION: 4 point compass indicator; north marked by a symbol, SEW by letter

21/8/11

WHITCHURCH

1814   1508M Devon/M&P/Whitchurch Maps 5a

Whitchurch Church SX 493727

TITLE: 'A Plan of the South and Southeastern Environs of Tavistock extending from thence to Harrowbridge; as enlarged from Col. Mudge's Map of Devon'

SURVEYOR: William Claringbull

SCALE: 'Chains of one Mile'; scale bar; 1"=20 chains; 1:15840

MATERIAL, SIZE & ORIENTATION: paper, slight colour; 48cms x 40.3cms; no direction although implied

CONTENT: Tavy River, Walkham River and streams, blue; Whitchurch Down, Shorts Down, Plaster Down and West Down outlined in blue, coloured grey; gardens and house plots outlined with hedge symbols, grey; tree symbols showing orchard and with stippling woodland, all outlined with hedge symbols; roads, fenced and unfenced; buildings in plan, red; principal settlements named; Tavistock buildings and garden plots shown in detail

21/8/12

WHITCHURCH

1825   1262M/E22/45

Whitchurch Church SX 493727

See entry under Brentor, 2/33/2

21/8/13

WHITCHURCH

1830   1508M Devon/M&P/Whitchurch A1

Brook SX 478729 Tor SX 472716

Leather-bound volume 29cms x 33.5cms; 2 maps

TITLES:

Map 1 'Brook otherwise Skoyns' Tenement'

Map 2 'Middle Tor in the Parish of Whitchurch'

SURVEYOR:

Map 1 'Survey'd &c by W:T: Stentaford Walkhampton Devon 1830'

Map 2 not named, presumably also W:T: Stentaford

SCALE:

Map 1 'Scale of Chains'; scale bar; 1"=6 chains 1:4752

Map 2 'Statute Chain'; scale bar; 1"=6 chains; 1:4752

MATERIAL, SIZE & ORIENTATION: parchment, slight colour; 28cms EW x 32.5cms NS; Map 1 north to top, Map 2 north-west to top

CONTENT: River Tavy, stream lines, arrows indicating direction of flow; fields outlined by hedge symbols; numeric reference to list giving names of closes, content of 'Tillageable', 'Waste' and total content; asterisks indicating hedge ownership; tree symbols showing woods and orchards; stippling marking waste; roads, direction given; buildings in plan, red; peripheral owners named

DECORATION: surveyor's name on scroll supported by a tree; map 1, 8 point compass rose, acanthus leaves and line shading; north marked by fleur-de-lys; map 2, 8 point compass rose, shaded line; north marked by fleur-de-lys

21/9/1

WHITESTONE
1756	ECA Book 58

Whitestone SX 869943
See entry under Exeter Chamber Map Book, 5/3/49

21/9/2

WHITESTONE
1787	Powderham Archive

Whitestone SX 869943
See entry under Powderham, 16/12/7

21/9/3

WHITESTONE
1798	Z17/3/7

Whitestone SX 869943
See entry under Dunsford, 4/13/5

21/9/4

WHITESTONE
late 18th cent.	1508M Devon/M&P/Whitestone Maps 1

Cutteridge SX 876923
TITLE: not given
SURVEYOR: not named
SCALE: no unit of measurement states; vertical and horizontal scale bars to be read from opposite sides of the map; 1"=2 ?chains; 1:?1584
MATERIAL, SIZE & ORIENTATION: paper, watermark, ink; c.154cms EW x 48.5cms NS; north-south line marked 'magnetic meridian'; south to top

CONTENT: draft plan only; river with old and new courses marked; arrows indicating direction of flow; fields named, with content and land use; asterisks indicating fence ownership; gates; areas of coppice separated from fields by broken lines, named; roads; buildings in plan with courtlage and garden attached, named; peripheral owners, commons, woods and parishes named
ENDORSED: Field Map of Cuttridge
NOTE: survey lines in pencil

21/10/1

WIDECOMBE IN THE MOOR
1786/7/9	Z17/3/20–21

Lizwell SX 706744 Jordan SX 701751
See entry under Ashburton, 1/8/2

21/10/2

WIDECOMBE IN THE MOOR
1800	PWDRO 1957/

Widecombe Church SX 719768
See entry under Buckland-in-the-Moor, 2/47/1

21/10/3

WIDECOMBE IN THE MOOR
1810	DCO 230

Widecombe Church SX 719768
TITLE: 'Laughter-Hall in the Parish of Widdicombe-in-the-Moor Property of Henry Browse, gent. 1810'
SURVEYOR: not named
SCALE: 'A Scale of Chains'; scale bar; 1"=4 chains; 1:3168
MATERIAL, SIZE & ORIENTATION: paper, coloured; 34cms x 44.5cms; no direction
CONTENT: East Dart River, green with stream lines; arrow indicating direction of flow; ford named; fields, green with field names and content; crosses indicating hedge ownership; gateways; tree symbols showing isolated trees; footpaths, buff, pecked lines; buildings in plan, red; peripheral owners and estates named

21/10/4

WIDECOMBE IN THE MOOR
early 19th cent.   48/14/142/1a–b

Spitchwick Manor SX 709725
TITLE: 'Manor of Spitchwich'
SURVEYOR: not named
SCALE: 'Scale of Chains'; scale bar; 1"=4 chains; 1:3168
MATERIAL, SIZE & ORIENTATION: tracing mounted on card, slight colour; 29.6cms x 37.3cms; no direction
CONTENT: River Dart and streams, mauve; arrows indicating direction of flow; bridges; tors in profile; fields outlined in various colours; tree symbols showing ?woods; roads, yellow, fenced and unfenced; footpaths, broken lines; buildings shown by red dots and properties named
NOTE: there are two almost identical copies of this map

21/10/5

WIDECOMBE IN THE MOOR
19th cent.   48/14/142/2a–b

Leigh Tor SX 710716
TITLE: 'Leightor in Withecombe'
SURVEYOR: not named
SCALE: 'Scale of Chains'; scale bar; 1"=4.25 chains; 1:3366
MATERIAL, SIZE & ORIENTATION: tracing mounted on paper, slight colour; 21.8cms EW x 30.3cms NS; north to top
CONTENT: stream, ink line, arrows indicating direction of flow; fields outlined in pink; numeric reference [to Survey Book]; gates; tree symbols on green-lined background showing ?wood; road, buff, directions given; buildings in plan, pink
DECORATION: 4 point compass indicator, green/pink; north marked by fleur-de-lys, green/pink
NOTE: There are two almost identical copies of this map

21/11/1

WIDWORTHY
1780   281M/E4

Widworthy Church SY 213993
See under Dalwood, 4/1/4

21/11/2

WIDWORTHY
1781   Antony Muniments PP/FX/23

Widworthy Church SY 213993
See entry under Colyton, 3/27/5

21/11/3

WIDWORTHY
1826   5556Z/ME1

Widworthy Church SY 213993
See entry under Farway, 6/2/4

WIDWORTHY see also C193

21/12/1

WINKLEIGH
1769   211M/P1

Winkleigh Church SS 632081 Coulson SS 639057 Cadditon SS 644050 Stabdon SS 658067 Collacott Barton SS 653075 Chittlehampton Church SS 636255
TITLE: 'A Map or Plan of several Estates called Colston, Cadditon, Stabdon, Shrievland alias Shorland, Collacott and Chittlehampton; part of the Manor of Winckley=Tracey, in the Parish of Winckley and County of Devon the Lands of the Revd Mr Henry Hawkins Tremayne Survey'd and Mapp'd in 1769 By Wm Hole and Thos Call'
SURVEYORS: William Hole and Thomas Call
SCALE: 'A Scale of Chains each containing 4 Statute Perches'; scale bar; 1"=3.6 chains; 1:2851
MATERIAL, SIZE & ORIENTATION: parchment on rollers, coloured; 145cms EW x 127.5cms NS; north to top
CONTENT: pond, streams, blue; fields outlined in various colours and with hedge symbols; alpha-numeric reference to table giving field names, land use – Arable & Pasture; Moorassy Pasture; Fursey Pasture; Timber & Coppice; Hedges & Waste – content and total content; 'asterisms' indicating hedge ownership; gates, red; tree symbols showing isolated trees, orchards and with stippling marking

furze and coppice; roads, buff, directions given; buildings, red with courtlages and gardens; peripheral landowners named

DECORATION: title cartouche: scrolls with acanthus leaves, flowers, fruit, shell, ruched fabric superimposed on hunting scene with huntsmen, hounds and fox; 8 point compass rose, light/dark grey; north marked by fleur-de-lys, east by cross

21/12/3

WINKLEIGH

1817   Ex. D&C Ch. Comm. 98/8791

Nethercott, now Narracott SS 603030

See entry under Aylesbeare, 1/18/2

Exeter D&C 3577 Chapter Act Book p.667 14 March 1817 various estates were ordered to be surveyed. Last in the list, Winkleigh … 'and the latter Estate to be mapped'

21/12/2

WINKLEIGH

1769   211M/P2

Winkleigh Church SS 632081

TITLE: 'A Map or Plan of severall Messuages or Tenements called Crought, Ward, Bowd-Hills, Hurdwicke, Lifton, Heckpen and Pope-houses, West-Heath, South Weekhouse Winckley-Moor, Gerradon, Copta Furse and Joynts, North Weekhouse, Wheatland, Hole & Punchedon, East Heath, Horrey-Mill, and Timbridge Wood, part of the Manor of Winckley-Tracey in the Parish of Winckley & County of Devon The Lands of the Revd Mr Henry Hawkins Tremayne. Survey'd and mapp'd in 1769 By William Hole & Thos Call'

SURVEYORS: William Hole and Thomas Call

SCALE: 'A Scale of Chains each containing 4 Statute perches'; scale bar; 1"=3.6 chains; 1:2851

MATERIAL, SIZE & ORIENTATION: parchment on rollers, coloured; 185.3cms EW x 138cms NS; north to top

CONTENT: pond, blue; fields outlined in various colours and with hedge symbols; alpha-numeric reference to table giving names of tenements and parcels, field names; land use (as in 211M/P1); 'asterisms' indicating hedge ownership of tenement boundaries; gates, red; tree symbols showing orchards and with stippling furze and coppice; roads, buff, fenced and unfenced, directions given; buildings, some in plan, outlined in red with courtlages and gardens; some houses in elevation including village of Winkleigh and its church, Winkleigh Court and Castle; peripheral landowners named

DECORATION: title cartouche: scrolls with acanthus leaves, flowers, ruched fabric superimposed on scene with views of village with church, Court and castle set in landscape of hills, shaded light and dark grey; 8 point compass rose, shaded light/ dark grey; north marked by fleur-de-lys, east by cross

21/13/1

WITHERIDGE

1769   211M/P3

Witheridge Church SS 803145

TITLE: 'A Map or Plan of the several Messuages Lands and Tenements of and belonging to The Revd Mr Henry Hawkins Tremayne in the Parish of Witheridge and County of Devon Taken in 1769 By Wm Hole & Thos Call'

SURVEYORS: William Hole and Thomas Call

SCALE: 'A Scale of Chains each containing 4 Statute perches'; scale bar; 1"=3.6 chains; 1:2851

MATERIAL, SIZE & ORIENTATION: parchment on rollers, coloured; 90cms EW x 104cms NS; north to top

CONTENT: pond, blue; river Dart grey with dark margins; arrow indicating direction of flow; bridge in elevation, red; fields outlined in various colours and with hedge symbols; alpha-numeric reference to table giving names of fields or parcels of ground and land use – Arable & Pasture, Moorassy Pasture, Fursey Pasture, Timber & Coppice, Hedges & Waste – content and total content; 'asterisms' indicating hedge ownership; gates, red; tree symbols showing orchards and with stippling woods, coppice and furze; roads outlined in buff, some directions given; footpaths, pecked lines; buildings, some in plan, red, some in elevation; church drawn in some detail with accurate scenic detail of churchyard and village centre; peripheral owners named

DECORATION: title cartouche: scroll with acanthus leaves, flowers and ruched fabric with rural scene of village with moors in the background, shaded light and dark grey; 8 point compass rose, light/dark grey; north marked by fleur-de-lys, east by cross

21/14/1

WITHYCOMBE RALEIGH
1756   ECA Book 58

Approx. position SX 998808
See entry under Exeter Chamber Map Book, 5/3/51

21/14/2

WITHYCOMBE RALEIGH
1768   Z2/4

Approx. position SY 005816
TITLE: 'A Map of Marpool Hall, the Seat of Thomas Hull Esqr'
SURVEYOR: 'survey'd and Mapp'd by William Hayman Land-Surveyor, in Exeter 1768'
SCALE: 'A Scale of Chains'; scale bar; 1"=1.2 chains; 1:950
MATERIAL, SIZE & ORIENTATION: parchment, coloured; 77cms EW x 81cms NS; east to top
CONTENT: river, grey-shaded margins, stream lines; arrows indicating direction of flow; leat taken off leading to ornamental lake; tree symbols distinguishing coniferous and deciduous trees; – regularly spaced for orchards, closely arranged for woods; isolated trees; ornamental groups of trees, fenced; some areas referred by letter to list in ornamental book, lower left; stippling for lawns and gardens in front of house and meadows; roads indicated by hedge symbols, trees and green shading; footpaths, pecked lines; path to Withycombe Chapel named; lanes named; gates; fence symbols at boundary of park with ornamental gates in elevation; buildings in plan, black; peripheral owners named
DECORATION: title cartouche: title in ribbon with surveyor's name in a medallion of palm leaves and flowers; coat of arms, black and gold; scale surmounted by dividers in black and gold with decoration similar to that on gatepost pillars; 16 point compass rose, black/plain, black/gold centre; north marked by fleur-de-lys, east by cross, south by arrowhead; border: 1 wide grey-shaded band, 2 fine lines inside, 1 fine line outside, 3 blue and gold rings above
PUBLICATION: Todd Gray, *The Garden History of Devon* (Exeter, 1995), 151–2

21/15/1

WOLBOROUGH
1790   1508M/Surveys/V5

Wolborough Church SX 855703
See entry under Bovey, North, 2/21/2

21/15/2

WOLBOROUGH
18th cent.   1508M/Devon/Parish Wolborough 7

Wolborough Church SX 855703
TITLE: not given; sketch plan only
SURVEYOR: not named
SCALE: not given
MATERIAL, SIZE & ORIENTATION: paper, ink, (no colour but colour mentioned in annotation); 22.4cms x 19.7cms; south-east to top
CONTENT: courtlages and fields outlined in ink, named with present and previous owners named; orchard indentified with parallel lines; 2 roads, named; houses in elevation on opposing horizons with owners' names
NOTE: top left, 'The Red part is claimed J Lake'
DECORATION: 4 point compass indicator composed of 2 fletched arrows pointing east and south; directions spelt out

21/16/1

WOODBURY
1783   346M/E834

Road SX 993852
TITLE: not given [map shows old road between Exeter and Lympstone and proposed new road]
SURVEYOR: not named
SCALE: not given
MATERIAL, SIZE & ORIENTATION: paper, ink; 39.4cms x 30.7cms; no direction
CONTENT: fields outlined in ink, named; tree symbols along 'old Footway'; roads, buff, direction given; new road outlined by pecked lines; one road gated; 'sand pitt'; note giving measurements concerning old and proposed new road and footpath
NOTE: the plan is annexed to a document

ENDORSEMENT: 3d March 1783. Copy Order diverting Highway &
Footway & for making new Highway & Footway in Lieu & plan
Annexed
    Copy of Sir Francis Drake's Consent
    Copy of Agreemt bet[ween] him & Surveyors of Woodbury

21/16/2

WOODBURY
1785   346M/E838

Parsonage Stile SX 988843

TITLE: not given [map shows area between the Exeter road and the river
Exe, roads between Exeter and Lympstone forming the boundary of
the Nutwell estate]

SURVEYOR: not named

SCALE: not given

MATERIAL, SIZE & ORIENTATION: paper, coloured; 90.5cms x 36.7cms; no
direction

CONTENT: River Exe, blue with grey left bank; 'Exon Brook' named;
fields outlined in green, named; some owners named; glebe and
parsonage fields distinguished; gates; roads, pink; old and new roads
demarcated with new roads and footpaths outlined with pecked lines;
Brice's Yard named; buildings in plan, yellow, named; one road
'Private Way of Sir Francis Henry Drake Bart'

NOTE: on map describing route and length of old and new footpaths;
also 'June 6th 1785 This is the Plan referred to us in our Order
hereunto annexed. Samuel Eyle John B Cholwich'

ENDORSEMENT: Plan and order for turning a Footway in Nutwell June 6
1785

PUBLICATION: M.G.Dickinson, compiler and ed., *A Living from the Sea*
(Devon Books, 1985), 39

21/16/3

WOODBURY
1798   1077/6/15

Woodbury Salterton Church SY 012891

TITLE: 'A Plan of the Manor of Woodbury Salterton in the County of
Devon the Property of Reymundo Putt Esqr'

SURVEYOR: 'Wm Pilkinton, Landsurveyor, Exeter, 1798'

SCALE: scale bar, no figures or unit of measurement

MATERIAL, SIZE & ORIENTATION: parchment, slight colour; 91cms EW x
131.5cms NS; north to top

CONTENT: streams, ink stream lines; arrows indicating direction of flow;
spring head marked; fields outlined in ink; individual farms outlined
in colour; alpha-numeric reference to Survey Book; gardens in plan;
green tree symbols showing orchards and with stippling, coppice;
roads, buff, fenced and unfenced; directions given; buildings in plan,
red; peripheral owners named

DECORATION: title cartouche: delicately-drawn trees and plants
surrounding medallion; milestone showing 'VI Miles from Exeter';
cartographer's name inscribed on log below; scale: ribbon decoration;
8 point compass rose with female head in profile in centre; north
marked by fleur-de-lys; border: decorative ribbon entwined with
leaves broken by spheres and bars

NOTE: This map is the complete survey mapped and described in detail
in the Survey Book 1077/6/6

21/16/4

WOODBURY
1798   1077/6/6

Woodbury Salterton Church SY 012892

Leather-bound volume tooled in gold, 24.3cms x 15.5cms. 11 maps
with details of land use, content and value followed by 'Survey of
Timber taken in 1798'

TITLE: 'Plans of Farm's in Woodbury Salterton Manor in the County of
Devon the Property of Reymundo Putt Esqr 1798'

SURVEYOR: 'Willm Pilkinton Land Surveyor Exeter'

SCALE: 'Scale of Chains'; scale bar; 1"=14 chains; 1:11088; later maps
have scale bars drawn on handles of pitchforks, spades and rakes but
with figures only, no unit of measurement

MATERIAL, SIZE & ORIENTATION: paper, ink, slight colour; maps on single
page, north to top

CONTENT: streams, ponds outlined in ink with stream lines; fields outlined
in ink with total holding outlined in colour; numeric reference to
table on facing page giving field names, content, 'Present Value per
Acre, Value per Piece'; tree symbols showing orchards, and with
stippling marking coppices; roads, buff; buildings in plan, brown

11 MAPS AS FOLLOWS:-
  1 A Plan of Mr Butters Farm in Woodbury
  2 A Plan of Mr Butter's Farm called Gigeon's Overland
  3 A Plan of Mr Force's Farm in Woodbury
  4 A Plan of Mr Sander's Farm in Woodbury

5 Davy & Parrot's Cottages & Orchard

6 A Plan of Mr Rew's Farm in Woodbury

7 A Plan of Jno Ellis's Cott and Orchard with 3 other orchards

8 A Plan of Mr Cox's Farm

9 A Plan of Mr Westcomb's Farm in Woodbury

10 A Plan of Mrs Beavis's Farm in Woodbury

11 A Plan of Mr Perry's Farm in Woodbury

DECORATION: title cartouche: rural scene with agricultural implements above and surveyor's instruments below; individual maps, titles superimposed on rural scenes and agricultural implements; variety of decorative borders surround each map and each reference page; leaf inserted before title page: 'Survey and Valuation of Grindle Farm in the Parish of Woodbury in the County of Devon Property of Reydo Putt Esqr Taken in 1800 by Alexr Law'

NOTE: annotations to text opposite map 2 dated 1843

21/16/5

WOODBURY

1790s   Private hands

Woodbury Church SY 009871

TITLE: 'A Map of the Manor of Woodbury Property of Denys Rolle Esqr'

SURVEYOR: not named

SCALE: scale bar; 1"=4 chains; 1:3168

MATERIAL, SIZE & ORIENTATION: paper, mounted on linen, ink; 185.5cms x 214cms; north-west to top

CONTENT: streams including 'Topsham Back River'; marshes and tide marks with high and ordinary tide levels indicated; fields with alpha-numeric reference [to Survey Book]; 'asterisms' indicating hedge ownership; tree symbols showing orchards; roads, fenced and un-fenced; directions given; buildings in plan, hatched black and in elevation including the church; Woodbury Castle marked; peripheral owners estates and parishes named

DECORATION: 4 point compass indicator and an 8 point compass indicator with north marked by a symbol on the latter

21/16/6

WOODBURY

early 19th cent.   96M/Box 93/50–51

Woodbury Church SY 009871

TITLE: 'Barons in the Parish of Woodbury'

SURVEYOR: not named

SCALE: not given

MATERIAL, SIZE & ORIENTATION: paper, mounted, ink; 44.8cms EW x 42.8cms NS; north to top; fletched arrow marking NS line

CONTENT: river, stream lines; fields with numeric reference to list giving field names and internal content; external content column blank; tree symbols showing orchard; roads, solid and pecked lines; buildings, some in plan, hatched; some in elevation

WOODBURY see also C194

21/17/1

WOODLAND

1790   1508M/Surveys/V5

Woodland Church SX 791688

See entry under Bovey, North, 2/21/2

WOODLAND see also C195

WOODLEIGH see C40, C196–97

WORLINGTON, EAST see C198

22/1/1

YARCOMBE

1817   Encl. Award 82

Peter Hayes Farm ST 245064

This is a badly damaged map being a copy of part of the map showing the Enclosure Award at Yarcombe

TITLE: Peter Hayes the only words legible

SURVEYOR: not named

SCALE: scale bar showing 1"=7 chains; (the scale on the Enclosure Map is 1"=6 chains)

MATERIAL, SIZE & ORIENTATION: parchment, coloured; size cannot be measured; north to top

CONTENT: stream, blue; relief shown by hill shading; fields in various colours with hedge symbols indicating ownership; numeric reference (different from Enclosure Map) to list now unreadable; tree symbols showing orchard, woods, copses and isolated trees; roads, direction given; buildings in plan, red; peripheral owners named

DECORATION: 8 point compass rose, black plain; north marked by fleur-de-lys but mostly torn away

NOTE: it would appear that this map was developed from the Enclosure Map by the same map-maker for the use of one landowner

YARCOMBE see also B16, B51, B108, C199

22/2/1

YARNSCOMBE

1821   96M/Box 87/5

Yarnscombe Church SS 562236

TITLE: 'A Plan of the Common Wood belonging to West Delay & Whitley and East or Lower Dellay situate in the Parish of Yarnscombe, Devon'

SURVEYOR: not named

SCALE: 'A Scale of Chains'; scale bar; 1"=2 chains; 1:1584

MATERIAL, SIZE & ORIENTATION: parchment, slight colour; 18.3cms EW x 31.5cms NS; north to top

CONTENT: brook, arrows indicating direction of flow; fields outlined in green or red; alphabetic reference to list giving field names and content and detailing those lands to be exchanged; tree symbols showing isolated trees; road, broken line; peripheral owners named

DECORATION: 4 point compass indicator; north marked by fleur-de-lys

ASSOCIATED DOCUMENT: map part of Conveyance dated 12 Sept. 1821. Land exchanged between Lord Rolle and Anthony Loveband

22/3/1

YEALMPTON

1785   PWDRO 1957/2

Lotherton bridge SX 585539

TITLE: 'A Plan of Lotherton in the Parish of Yealmpton, and County of Devon belonging to M.T. Edwards'

SURVEYOR: 'Survey'd & Planned by R. Cowl, Plymo 1785'

SCALE: not given

MATERIAL, SIZE & ORIENTATION: paper, mounted on linen, slight colour; 47.3cms x 29.5cms; north-east to top

CONTENT: river, grey with stream lines; bridges; ponds; fields outlined with hedge symbols; meadow, green; arable, parallel lines; alphabetic reference to list giving field names and content; gates, red; tree symbols, black; roads, buff, outlined with hedge symbols; buildings in plan outlined in red; 'Part of Ermington' parish named

DECORATION: title cartouche: scrolls with acanthus leaves and lady's portrait at top; 4 point compass indicator, plain/grey; north marked by fleur-de-lys

22/3/2

YEALMPTON

*c.*1804   PWDRO 1957/4

Dunstone SX 594515

TITLE: 'A Map of Dunstone in the Parish of Yealmpton'

SURVEYOR: 'R. Fox fecit'

SCALE: 'A Scale of 20 Chains or 1 Quarter of a Mile'; scale bar; 1"=4 chains; 1:3168

MATERIAL, SIZE & ORIENTATION: paper, coloured; 81.6cms EW x 48.1cms NS; south to top

CONTENT: fields, some in various colours; some with initials denoting ownership; numeric reference to Reference Table giving field names, content and hedge content; crosses indicating fence ownership; tree symbols, green showing orchards; stippling marking gardens and common; quarry, blue; roads, plain, some directions given; buildings in plan, shaded black, red or blue; peripheral owners named

DECORATION: title cartouche: leaf pattern; 8 point (plain) compass rose; north marked by fleur-de-lys

22/3/3

YEALMPTON
1824   PWDRO 1957/11

Hurdlecombe SX 601518

TITLE: 'Map of Lands at Hurlcombe Lake 1824'

SURVEYOR: not named

SCALE:'Scale of Chains'; scale bar; 1"=1 chain; 1:792

MATERIAL, SIZE & ORIENTATION: paper, slight colour;76cms EW x 55.4cms NS; north to top

CONTENT: river, blue, named (Hurlcombe Lake); arrows indicating direction of flow; culvert; fields outlined in black with owners' names and content; gates, red; roads, fenced; directions given; peripheral owners named

DECORATION: 4 point compass indicator; fletched arrow marking NS line

22/3/4

YEALMPTON
1827   113A/33/2

Coffleet House (now disappeared) SX 551511

See entry under Brixton, 2/38/10

22/3/5

YEALMPTON
1829   PWDRO 1957/14

Hurdlecombe SX 601518

TITLE: 'Map of Huddlecombe in the Parish of Yealmpton'

SURVEYOR: not named

SCALE: not given

MATERIAL, SIZE & ORIENTATION: paper, coloured;55.4cms EW x 43.7 NS; north to top

CONTENT: stream, black; arrows indicating direction of flow; fields outlined with hedge symbols; coloured green or brown according to land use; crosses indicating fence ownership; numeric reference to list giving field names and content; tree symbols, green showing orchards and isolated trees; roads, buff; directions given; footpaths, dotted lines; buildings in plan, red; peripheral owners named

DECORATION: 4 point compass indicator with flower in centre and leaves marking the 4 directions

YEALMPTON see also C200

23/1/1

ZEAL MONACHORUM
1765–1770   Z17/3/42

Aller Farm SS 735030

See entry under Down St Mary, 4/8/1

23/1/2

ZEAL MONACHORUM
1772   63/2/3/3/1

Zeal Monachorum Church SS 720040

TITLE: 'A Plan of the Manor of Zealmonachorum near Craiditon in the County of Devon belonging to T Parker Esqr Taken in 1772'

SURVEYOR: not named

SCALE: 'A Scale of Chains'; scale bar; 1"=8 chains; 1:6336

MATERIAL, SIZE & ORIENTATION: paper, damaged and in 2 pieces, slight colour; c.64.2cms EW x c.72cms NS; east to top

CONTENT: river, bridges; fields outlined in ink, some named; numeric reference in red [to Survey Book]; tree symbols on green areas showing ?woods, ?orchards; roads, brown, fenced and unfenced, directions given; buildings in plan, black; peripheral owners named

DECORATION: title cartouche: rococo with acanthus leaves and part of Parker arms above; top right 'No 5' surrounded by acanthus leaves; 16 point compass rose, plain/black, solid and pecked lines; north marked by fleur-de-lys

23/1/3

ZEAL MONACHORUM
1782   317M/T66

Burston SS 713023

TITLE: 'A Map of the Barton and Farms of Higher Bourston and Limerise and Overland called Higher Burrow and Farms called Reeve Lane and Oxendowns Arscotts and Maidenhays and Farms called Pitt and Traceys all situate in the Parish of Zealmonachorum in the County of Devon Parts of the Manor of Bourston there. And all which are purchased by Mr John Wreford of Bow alias Nymet Tracey of Mr

Thomas Hole by certain Indentures hereto Annexed and which Refer Hereto'

SURVEYOR: not named

SCALE: 'a scale of chains and links'; scale bar; 1"=2.5 chains; 1:1970

MATERIAL, SIZE & ORIENTATION: parchment, ink; 70cms EW x 82cms NS; north to top

CONTENT: Bow River; fields outlined in ink, named; some with content and some with alpha-numeric reference to table repeating field names; hedge symbols indicating fence ownership; tree symbols showing isolated trees; roads and footpaths; buildings in plan, black; peripheral owners named

ASSOCIATED DOCUMENT: map part of Conveyance dated 27 March 1782

23/1/4

ZEAL MONACHORUM

   post 1803   3068Z/1

Fold Hay SS 708042

TITLE: not given

SURVEYOR: not named

SCALE: not given

MATERIAL, SIZE & ORIENTATION: paper, watermark (1803), damaged, coloured; 38.8cms x c.24.5cms; no direction

CONTENT: watercourse [?Gissage Lake] and tributaries, blue; arrows indicating direction of flow; relief shown by hill shading; fields in various colours outlined in red; alphabetic or numeric reference to list giving field names and content; some fields have asterisks in addition to reference numbers or letters; gates; tree symbols showing orchards, groves and isolated trees; roads, red lines; footpaths, red lines and pecked red lines; directions given; buildings in plan, red; peripheral owners and estates named

NOTE: below map explanatory note concerning significance of asterisks and use of colour but major part torn away

23/1/5

ZEAL MONACHORUM

   1826   SRO DD/WY/Box 121

Zeal Monachorum Church SS 720040

See entry under Bondleigh, 2/19/2

24/1/1

UNIDENTIFIED

   [1694/99]   1948 Pearse/Maps

2 maps of equal size on one sheet of parchment

TITLE: not given

SURVEYOR: not named [Joel Gascoyne, on stylistic grounds]

SCALE: not given

MATERIAL, SIZE & ORIENTATION: parchment, coloured; 68cms x 50cms; each map 34cms x 50cms; compass rose on each map but north not indicated

CONTENT: streams, blue; fields outlined in green and washed in two shades of green; parallel brown lines indicate arable land; various forms of green shading differentiating meadow and moorland; numeric reference to table giving 'Names Quantityes and Qualityes of the feilds conteyned in this Scheame' in statute and customary measure

DECORATION:

   left map: 16 point compass rose, plain/red, plain/blue, light and dark green; centre, turquoise and yellow stylised flower; yellow outer circle

   right map: 8 point compass rose, plain/red, blue; yellow centre and outer circle

Border to each map, two shades of yellow

NOTE: there is some evidence that this map was guarded for insertion into an Atlas

24/1/2

NORTH DEVON

   1768   PRO 30/8/86 (8) 'Planche 6' (MR 1111)

Taw and Torridge estuaries

TITLE: 'Plan de L'Ebouchere des Riverres de Taw, et de Torridge dans le Canal de Bristol figure de memoire les 21 et 22 Octobre 1768'

SURVEYOR: not named

SCALE: not given

MATERIAL, SIZE & CONTENT: Bristol Channel, estuaries and rivers, green; direction of flow indicated; sands, buff, keyed (with some buildings) to reference list A–P where they are further described; fields, plain with hedge boundaries and marked 'bien cultive'; green tree symbols showing 'Perspective du chateau'; roads, plain, directions given; buildings in plan, red, including 'Ipcot chateau' and towns of Barnstaple, Appledore, Pilton and Bradford

24/1/3

NORTH DEVON

19th cent.   Z2/10

TITLE: 'The River Ex[e] from its Rise at Exhead on Exmoor to Tiverton
and the River Barle from its Rise in Challacombe to its influx into
the Ex[e] above Exbridge'

SURVEYOR: not named

SCALE: not given

MATERIAL, SIZE & ORIENTATION: paper, slight colour; 55cms x 45cms; no
direction

CONTENT: rivers, dark green; springs at sources, fine lines converging to
form rivers; bridges; Bristol Channel named but no coastline indicated; principal villages and landscape features named; numeric
reference at various points along the rivers to 2 lists; one referring to
River Barle, the other to the River Exe; roads, red

Supplement

Maps added to the carto-bibliography up to the end of May 2002

BLACKAWTON

1818 or later   DD 69253

Fuge SX 831481

TITLE: not given

SURVEYOR: not named

SCALE: not given

MATERIAL, SIZE & ORIENTATION: paper, watermark, 1818, ink; 37.2cms x 32.7cms; no direction

CONTENT: fields outlined in ink, some with field name and content, some with owners' names; hedge ownership indicated by symbols; roads, directions indicated; Fuge House shown in elevation

BUCKERELL/FENITON

1798   CRO R 5295/1

Deer Park Hotel ST 132001

TITLE: 'A Plan of an estate called the Barton with Overland called Downs Situate in the Parishes of Buckerell and Feniton Property of R. Northcot Esq. Surveyed in April 1798 WW Fecit'

SURVEYOR: WW

SCALE: map damaged and no scale present

MATERIAL, SIZE & ORIENTATION: paper, slight colour; 93cms x 61.5cms; south-west to top

CONTENT: streams, blue with arrows indicating direction of flow; fields outlined in green and some fields in colour; alphabetic reference to separate tables of Barton and Downs giving field names and content; gates; tree symbols, green, showing orchards and isolated copse; tree symbols, green with varied canopies showing isolated trees; roads, fenced and unfenced, some named and some directions given; buildings in plan and elevation including large mansion; peripheral owners and parishes named

DECORATION: title on scroll; 16 point compass rose, plain/blue, plain/red, plain/pale blue; north marked by fleur-de-lys, east by arrow

COLEBROOKE

1736   CRO CY/6737

Colebrooke Church SS 769000

TITLE: 'A Plan of the Manor of Colebrooke in the County of Devon. Being Part of the Estate of the Honble. Sr. John Coryton Bar: Survey'd Septemr. MDCCXXXVI By Will. Doidge Surveyr.'

SURVEYOR: William Doidge

SCALE: 'Scale of Chains'; divided scale; 1"=6 chains; 1:4752

MATERIAL, SIZE & ORIENTATION: parchment, ink; 66.7cms EW x 82.5cms NS; north to top

CONTENT: streams, ink stream lines; fields outlined with hedge symbols; alphabetic reference to tables arranged by tenement giving field names and content; symbols indicating marl and moor; tree symbols showing orchards and isolated trees; roads, directions given; buildings in plan, grey; peripheral owners named

DECORATION: title cartouche; swag of cloth; 4 point compass indicator; north marked by fleur-de-lys; Tables in panels with semi-circles at the top

S4

HAWKCHURCH (formerly in Dorset)
and other Dorset parishes

1769   Dors RO/D/WFP (unlisted)

Hawkchurch Church ST 343014 Abbotts Wootton Farms ST 380964 Berne Farm ST 384946   Morecombelake ST 400942

Leather-bound volume, tooled in gold, 37.8cms x 53.4cms. On spine 'ABBOTTS WOOTTON HAWK CHURCH &c'

GENERAL TITLE: 'Distinct Plans of all the Leasehold Copyhold and Demesne Farms & Tenemts. in the Manor and Liberty of Abbotts Wootton Hawk Church Berne and Moorcombes Blake now calld Moorcombes Lake The whole being a Freehold Estate belonging to The Right Honorable Lord Milton and situate in Dorsetshire Survey'd Valued and Plan'd in the Year 1769 by William Woodward'

SURVEYOR: William Woodward

Atlas contains 208 pages and three unnumbered maps. Within the numbered pages there are maps and written descriptions of some 100 tenements, all part of the above premises, which are keyed to a square (see [map 3] below) and to 'The Great Plan'. Where present, orientation is usually west to top, shown by a line with a fleur-de-lys. The three unnumbered maps, which show the entire estate, are described briefly as follows:-

[Map 1]

TITLE: 'A Plan of the Perambulation of the Manor and Liberty of Abbotts Wootton and Hawkchurch as also of Berne and Moorcombes Blake now called Moorcombes Lake made or taken August 2'o" and 3'o" in the Year 1769'

SCALE: 'A Scale'; scale bar marked in chains and miles; 1"=20 chains; 1:15840

MATERIAL, SIZE & ORIENTATION: parchment, coloured; 62cms x 51.5cms; west to top

CONTENT: 'Bristol Channel' and 'Black Water' named; rivers outlined in ink; the three tenements outlined in blue, green and yellow; some farms named and field names given; commons, named; roads, fenced and unfenced, some named; houses in elevation; buildings in plan, black; peripheral parishes named

Note: 'For a more exact measurement of particulars, apply the enlarg'd Scale inserted in the General Large Plan to the respective Boundarys etc.'

DECORATION: 16 point compass rose, north shown by fleur-de-lys, SEW and half cardinals by letter

ASSOCIATED DOCUMENTS: (a) 'August 3 1769 made a Perambulation of the Parish of Hawkchurch in the Manor and Liberty of Abbotts Wootton' and (b) Index of tenants, giving situation of tenement, how held, page in atlas and 'how to be thrown together'

[Map 2]

TITLE: 'A Plan or Scheme to facilitate the Uniting of small Farms and Tenements in the Manor and Liberty of Abbotts Wootton'
Scale and orientation as in [Map 1]. Parchment, coloured, size 64cms x 51.3cms

[Map 3]

TITLE: 'A Diminish'd Plan of the extensive Manor and Parish of Hawk Church Abbotts Wootton Moorcombe's Blake and detach'd Farms in Marshwood Vale & situate in Dorsetshire belonging to the Right Honorable Lord Milton. Note the use of this Plan to shew the Situation, Connexion and Boundary Line of each Farm and refers to the foregoing Plans'

SCALE: 'A Scale of Poles Chains and Miles'; scale bar; 1" = 20 chains; 1:15840

MATERIAL, SIZE & ORIENTATION: paper, coloured; 64cms x 52.2cms; west to top

CONTENT: much of detail as in [Map 1]; relief shown by grey shading; green tree symbols marking avenues of trees; peripheral parishes and manors named

Grid reference A–T and 1–16

DECORATION: cartouche: medallion surrounded by blue and yellow ribbons and acanthus leaves (similar to that on General Title); 16 point compass rose, plain/red, north shown by fleur-de-lys and NSEW by letter

PUBLICATION: Jack Banfield and Harry Austin, *Where Dorset meets Devon. Hawkchurch* (Hawkchurch, 1996), p.10

S5

KINGSTEIGNTON

1740   Private hands

Kingsteignton Church SX 871730

TITLE: 'A Plan of the Manor of Kingsteignton lying in ye Parish of Kingsteignton in ye County of Devon belonging to ye Rt Honble Lord Clifford Survey'd Novemr MDCCXXXX by Wm Doidge Surveyor'

SURVEYOR: William Doidge

SCALE: 'Scale of Chains each 66 feet'; scale bar; 1"=4 chains; 1:3168
MATERIAL, SIZE & ORIENTATION: parchment; 89cms x 59cms

[Late entry – no fuller details available as compiled from an old list]

S6

PLYMTREE

1788	Private hands

Woodbeer Court ST 065040
TITLE: 'A Plan of the Manor and Farm of Woodbear in the Parish of Plymtree and County of Devon The Property of Wm Southcote Young Survey'd by Jas Foster Ashburton Devon 1788'
SURVEYOR: James Foster
SCALE: 'A scale of chains'; scale bar; 1"=3.5 chains; 1:2772
MATERIAL, SIZE & ORIENTATION: parchment, coloured; framed, approx. 65cms EW x 76cms NS; east to top
CONTENT: river, black stream lines, arrow indicating direction of flow; ford, mill leat, pond; fields outlined in various colours with alpha-numeric reference to contents list giving field name and content and listed by tenement; tree symbols, black, showing orchards, woods and isolated trees; gardens in detail; gates; roads, some gated, buff, directions given; footpaths, pecked lines; marlpits; buildings in plan, named; 'Danes Mill'; peripheral owners named
INSET: 'A Plan of the Manor of Woodbeer'
SCALE: 'A Scale of Poles'; scale bar; 1"=12.5 poles; 1:2475

SIZE & ORIENTATION: 21.5cms EW x 26cms NS; east to top
NOTE: some of detail included is spatially incorrect
DECORATION: title cartouche: rectangular panel decorated by ferns and ribbon at the bottom with brackets supporting an overmantel below which is a shield depicting surveyor's instruments – dividers, set square and pole; 32 point compass rose, red/blue/black superimposed on yellow centre circle, north shown by coloured fleur-de-lys

S7

SHEBBEAR

[1799–1800]	DQS Box 328

Shebbear Church SS 438092
TITLE: 'A Sketch of the Roads leading from Great Libbear in the Parish of Shebbear in the County of Devon to the several places mentioned below part of which is presented by The Revd. William Walters (that is to say) From Great Libbeer to the Book (near the Tenemt. called New Inn) being one mile & 20 Poles in Length & about [blank] Feet in Breadth'
SURVEYOR: not named
SCALE: not given but distances between various points indicated
MATERIAL, SIZE & ORIENTATION: paper, ink; 33.1cms x 41.6cms; no direction
CONTENT: gates; roads outlined in ink, directions given; 'The Road presented' marked; footpath, pecked lines; 'New Inn Cross' marked; houses and church in elevation

Surveyors mentioned in the Main Text, the Supplement, and in Appendices B and C

Notes: This appendix gives references to maps in this volume produced by surveyors working in Devon, their biographical details where found and the maps' date span. Supplementary information in A. Sarah Bendall, *Dictionary of Land Surveyors and local map-makers of Great Britain and Ireland 1530–1850*, is given between braces { } together with the reference number of the surveyor in the Bendall volume.

A1. AISLABIE, Gilbert (also appears as George)
m. Prothesia Edgcumbe, Tavistock, 1773; d. Tavistock, Oct. 1778; maps dated 1750–1770 (and map used by T. King in 1793); refs 2/6/3; 13/13/2; 13/13/3; 15/5/1; 16/5/5; 19/3/2; 19/3/12; 19/3/20; 19/3/21; 19/3/22; 19/3/23; assistant to John Wynne, who was agent to the 4th Duke of Bedford
Bendall: A 049

A2. ANDERSON, William {of London}
Maps dated 1832 {1829–d. 1843/4}; refs B76; associates: Dymond and Dawson; Engineer with Exeter Water Company, 1833 (BMI)
Bendall: A 110

A3. ANDREWS, Henry
bap. Modbury, 1800; maps dated 1826–1837 {1838–50}; refs 1/6/6; 2/38/2; 4/5/8, 16/8/7; B50; B54; B99; B103; associate: George Cumming; Surveyor for Mr Templer; belonged to firm of Messrs Andrews and Otton
Bendall: A 118.8

A4. ANDREW(S), John of Plympton St Mary
Maps dated 1839–40; refs 3/7/2; 3/31/2

A5. ANDREWS, Richard of Poundwell, Modbury
bap. Modbury, 1784, m. Elizabeth Harvey, Modbury, 1804 (IGI); d. Sept. 1833 (EFP); maps dated 1823 {1830}; refs B39; worked under the direction of James Green
Bendall: A 125

A6. BAILEY, Charles {of Nynehead, Somerset
bap. 1766/7, d. Sept. 1855}; maps dated 1823–6; refs B44; B49
Bendall: B 016

A7. BALLMENT, Hugh of Barnstaple
bap. Barnstaple, 1807, son of Robert (*see* A8) and Tabitha; maps dated 1831–40 (and additions to map of Challacombe, 1859); refs 3/10/2; 13/18/8; B118
Bendall: B 070.9

A8. BALLMENT (BALLMONT), Robert
bap. East Down, 1764; m. Tabitha Squire, Barnstaple, 1803; d.1823 (Hugh Fortescue, *A Chronicle of Castle Hill*); maps dated 1788–1810 and work used by Ethelred Still in 1815 {1791–4}; refs 1/6/4; 2/22/12; 2/24/1; 3/4/1; 3/4/2; 3/15/4; 3/33/3; 6/4/1; 6/4/4; 6/5/4; 8/7/3; 8/13/4; 8/19/2; 12/11/2; 13/5/1; 13/18/6; 18/33/1; 18/32/2; associates: worked with James Pitts, William Hole and Alexander Law and his

work used by Ethelred Still; collector of rents for Sir Bourchier Wrey, 1798–1802; accountant at salary of £40 per annum for Sir Bourchier Wrey, 1802–07; estate steward for Fortescue family for 21 years
Bendall: B 071

A9. BARING-GOULD, Edward [E.B.G.] of Bratton Clovelly
b. 1803/4; m. Sophia Charlotte Bond, 1832; d. 26 May 1872; maps dated 1834/36; refs 12/4/1; letter of Juliana Bond, his sister-in-law, dated 23 May 1836, states that 'Lately he has been employing himself in surveying some of Mr. Baring-Gould's property' (S. Baring-Gould, *Early Reminiscences 1834–1864*)
Bendall: B 095.5

A10. BEAR, William of Bideford, Buckland Brewer and Monkleigh
bap. Monkleigh, 1770; bur. Bideford 1839 (?aged 63); maps dated 1803–39; refs 1/7/1; 1/14/4; 1/14/5; 2/2/4; 2/8/2; 2/14/7; 8/8/3; 8/13/2; 12/6/1; 13/19/2; schoolmaster of Monkleigh, 1827; 'copyist'
Bendall: B 196.2

A11. BEARD, R.
Maps dated 1781; refs 3/5/1; associate: Samuel Donne

A12. BEARNE, Edward Snelling of Teigngrace
Maps dated 1840 {1838}; refs 9/3/8
Bendall: B 200.2

A13. BENTLEY, George
Maps dated 1794–5 {1792}; refs B5
Bendall: B 282

A14. BERMINGHAM, James {of London 1740}
Maps dated [1739] {1735–48}; refs 1/17/3
Bendall: B 287

A15. BERRY, Miles of 'Newtons and Berry', Chancery Lane, London
Maps dated 19th cent.; refs 5/9/5; associate: William Newton

A16. [BERRY, Thomas]
bap. Marwood, 1607; bur. Marwood, 1679; maps dated [1649–1654]; refs 2/8/1; 2/23/1; 9/4/1; 12/2/1

A17. BINDON, John of Runnington Farm, ?Wellington
Maps dated 1820; refs 3/35/10; mentioned as surveyor, 1828–30 (EFP)
Bendall: B 321.5

A18. BLACKAMORE, James (also J. or I), of Exeter and Taunton
Maps dated 1773 {1764–1776}; refs 20/5/1; taught surveying, etc. at school in Exeter with Matthew Blackamore and in Cornwall (advertisements in EFP from 1763 onwards)
Bendall: B 371

A19. BLACKAMORE, Matthew of Exeter 1763–c.1794
Maps dated 1763–1777; refs 1/16/2; 1/16/3; 1/16/4; 1/16/5; 1/16/6; 2/39/5; 2/44/1; 18/9/1; 19/16/5; 19/16/6;19/16/7; 19/16/8; 20/6/1; taught surveying, etc. at school in Exeter with James Blackamore (advertisements in EFP 1763–1789); schoolmaster for Company of Weavers, Fullers and Shearmen of Exeter, replaced by 1794; produced map of Robert Palk's estate at Torquay, 1770 and probably acted as steward there; original map not now extant – see *Transactions of Torquay Natural History Society*, IV, 50
Bendall: B 367.3 and possibly B 367.2

A20. BLAKE, J.
Maps dated 1796; refs 8/7/7; 8/7/8
Bendall: B 381.6

A21. BOLTON, Thomas {of Birmingham, mathematical instrument-maker}
Maps dated 1793–95 {1808–45}; refs B3; B5
Bendall: B 423

A22. BOND, William of Axminster and Axmouth
bap. Axminster, 1765; d.14 May 1834 (*Gent. Mag.*); maps dated 1793–97 {1788–1830}; refs 2/50/1; 3/27/8; 4/1/3; 4/12/1; 19/12/1; B6; B16; associate: — Pickering; advertisement for surveying, valuing and selling estates, 1788 (SM); agent, 1791–4 and 1804–05 (EFP); land valuer at Salcombe Regis, 1819 (BMI); County Surveyor of Devon; agent to re-survey railway line, 1824; will perambulate wasteland boundaries, 1828; agent for farm sale, 1828 (EFP)
Bendall: B 427

A23. BOWMAN, Robert
Maps dated 1833; refs 7/1/6

A24. BOWRING, John of Chulmleigh
born 1690 (IGI unattributed source); Will proved 1774; maps dated 1745–c.1760; refs 2/2/1; 2/14/3; 2/46/1; 3/15/2; DNB gives details of Sir John Bowring (1792–1872), linguist, writer and traveller, born in Exeter and descended from an old Devonshire family. An ancestor coined tokens to pay his workmen (in the woollen trade) bearing the

inscription 'John Bowring of Chulmleigh his half penny' with device of a wool comb

A25. BOYCE, Gideon Ackland {of Tiverton architect, 1830
b. 1796/7; d.16 Jan.1861}; maps dated 1826–40; refs 6/2/4; B96; B117; produced designs for Blue Coat School (Middle School), Tiverton and Heathcoat School, Westexe, 1841–42 (*Kelly's Directory*)
Bendall: B 502

A26. BOYCOT, William of Fordwich and Canterbury, Kent
Maps dated 1641 {1615–48}; refs 2/22/1
Bendall: B 504

A27. BRADLEY, Thomas of Launceston, Cornwall
Maps dated 1802–09 {1805–58 if correct identification}; refs 2/3/1; 3/36/3; 8/8/4; 9/1/2; 18/1/3; associate: Alexander Law
Bendall: ?B 524 but no evident Devon connection

A28. BRAUND, J.W. of Sidney Place, Alphington
Maps dated 19th cent.; refs 3/24/5; possibly related to George Braund of Exeter (Bendall B 548)

A29. BREMRIDGE, John
?bap. Heanton Punchardon, 1764; maps dated 1787; refs 2/2/6; possibly of Barnstaple, merchant, partnership with W. Bowhay dissolved 1794 (EFP)

A30. BRIGHT, William {of Shropshire; d. 1839/44}
Maps dated 1824 {1800–1839/44}; refs 12/13/1
Bendall: B 574

A31. BRIMACOMBE, J. of Stoke Climsland, Cornwall
Maps dated 1831; refs 8/14/1

A32. BRINSDEN (BRINSDON), John {of the Quay, Newcastle}
Maps dated 1836–37 {1846}; refs 11/4/20; 16/12/12
Bendall: B 577.3

A33. BRISTOW, Thomas of Kentisbeare
bap. Tiverton, 1734; d. Kentisbeare, 1770 ; maps dated 1769; refs 11/3/2; proxy for Overseers in Kentisbeare, 1766 and 1768 and resident Excise Officer, Kentisbeare (E.S. Chalk, *Kentisbeare*)

A34. BUCKBERTE, William of the Inner Temple, London, gent.
Maps dated 1574; refs 1/17/1; associate: Barnard Drake; granted lease of land in Axminster for his work on the survey, 1575 (DRO 123M/TB557–8)

A35. CALL, Thomas
b. *c.*1749; younger son of Richard and Mary Call of Priestacutt, Launcells, Cornwall; m. Bethia Blackburne of Sneaton, Yorks.; d. Dec. 1788 at sea; maps dated 1769–*c.*1770; refs 3/1/1; 12/5/2; 13/18/4; 13/19/1; 21/4/1; 21/12/1; 21/12/2; 21/13/1; Chief Engineer in Bengal; Ensign 1771; succeeded James Rennell as Surveyor General of Bengal 1777; reported that he had in hand an Atlas of India; promoted Lieut. Col. 1786; resigned because of poor health, 1788; sailed from Calcutta taking with him a copy of his Atlas; died at sea 15 Dec. 1788; executors John Call and William Hole; monument in Exeter Cathedral; associate: William Hole

A36. CARSLAKE, J.
Maps dated 1828; refs C152

A37. CARTWRIGHT, H.
Maps dated 1829; refs B67

A38. CARTWRIGHT, Robert
bap. Exminster, 1773; maps dated 1793–1805; refs 1/4/16; 1/4/17; B7; of Haldon House, Kenn, second son of William Cartwright late of Exminster, deceased (*Gray's Inn Admissions*); steward to Sir L.V. Palk, 1810 (BMI)
Bendall: C 082

A39. CARTWRIGHT, William
bap. Exminster, 1769; d.1806; maps dated 1787; refs 16/12/8; steward to Viscount Courtenay, 1806 (BMI)

A40. CARTWRIGHT, William
Maps dated 1810; refs 4/5/6; eldest son of William Cartwright late of Exminster, deceased (*Gray's Inn Admissions*); of New Bridge Street, Exeter, 1816 (EPJ); steward to Lord Rolle, 1823 (*Pigot's Directory*); resident in New Street, Great Torrington (BMI)

A41. CASE, John
Maps dated 1766; refs 2/39/4; 19/20/3

A42. CHANNON, James of Honiton
bap. ?Talaton, 1738; maps dated 1772; refs 7/5/1; associate: Francis King

A43. CHAPPLE, Charles {of Stonehouse, architect}
Maps dated 1829 {1825–43}; refs B64; a Charles Chapple of Plymouth, builder, in partnership with John Bidcook, 1798 (EFP) may be his father
Bendall: C 164.5

A44. CHAPPLE, William of Cathedral Close, Exeter
bap. Witheridge, 1718; m. Elizabeth Pollard, Exeter Cathedral, 1747;
bur. Exeter St Mary Major, 1781; maps dated 1748–61; refs 1/4/1;
1/4/2; 1/4/4; 1/4/10; 5/11/1; 8/21/1; 8/21/2; 8/21/3; 11/4/2; 19/17/1;
clerk to John Richards, surveyor, 1743 and married his master's niece;
superintended the building of the Devon and Exeter Hospital, 1741;
secretary to the Devon and Exeter Hospital, 1741–1781; steward to
the Courtenay family and resigned owing to ill health; antiquarian;
admitted to Freedom of the City of Exeter, 8 June 1767

A45. CHARLTON, F.
Maps dated 1796; refs 18/3/1; may be related to John Charlton of
Stourton, Wilts.

A46. CLACK, Thomas
bap. Okehampton, 1774; d.1852; maps dated 1827; refs 13/14/5; son
of Rev. Thomas Clack, Rector of Kenn and Moretonhampstead, who
died 1805; matric. Exeter College Oxford 1792, BCL 1804; Rector
of Milton Damerel 1799–1852; *View of the Revd. W.H. Coham's weir
at Black Torrington, Devonshire*, by Neale after T. Clack, published
*c.*1800 (WCL, S.C.222) may be ascribed to him

A47. CLARINGBULL, William of Plymouth
Maps dated 1814; refs 21/8/11; connected with construction of
Plymouth Breakwater, 1819 and Assistant Surveyor, 1823 (BMI)

A48. CLODE, Samuel, senior of Southleigh
Maps dated between 1684 and 1707; refs 18/21/1; associates: Samuel
Clode, junior, Thomas Cookney and John Coffyn
Bendall: C 279.95

A49. CLODE, Samuel, junior of Southleigh
Maps dated between 1684 and 1707; refs 18/21/1; associates: Samuel
Clode, senior, Thomas Cookney and John Coffyn
Bendall: C 279.96

A50. CODDLE, Robert J.
Maps dated 1817; refs C126

A51. COFFYN, John of Southleigh
Maps dated between 1684 and 1707; refs 18/21/1; associates: Samuel
Clode, junior, Samuel Clode, senior, Thomas Cookney
Bendall: C 313

A52. COGGAN, Samuel, of St Thomas, Exeter, 1794 (UBD), of Alphington Street, 1796 (EPJ)
d. Exeter St. Thomas, 31 March 1803; maps dated 18th cent.; refs
4/13/5; associate: William Greenslade; Assistant secretary to Devon
& Exeter Hospital (BMI)

A53. COLDRIDGE, John of Fore Street, Exeter, 1816 (UBD), of
Larkbear, 1822 (EPJ), of Magdalen Street, Exeter, 1827–38 (EPJ)
son of Richard and Ann, bap. Doddiscombsleigh, 17 Sept. 1777;
maps dated 1802–25 {1808–42}; refs 1/18/2; 3/14/12; 5/3/22; 5/4/10;
5/4/12; 6/1/3; 6/3/3; 8/1/3; 15/7/4; 18/23/7; 18/28/2; 19/13/4; 19/13/5;
19/13/6; 19/16/24; B10; B11; B15; B22; B70; office on Holloway
[Exeter], 1804; surveyor for Commissioners for Improvement Act,
1810; surveyor of rectorial tithes of Pinhoe, 1811 (Z17/2/11); offers
himself for road surveyor's post, 1816; survey plan of Exeter to be
published, 1819; surveyor for tithes, 1823; letter of resignation (from
tithes) 1824 (all EFP); conveyance to him of 46 Magdalen Street,
Exeter, 1824 (D7/929/13a–b); Surveyor to Exeter Dean and Chapter;
ordered by Dean and Chapter to survey land for possible railway
line through Stoke Canon, 1836; received annual salary as
woodwarden from Dean and Chapter (Ex. D&C Act Books); see
Christopher Couldridge, 'John Coldridge of Exeter, Land Surveyor',
unpublished thesis, Oxford Brookes University, 2001 for details of
John Coldridge and his family
Bendall: C 325

A54. COLDRIDGE, Samuel T. of Magdalen Street, Exeter, 1827–38
(EPJ)
bap.as John Taylor Coleridge, Exeter St Thomas, 1800, son of John
(*see* A53); m. Elizabeth Powning, Exeter Holy Trinity, 1826; of 28
South Street, Exeter, auctioneer, 1832 (EPJ); d. 20 April 1871
(D7/929/14); maps dated 1827 {1828–30}; refs 1/9/1; 6/3/3; 19/17/6;
B70
Bendall: C 325.1

A55. COLE, [Samuel] of Lower Northernhay, Exeter, 1827, of Goldsmith
Street, Exeter, 1830, of Paul Street, Exeter, 1831–34 (all EPJ);
maps dated 1831 {1830}; refs 5/4/16
Bendall: C 336

A56. COLES, S.
Maps dated 1827; refs 5/8/10

A57. COOKNEY, Thomas of Southleigh
Maps dated between 1684 and 1707; refs 18/21/1; associates: Samuel Clode, junior, Samuel Clode, senior, John Coffyn
Bendall: C 420.2

A58. CORBRIDGE, James {of Norwich}
Maps dated 1737 {1720–37}; refs 2/6/2
Bendall: C 442

A59. CORNISH, Hubert
bap. ?West Teignmouth, 1757; d.1802 (EFP); maps dated 1778; refs 2/23/3; 3/28/1; associate: Christopher Hamlyn

A60. CORNISH, 'Mr'
Maps dated c.1690; refs 7/1/1; 7/1/2; 7/1/3

A61. CORNISH, Robert of Bartholomew Yard, Exeter, 1796 (EPJ) {b. 1759/60}; m. 1785; {d. 9.1.1844}; maps dated 1812 {1800–1838}; refs 3/33/8; of Exeter, builder, 1785 and various refs. 1795–1812 (EFP); surveyor of works for Exeter Cathedral for 32 years (noted in 1838); admitted to the Freedom of the City of Exeter, 25 Sept. 1820
Bendall: C 449

A62. CORNISH, Robert Stribling of Exeter
b.1788; m. Marianne Powning of Hill's Court, Exeter, 1844; d.1871; maps dated 1836; refs 5/3/25; of 139 Fore Street, Exeter, 1850 and 1857 (Directories); appointed surveyor of the works and fabric of Exeter Cathedral, 1838

A63. CORRIS, John
Maps dated 1779 {1777–93}; refs 15/5/2; 15/5/3
Bendall: C 452

A64. COUCH, Richard, alias 'Dick the plowman'
bap. Newton St Cyres, 1715; maps dated 1782; refs 14/3/1

A65. COWL, Richard of Plymouth
d.1789; maps dated 1781–1789 {1777–89}; refs 2/38/4; 5/1/1; 19/2/2; 19/2/3; ?19/2/4; 21/8/4; 22/3/1; map of Plymouth to be published, 1779; map banned by the Admiralty, 1783; apprentice wanted, 1783; reference to his water engine, 1785; advertisement for his map of Devon, 1788; report of his death, 1789 (all EFP)
Bendall: C 490

A66. CREAGH, H[enry] C[ouch] of Widecombe
m. Mary Caroline Luscombe, Rattery, 1818; maps dated 1834 {18?39}; refs B85; surveyed measured distance from Plymouth to

Exeter by two routes, 1827 (EFP); surveyor at the first Widecombe Fair, 1850 (*Widecombe*, p.xi, DCRS, Exeter, 1938); auctioneer and surveyor, of West Street, Ashburton, 1850; of Staverton Place, Ashburton, 1857 and 1878 (Directories)
Bendall: C 528.3 where the name is given as H.C. Creach

A67. CRIDGE, John ?of Barnstaple
schoolteacher, April 1819 (EFP); maps dated 1823; refs 2/2/8

A68. CROCKER, I.
?John Crocker d. 1844 aged 54 at Plymouth (*Gent. Mag.*); maps dated 1835; refs 18/31/3

A69. CROOTE, William of Lapford and Chulmleigh
Maps dated 1811; refs 19/6/1; 19/6/2; measured and mapped estates in Coryton for Arthur Tremayne, 1801 (map not now extant), (158M/E363); selling land and timber, 1805–28 (EFP); aged 30, landsurveyor, only son of John Croote of Chulmleigh, landsurveyor, 1806 (*Gray's Inn Admissions*)

A70. CUMING[S], N.
Maps dated 1830–34 {1841}; refs 5/2/5; 8/7/14
Bendall: C 600.6 (N. Cuming)

A71. CUMMING, George W. {of Oundle and Trumpington}; of [St] David's Hill, Exeter, 1838 (EPJ)
Maps dated 1837–39 {1820–d.1871/4}; refs B103; B113; C156; at Post Office Chambers, Exeter, 1857 (Billings Directory); View from Rowden's, by W. Spreat, after G.W. Cumming, publ. c.1850 (Somers Cocks, *Topographical Prints*); associate: Henry Andrews
Bendall: C 600

A72. D., W.P.
?possibly William Dawson of Exeter, *q.v.*
Maps dated 1840; refs 13/23/2

A73. DARCH, J.
Maps dated 1792; refs 14/3/3
Bendall: D 036

A74. DARE, Barnabas
Maps dated 1720 {1700–24}; refs 3/27/2; family appears to have been resident in West Dorset (Dorset IGI)
Bendall: D 037

A75. DAVIS, Richard of Lewknor, Oxon.
{bap.Windsor, Berks., 1750; bur. Lewknor, Oxon., 1814}; maps dated 1788–89 {1781–1814}; refs 2/35/6; {Topographer to His Majesty 1786–94}
Bendall: D 087

A76. DAWSON, William of Exeter; of St Sidwells, Exeter, 1830 and 1858; of 7 Northernhay Place, Exeter, 1836–37 (EPJ)
Maps dated 1835–39 {183(?0)–1858}; refs B91; B93; B108; B110; associate: Robert Dymond; *see* separate entry for Dymond and Dawson; Explanatory key to Map of England and Wales with miscellaneous information Historical and Geographical, 1829 (BMI); artist, 1840 and later lithographs published by Spreat; coloured aquatint of Teignmouth and Shaldon Bridge, 1828; drew map and view of Bicton Park, 1845, which was produced in Chancery case, Drake v. Trefusis, 1847; of 7 Northernhay Place, Exeter, 1850 and of Dix's Field, Exeter (Directories)
Bendall: D 116

A77. DAY, William {of Blagdon, Somerset}
Maps dated 1789–*c*.1800 {1767–82}; refs 1/16/7; 18/18/2; 18/22/3
Bendall: ?D 120

A78. DEAN, Charles of Heavitree, Exeter; of Castle Street, Exeter, 1831–38 (EPJ)
?d. 1845 aged 48; maps dated ?1812–29 {1824–(?41)}; refs ?2/7/1; 8/26/1; 19/16/25; C54; used by William Faden, 1814; of Exeter, surveyor, 1825–1832, plans for street alterations, 1830 (EFP); possibly the C. Dean of Exeter, agent to the Earl of Devon, who died from injuries in a railway accident near Chalk Farm, London in 1845, aged 48 (*Gent. Mag.* 1845/433)
Bendall: D 126

A79. DEAN, [possibly James*] of Heavitree, 1816 (EPJ)
Maps dated 1812–13 {1810–29}; refs ?2/7/1; surveyor, Tiverton roads, 1810; large plan of manor of Doddiscombsleigh 1814, sold 1930 [not now traced]; of Exeter, surveyor, refs. 1803–14 (EFP)
Bendall: *D 127

A80. DOE, John
Maps dated 1837; refs C141; a George Doe, Devon, tithes, is listed in Bendall D 224.7

A81. DOIDGE, Thomas
born Lamerton, 1720; maps dated 1751; refs 19/3/1

A82. DOIDGE, William
Maps dated 1736–49 {1730–52}; refs 1/10/2; 2/17/2; 3/14/1; 16/8/1; 18/30/1; 18/31/1; 19/3/1; S3; S5
Bendall: D 226

A83. DONNE (DOUNE), Samuel of Melbury Osmond, Dorset
m. Susanna Daw, Melbury Osmond, 1738; maps dated 1772–81 {1754–86}; refs 3/5/1; 3/26/2; 3/35/3; 8/12/1; a cousin of Benjamin Donn
Bendall: D 246

A84. DOSWELL, Richard {?of Southampton}
Maps dated 1834 {1835–}; refs B84; B89
Bendall: D 265

A85. DOWLING, George
Landsurveyor, Andover, Hants.; maps dated 1834; refs 15/7/6
Bendall: D 292

A86. DRAKE, Sir Barnard of Musbury
bap. 1551; m. Gertrude Fortescue; bur. Crediton, 1586; maps dated 1574; refs 1/17/1; associate: William Buckberte; admitted to Inner Temple; land transaction, Offwell, Northleigh and Farway, 1567; expedition to Newfoundland with Carew and Raleigh, 1585 (*DCNQ* XVIII, 186); muster captain, 1572, knighted Jan. 1586 (Prince's *Worthies; The Antiquary* II, 237–8); buried 12 April 1586 at Crediton after catching pestilential fever at Exeter Assizes

A87. DRAYTON, John of Chardstock
Maps dated 1797; refs 3/5/2; {assistant to William Bond}
Bendall: D 310

A88. DUNSTONE, James
Maps dated 1814; refs 3/18/1; of Holsworthy, surveyor, 1812 (EFP)

A89. DYMOND, Robert of Bartholomew Yard, Exeter, 1836–38 (EPJ)
b. Exeter, *c*.1800 (IGI unattributed); m. Anne Priscilla Williams, 1823; d.1866; maps dated 1825–39 {1838–?60}; refs 2/10/2; 5/3/24; 5/3/54; 6/3/3; 11/4/22; 16/12/11; associate: Thomas Michelmore; *see also* Dymond and Dawson; of 10 Bridge Street, Exeter, 1821 (EFP); of Bedford Street, Exeter, 1850 (Directory); of 3 Southernhay, Exeter, 1857 (Directory); his article on 'Devon Fields and Hedges' in *Journal of the Bath and West of England* {Society,} 1856, 132–48
Bendall: D 385

A90. DYMOND AND DAWSON of Bartholomew Yard, Exeter, 1830–
34 (EPJ)
Maps dated 1829–34; refs B63; B76; B87; associates: *see also*
Dawson, William and Dymond, Robert; plan for bringing water to
Exeter from Shutterton Brook, 1834 (BMI)
Bendall: D 384

A91. E., M.,
Maps dated 1761; refs 3/35/2
Bendall: nothing identifiable

A92. EASTON, John (?alias R.J. EASTON) of Taunton, Somerset
{b. 1788; d.1860}; maps dated 1812–21; 2/51/4; 3/35/9; B17; B23
Bendall: E 022

A93. EASTON, Josiah {of Pawlett
b.1790}; maps dated *c.*1838 {?1838–42}; refs B107; his sworn
statement as surveyor with John Perratt on tithes of Crediton, Sandford
and Exminster belonging to Crediton Governors (G. Oliver, *Eccles.
Antiq.* II, 26n.); two entries to – Easton, no Christian name given,
may refer to him (a) Tide Surveyor of Plymouth, married 1801 (b) of
Wimborne, surveyor, notice that the River Frome is to be rendered
navigable, 1831 (both EFP)
Bendall: E 024

A94. ELLIOT(T), Samuel {of Plymouth, 1820–32}
Maps dated 1817–28 {1816–32}; refs 2/7/2; 2/38/8; 4/2/4; 8/15/4;
9/5/3; B60; associates: *see* Rendle and Elliott of South Brent;
surveyor, agent for sale of tithes, 1827 (EFP)
Bendall: E 069

A95. ELLIOTT, W.
Maps dated 1781; refs 1/15/1

A96. FEWELL, Mr
Maps dated late 17th cent.; refs 2/6/1; the Fewells appear to have
been a Plymouth family: a Mr Fewell was Town Clerk of Pymouth
in 1637 (*State Papers Domestic*). It is possible that Mr Fewell was
the owner or patron of the map and not its surveyor.

A97. FINNIMORE, Richard King
born Halberton 13 June 1797; bap. Halberton 1 June 1798; bur.
Halberton Jan. 1820 aged 22; maps dated 1814; refs 8/2/7

A98. FOSTER, James of Ashburton; {of Axminster 1800}
m. Mary Eales, Ilsington, 1764; bur. Ashburton Sept. 1810; maps

dated 1781–1810 {1781–1800}; refs 1/8/2; 1/12/1; 2/17/3; 3/14/7;
3/27/5; 8/4/3; 9/3/1; 18/12/2; S6; signs petition to give bounties to
seamen, 1793 (BMI)
Bendall: F 156

A98a. FOX, R. [Late Entry]
Maps dated *c.*1804; refs 22/3/2

A99. FULLER, Edward
Maps dated 1817 {1816–51}; refs 5/10/4
Bendall: F 235

A100. FULTON, Hamilton {of London}
d.1834; maps dated 1832–33 {1810–1834}; B77; B80; worked under
the supervision of G. and J. Rennie for map of 1832
Bendall: F 242

A101. G., F.
Maps dated 1810; refs 21/2/2
Bendall: nothing identifiable

A102. GARDNER, William
{d.1800}; maps dated 1785 {1762–1800}; refs 2/38/3
Bendall: G O34

A103. GARRETT, James (also J. and Jo)
d.1776; maps dated 1760–*c.*1776; refs 1/4/6; 1/4/12; 1/4/13; 1/4/14;
?the joiner who worked on wooden staircases at Powderham, 1754–
56 (Cherry/Pevsner, *Buildings of Devon*, p.694); estimated damage
caused by Honiton fire, 1765; a joiner in St Thomas, 1766 (EFP);
agent for re-sale of property, 1772 and 1774 (EFP)

A104. GASCOYNE, Joel
bap.1650; d.1705; maps dated [1694–1700]; refs 2/14/1; 24/1/1
Bendall: G 047

A105. GILBERT, R. of Crediton
Maps dated early 19th cent.; refs 18/5/5

A106. GLIDDON, William
Maps dated 1824–25; refs 2/46/3; 3/15/7; steward at Castle Hill
succeeding Robert Ballment, 1823 (*Chronicles of Castle Hill*)

A107. GOULD, George, senior {?of Welcombe}
Maps dated 1802; refs 1/14/1; 2/30/2; 8/13/1
Bendall: G 213.9

A108. GOULD, George, junior, of Okehampton
 Maps dated 1807–32 {1842–49}; refs 1/13/1; 3/21/2; 9/5/4; associate:
 T. Jenn of Okehampton, land surveyor, 1820 (BMI)
 Bendall: G 213.95

A109. GRANT, John of Torpeek, Ugborough
 Maps dated 1839–40 {1838–*c.*1850}; refs 3/17/1; 3/21/3; 11/2/12; a
 John Grant, surveyor, Castle Street, Exeter, listed in Directory for
 1850; there is no entry for him under surveyors in Ugborough
 Bendall: G 234.7

A110. GRAY (Grey), Thomas, of Haven Banks and Exe Island, Exeter
 d.1822; maps dated *c.*1775–95/6; refs 5/3/27; 16/12/5; 20/1/3; C194;
 appointed Exeter City Surveyor, 1792 (ECA, Act Book 16, p.384);
 of Exe Island, surveyor, 1794 (UBD); of Exeter, surveyor, agent for
 letting, 1795 (EFP); of Haven Banks, 1796, 1816 and 1822 (EPJ);
 admitted to the Freedom of the City of Exeter, 1802; died, aged 82,
 March 1822 (EFP); a Thomas Gray of Mamhead, advert. as landscape
 gardener, 1779 (EFP), may refer to him
 Bendall: ?G 249 (1813)

A111. GREAVES, C[harles]
 {b.1816, d.1883}; maps dated 1837; refs B105; {apprenticed to James
 Meadows Rendel 1831–37}
 Bendall: G 255.5

A112. GREEN, James of (St) David's Hill, Exeter, 1816, of Southernhay
 Place, Exeter, 1831, of Magdalen Street, Exeter, 1832–37, of
 Alphington, 1838 (all EPJ)
 {b. Birmingham, 1781; d. London, 1849}; maps dated *c.*1814–32;
 refs 5/3/21; 5/11/6;16/12/15; B25; B28; B29; B34; B39; B55; B58;
 B71; B79; associates: worked with James Shearm and directed
 Richard Andrews; {Devon County Surveyor 1808–41}; published
 Report on the alteration and improvement of turnpike road between
 Exeter and Plymouth, n.d.; Report on canal from Bude Haven, 1818;
 Report on canal between East and West Looe and Liskeard, 1823;
 died in reduced circumstances at Westminster aged 67 in Feb. 1849
 (biography in W. Buckingham); plan for alteration of Bideford Bridge,
 1807 (*TDA* 34/232); informs public of residence in Exeter, 1808,
 elected a Freeman of Exeter, 1830 and presented with Freedom of
 the City, 1832 (all EFP); lived at Elmfield House, Exeter; see also
 Brian George, *James Green: Canal Builder and County Surveyor*
 Bendall: G 262

A113. GREENSLADE, William of Exeter
 Maps dated *c.*1800; refs 2/49/4; 4/13/5; associate: Samuel Coggan;
 drawing master, Fore Street, Exeter, 1799–1801, in partnership with
 Coggan; partnership dissolved and Greenslade continued to run
 business, 1793 (EFP)

A114. HALLORAN, E.C.P.
 bap. Tamerton 1814; maps dated 1835; refs 2/11/1; later map (1836)
 of Bickleigh Glebe mentioned in J.G. Commin's book catalogue
 no.361, p.49

A115. HAMLYN, Christopher of Paschoe, Colebrooke
 ?bap. Exeter, 1730; m. Elizabeth Mary Calmady, 1775; d. 1815
 Colebrooke (*Gent. Mag.*); maps dated 1750–87; refs 2/23/2; 2/23/3;
 3/26/4; 19/8/3; associate: Hubert Cornish; paid male servant tax in
 Colebrooke parish, 1780
 Bendall: H 075.2

A116. HARRES, Thomas, Public Notary
 Maps dated 1499; refs 5/3/1

A117. HARRIS, William of Barnstaple
 bap. 1716; d. May 1791 (EFP); maps dated 1783/4 {1779}; refs 8/7/3;
 steward to Earl Fortescue at Castle Hill (EFP)
 Bendall: H 156

A118. HARRISON, William
 Maps dated 1785; refs 5/10/3

A119. HASSALL, Charles{of Pembrokeshire and London
 b. 1754; d. by 19.8.1814}; maps dated 1777; refs 3/24/1; artist, views
 (aquatints) of Berry Pomeroy Castle, Ivybridge, Okehampton and
 Shaugh Bridge, 1801, 1807 and 1813 (BMI)
 Bendall: H 195

A120. HATCHER, Stephen
 Maps dated 1840; refs 3/33/18

A121. HAWKES, Thomas {I AND II} of Williton, Somerset
 Maps dated 1825–28 {1820–51}; refs 2/39/8; 3/35/13; 11/3/7; 11/3/8;
 11/3/10; 17/3/2; 18/19/3; 19/16/28
 Bendall: H 211

A122. HAYMAN, John of Bartholomew Yard, Exeter, 1794 (UBD)
 m. Mary —; d. 1847; maps dated 1802/11 {1786–90}; refs 5/7/1;
 nephew of William Hayman and his partner (*see* A123); will proved

February 1847 (IRW, H 553); proposal for publishing map of Exeter, 1789 (BMI)

Bendall: H 226

A123. HAYMAN, William of Exeter

b. 1716; d. Modbury, 1793; maps dated 1762–85 {1770–86}; refs 2/39/3; 5/3/52; 5/3/53; 5/5/4; 19/7/1; 21/14/2; appointment as Exeter City Surveyor, 1760 and resigned for reason of ill health, 1791; advertisements as agent for sale of timber and houses, St Mary Arches parish, Exeter, 1770–78; admitted to the Freedom of the City of Exeter, 1777; partnership with J. Hayman, 1786 (EFP); Musgrave's obituary of William Hayman (BMI)

Bendall: H 226.4

A124. HAYWOOD (HEYWOOD), James

d. 1784 at Kemsey nr. Worcester, 'only son of James Modyford Heywood of Maristow' (*Gent. Mag.)*; maps dated 1773–78; refs 1/17/4; 3/14/4; 3/14/6; 18/21/2

Bendall: H 250.5

A125. HEATH, Thomas {of London 1720–50

b.1698; d.1773}; maps dated 1755–60; refs 1/4/7; 16/8/2; compiler of *Heath's Scale*

Bendall: H 264 (if correct identification with the Devon map-maker)

A126. HILES, F.G. of Great Torrington and Barnstaple

Maps dated 1810–11; refs 1/7/2; C148

A127. HILES, John

Maps dated 1808; refs 1/13/2; 8/19/4; undertook 'A Survey of Sundry Manors and Estates in the County of Devon. Davidson Collection' (BMI)

A128. HITCHEN(S), J. {HITCHINS, JOHN) of Tavistock}

b. *c*.1778; d. 30 March 1842, aged 74, at Tavistock (*Gent. Mag.*); maps dated *c*.1840 {1813–30}; refs 16/8/8; 19/3/1; B31; associate: T.H. Lakeman; mentioned as a painter, 'the Ruysdael of his native scenery', Dec. 1832 (*Gent. Mag.*)

Bendall: H 397

A129. HITCHINS, Malachy(i)

bap. Gwennap, Cornwall, 1741; d.1809; maps dated 18th cent.; refs 13/11/1; astronomer; matric. Exeter College Oxford, 1763, aged 22, BA 1781, Cambridge BA 1785, MA 1785, Deacon 1765, Priest 1765 (*Alumni Cantab.*); Curate at Lustleigh, 1775; Vicar of Hennock, 1772–

75; wrote 'Account of a remarkable meteor. Dated Bideford' (*Annual Register 1762*)

Bendall: H 399

A130. HODGE, Thomas of Silverton

bap. Silverton, 1714/15; bur. Silverton 1773; maps dated 1752–64; refs 2/39/2; 16/11/1; 18/19/1

A131. HOLE, William of Bovey Tracey and Barnstaple

bap. Bovey Tracey, Feb. 1736/7; d. Bovey Tracey, Jan.1812; maps dated 1756–94 {1761–95}; refs 1/6/3; 2/22/2; 2/22/3; 2/22/5; 2/22/6; 2/22/7; 2/22/8; 2/30/1; 2/39/6; 3/1/1; 4/5/2; 9/6/1; 10/1/1; 11/4/3; 11/4/4; 11/4/5; 11/4/6; 11/4/7; 13/18/4; 13/19/1; 16/12/3; 18/5/3; 18/23/1; 18/33/2; 19/8/2; 20/7/1; 21/4/1; 21/12/1; 21/12/2; 21/13/3; associates: Thomas Call and Alexander Law; steward at and worked for Castle Hill, 1762–1790s; in partnership with Robert Lewis Barnstaple, 1775–82; executor of Will of Thomas Call, 1788; monument to him and other members of his family, Bovey Tracey Church

Bendall: H 446

A132. HOOKER, John of Exeter

b. Exeter, 1525; d. Exeter, 1601; maps dated *c*.1568–*c*.1600; refs 4/3/4; 5/3/2; 5/3/3; 5/3/4; 5/3/5; 5/3/6; 5/3/7; held various offices in City of Exeter including M.P. and City Chamberlain; antiquarian and historian, several of his manuscripts survive in the Exeter Dean and Chapter archives and Exeter City archives

Bendall: H 486.8

A133. HOOPER, Henry junior of Exeter, builder

bap. Exeter, 1794; maps dated 1826; refs 5/4/14; associate: William Hooper

A134. HOOPER, William of 13 Paris Street, Exeter, builder

d. Exeter, 1831 (EFP); maps dated 1826; refs 5/4/14; associate: Henry Hooper junior; built Higher Summerlands, 1804, Baring Place, 1808, Lower Summerlands, 1814, Chichester Place, 1824–5 and much of St Leonard's Road, 1828 onwards

A135. HOPKINS, Roger and Son of Bodmin, Cornwall {of Plymouth, 1825–41, of Bath, 1836}

Maps dated 1825–33 {1807–?51}; refs 2/14/9; B46; B61; Report on projected railway between Okehampton and Bideford in *Exeter and Plymouth Gazette* Oct. 1832 (BMI); Roger Hopkins, architect, Brunswick Terrace, Plymouth (Thomas's *Plymouth Directory*, 1836)

Bendall: H 497

A136. HUGGINS, Thomas
    Maps dated 1789–92 {1787–1815}; refs 19/16/11; 19/16/12; 21/1/2; 21/1/3
        Bendall: H 570

A137. HUNT, Thomas
    Maps dated 1839; refs 16/1/3

A138. IRISH, [Thomas B.] of Buckfastleigh and Winkleigh
    Maps dated *c.*1840 {1841–58}; refs 4/9/1; associate: A.S. Parker
        Bendall: I 022.5

A139. ISAAC, William
    Maps dated 1802–06; refs 3/11/2; 18/33/3; 18/33/4

A140. J., F.
    Maps dated 1798; refs 15/5/7

A141. JENN, T. ?of Okehampton
    Maps dated 1832; refs 9/5/4; associate: G. Gould

A142. JEWELL, S.
    ?bap. Bideford, 1723; maps dated 1776; refs 2/14/4; a Samuel Jewell was a Churchwarden at Hartland, 1744 (DCRS *Hartland*, p. 498); note also a map of Great Torrington by JOHN Jewell, 1777, is referred to in *DCNQ*, XVIII, 151 as being in the possession of the Conservators of Great Torrington Commons

A143. JONES, J.
    Maps dated 19th cent.; refs 8/16/1; possibly John Jones of Liskeard, Cornwall, surveyor, who was agent for timber sale, 1797 (EFP)
        Bendall: possibly Joshua Jones at J 174, but *see above*

A144. JOPE, John of Tavistock
    ?bap. Okehampton, 1705; maps dated 1763; refs 19/3/2; possibly father of Thomas Jope (*see* A145)

A145. JOPE, Thomas of Tavistock
    d.1814; maps dated 1779–1811; refs 19/2/7; 19/2/9; 19/3/2; 19/3/24; 19/3/33; C161; advertisement as land surveyor and teacher of the same, 1778 (SM) ; agent for a sale, March 1814 (EFP); inquest into his death (cut his throat), 28 July 1814 (EFP)
        Bendall: J 200

A146. KING, F(rancis) of Honiton
    Maps dated 1772–92; refs 1/8/3; 7/5/1; associate: James Channon

A147. KING, Henry
    Maps dated 1823; refs 2/37/4; possibly Henry King son of William King of Brixham, schoolmaster, 1818 (BMI)

A148. KING, J(AMES)
    Maps dated 1781–92; refs 2/37/2; 2/37/3; B1; B2; original plan of Brixham taken by J. King, 1781, double-sheet folio, coloured, 3s.6d. (BMI); agent for house sale, 1797, described as of Dartmouth, surveyor (EFP)

A149. KING, T.
    Maps dated 1793; refs 2/6/3 (4 items)

A150. KINGDON, Samuel {of Milverton, Somerset, 1753–1785/7}
    d. 1797 (EFP); maps dated 1774 {1748–94}; refs 2/5/1; sale of property, 1767 and similar references 1780–94 (EFP)
        Bendall: K 155

A151. LAKEMAN, T(homas) H(awkins) {of Milton Abbot, 1830}
    Maps dated 1813–25 {1830}; refs 2/22/13; 2/33/3; 21/8/10; B31; B45; associate: John Hitchen
        Bendall: L 013

A152. LAMPREY, —
    Maps dated 1821–22; refs 2/2/4 (maps 10–12); associates: others working on the Barnstaple atlas

A153. LANG, George of Leyland, Lancs.
    bap. Leyland, Lancs., 1756 (IGI); maps dated 1777–87; refs 1/6/1; 1/6/2; 3/29/1; 8/21/4; 8/24/2; 11/4/8; 16/10/2; 16/12/6; 16/12/7
        Bendall: L 043.9 and L 043.95

A154. LAW, Alexander of Barnstaple, Truro and Littleham (Exmouth)
    b. 1753 possibly bap. Aberdeen, 1755; m. Elizabeth Davey, Truro, 1780; d. Littleham Exmouth, March 1840; maps dated 1773–1809; refs 1/8/4; 1/8/6; 2/3/1; 2/28/3; 2/31/3; 2/31/4; 2/40/3; 2/41/2; 2/44/4; 2/51/2; 3/20/1; 3/20/2; 3/25/2; 3/26/5; 3/33/3; 3/33/7; 3/36/3; 4/5/4; 4/10/1; 4/11/4; 5/4/9; 5/8/6; 8/12/3; 8/15/3; 9/1/2; 10/1/1; 18/1/3; 18/5/3; 18/13/1; 18/23/1; 18/28/1; 19/9/5; 19/16/17; 21/3/2; associates: Robert Ballment; Thomas Bradley; William Hole; John Pascoe; his map used by John Coldridge; assistant to William Hole of Barnstaple, 1773–78; carrying on business in Truro, 1778–*c.*1785; carrying on business in Exmouth, from 1785; worked for Exeter Dean and Chapter, 1776–1810; advertisements for sales, etc., 1795–1819

(EFP); advertisements for his work, 1777–82 (SM); admitted member of Gray's Inn, 1805; will proved 4 May 1840
Bendall: L 074 and L 074.2

A155. LAW, Charles of Exmouth
Maps dated 1787; refs 4/5/3; 4/5/4

A156. LEAVE, Robert of Exeter
bap. Exeter St Pancras, 1748; d. 1794; maps dated 1770; refs 18/32/3; theatre ticket agent, 1768 (EFP)
Bendall: L 111.8

A157. LETHBRIDGE, John King
Maps dated 1836; refs 19/3/38
Bendall: L 165.5

A158. LO, Thomas [possibly Thomas Loring of Axminster]
Maps dated 1616; refs 1/17/2

A159. LOBB, Henry of 18 Lincoln's Inn Fields, London
Maps dated 1839; refs 5/11/7

A160. LOCK, J.
Maps dated 1837; refs B104; may be identified with John Lock, surveyor, of Herne Hill, whose son was admitted pensioner at Trinity College Cambridge, 1824 (*Alumni Cantab.*)

A161. LOCK, Thomas, junior {of Instow}
d. Instow, March 1860, aged 81 (*Gent. Mag.*); maps dated 1840 {1840–44}; refs B121
Bendall: L 234.5

A162. MALLET(T), John of Torrington {Meeth}
d. Peters Marland, 1847, aged 79 (*Gent. Mag.*); maps dated 1823 {1839}; refs 18/27/2; of New Street, Great Torrington, 1847 (*Gent. Mag.*); of Little Torrington, auctioneer, 1798, of Torrington, auctioneer, 1834 (both EFP)
Bendall: M 142.2

A163. MARTIN, William
Maps dated 1804 {1801–34}; refs 19/3/33;
resigned as Surveyor of Bridges, South Grand Division, 1800 (EFP); Portreeve of Tavistock, 1825 (BMI)
Bendall: M 213

A164. MARTYN, Richard
Maps dated 1751–58 {1754–64}; refs 12/5/1; 19/3/1 (3 items)
Bendall: M 216

A165. MICHELL, Ralph 'philo-mat' {of Epsom}
Maps dated 1700 {1696–1725}; refs 19/21/3
Bendall: M 319

A166. MICHELMORE, Thomas ?of Totnes
Maps dated 1839; refs 11/4/22; associate: Robert Dymond; book by T.M. 'junior' – 'On the Value of the Farm Labourer' 1855

A167. MOORE, John
Maps dated 1657; refs 5/10/1
Bendall: ?John More at M 430 (?and M 448)

A168. MURRAY, James
Maps dated 1794–95 {1796–d. 1807}; refs B5
Bendall: M 531

A169. NEWCOURT, Richard {of Somerton, Somerset}
bap. Tiverton 1599; {d. 1679}; maps dated 1652; refs 4/11/1; published plans of London and Westminster, 1658 (DNB)
Bendall: N 054.5

A170. 'NEWTONS AND BERRY' of Chancery Lane, London
See also BERRY, Miles
Maps dated 19th cent. {?c.1830–41}; refs 5/9/5; Clerk to the Ordnance Office, Plymouth, 1823 (BMI)
Bendall: possibly William Newton, 1786–1861 at N 074

A171. NORDEN, John, senior
b. 15(?48); d.1626; maps dated 1598–1617; refs 3/33/1; 5/3/12; 5/3/13; associate: John Norden, junior; {Surveyor to Duchy of Cornwall}; Surveyor of Crown Lands; possibly BA (Oxford) 1568–9, MA (Oxford) c.1573, MA (Cambridge, incorp. from Oxford) 1581, MD (Oxford) 1581 (*Alumni Cantab.*)
Bendall: N 113

A172. NORDEN, John, junior
Maps dated 1617 {161(?1–40)}; refs 5/3/13; associate: John Norden, senior; {Surveyor of Crown Lands}
Bendall: N 114

A173. OSMOND, Edward of Newton St Cyres
Maps dated 1823; refs 4/11/4; 11/2/9; 18/13/1; associates: Alexander

Law and John Pascoe; auctioneer, 1815–26, started business as auctioneer and land agent, 1830 and reference to this, 1832 (EFP)

A174. OTTON, Joseph
bap. Alphington 1795; maps dated 1823–35 {1822–30}; refs 2/50/2; 4/5/8; 17/3/1; surveyor starting own business, 1832 (EFP); of Cowick Street, 1850 and Alphington Street, 1857 (Directories)
  Bendall: 0 079

A175. PADDON, J.
Maps dated 1777; refs 18/12/1; 19/15/1; associate: E. Reed; ?John son of George Paddon of Chawleigh matric. Exeter College Oxford 1774 aged 19, B.A. 1778, Minister of St Mary Bungay at his death in 1823 (*Alumni Oxon.*) may refer to this surveyor as his father was Rector of Chawleigh in 1743

A176. PALKE, Samuel
Maps dated 18th cent.; refs 5/11/5

A177. PALMER, David of Launceston, Cornwall
maps dated 1780–1810 {1787–1812}; refs 3/3/1; 6/5/6; 8/8/2; 13/8/4; 16/4/1; 19/2/5
  Bendall: P 031

A178. PALMER, Edwin
Maps dated 1838 {1839–44}; refs 19/16/31
  Bendall: P 032

A179. PARKER. A.S. of Buckfastleigh and Winkleigh
Maps dated *c.*1840 {1841–44}; refs 4/9/1; associate: Thomas B. Irish
  Bendall: P 050.5

A180. PARKER, T. of Willand
Maps dated 1839; refs 8/2/12
  Bendall: P 063.5

A181. PARKYNS, George J.
Maps dated 1820; refs 12/10/1; author of *Monastic and Baronial Remains*

A182. PARMINTER, G.
Maps dated 1834; refs 2/7/3

A183. PARR, W.
d. Moretonhampstead, Nov. 1800 (EFP); maps dated 1795; refs 15/5/5

A184. PASCOE, John of Palace (Paris) Street, Exeter, 1816 and 1822, of Maddocks Row, Exeter, 1830–36, of Southernhay Place,.Exeter, 1838 (all EPJ)
b. *c.*1765; d. Crediton, July 1852 (BMI); maps dated 1797–1831 {1809–30}; refs 2/27/1; 2/31/3; 2/31/4; 3/1/5; 3/33/11; 4/5/5; 11/2/8; 11/2/9; 11/2/10; 11/2/11; B9; B13; B24; B32; B37; B40; B48; B57; B65; B72; B73; associates: Alexander Law; Edward Osmond; land steward to Richard Hippisley Tuckfield of Shobrooke Park (*Gent. Mag.*, 1852); land agent and surveyor of Theatre Lane, Exeter, moved from Honiton 1808 (EFP); plan of new road, 1828 (EFP)
  Bendall: P 101

A185. PASSMORE, R. of Braunton, landsurveyor
Maps dated [1821]–1835; refs 1/14/2; 1/14/3; 2/31/5; 2/31/6; 8/9/5; schoolmaster, mentioned in Will of John Elliott of Braunton, 1814 (BMI); agent for sale of house, 1808 and described as of Braunton, teacher (EFP)

A186. PATERSON, I(J)
Maps dated 1798 {1799}; refs 1/5/2; a J. Paterson described as Additional Lieutenant in 1787 in 20th Foot (*Army List 1787*)
  Bendall: P 103.5

A187. PEARSE, William
Maps dated 1781–*c.*1788; refs 3/27/6; 7/5/4

A188. PECKHAM, T., junior
Maps dated 1741; refs 4/4/3

A189. PERER, J. {PER, J.}
Maps dated 1836; refs 12/1/6
  Bendall: P 170.5

A190. PHILLIPS, Joseph
Maps dated 1721–26 {?1751–68*}; refs 21/2/1 (3 items); surveyor of bridges, resigns post, May 1783 (EFP)
  Bendall: possibly P 200.5 but maps are later*

A191. PHILP, J. of 107 Fore Street, Exeter, 1836 (EPJ) and of Moreton-hampstead
Maps dated 1837 and 19th cent. {1838–43}; refs 2/22/14; 2/22/15; 2/22/16
  Bendall: P 207.6

A192. PICKERING, [T.] of Axminster
Maps dated 1812 {1845}; refs B16; associate: William Bond; Messrs

Pickering and Bond of Axminster, land surveyors, agents in land sales, 1814 and 1816 (EFP)
Bendall: P 211

A193. PIERCE (PIERSE), Mark of Sandhurst, Kent and London
Maps dated 1633 {c.1600–1635}; refs 2/25/1
Bendall: P 221

A194. PILKINTON (WILKINTON), W. of Exeter
Maps dated 1797–98 and late 18th cent.; refs 3/14/10; 19/16/13; 21/16/3; 21/16/4; won Award at Okehampton, 1798 and was aged 37 in 1800 (*Gent. Mag.*, 1831) ; agent for sale of houses and timber, 1796–99; of Paris Street, 1799; opens warehouse to sell clover and grass seed, 1796; of Fore Street, turnip seed for sale, 1802; opened hop and seed warehouse, 1802; bankrupt and goods auctioned, 1803 (all EFP); wrote treatise on agriculture, 1818
Bendall: P 236

A195. PITTS, James
Maps dated 1791; refs 3/15/3; 18/33/2

A196. POOLE, I.(J) of Sherborne, Dorset
Maps dated 1836 {1809–49}; refs 19/17/7
Bendall: P 274

A197. PRICKETT, John of Highgate, Middlesex
Maps dated 1796 {1775–1827}; refs 8/7/4; 8/7/5; 8/7/6
Bendall: P 333

A198. PRIDE, Thomas {of London and Oxford}
Maps dated 1761 {1758–1801}; refs 18/24/1; 18/24/2
Bendall: P 335

A199. PROWSE, Richard
?bap. West Teignmouth, 1684; maps dated 1727; refs 19/9/1; of West Teignmouth, 1710 (BMI)

A200. PRYDE, Thomas
Maps dated 1827 {1825}; refs 2/38/9
Bendall: P 356

A201. PUDDICOMBE, Richard
bap. Bovey Tracey, 1717; bur. Bovey Tracey 1775; maps dated 1740; refs 2/22/2; 2/22/3

A202. REED, E. of Kingsbridge
Maps dated 1777; refs 18/12/1; 19/15/1; associate: J. Padddon

A203. REED, William
Maps dated 1795; refs 2/31/2

A204. RENDEL(L), James Meadows
{b. nr. Okehampton 1799;} m. Catherine Jane Harris (DNB); {d. 21.11.1856}; maps dated 1822–39; refs ?5/11/7; B36; B38; B43; B74; B78; B81; B111; settled in Plymouth after previously working in Teignmouth and London (with Telford) (DNB); designed chain ferries at Dartmouth, worked with Telford in building roads in North Devon; erected Laira Iron Bridge, 1824; planned Milbay Docks, 1836/7; moved from Plymouth to London, 1838 (all BMI); partnership dissolved with Nathaniel Beardmore (DNB); proposed line of railway from Plymouth to Exeter over Dartmoor, printed map, 1840 (BMI)
Bendall: R 100

A205. RENDLE (RENDEL), James
See also RENDLE & ELLIOTT
{d. Okehampton, 1838}; maps dated 1815–29; refs 3/9/1; 5/11/7; B41; B62; {Father of James Meadows Rendel; assistant surveyor of highways}; letter book and ledger, 1810–31 (DRO, Z17/3/35)
Bendall: R 099

A206. RENDLE & ELLIOTT
Maps dated 1814; refs 4/10/2

A207. RENNELL, James of Chudleigh
b.1742; {d.1830}; maps dated c.1756; refs 3/14/3; entered the navy, 1756, marine surveyor and produced charts and plans of harbours for the East India Co., guardian was Rev. Gilbert Burrington of Chudleigh (all DNB)
Bendall: R 100.5

A208. RENNIE, George {of Christchurch and London}
{b.1791; d.1866}; maps dated 1832; refs B77; associate: John Rennie; supervisor of Hamilton Fulton
Bendall: R 101

A209. RENNIE, John (later Sir John)
{b. 1794; d. 1874}; maps dated 1832; refs B77; associate: George Rennie; supervisor of Hamilton Fulton
Bendall: R 102.2

A210. RENNIE, John
engineer; {b.1761; d.1821}; maps dated 1794–95; refs B5; B77; chart of Tor Bay, 1799; Report of Messrs Rennie and Whidby on Plymouth

Breakwater, 1806; Master in the navy; companion of Captain Cook of Woolwich (all BMI)
>Bendall: R 102

A211. RICE, James
?bap. Exeter St David 1745 (IGI); maps dated 1763 {1756–75}; refs 18/5/1; eldest son of John Rice of Exeter, hatter and received houses and land in Little Silver, St David's, Exeter under his father's will

A212. RICHARDS, John
bap. Mariansleigh, 1690; m. Elizabeth Voysey, widow, at Exeter St Thomas, 1711; bur. Mariansleigh, 1778; maps dated 1732–64; refs 1/4/11; 2/17/1; 2/38/1; 3/33/2; 4/13/3; 5/2/1; 5/3/19; 5/3/28; 5/3/29; 5/3/30; 5/3/31; 5/3/32; 5/3/33; 5/3/34; 5/3/35; 5/3/36; 5/3/37; 5/3/38; 5/3/39; 5/3/40; 5/3/41; 5/3/42; 5/3/43; 5/3/44; 5/3/45; 5/3/46; 5/3/47; 5/3/48; 5/3/49; 5/3/50; 5/3/51; 5/4/1; 5/4/2; 5/4/3; 5/4/4; 5/4/5; 18/17/2; published *The Gentleman's Steward*, 1730; published *Annuities on Lives*, 1739; published *Cask Gauging Perfected*, 1740; architect to Devon and Exeter Hospital (BMI); obituary, 1778 (EFP); library sold by Edward Score, 1779 (EFP)
>Bendall: R 133

A213. RICHARDS, Thomas of Totnes
Maps dated 1805–15; refs 2/45/3; 3/31/1; 17/2/2; plan of the Town of Plymouth Dock, 1810 by T. Richards of Totnes, draughtsman (BMI); agent in property sale, 1816 (EFP)

A214. RICHARDSON, T.
Maps dated 1773; refs 15/5/1; 18/24/2
>Bendall: R 149

A215. RISDON, Joseph of Black Torrington {of Speccott near Great Torrington}
?d. Buckland Filleigh, 1855, aged 84 (*Gent. Mag.*); maps dated 1835 {1838–50}; refs 1/11/2; letter book, 1832–48 (DRO, 57/6); agent for farm sale, 1834 (EFP)
>Bendall: R 163

A216. ROBERTS, E.R.
Maps dated (1779)–1822; refs 2/2/4 (maps 6–8); 19/20/6; 19/20/7; 19/20/8; 19/20/9; 19/20/10; 19/20/11; Customs Collector at Barnstaple, 1812 (*Gent. Mag.*); ?Edward Richards Roberts Mayor of Barnstaple, 1817 and 1830 (BMI)

A217. ROCH, Jerom
{16?77–1707}; maps dated 1707; refs 5/8/1; of Plymouth, artist, 1678 (BMI); paid for drawing map of Plymouth, 1678/9 (R. N. Worth, *Calendar of Plymouth Records*, p.169)
>Bendall: R 222.9

A218. ROWSE, Matthew
Maps dated 19th cent.; refs 11/4/17

A219. SALISBURY AND WARMINGTON
Maps dated 1840; refs B120; B122
>Bendall: possibly W 110.8, Augustus Henry Warmington of Honiton

A220. SHEARM, Thomas of Stowe and Stratton, Cornwall
bap. Kilkhampton, Cornwall, 1794 (IGI); maps dated 1816–19 {c.1817–54}; refs 2/14/8; 7/1/5; 18/5/6; 18/5/7
>Bendall: S 174

A221. SHEARM, James
Maps dated 1818; refs B25; associate: James Green

A222. SHERRIFF, James {?I AND II), of Birmingham}
Maps dated 1797 {1774–1830}; refs 13/21/2
>Bendall: ?S 198

A223. SHERWOOD (SHERWODDE), Robert of Exeter
bap. c.1552; m. Elizabeth Whetcombe, Exeter, 1584; d. Exeter, 1640; maps dated 1604–33; refs 5/3/9; 5/3/10 (2 items); 5/3/11; 5/3/14; 5/3/15; admitted to the Freedom of Exeter, 1580 and appointed City Surveyor for Exeter, 1616 (ECA); described as a merchant of Exeter, 1633 (BMI)
>Bendall: S 201.5

A224. SHILLI(A)BEER, W.
Maps dated 1805–18; refs 4/3/6; 4/3/9; B14; B26; possibly the same person as the William Shillabeer of Walkhampton, gent. who had a son H.B. Shillibeer of Taunton, civil engineer (BMI)
>Bendall: S 204.3

A225. SIMPSON, William {?of Somerset}
{d.1799}; maps dated 1788 {1771–}; refs 2/25/2
>Bendall: S 242

A226. SINGER, Josh. (Joseph) of Luppitt and Littletown in Honiton
Maps dated c.1800 {c.1760–1803}; refs 3/15/5; agent for sale of timber, 1799 (EFP); directed to survey land at Membury and prepare

a map (enclosure), 1807 (*TDA*, 1927, 240); {road-measurer to John Cary}

    Bendall: S 248

A227. SMITH, John

    Maps dated 1837 {*c.*1800–30}; refs 2/43/1

        Bendall: ?S 331

A228. SMYTH, George

    Maps dated *c.*1750 {1742}; refs 20/1/1

        Bendall: ?S 372.8

A229. SPRY, Henry of Boyton, Cornwall and Plymouth Dock

    bap. Boyton, 1747; maps dated 1786 {1775/84–1797/1815}; refs 4/14/1; 16/13/1 agent, 1804 (EFP)

        Bendall: S 426

A230. STENTAFORD, W.T. of ?Walkhampton and of Stoke Climsland, Cornwall

    Maps dated 1805–30; refs 21/8/13; 19/2/11

        Bendall: S 477

A231. STILL, Ethelred

    Maps dated 1823–32; refs 8/19/2; 18/33/1; 18/33/5; 21/8/13

A232. STRIBLING, Robert of Northgate Street, Exeter

    bap. Exeter St Thomas, 1727; d.1789 (EFP); maps dated 1762; refs 2/39/3; associate: William Hayman; property sales, 1767–81; dissolved partnership with Painter, 1781; statement re safety of theatre, 1781 (all EFP)

A233. STURGE, Jacob of Bristol

    {b.1754; d. 1811}; maps dated 1780–83; refs 2/5/2; 3/27/7; 4/1/2; 14/5/1; 15/2/1; 18/26/1

        Bendall: S 582

A234. SUMMERS, William {(senior) of Curry Mallet and Ilton, Somerset}

    Maps dated 1827–28 {1810–33}; refs B51; B53; B59; of Belmont House, Hatch Beaucham[p], surveyor, receiving tenders, 1819; estimated for Taunton/Chard railway, 1830 (both EFP)

        Bendall: S 597

A235. TAMLYN, John [of Barnstaple]

    possibly bap. Yarnscombe, 1717; d. Barnstaple, 1798 'a worthy man' (*Gent. Mag.*); maps dated 1776–79; refs 2/2/4; 6/5/1; 16/6/1

A236. TAPERELL, J.

    Maps dated 1829; refs 19/9/6; James Taperell of Blackboy Road, Exeter, 1857 (Directories); John Taperell of Higher Broad Street, Plymouth, auctioneer, 1808 (EFP)

        Bendall: T 020.8 (James Taperell); T 021 (John Taperell)

A237. TATHAM, Edmund {of Chorley, Lancs.}

    Maps dated 1790 {1793–1816/18}; refs 2/21/2

        Bendall: T 032

A238. TAYLOR, Isaac {of Ross-on-Wye, Herefordshire}

    Maps dated: 1765–70 {1750–77}; refs 2/4/1; 2/20/1; 4/8/1; 19/4/1; 19/4/2; 19/4/3; 19/5/1; 19/5/2; 19/5/3

        Bendall: T 049

A239. THOMAS, Lewis of Margam, Glamorgan

    b.1735; d.1817; maps dated 1772; refs 18/27/1

        Bendall: T 115

A240. THOMAS, Nicholas

    Maps dated 1714; refs 6/1/1

        Bendall: T 116

A241. THOMAS, William

    Maps dated 1836 {1839–41}; refs 15/5/9

        Bendall: T 120

A242. THOMPSON, John

    Maps dated 1775; refs 20/4/1

A243. TOLL, J.Y.

    Maps dated 1831; refs 2/19/5; John Yeo Toll of Black Torrington, farmer, insolvent debtor, 1832 (EFP)

A244. TOTHILL, John of Musgrave's Alley, Exeter, 1794 (UBD) and 1796 (EPJ), and of Bear Gate, Exeter

    bap. Exeter St Sidwell, 1728 (son of Robert) or bap. Exeter Bow Presbyterian Meeting, 1731 (son of Thomas); d. end of December 1799 (Ex. D & C 3575); maps dated 1763–95 {1759–}; refs 2/28/2; 3/16/1; 5/3/20; appointed Surveyor to Dean and Chapter of Exeter, 1759; appointed Steward of Exeter [Cathedral], 1793 (EFP)

        Bendall: T 215

A245. TOWNSEND, Nicholas

    m. Jane Heale at Dartmouth Townstal (St Clement), 1619; maps dated 1619; refs 4/4/1; 4/4/2; paid for drawing 4 plots of Dartmouth, Aug. 1620 (DD 61964)

        Bendall: T 224

A246. TOZER, Charles of Westerland, Marldon
m. Susanna Stephens; bur. Marldon, 3 Jan. 1826, aged 59 (Parish register, IRW/T518); maps dated 1789–c.1825; refs 1/8/2; 2/41/1; 6/3/3; 9/6/2; 18/26/2; 18/29/1; B30; C177; described as of Marldon, land surveyor, agent in farm sale, 1818 (EFP); associated with R. Cowl and was his assistant; Will proved 1826 – left books, maps and surveying instruments to his son (IRW, T518)
Bendall: T 229

A247. TREGELLES, Edwin Octavius of Frenchay near Bristol, later of Shotley Bridge, Gateshead (Boase, *Bibl. Cornub.*)
bap. Falmouth, Cornwall, 1806; d. Sept. 1886 (DNB); maps dated 1835; refs B90; associate: James B. West; report on water supply and sewerage of Barnstaple, 1849 (BMI); adviser about Bideford Bridge widening (*TDA*, 34, 237); biography entitled *Edwin Octavius Tregelles*; went to Hebrides to relieve distressed persons there, 1855 (BMI)

A248. TURNER, Richard
Maps dated 1762 & 18th cent.; refs 19/3/18; 19/3/31; agent to the Duke of Bedford, 1756–77; Portreeve of Tavistock (BMI)

A249. VEITCH (VETCH), John
b. Jedburgh, 1752; d.1839
Maps dated 1795; refs 6/3/2; steward to Acland estates from 1770

A250. VICARS, Murray of 241 High Street, Exeter, 1831–33 (EPJ) and of Upper Paul Street, Exeter, 1834–38 (EPJ)
Maps dated 1834–38 {1837–42}; refs 3/33/16; 18/13/2; 18/18/4; B88; B92
Bendall: V 025

A250a. W., W. [Late Entry]
Maps dated 1798; refs. S2

A251. WALLACE, William ?John, a 'sworn surveyor'
Maps dated 1821; refs 15/6/2

A252. WAPSHARE, William {of The Close, Salisbury, Wilts.}
Maps dated 1744 {1738–78/82}; refs 11/1/1
Bendall: W 088

WARMINGTON *see* SALISBURY & WARMINGTON

A253. WARREN, P. of Holne Cottage
Maps dated 1802–06; refs 1/8/7; 15/6/1; a Philip Warren described

as of Okehampton, maltster, 1797 (EFP); Philip Warren lived at Eastern Town, Okehampton, 1808 (BMI)

A254. WATKINS, William
possibly bap. Bideford, 1753; maps dated 1775–77; refs 1/11/1; 3/34/1; a subscriber to J. Watkins' *Bideford*, 1792 (BMI)
Bendall: W 145.5

A255. [WEBB, {Francis}]
{d.1812/15}; maps dated 1809; refs 18/2/1; 18/2/2; possibly the nonconformist minister and miscellaneous writer, born at Taunton 1735, married Hannah Milner at Wareham, 1764, settled at Lufton near Yeovil in 1811 and died at Barrington, Somerset, 1815 (DNB)
Bendall: W 183

A256. WEBB, John
{b.1753/4; d.1828}; maps dated 1825; refs 2/13/4
Bendall: ?W 189.5

A257. WEST, James B.
Maps dated 1834–40; refs B83; B90; B94; B100; B119; associate: Edwin Tregelles

A258. WHITAKER, Thomas of Bedford Street, Exeter, 1836–38 (EPJ)
Maps dated 1838–39 {1839–42}; refs B109; B112; B115; of Bampfylde House, Exeter, justifies his action as surveyor to the Improvement Commissioners, 1836 (EFP); at Hills Court, Exeter, 1850 and 1857 (Directories); County Surveyor and work on bridge at Great Torrington mentioned (Cherry/Pevsner, *Devon*, 460)
Bendall: W 273.6

A259. WHITE, 'Farmer' of Oakford
possibly Robert White, bap. Oakford 1721 or 1723; maps dated 1745; refs 15/1/1

A260. WHITE, John of Ugborough
b. c.1741; d. Ugborough, aged 87, 1828 (EFP); maps dated 1804; refs 1/15/2; agent for property sale, 1806 (EFP)

A261. WHITE, William
{b. c.1749; d.1817}; maps dated 1775–97; refs 2/36/1; 3/35/4; 7/2/3; 8/26/1; of Bristol, surveyor, agent for sale of houses, 1776; of Devon, surveyor, County Bridge Surveyor, 1802 (both EFP)
Bendall: W 296

A262. WHITTLESEY (WHITTLESEA), Robert
Maps dated 1723–*c.*1759; refs 11/4/2; 16/12/1
Bendall: W 321

A263. WIGHTWICK, George of Plymouth, architect
Maps dated 1835; refs 19/2/13; listed as architect, Athenaeum Street, 1836 (Thomas's *Plymouth Directory*) and surveyor and architect, 3 Athenaeum Terrace, Plymouth, 1844 (Pigot's *Directory*)

WILKINTON, W. *see* PILKINTON, W.

A264. WILLEY, Josh. {Joseph}
?bap. Cullompton Presbyterian Meeting, 1726 (IGI); maps dated 1743; refs 2/37/1
Bendall: W 313.8

A265. WITHIELL, George
Maps dated 1694 {1679–1708}; 13/14/1; recommended by Barnstaple and Bideford as having knowledge of the Newfoundland trade and to make a survey of Newfoundland (*Journal of Trade and Plantations*, 611 and *Calendar of State Papers Colonial and West Indies*, 1714/15, 22–23); undertook surveys in Cornwall and Somerset (*DCNQ*, XXXV, 45–58, 95–114)
Bendall: W 502

A265a. WOODWARD, William [Late Entry] {of London}
Maps dated 1769 {176(?2)–97}; refs. S4
Bendall: W 557

A266. WOOLCOTT, Josiah
?bap. South Molton, 1764; maps dated 1805; refs 2/15/1

A267. WOOLCOTT, Simon
Maps dated 1774–*c.*1775; refs 7/2/2; 13/18/5

A268. WRIGHT, Thomas
Maps dated 1831 {1830–?40}; refs 18/11/1; of Tiverton, land surveyor, agent for land and timber sales, 1819–35 (EFP)
Bendall: W 611

A269. WYNNE, John
?bap. Biggleswade, Beds., 1720 (IGI); m. Mary Pollard, Tavistock, 1755; maps dated 1740s– 1758; refs 5/3/18; 15/5/1; 19/3/1; 19/3/2; 19/3/9; 19/3/10; 19/3/11; 19/3/14; 19/3/15; associate: Gilbert Aislabie; Portreeve of Tavistock, 1756 (*TDA*, XLVI, 173); Freeman of Tavistock, 1768 (BMI); agent to the Duke of Bedford, 1743–56
Bendall: W 639

A270. YEAKELL, Edmund of Alphington
Maps dated 19th cent.; refs 19/1/4

Plans of Major Statutory Undertakings in Devon deposited with the Clerk of the Peace, Devon Quarter Sessions, 1792–1840

Plans of major statutory undertakings, such as roads, canals, railways, bridges, ferries and harbours, were deposited pursuant to a House of Commons order of 1792 with Devon Quarter Sessions. A fuller list, which also includes the much more numerous plans after 1840, beyond the scope of this volume, is in the Devon Record Office Search Room. In some cases, a copy of the plan also survives in the House of Lords Record Office, often with a slightly later date as this was the copy which accompanied the Local or Private Act of Parliament which enabled the work on the project to proceed. This copy is noted as 'HL' in the following list. Other copies sometimes survive in the Exeter City Archives (ECA) or in privately deposited family collections of archives (PD) where the project involved Exeter or a landowner's property.

Plymouth projects are included in this Appendix as the list of Plymouth maps in Elisabeth A. Stuart's *Lost Landscapes of Plymouth* covers the period up to 1800 only.

	DATE	DESCRIPTION	LOCATION
B1	1792	Ashburton to Totnes Canal, via Buckfastleigh and Staverton. Surveyor: J. King	DRO, DP8
B2	1792	Plymouth Dock water supply. Surveyor: J. King	DRO, DP7
B3	1793	Public Devonshire Canal, Topsham to Barnstaple via Crediton, Chulmleigh and Bishop's Tawton. Surveyor: T. Bolton	DRO, DP9; ECA
B4	n.d.	Seaton to River Tone (Somerset) Canal. Surveyor: not named (1793–4)	DRO, DP6a
B5	1794–5	Tamar Manure Canal. Morwellham (Devon) to Tamerton (Cornwall). Surveyors: George Bentley and Thomas Bolton John Rennie (engineer) and James Murray	DRO, DP11a–d; HL
B6	1795	Yarty Bridge Watercourse. Surveyor: William Bond	DRO, DP12
B7	1800	Exeter to Cediton Canal. Surveyor: Robert Cartwright	DRO, DP13; HL
B8	1803	Tavistock to Morwellham Canal and Tunnel. Surveyor: not named	DRO, DP14
B9	1809	Braunton Canal. Engineer: J. Green Surveyor: John Pascoe	DRO, DP17
B10	1810	Tiverton to Bampton Turnpike. Surveyor: J. Coldridge	DRO, DP16
B11	1810	Exeter to Tiverton Turnpike. Surveyor: J. Coldridge	DRO, DP18
B12	1811	Turnpike road over Dartmoor. Surveyor: not named	DRO, DP19

	Date	Description	Location
B13	1811	Brandy Cross to Sidmouth road. Surveyor: J. Pascoe	DRO, DP20
B14	1811	Buckland Monachorum to Two Bridges road. Surveyor: W. Shillabeer	DRO, DP21
B15	1812	Tiverton to Bampton road. Surveyor: J. Coldridge	DRO, DP22–23
B16	1812	Chard to Yarcombe road. Surveyors: Bond and Pickering	DRO, DP24
B17	1812	Cullompton to Broadclyst road. Surveyor: J. Easton	DRO, DP25
B18	1813	Plymouth Turnpike (Bittaford). Surveyor: not named	DRO, DP26
B19	1813	Chard to Upottery road. Surveyor: not named	DRO, DP27
B20	1813	Plymouth Eastern Turnpike. Surveyor: not named	DRO, DP29
B21	1813	Road, Farm Gate to Plympton. Surveyor: not named	DRO, DP30
B22	1814	Road near Ugbrooke. Surveyor: J. Coldridge	DRO, DP32; HL
B23	1814	Road, Upottery to Chard. Surveyor: R.J. Easton	DRO, DP33 HL
B24	1815	Brandy Cross to Sidmouth road. Enlarged version of DP20. Surveyor: J.Pascoe	DRO, DP34–35; HL
B25	1818	Canal, Bude Haven to Thornbury. Surveyors: James Green and James Shearm	DRO, DP36
B26	1818	Tramway, Dartmoor Prison to Crabtree. Surveyor: William Shillabeer	DRO, DP37
B27	1819	Tramway, Plymouth and Dartmoor. Surveyor: not named	DRO, DP38: HL
B28	1819	Exeter to Plymouth road. Surveyor: James Green	DRO, DP39; HL
B29	1820	Exeter to Crockernwell road. Surveyor: James Green	DRO, DP40; HL
B30	1820	Newton Abbot to Torquay road. Surveyor: Charles Tozer	DRO, DP41; HL
B31	1821	Railway, Leigham to Jump. Surveyors: T.H.Lakeman and John Hitchen	DRO, DP43a–b
B32	1821	Exeter to Chudleigh road. Surveyor: John Pascoe	DRO, DP44
B33	1821	Honiton to Cullompton and Sidmouth roads. Surveyor: not named	DRO, DP45; HL
B34	1821	Canal, Broad Pill to North Sluice, Braunton. Surveyor: James Green	DRO, DP46
B35	1822	Axminster to Charmouth and Lyme Regis road. Surveyor: not named	DRO, DP47
B36	1822	Teignmouth to Haldon roads. Surveyor: James M. Rendell	DRO, DP50
B37	1822	Exeter to Teignmouth road. Surveyor: John Pascoe	DRO, DP51; HL
B38	1823	Plymouth roads. Surveyor: James Rendell	DRO, DP53a–b; HL
B39	1823	Plymouth and environs, roads. Surveyors: Richard Andrews under the direction of James Green	DRO, DP54; HL
B40	1823	Exeter to Teignmouth road. Surveyor: John Pascoe	DRO, DP55
B41	1823	Okehampton to Hatherleigh road. Surveyor: James Rendle	DRO, DP56; HL
B42	1823	Totnes Turnpike road. Surveyor: not named	DRO, DP58
B43	1823	Dartmouth to Salcombe roads. Surveyor: James Rendel	DRO, DP59 & 62
B44	1823–4	Wiveliscombe to South Molton roads. Surveyor: Charles Bailey	DRO, DP60 & 63; HL
B45	1824	Tavistock Turnpike roads. Surveyor: T.H. Lakeman	DRO, DP64; HL
B46	1825	Roads near East Teignmouth. Surveyor: Roger Hopkins	DRO, DP65; HL
B47	1825	Roads, Shaldon–Torquay. Surveyor: Henry Andrews	DRO, DP67
B48	1825	Exeter Turnpike Trust. Surveyor: John Pascoe	DRO, DP68; HL; ECA
B49	1826	Roads, Ilfracombe and Barnstaple. Surveyor: Charles Bailey	DRO, DP69; HL
B50	1826	Road, Newton Abbot to Whiddon Down. Surveyor: Henry Andrews of Modbury	DRO, DP70; HL
B51	1827	Roads near Yarcombe and Chard. Surveyor: William Summers	DRO, DP71
B52	1827	Road, Bideford to Peters Marland. Surveyor: not named	DRO, DP73; HL
B53	1827	Road, Somerset to Dalwood. Surveyor: William Summers	DRO, DP74

	Date	Description	Location
B54	1827	Kingsbridge roads. Surveyor: Henry Andrews	DRO, DP75
B55	1827	Canal, Newton Abbot to River Teign. Surveyor: James Green	DRO, DP76
B56	1828	East and West Teignmouth water supply. Surveyor: not named	DRO, DP77
B57	1828	Road, Braunton to Barnstaple. Surveyor: John Pascoe	DRO, DP78
B58	1828	Exeter canal. Surveyor: James Green	DRO, DP79; HL; ECA
B59	1828	Chard Turnpike. Surveyor: William Summers	DRO, DP81; HL
B60	1828	Road, Modbury to Plymouth. Surveyor: S. Elliott	DRO, DP82; HL
B61	1828	Water tunnel at St Andrew, Plymouth. Surveyor: Roger Hopkins	DRO, DP83
B62	1829	Road and ferry, Brixham to Dartmouth. Surveyor: James Rendel	DRO, DP84; HL
B63	1829	Exeter to Crediton Turnpike. Surveyors: Dymond and Dawson	DRO, DP85; ECA
B64	1829	Bridge over Stonehouse Mill Pool. Surveyor: Charles Chapple	DRO, DP86
B65	1829	Road, Braunton to Barnstaple. Surveyor: John Pascoe	DRO, DP87; HL
B66	1829	Tiverton roads. Surveyor: not named	DRO, DP89; HL
B67	1829	Roads from Little Torrington to Great Torrington. Surveyor: ?H. Cartwright	DRO, DP90; HL
B68	1829	Ashburton and Totnes roads. Surveyor: not named	DRO, DP91
B69	1830	Teignmouth to Dawlish Turnpike roads. Surveyor: not named	DRO, DP92; HL
B70	1830	Improvements to Exeter Turnpike Trust roads. Surveyor: not named [John & Samuel T. Coldridge in ECA copies]	DRO, DP93; HL; ECA
B71	1830	Road, Topsham to Exeter. Surveyor: James Green	DRO, DP94
B72	1830	Road, Crediton to Chudleigh Bridge. Surveyor: John Pascoe	DRO, DP95; HL
B73	1831	Exeter Turnpike road, Lympstone to Exmouth. Surveyor: John Pascoe	DRO, DP96; HL
B74	1831	Sutton Pool near Plymouth. Surveyor: James M. Rendel	DRO, DP97; HL
B75	1831	Railway, Exeter to Crediton. Surveyor: not named	DRO, DP99; HL
B76	1832	Exeter waterworks. Surveyors: William Anderson and Dymond and Dawson	DRO, DP100 &100A; HL; ECA
B77	1832	River Dart from Totnes to Anchor Stone. Surveyor: Hamilton Fulton under the supervision of G. and J. Rennie	DRO, DP101
B78	1832	Turnpike Trust, Saltash and Plymouth. Surveyor: James M. Rendel	DRO, DP103
B79	1832	Railway, Newton Abbot to Torquay. Surveyor: James Green	DRO, DP104
B80	1833	River Dart to Langham Wood Point. Surveyor: Hamilton Fulton	DRO, DP106; HL
B81	1833	Kingsbridge Turnpike Trust. Surveyor: James M. Rendel	DRO, DP108; HL
B82	1834	Exeter Canal Basin. Surveyor: not named	DRO, DP109; HL; ECA
B83	1834	Teignmouth waterworks. Surveyor: J.B. West	DRO, DP110
B84	1834	Newton Abbot roads. Surveyor: Richard Doswell	DRO, DP111
B85	1834	Road, Dean Prior to Dartington and Totnes. Surveyor: H.C. Creagh	DRO, DP112; HL
B86	1834	Road, Newton Abbot, Kingsteignton and Exeter. Surveyor: not named	DRO, DP113
B87	1834	Exeter water supply. Surveyors: Dymond and Dawson	DRO, DP114; ECA
B88	1834	Launceston roads and some in Devon. Surveyor: Murray Vicars	DRO, DP115
B89	1834	Teignmouth Turnpike. Surveyor: Richard Doswell	DRO, DP116
B90	1835	Teignmouth waterworks. Surveyors: J.B. West and Edwin Tregelles	DRO, DP117
B91	1835	Honiton and Ilminster Turnpike. Surveyor: William Dawson	DRO, DP118
B92	1835	Teignmouth and Dawlish Turnpike Trust. Surveyor: Murray Vicars	DRO, DP120; HL
B93	1835	Road from Upottery to Seaton. Surveyor: William Dawson	DRO, DP121

	DATE	DESCRIPTION	LOCATION
B94	1835	Teignmouth Harbour. Surveyor: J.B. West	DRO, DP122; HL
B95	1835	Bristol and Exeter Railway. Surveyor: not named	DRO, DP123; HL; ECA
B96	1836	South Molton Turnpike Trust. Surveyor: G.A. Boyce	DRO, DP124
B97	1836	London, Exeter and Falmouth Railway. Surveyor: not named	DRO, DP125
B98	1836	Taw Vale Railway. Surveyor: not named	DRO, DP126; HL
B99	1836	Roads from Newton Abbot, Shaldon to floating bridge. Surveyor: Henry Andrews	DRO, DP127
B100	1837	Paignton Harbour. Surveyor: James B. West	DRO, DP128
B101	1837	Taw Vale Railway. Surveyor: not named	DRO, DP129; HL
B102	1837	South Molton Turnpike Trust. Surveyor: not named	DRO, DP130
B103	1837	Torquay roads. Surveyors: George Cumming and Henry Andrews	DRO, DP131
B104	1837	Combmartin Turnpike Trust. Surveyor: J. Lock	DRO, DP132
B105	1837	Brixham roads and quay. Surveyor: C. Greaves	DRO, DP133; HL
B106	1838	South Molton Trust new roads. Surveyor: not named	DRO, DP134; HL
B107	n.d.	Roads in Culmstock (Devon) and Sampford Arundel (Somerset) Surveyor: Josiah Easton	DRO, DP135
B108	1838	Turnpike roads, Upottery and Yarcombe. Surveyor: William Dawson	DRO, DP136
B109	1838	Road at Topsham. Surveyor: Thomas Whitaker	DRO, DP137
B110	1839	Honiton and Ilminster Turnpike. Surveyor: William Dawson	DRO, DP138
B111	1839	Plymouth, Millbay Pier. Surveyor: James M. Rendel	DRO, DP139
B112	1839	Exeter Turnpike. Surveyor: not named [J. Whitaker in ECA copy]	DRO, DP140; ECA
B113	1839	Roads, St Marychurch, Torquay. Surveyor: George Cumming	DRO, DP141; HL
B114	1839	Railway, St David's, Exeter. Surveyor: not named	DRO, DP142–3
B115	1839	Exeter Turnpike. Surveyor: T. Whitaker	DRO, DP144–7; HL
B116	1840	Plymouth, Devonport and Exeter Railway over Dartmoor with branch to Tavistock. Surveyor: not named	DRO, DP148
B117	1840	Bideford Turnpike Trust. Surveyor: G.A. Boyce	DRO, DP149
B118	1840	Barnstaple and Braunton Turnpike to Ilfracombe. Surveyor: Hugh Ballment	DRO, DP150
B119	1840	Dartmouth improvement. Surveyor: James B. West	DRO, DP151
B120	1840	Honiton Turnpike Trust. Surveyors: Salisbury and Warmington	DRO, DP152–3
B121	1840	Barnstaple Turnpike Trust. Surveyor: Thomas Lock, junior	DRO, DP154
B122	1840	Road from Honiton to Exeter. Surveyors: Salisbury and Warmington	DRO, DP155

APPENDIX C

Plans of 'Highways Diverted' enrolled at Devon Quarter Sessions before 1840

Plans relating to the enrolment of records of the diversion and stopping up of roads, bridleways and footpaths under the Act of 1773 and subsequent legislation. Please note that only the pre 1840 plans and sketches in these records are listed here. For a fuller list, see the relevant folder on the Search Room shelves in the Devon Record Office.

	DATE	PARISH AND DETAIL	DRO REFERENCE
C1	1829–30	East Allington. Plan.	113A/1/1
C2	1812	West Alvington and Dodbrooke. Two sketches.	113A/3/1
C3	1812	West Alvington and Dodbrooke. Sketch.	113A/3/2
C4	1813	West Alvington and Charleton. Sketch.	113A/3/3
C5	1813	West Alvington and Charleton. Sketch.	113A/3/4
C6	1824	West Alvington. Plans.	113A/3/5A–B
C7	1828	Arlington. Plan.	113A/6/1
C8	1800	Ashburton. Plan.	113A/7/1
C9	1834–5	Ashreigney. Plan.	113A/9/1
C10	1784	Awliscombe and Combe Raleigh. Plan.	113A/11/1.
C11	1806	Awliscombe. Plan.	113A/11/2
C12	1810	Awliscombe. Plan.	113A/11/3
C13	1839–40	Axminster. Plans.	113A/12/1A–B
C14	1820	Axmouth. Sketch.	113A/13/1
C15	1831	Berrynarbour. Plans.	113A/19/1
C16	1837	Berrynarbour. Plan.	113A/19/2
C17	1808	Bicton, Colaton Raleigh and Otterton. Plans.	113A/21/1
C18	1836	Blackawton. Plan.	113A/23/1

	DATE	PARISH AND DETAIL	DRO REFERENCE
C19	1829	Bovey Tracey. Sketch.	113A/24/1
C20	1837	Bovey Tracey. Plan.	113A/24/2
C21	1838	Bovey Tracey. Plan.	113A/24/3
C22	1840	Bovey Tracey. Plan.	113A/24/4
C23	1793	Bradworthy. Plan.	113A/26/1
C24	1820	Bridestowe and Lew Trenchard. Plan.	113A/30/1
C25	1812	Brixton. Plan.	113A/33/1
C26	1827	Brixton. For description see main series of maps in this volume under Brixton parish	113A/33/2
C27	1812	Broadclyst. Plan.	113A/34/1
C28	1832	Broadclyst. Plan.	113A/34/3
C29	1798	Broadhembury. Sketch.	113A/35/1
C30	1796	Buckerell and Awliscombe. Plan.	113A/36/1
C31	1797	Buckerell. Plan.	113A/36/2
C32	1782	Buckland Monachorum. Plan.	113A/40/1
C33	1808	Burlescombe. Plan.	113A/42/1
C34	1821	Cadeleigh. Plan.	113A/44/1
C35	1811	Chagford. Plan.	113A/46/1
C36	1833	Chagford and Throwleigh. Plan.	113A/46/2
C37	1813	Charleton and West Alvington. Sketch.	113A/48/1
C38	1813	Charleton and West Alvington. Sketch.	113A/48/2
C39	1813	Charleton and Moreleigh. Sketch.	113A/48/3
C40	1813	Charleton and Woodleigh. Sketch.	113A/48/4
C41	1826	Chawleigh. Plan.	113A/49/1
C42	1822	Chivelstone. Plan.	113A/51/1
C43	1840	Christow. Plan.	113A/52/1
C44	1824	Churston Ferrers. Sketch.	113A/56/1
C45	1829	Churston Ferrers. Plan.	113A/56/2
C46	1834	Clyst St George. Plan.	113A/58/1
C47	1809	Clyst Honiton. Plan.	113A/59/1
C48	1805	Clyst Hydon. Plan.	113A/60/1
C49	1820	Clyst Hydon. Plan.	113A/60/2
C50	1802	Colyton. Plan.	113A/62/1
C51	1816	Combeinteignhead. Sketch.	113A/63/1
C52	1803	Combe Raleigh. Plan.	113A/64/1
C53	1827	Crediton. 3 Plans.	113A/66/1
C54	1829	Crediton. Plan. Surveyor: C. Dean	113A/66/2
C55	1802	Cullompton. Plan.	113A/67/1
C56	1817	Cullompton. Plan.	113A/67/2
C57	1809	Dawlish. Sketch.	113A/70/1
C58	1810	Dawlish. Plan.	113A/70/2
C59	1815	Dawlish. Sketch.	113A/70/3

	DATE	PARISH AND DETAIL	DRO REFERENCE
C60	1830	Dawlish. Plans.	113A/70/4
C61	1831	Dawlish. Plans.	113A/70/5A–B
C62	1840	Dawlish. Plan.	113A/70/7
C63	1821	Dunchideock, Kenn & Exminster. Plan.	113A/73/1
C64	1829–30	Exeter, Heavitree. Plan.	113A/74/1
C65	1837	Exeter, Heavitree. Plan.	113A/74/2
C66	1834–40	Exeter, Heavitree. Plan.	113A/74/3
C67	1813	Exeter, St Thomas. Plan.	113A/75/1
C68	1803	Exminster. Plan.	113A/76/1
C69	1825	Exminster. Plan.	113A/76/2
C70	1829	Exminster. Plan.	113A/76/3
C71	1804	Farringdon. Plan.	113A/78/1
C72	1810	Farringdon. Sketch.	113A/78/2
C73	1792–3	Fremington. Sketches.	113A/80/1A–B
C74	1818	Frithelstock. Plan.	113A/81/1
C75	1817	Gittisham. Plan.	113A/83/1
C76	1823–4	Gittisham. Plan.	113A/83/2
C77	1836	Gittisham. Plan.	113A/83/3
C78	1781–2	Halberton & Uffculme. Plan.	113A/85/1
C79	1821	Harberton. Plan.	113A/87/1
C80	1777	Hartland. Plan.	113A/89/1
C81	1830	Hatherleigh. Plans.	113A/90/1
C82	1827	Hemyock, Culmstock & Churchstanton. Plan.	113A/91/1A–B
C83	1836	Hockworthy. Plan.	113A/93/1
C84	1830	Holbeton & Newton Ferrrers. Plan.	113A/94/1
C85	1817	Holcombe Rogus. Plan.	113A/95/1
C86	1808	Honiton. Plan.	113A/98/1
C87	1825	Honiton. Plans.	113A/98/2A–C
C88	1825	Honiton. Plans.	113A/98/3A–B
C89	1824	Huish, Meeth & Merton. Plan.	113A/99/1
C90	1816	Huntsham. Plans.	113A/100/1
C91	1813	Ilsington & Highweek. Sketch.	113A/103/1
C92	1815	Ilsington & Highweek. Sketch.	113A/103/2
C93	1798	Instow. Plan.	113A/104/1
C94	1828–9	Inwardleigh. Plan.	113A/105/1
C95	1780	Kenn. Sketch.	113A/106/1
C96	1787	Kenn. Sketch.	113A/106/2
C97	1797	Kenn. Sketch.	113A/106/3
C98	1818	Kenn, Exminster & Shillingford St George. Sketch.	113A/106/4
C99	1829	Kenn. Plan.	113A/106/5
C100	1786	Kilmington. Sketch.	113A/107/1
C101	1793	Kilmington. Plan.	113A/107/2

	Date	Parish and Detail	DRO Reference
C102	1803	Kilmington. Sketch.	113A/107/3
C103	1819	Lympstone. Sketch.	113A/115/1
C104	1834	Lympstone. Plan.	113A/115/2
C105	1815	Malborough. Sketch.	113A/117/1
C106	1828	Marwood. Sketch.	113A/121/1
C107	1818	Milton Abbot. Sketch.	113A/126/1
C108	1836–7	South Milton. Plan.	113A/127/1
C109	1826	North Molton. Plans.	113A/128/1
C110	1815–6	Monkleigh & Frithelstock. Plan.	113A/129/1
C111	1833	Monkleigh. Plan.	113A/129/2
C112	1828	Morchard Bishop. Plan.	113A/130/1
C113	1824	Moreleigh & Halwell. Plan.	113A/132/1
C114	1807	Newton Ferrers. Sketch.	113A/137/1
C115	1827	Newton Ferrers & Holbeton. Plan.	113A/137/2
C116	1835	Northam. Plan.	113A/138/1
C117	1826	Offwell. Plans.	113A/139/1A–B
C118	1800	Okehampton. Plan.	113A/140/1
C119	1820	Ottery St Mary. Plan.	113A/142/1
C120	1822	Paignton. Sketch.	113A/143/1
C121	1789	Parkham & Alwington. Plan.	113A/144/1
C122	1793	Pilton. Sketch.	113A/146/1
C123	1822	Pilton. Plan.	113A/146/2
C124	1807	Plymouth, Charles. Plan.	113A/148/1
C125	1825	Plymouth, Egg Buckland. Plan.	113A/150/2
C126	1817	Plymouth, Stoke Damerel. Plan. Surveyor: Robert J. Coddle	113A/153/1
C127	1833	Plymouth, Stoke Damerel. Plan.	113A/153/2
C128	1836	Plymouth, Stoke Damerel. Plan.	113A/153/3
C129	1800	Plympton St Mary. Plan.	113A/155/1
C130	1813	Plympton St Mary. Sketch.	113A/155/2
C131	1817	Plympton St Mary & Shaugh Prior. Plan.	113A/155/3
C132	1817	Plympton St Mary. Plan.	113A/155/4
C133	1824	Plympton St Mary. Plans.	113A/155/5
C134	1831	Plympton St Mary. Plan.	113A/155/6
C135	1831	Plympton St Mary. Plan.	113A/155/7
C136	1833	Plympton St Mary. Pictorial map.	113A/155/9
C137	1813	Plymstock. Plan.	113A/157/1
C138	1840–1	Plymstock. Plan.	113A/157/2
C139	1835	Poltimore & Broadclyst. Plan.	113A/158/1
C140	1839	Puddington. Plan.	113A/159/1
C141	1837	Roborough & St Giles in the Wood. Plan. Surveyor: John Doe	113A/162/1
C142	1791	Rockbeare. Plan.	113A/163/1
C143	1806	Salcombe Regis. Plan.	113A/166/1

	DATE	PARISH AND DETAIL	DRO REFERENCE
C144	1828	Salcombe Regis. Plan.	113A/166/2
C145	1821	Sandford. Plans.	113A/168/1
C146	1819	Seaton & Beer. Plan.	113A/169/1
C147	1834	Seaton & Beer. Plan.	113A/169/2
C148	1810	Shirwell. Plans. Surveyor: F. Hiles, surveyor, Barnstaple	113A/172/1
C149	1829	Shirwell. Plan.	113A/172/2
C150	1794	Shute. Sketch.	113A/174/1
C151	1814	Sidbury. Plan.	113A/175/1
C152	1828	Sidbury. Plan. Surveyor: J. Carslake	113A/175/2
C153	1794	Sidmouth. Plan.	113A/176/1
C154	1827	Sidmouth. Plans.	113A/176/2
C155	1833	Sidmouth. Plans.	113A/176/3
C156	1838	Silverton. Plans. Surveyor: G.W. Cumming	113A/177/1–2
C157	1831	Stokeinteignhead & Shaldon (St Nicholas). Sketches.	113A/183//1
C158	1833	Stokenham. Plan.	113A/184/1
C159	1820	Talaton. Plan.	113A/186/1
C160	1833–5	Tamerton Foliot. Plan.	113A/187/2
C161	1798	Tavistock. Plan. Surveyor: Thomas Jope	113A/188/1
C162	1839	Tavistock, Milton Abbot, Lamerton & Brentor. Plan.	113A/188/2/1–2
C163	1805	Tawstock. Plan.	113A/189/1
C164	1813	North Tawton. Plan.	113A/190/1/1–2
C165	1802	West Teignmouth. Sketch.	113A/192/1
C166	1823	West Teignmouth. Sketch.	113A/192/2
C167	1840	Thorverton. Plan.	113A/194/1
C168	*c.*1820	Tiverton. Sketch.	113A/196/1
C169	1804	Topsham. Plan.	113A/197/1
C170	1808	Topsham. Plan.	113A/197/2
C171	1813	Topsham. Plan.	113A/197/3
C172	1839	Torquay, Cockington. Plan.	113A/198/1
C173	1831	Torquay, Cockington & Paignton. Sketch.	113A/198/7
C174	1822	Torquay, St Marychurch. Plan.	113A/199/1
C175	1826	Torquay, St Marychurch. Sketch.	113A/199/2
C176	1807	Torquay, Tormoham & St Marychurch (also Haccombe & Coffinswell) Plan.	113A/200/1
C177	1807–8	Torquay, Tormoham. Plan. Surveyor: Charles Tozer	113A/200/2
C178	1810	Torquay, Tormoham. Plan.	113A/200/3
C179	1822	Great Torrington. Plan.	113A/202/1
C180	1824	Totnes. Plan.	113A/203/1
C181	1809	Uffculme. Sketch.	113A/205/1
C182	1816	Ugborough. Sketch.	113A/206/1
C183	1820	Ugborough. Sketch.	113A/206/2
C184	1830	Ugborough. Plan.	113A/206/3

	Date	Parish and Detail	DRO Reference
C185	1790	Uplyme. Plan.	113A/207/1
C186	1797	Upottery. Sketch.	113A/208/1
C187	1808–9	Upottery. Plans.	113A/208/2–3
C188	1816–7	Upottery. Plan.	113A/208/4
C189	1826	Upottery. Plans.	113A/208/5
C190	1821	Upton Pyne. Plan.	113A/209/1
C191	1827	Warkleigh. Plans.	113A/211/1
C192	1809	Whimple. Sketch.	113A/215/1
C193	1832	Widworthy. Plan.	113A/216/1
C194	1795–6	Woodbury. Plan. Surveyor: Thomas Gray	113A/217/2
C195	1815	Woodland. Sketch.	113A/218/1
C196	1813	Woodleigh & Charleton. Sketch.	113A/219/1
C197	1813	Woodleigh & Moreleigh. Sketches.	113A/219/2–3
C198	1789	East Worlington. Sketch.	113A/220/1
C199	1817	Yarcombe. Plans.	113A/221/1
C200	1785	Yealmpton. Plan.	113A/222/1

APPENDIX D

List of Repositories whose Maps are Represented in this Volume

Antony Muniments *see* Cornwall Record Office
Balliol College Oxford
Blundell's School Tiverton
Bristol Record Office [Bristol RO]
British Library [BL]
Corporation of London Record Office [CLRO]
Cornwall Record Office [CRO]. Includes Antony Muniments.
Devon Record Office [DRO]. All maps which are not specifically described as being in another record office are held in the Devon Record Office. These include documents with the prefixes DD, CR, TD, MFM (microfilm), Z, Pearse and DPQ. The collection of Exeter City Archives [ECA] is also lodged there as are the Diocesan Archives which include Glebe Terriers.
Dorset Record Office [Dors. RO]
Duchy of Cornwall Office [DCO]
Exeter Dean and Chapter Archives [Exeter D&C and Ex. D&C]
Gonville and Caius College Cambridge
House of Lords Record Office [HL]
Kent Archives Office [KAO]
King's College Cambridge
Knightshayes Estate Office, Tiverton
London Metropolitan Archives [LMA]

National Library of Scotland
North Devon Record Office [NDRO]
Northamptonshire Record Office [Northants RO]
Plymouth and West Devon Record Office [PWDRO]
Powderham Archive
Public Record Office [PRO]
Rolle Estate Office
Royal Geographical Society [RGS]
Royal Institution of Cornwall [RIC]
Somerset Record Office [SRO]
Tiverton Library
Tiverton Museum
Trinity House, London
Wiltshire Record Office [Wilts RO]

Maps in Private Hands

In some cases, maps described as being 'in private hands', may be seen by appointment. Searchers wishing to view items which are thus described should apply to the County Archivist, Devon Record Office, to enquire.

Index of Personal Names

to references in the Introduction, the Carto-bibliography,
the Supplement (prefix S), and Appendices A to C (prefixes A to C)

ACLAND (ACKLAND), family, 23, 32, 33, 41, 43, A249; Sir Thomas (Dyke), 24, 32, 2/3/1, 2/39/4, 2/39/6, 2/39/9, 3/15/2, 18/25/2; Thomas Palmer, 13/18/6

Addington, Henry, 1st Viscount Sidmouth, *see* Sidmouth

Addison, Thomas, 30

Aislabie (Aiselby, Aisleby), Gilbert (George), 5, 16, 21, 31, 2/6/3, 13/13/2, 13/13/3, 15/5/1, 15/5/3, 16/5/5, 19/3/1, 19/3/2, 19/3/3, 19/3/12, 19/3/20, 19/3/21, 19/3/22, 19/3/23, A1, A269

Alford, William, 2/35/6

Amerideth, Edward, 5/3/51; Griffin, 5/3/51

Anderson, William, A2, B76

Andrew(s), Henry, 1/6/6, 2/38/2, 4/5/8, 16/8/7, A3, A71, B47, B50, B54, B99, B103; John, 3/7/2, 3/31/2, A4; Richard, A5, A112, B39

Andrews & Otton, A3

Archer, Samuel, 8/2/6

Arnold, George, 8/8/3

Arthur, Rev. James, 1/14/4, 1/14/5

Arundell, Hon. James Everard, 19/12/1; Lady, 19/12/1

Atherley, Arthur, *see* Heavitree, Vicar of

Atwell, Lawrence, 5/3/49

Atwyll, John, 5/3/1

Austin, Benjamin, 5/4/15

Axworthy, John, 19/3/28

BABB, Thomas, 8/2/5, 8/2/9

Babbage, B., 9/6/2

Bailey, Charles, A6, B44, B49

Ballment, Hugh, 15, 3/4/1, 3/4/2, 3/10/2, 13/18/8, A7, B118; Robert, 15, 21, 23, 32, 1/6/4, 2/22/12, 2/24/1, 3/4/1, 3/4/2, 3/10/2, 3/15/4, 3/33/3, 6/4/1, 6/4/4, 6/5/4, 8/7/3, 8/13/4, 8/19/2, 12/11/2, 13/5/1, 13/18/6, 18/33/1, 18/33/2, A7, A8, A106, A154; Tabitha (nee Squire), A7, A8

Baring-Gould, Edward, 12/4/1, A9

Baring, Sir Thomas, 5/4/12

Barnes, Ralph, 16, 3/14/12, 16/1/3, 19/16/29, 19/16/30; Rev. Archdeacon, 19/16/24

Bartholomew, Rev. J., 13/22/1

Bartlett, Humphry, 2/37/3; John, 8/15/3; Rev. Nicholas Adams, 5/2/4, 5/2/6

Basset (Bassett), Arthur, 2/10/1; (Sir) Francis, 23, 2/8/2

Bastard, E.P., 2/38/7; Edmund P., 2/47/1; J.P., 1/6/5

Bath, Lord, (mid-16th cent.), 4/3/3

Batty, Dr, 19/3/12

Bear, William, 18, 1/7/1, 1/14/4, 1/14/5, 2/2/4, 2/8/2, 2/8/3, 2/14/7, 8/8/3, 8/13/2, 12/6/1, 13/19/2, A10

Beard, R., 3/5/1, A11

Beardmore, Nathaniel, A204

Bearne, E.S., 9/3/8, A12; Mr, 8/15/1

Beavis, Mr, 21/16/4; *see also* Bevys

Bedford, Duchess of, 16/4/5 (1771)

Bedford, John, 4th Duke of, 13, 16, 21, 5/3/18, 13/13/3, 16/8/2, 18/24/1, 18/24/2, 19/3/1, 19/3/2, 19/3/3, 19/3/5, 19/3/12, 19/3/14, 19/3/15, 19/3/16, 19/3/17, 19/3/18, 19/3/19, 19/3/20, 19/3/22, 19/3/23, A1, A248, A269

Bedford, Duke of, (late 18th cent.), 19/3/28

Bedford, Duke of, (19th cent.), 21/8/8

Bedford, Dukes of and Earls of (Russell family), 3, 15, 30, 31, 37

Benese, Richard, 4

Bentall, Thornton, 2/45/3; William Searle, 2/45/3

Bentley, George, A13, B5

Bermingham, James, 3, 11/17/3, A14

Bernard, James, 3/29/3

Berry, Miles, A15, A169; Samuel, 2/45/3; Thomas, 2/8/1, 2/23/1, 9/4/1, 12/2/1, A16

Bevys, Richard, 38

Bickford, Arscott, 1/13/2, 2/24/1, 8/19/4; Mr, 1/6/3, 3/14/10

Bidcook, John, A43

Bidlake, family, 2/35/4; Henry, 5, 2/35/1; John, 4/2/4; Phillippa, 2/35/4
Biggliston, Mr, 5/3/12
Billingsley, Sir Henry, 4
Bindon, John, 3/35/10, A17
Bion, Mr, 14/3/1
Blackamore, I. (J.) James, 7, 17, 20/5/1, A18, A19; Matthew, 7, 8, 13, 17, 1/16/2, 1/16/3, 1/16/4, 1/16/5, 1/16/6, 2/39/5, 2/44/1, 18/9/1, 19/16/5, 19/16/6, 19/16/7, 19/16/8, 20/5/1, 20/6/1, A18, A19
Blackburne, Bethia, A35
Blake & Sons, 3/35/11; J., 8/7/7, 8/7/8, A20
Blanchard, James, 19/3/32
Blessington, Mr, 13/18/1
Bluett, B. Nutcombe, 8/17/1; Mr, 5/3/9; Peter, 8/17/2
Blundel(l), Peter, 19/16/7; —, 13/18/1
Bodley, Mr, 5/3/27
Boen, Mr, 13/18/1
Bolt, John, 3/9/1
Bolton, Thomas, A21, B3, B5
Bond, Charles, 4/12/1; Juliana, A9; Sophia Charlotte, A9; William, 2/50/1, 3/27/8, 4/1/3, 4/12/1, 19/12/1, A22, A87, A192, B6, B16
Bonvile, —, 5/3/51
Border, Christopher, 8/15/1
Bourne, William, 5
Bowhay, W., A29
Bowman, Robert, 7/1/6, A23
Bowring, John, 6, 7, 13, 32, 33, 2/2/1, 2/14/3, 3/15/2, 2/46/1, A24; Sir John, A24
Boyce, Edward, 19/16/21; G.A., 6/2/4, A25, B96, B117
Boycot, *Gulielmus* (William), 4, 2/22/1, A26
Bradley, Arthur, 33; Thomas, 16, 2/3/1,

3/36/3, 8/8/4, 9/1/2, 18/1/3, A27, A154
Braund, George, A28; J.W., 3/24/5, A28
Bray, Lord, (mid-16th cent.), 4/3/3
Bredall, William, 19/3/21
Bremridge, John, 2/2/6, A29
Brewer, Richard, 8/15/3
Bridham, Jasper, 2/10/1
Bright, William, 12/13/1, A30
Brimacombe, J., 8/14/1, A31
Brinsden (Brinsdon), J., 11/4/20, 16/12/12, A32
Bristow, Thomas, 21, 11/3/2, A33
Brown(e), 'Capability', 32; Edward, 20/1/7; J.L., 2/40/1; Robert, 1/10/1
Browning, Mr, 5/3/17
Browse, Henry, 21/10/3
Brune, Charles Prideaux, 19, 23, 24, 25
Brut(t)on, Charles, 5/3/25, 5/3/52, 9/3/8
Buck, Lewis William, 2/14/9
Buckberte, William, 31, 1/17/1, A34, A86
Budd, John, 2/2/9
Buller, family, 33; James, 3/33/4, 5/8/6; James Wentworth, 3/33/11, 3/33/13, 3/33/15, 3/33/17; Mrs, 3/33/7
Bulteel, Mr, 19/3/14
Burgess, Miss, 1/16/6; William, 2/49/1, 2/49/2
Burnett, A.F., 19/17/5
Burrington, Rev. Gilbert, 3/14/3, 3/14/12, A207
Burrough, Rev. John, 6/3/1
Burton, John, 10/1/1
Butter, Mr, 21/16/4

CALL, John, 22, 23, A35; Mary, A35; Richard, A35; Thomas, 14, 16, 20, 21, 22, 23, 3/1/1, 12/5/2, 13/18/4, 13/19/1, 21/4/1, 21/12/1, 21/12/2, 21/13/1, A35, A131
Callow, William, junior, 14/4/3
Calmady, Charles Holmes (Everitt),

2/35/6; Elizabeth Mary, A115; family, 32; James, 21/3/2; Pollexfen, 2/35/6; —, 19/3/12
Campion, R.C., 3/35/16
Cann, Phillip, 19/6/3
Carew, family, 32, 8/1/3, A86; Sir John, 18/32/1, 18/32/2; Sir Thomas, 19/16/9, 19/16/13, 19/16/16
Carlyon, Col. Edward, 3/17/1
Carpenter, Mr, 19/3/33, 19/3/36
Carslake, J., A36, C152
Carter, Charles, 2/2/9
Cartwright, family, 21; H., A37, B67; Robert, 15, 1/4/16, 1/4/17, 11/2/4, A38, B7; William, senior, 15, 30, 16/12/8, A38, A39, A40; William, junior, 15, 4/5/6, A40
Cary, George, 1/13/1, 3/24/1; John, A226; Mr, 3/23/1, 3/23/5
Case, John, 2/39/4, 19/20/3, A41
Caunter, Roger, 1/8/1; William, 1/8/1
Cave, Daniel, 20/1/5
Chalk, Rev. E.S., 11/3/2
Champernowne, Henry, 4/2/4; Mr, 4/2/1
Channon, James, 7/5/1, A42, A146
Chapple, Charles, A43, B64; William, 16, 21, 29, 30, 1/4/1, 1/4/2, 1/4/4, 1/4/10, 5/11/1, 8/21/1, 8/21/2, 8/21/3, 11/4/2, 19/17/1, A44
Charley, John, 2/8/3
Charlton, F., 18/3/1, A45; John, A45
Chichester, Sir Arthur, 2/1/1; Charles, 8/2/4, 18/33/1; J.P.B., 2/2/9; Mrs, 2/8/1
Cholwich, John B., 21/16/2
Chop(e), Thomas, 8/7/9, 8/7/11
Clack, Thomas, 20, 13/14/5, A46; Rev. Thomas, 20, A46
Clamp, R., 2/7/3
Clampit, Mr, 3/13/1
Clapp, Gilbert, 8/15/3; William, 17/3/1
Claringbull, William, 20, 21/8/11, A47

also Davie and Davy

Davie, Catherine, 2/39/6; Sir Humphry, 3/10/2; Sir H.R.F., 18/5/4; Sir John, 2/39/6, 3/1/1, 3/33/3, 8/19/2, 12/11/2, 13/5/1, 18/5/6, 18/5/7, 18/27/1, 18/27/2; Joseph, 2/8/2; William, 2/39/6; *see also* Davy

Davis, Richard, 2/35/6, A75

Davy, Joseph, 20/1/7; Thomas, 20/1/7; —, 21/16/4; *see also* Davie

Daw, John, 2/35/6

Dawson, William, A76, A90, B91, B93, B108, B110

Day, William, 1/16/7, 18/18/2, 18/22/3, A77

Dean, Charles, 2/7/1, 2/7/2, 8/26/1, 19/16/25, A78, C54; James, 2/7/1, A79

Dee, John, 4

Dennys, Nicholas, 19/16/10

Devon, Earls of, *see* Courtenay

Dickinson, Benjamin, 19/16/7

Digby, Hon. Edward, 20/1/1

Digges, Leonard, 4; Thomas, 4

Diggon, Margaret, 1/8/1

Ditrey, —, 5/2/7

Doe, George, A80; John, A80, C141

Dobson, Richard, 19/3/21

Doidge, Maurice, 12/1/6; Thomas, 19/3/1, A81; William, 6, 13, 31, 43, 1/10/2, 2/17/2, 3/14/1, 16/8/1, 18/30/1, 18/31/1, 19/3/1, A82, S3, S5

Dolling, Mrs, 3/15/1

Donn(e), Benjamin, 1, 17, 20, 43, A83; George, 17; Samuel, 3/5/1, 3/26/2, 3/35/3, 8/12/1, A11, A83; —, 21/7/3; *see also* Dunn, Samuel

Doswell, Richard, A84, B84, B89

Dowling, George, 15/7/6, A85

Downe, Henry, 14/4/2

Downman, Mr, 1/4/14

Drake, Barnard, 31, 1/17/1, A34, A86; Sir

Francis, 21/16/1; Sir Francis Henry, 21/16/2; Henry, 6//5/4; —, 3/33/9, A86

Drayton, John, 3/5/2, A87

Drewe, Robert, 3/21/3; —, 1/16/8

Drury, Rev. J., 4/5/11

Duck, —, 2/31/1

Duncombe, Mr, 18/12/1

Dunn, Samuel, 17

Dunstanville, Lord de, 3/33/7

Dunstone, James, 3/18/1, A88

Duntze, Sir John, 15/7/2

Dyer, Rev. Nicholas, 2/49/1, 2/49/2

Dyke, Elizabeth, 32

Dymond, Robert, 2/10/2, 5/3/24, 5/3/54, 6/3/3, 11/4/22, 16/12/11, A76, A89, A90, A166

Dymond & Dawson, A2, A89, A90, B63, B76, B87

E., M., 3/35/2, A91

Eales, Richard, 1/8/3, 4/5/7, 4/5/11; —, 4/5/10

East, E.H., 2/30/3

Eastabrooke, John, 15/5/9

Eastcott, Richard, 2/43/1; *see also* Exeter, St Edmunds, Rector of

Easton, John, 2/51/4, 3/35/9, A92, B17, B23; Josiah, A93, B107; R.J., A92

Eastly, Yarde, 3/24/5

Edgcumbe, Lord, 4/1/1, 13/1/1; Prothesia, A1

Edwards, John, 9/3/13; Mrs, 18/23/6; T., 22/3/1

Egremont, Charles, Earl of, 3/35/2

Elford, Jonathan, 19/2/9

Elizabeth I, Queen of England, 3/33/1

Ellicombe, Mr, 4/11/3

Elliott, Elizabeth, 1/8/1; John, A185; Samuel, 2/7/2, 2/38/8, 4/2/4, 8/15/4, 9/5/3, A94, B60; W., 1/15/1, A95; *see also* Rendle & Elliott

Ellis, John, 21/16/4

Elwes family, 4/4/4

Elwill, Sir John, 7/5/1

Evans, Nicholas, 5/3/10; —, 19/16/17

Ewings, Thomas, 19/16/9

Exeter, Bishop of, [Stephen Weston], 13/8/2

Exeter, St Edmunds, Rector of [Richard Eastcott], 3/14/10

Eyde, John, 2/50/1

Eyere, Baron, [James Eyre, Baron of the Exchequer], 8/17/1

Eyle, Samuel, 21/16/2

FADEN, William, A78

Falvey, Luke, 40

Farrant, Samuel, 3/35/10

Farwell, George, 4/2/4

Fewell, Mr, 2/6/1, A96

Filliter, Mr, 25

Finnimore, Richard King, 8/2/7, A97

Fitzherbert, John, 4

Flay, Elizabeth, 5/3/51; Thomas, 5/3/51

Flood, Christopher, 4/12/1; —, 2/22/7

Floyd, Mrs, 17

Folkes, Sir Martin, 18/23/1

Folkingham, William, 5, 12

Follett, John, 18/26/2

Force, Mr, 21/16/4

Ford(e), Charles, 1/18/2; Thomas, 1/8/1

Fortescue, Hugh, 1st Earl Fortescue, 2/33/3, 2/46/3, 3/15/3, 3/15/4, 3/15/7, 3/18/1, 3/18/6, 3/18/8, 6/4/4, 7/1/6, 13/18/7; Hugh Fortescue, 14th Baron Cinton, *see* Clinton

Fortescue, Matthew, 2nd Baron Fortescue, 32, 13/18/4

Fortescue, Earl, 3, A117; family, 3, 15, 21, 22, 32, A8; Gertrude, A86; John (Inglett), 4/5/3, 4/5/4, 4/5/9

Fortibus, Isabella de, 38, 5/3/6

Parkyns, George J., 12/10/1, A181

Parminter, G., 2/7/3, A182

Parr, W., 15/5/5, A183

Parrot, —, 21/16/4

Parsons, Robert, 3/16/3

Pascoe, John, 16, 2/27/1, 2/31/3, 2/31/4, 3/1/5, 3/33/11, 4/5/5, 11/2/8, 11/2/9, 11/2/10, 11/2/11, A154, A173, A184, B9, B13, B24, B32, B37, B40, B48, B57, B65, B72, B73; John (clerk), 3/20/1

Pass(e)more, George, 39; R., 1/14/2, 1/14/3, 2/31/5, 2/31/6, 8/9/5, A185

Paterson, I [J]., 1/5/2, A186

Peacham, Henry, 12

Peake, David, 2/8/1

Pearse, William, 3/27/6, 7/5/4, A187; —, 1/16/8

Peckham, T., junior, 4/4/3, A188

Penneck, Mr, 5/8/3

Penny, Mr, 42

Per[er], J., 12/1/6, A189

Periam, Mr, 5/4/1

Perratt, John, A93

Perry, Mr, 21/16/4

Petre, Thomas, 6th Baron Petre, 18/21/1; Robert James, 8th Baron Petre, 1/17/3, 3/27/2; Robert Edward, 9th Baron Petre, 1/17/4, 2/28/2, 18/21/2; Lord, 1/8/2; Thomas, Lord, 31; Sir William, 18/21/1

Phillips, Joseph, 21/2/1, A190

Philp, J., 2/22/14, 2/22/15, 2/22/16, A191

Pickering, [T], A22, A192, B16

Pierce (Pierse), Mark, 4, 2/25/1, A193

Pilkinton (Pilkington, Wilkinton), William, 7, 14, 32, 3/14/10, 19/16/13, 21/16/3, 21/16/4, A194

Pinson, Andrew, 18/29/1

Pitfield, William, 1/4/8

Pitman, James, 4/11/3

Pitts, James, 3/15/3, 4/10/2, 18/33/2, A8, A195

Plea, John, 5/3/51

Pococke, Dr, 3/33/5

Pode, John Spurrell, 21/3/2

Pole, Rev. Edward, 19/10/1; Sir John William, 3/27/4; Sir William, 3/27/4; Sir William Templer, 3/27/8

Pollard, Elizabeth, A44; Mary, A269

Poltimore, Lord, (1832), 16/9/1

Polwhele, Richard, 1/16/6

Ponsford, Mr, 14/3/1; William, 5/4/1

Poole, I[J]., 19/17/7, A196

Popham, Francis, 13, 3/19/1

Poulett, John, 4th Earl Poulett, 18/3/1

Powning, Elizabeth, A54; Marianne, A62

Praed, Humphrey Mackworth, 2/39/6; William Mackworth, 2/39/6, 8/15/3, 19/9/5; William Mackworth, junior, 8/15/3

Preston, Sally, 23

Prickett, John, 8/7/4, 8/7/5, 8/7/6, A197

Pride, Thomas, 18/24/1, 18/24/2, A198

Prideaux, Sir John, 6/2/4

Prince, James, 14/3/1

Prowse, Richard, 19/9/1, A199; William, 40

Pryde, Thomas, 2/38/9, A200

Puddicombe, Richard, 21, 2/22/2, 2/22/3, A201

Putt, Reymundo, 21/16/3, 21/16/4; Thomas, 3/35/2, 7/5/1, 7/5/4

RADCLIFFE (Ratcliffe), family, 32; Walter, 19/2/2, 19/2/3, 19/2/9, 19/2/13

Raleigh, —, A86

Rashleigh, Philip, 18

Rathborn(e), Aaron, 7, 8, 40, 41

Rawling, Mr, 11/2/4

Recorde, Richard, 4

Reed, E., 18/12/1, 19/15/1, A175, A202; William, 2/31/2, A203

Rendel (Rendell, Rendle), family, 21; James, 24, 3/9/1, 5/11/7, A205; James

Meadows, A111, A204, A205, B36, B38, B43, B74, B78, B81, B111

Rendle & Elliott, 4/10/2, A94, A206

Rennel(l), James, 20, 22, 23, 3/14/3, A35, A207

Rennie, family, 21; G., A100; George, A208, A209, B77; J., A100; John, A210, B5, B77; John (later Sir John), A208, A209, B77

Rennie & Whidby, Messrs., A210

Rew, Mr, 21/16/4

Rice, James, 18/5/1, A211; John, A211

Richards, Edward, 15/7/6; John, 6, 7, 13, 14, 16, 18, 21, 30, 31, 37, 40, 41, 1/4/11, 2/17/1, 2/38/1, 3/33/2, 4/13/3, 5/2/1, 5/3/19, 5/3/28, 5/3/29, 5/3/30, 5/3/31, 5/3/32, 5/3/33, 5/3/34, 5/3/35, 5/3/36, 5/3/37, 5/3/38, 5/3/39, 5/3/40, 5/3/41, 5/3/42, 5/3/43, 5/3/44, 5/3/45, 5/3/46, 5/3/47, 5/3/48, 5/3/49, 5/3/50, 5/3/51, 5/4/1, 5/4/2, 5/4/3, 5/4/4, 5/4/5, 11/4/6, 12/5/2, 18/17/2, A44, A212; Thomas, 2/45/3, 3/31/1, 17/2/2, A213

Richardson, Francis, 2/35/6; T., 15/5/1, 18/24/2, A214

Riche, Thomas, 1/8/1

Ridler, Robert, 5/8/2

Ridout, J., 21/8/3

Rigg, William, 5/3/20

Risdon, George Smale, 2/19/5; Joseph, 1/11/2, A215

Roath, Jerom, *see* Roch, Jerom

Robbins, John, senior, 1/8/1; John, junior, 1/8/1

Roberts, Charles, 19/20/3; Edmund, 20/7/1; E.R., 2/2/4, 19/20/6, 19/20/7, 19/20/8, 19/20/9, 19/20/10, 19/20/11, A216; Messrs, 19/20/4

Robinson, Nicholas, 40

Roch (Roath), Jerom, 40, 5/8/1, A217; Monnier, 2/2/2

Bibliography of Printed Works Cited in the Text

Annual Register 1762.

The Antiquary II.

Archaeologia 85.

Army List 1787.

Ashton, R., *The Crown and the Money Market 1603–1640* (Oxford: Clarendon Press, 1960).

Baker, A.H.R., 'Field Patterns in Seventeenth-Century Kent', *Geography* 50 (1965), 18–30.

Banfield, Jack, and Austin, Harry, *Where Dorset meets Devon. Hawkchurch* (Hawkchurch: Hawkchurch History Society, 1996).

Baring-Gould, S., *Early Reminiscences* (London: John Lane & The Bodley Head, 1923).

Beer, E.J., *Buckfastleigh Remembered* (Plymouth: Privately published, 1981).

Bendall, A. Sarah, *Maps, Land and Society* (Cambridge: Cambridge University Press, 1992).

Bendall, A. Sarah, *Dictionary of Land Surveyors and Local Map-makers of Great Britain and Ireland 1530–1850* 2 vols (London: The British Library, 1997).

Benese, Richard, *This boke sheweth the Manner of measurynge of all maner of lande…* (Southwarke: James Nicolson, 1537).

Billings Directory.

Billingsley, Sir Henry, *The Elements of Geometrie of…Euclide…* (London: John Daye, 1570).

Boase, George Clement, *Collectanea Cornubiensis* (Truro: Netherton & Worth, 1890).

Boase, George Clement, and William Prideaux Courtney, *Bibliotheca Cornubiensis* 3 vols (London: Longman Green, 1882).

Bourne, William, *A booke called the Treasure for Traveilers* (London: Thomas Woodcooke, 1578).

Buckingham, W., *A Turnpike Key* (Exeter: James Townsend, 1885).

Camden, William, *Britannia* (London, 1610).

Chalk, E.S., *Kentisbeare* (Devonshire Association, 1934).

Cherry, Bridget, and Nikolaus Pevsner, *The Buildings of England Devon* (London: Penguin Books, 1989 and 2nd edition reprint, 1991).

Clark, E.A.G., *The Ports of the Exe Estuary* (Torquay: University of Exeter and Devonshire Press, 1960).

Cocks, J.V. Somers, *Devon Topographical Prints* (Exeter, 1977).

Cocks, J.V. Somers, 'Dartmoor Devonshire' in *Local Maps and Plans from Medieval England* R.A. Skelton and P.D.A. Harvey, eds, (Oxford: Clarendon Press, 1986), 293–302.

Constable, K.M., 'The Early Printed Plans of Exeter 1587–1724', *TDA* 65 (1932), 455–73.

Cook, Andrew, 'James Rennell's Manuscript Maps in the RGS Collection', *Geographical Journal* 144 (1) (March, 1978), 157–9.

Couldridge, Christopher, John Coldridge of Exeter, Land Surveyor, unpublished PhD thesis (Oxford, Brookes University, 2001).

Curtis, Muriel, *Some Disputes between the City and the Cathedral Authorities of Exeter* (Manchester: Manchester University Press, 1932).

Devon Archaeological Society Transactions.

Devon and Cornwall Notes and Queries.

Devon County Surveyor 1808–1841.

Dictionary of National Biography.

Dickinson, M.G., ed., *A Living from the Sea* (Tiverton: Devon Books, 1985).

Dredge, John Ingle, and R. Pearse Chope, transcribers and eds, *The Register of Baptisms, Marriages & Burials of the Parish of Hartland, Devon, 1558–1837* (Exeter: DCRS, 1930–34).

Digges, Leonard, *A boke named Tectonicon...* (1556).

Dymond, Robert, 'Devon Fields and Hedges', *Journal of the Bath and West of England Society* (1856), 132–48.

Erskine, Audrey, 'The Western Part of the Close in the Sixteenth Century', *Friends of Exeter Cathedral Forty-seventh Report: 31 March 1977.*

Erskine, Audrey, Brian Harley and William Ravenhill, 'A Map of "the way to Deartmoore forest the Comen of Devonshire" made circa 1609', *DCNQ* 33 (1976), 229–36.

Exeter Flying Post.

Exeter and Plymouth Gazette 1832.

Exeter Pocket Journal.

Fitzherbert, John, *...the Boke of Surveying and improuvements* (London, 1523).

Fleming, Laurence and Alan Gore, *The English Garden* (London: Michael Joseph, 1979).

Folkingham, William, *Feudigraphia* (London, 1610).

Fortescue, Hugh, 4th Earl, *A Chronicle of Castle Hill* (Privately printed, 1929).

Fox, Harold, 'Medieval Towns', in *Historical Atlas of South West England* Roger Kain and William Ravenhill, eds, (Exeter: University of Exeter Press, 1999), 400–7.

Fox, H.S.A., 'An Exeter Tenter-framed map, 1420' in *Local Maps and Plans from Medieval England* R.A. Skelton and P.D.A. Harvey, eds, (Oxford: Clarendon Press, 1986), 163–9.

Fox, H.S.A., 'A Map of 1499 dispute in Mary Arches' in *Local Maps and Plans from Medieval England* R.A. Skelton and P.D.A. Harvey eds, (Oxford: Clarendon Press, 1986), 329–36.

Fox, Sarah E., *Edwin Octavius Tregelles Civil Engineer and Minister of the Gospel* (1892).

Foster, Joseph, ed., *Alumni Oxoniensis* 8 vols (Oxford: Parker, 1888–92).

George, Brian, *James Green: Canal Builder and County surveyor (1791–1849)* (Tiverton: Devon Books, 1997).

Gentleman's Magazine.

Gray's Inn Admissions.

Gray, Todd, *The Garden History of Devon* (Exeter: University of Exeter Press, 1995).

Gray, Todd, ed., *Devon Household Accounts, 1629–59* DCRS New Series 39 (Exeter, 1996).

Gray, Todd, *Devon Country Houses and Gardens Engraved* (Exeter: The Mint Press, 2001)

Gray, Todd, and Margery M. Rowe, eds, *Travels in Georgian Devon* 4 vols (Tiverton: Devon Books, 1997–2000).

Goss, E.J., *Biographical History of Gonville and Caius College* 4 (Cambridge, 1912).

Green, John, *The Construction of Maps and Globes* (London, 1717).

Hamil, John, and R.A. Gilbert, *World Freemasonry* (London: Aquarius Press, 1991).

Hans, Nicholas, *New Trends in Education in the Eighteenth Century* (London: Routledge, Kegan & Paul, 1951).

Harding, William, *The History of Tiverton in the County of Devon* 2 vols (Tiverton and London: F. Boyce, 1845).

Harley J.B., and Yolande O'Donoghue, eds, *The Old Series Ordnance Survey Maps of England and Wales* 2 Devon, Cornwall and West Somerset (Lympne Castle, Kent: Harry Margary, 1977).

Harley, J.B., and E.A. Stuart, 'George Withiell – a West Country Surveyor of the late seventeenth century' *DCNQ*, 25 Part II (Autumn, 1982), 45–8 and Part III (Spring, 1983), 95–115.

Harley, R.D., *Artists' Pigments 1600–1835* (London: Butterworth, 1970).

Harris, J, Delpratt, The Royal Devon and Exeter Hospital (Exeter: Eland Brothers, 1922).

Harvey, P.D.A., *Maps in Tudor England* (London: The Public Record Office and The British Library; Chicago: University of Chicago Press, 1993).

Haslam, Graham, 'Patronising the Plotters: the Advent of Systematic Estate Mapping' in *Maps and History in South-West England* Katherine Barker and Roger J.P. Kain, eds, (Exeter: University of Exeter Press, 1991), 55–73.

Headlam, Cecil, ed., *Calendar of State Papers Colonial America and West Indies 1714/15* 2 (London: PRO, 1929).

Heriz-Smith, Shirley, 'The Veitch Nurseries of Killerton and Exeter *c.*1780 to 1863', Part 1 *Garden History* 16 (Spring, 1988), 41–57.

Holwell, John, *A Sure Guide to the Practical Surveyor* (London, 1678).

Hoskins, W.G., The Ownership and Occupation of Land in Devonshre 1650–1800, unpublished PhD thesis (University of London, 1938).

Hoskins, W.G., *Devon* (London: Collins, 1954).

Hoskins, W.G., *Two Thousand years in Exeter* (Exeter: James Townsend, 1960).

James, John, *The Theory and Practice of Gardening* (London, 1712).

Journal of the Commissioners for Trade and Plantations from February 1708–9 to March 1714–15 2 (London: PRO 1925).

Kain, Roger J.P., and Richard Oliver, *The Tithe Maps of England and Wales* (Cambridge: Cambridge University Press, 1995).

Kain, Roger J.P., John Chapman and Richard Oliver, *The Enclosure Maps of England and Wales* (Cambridge: Cambridge University Press, forthcoming).

Kain, Roger, and William Ravenhill, eds, *Historical Atlas of South-West England* (Exeter: University of Exeter Press, 1999).

Kellys Directory.

Kew, John, 'The Disposal of Crown Lands and the Devon Land Market 1536–1568', *Agricultural History Review* 18 (1970), 93–105.

Kiely, Edmond R., *Surveying Instruments Their History* (Ohio: Carben Surveying Reprints, 1979)'.

Lamplugh, Lois, *Barnstaple: Town on the Taw* (Chichester: Phillimore, 1983).

Leybourn, William, *The Compleat Surveyor...* (London, 1653).

Love, John, *Geodaesia* (London, 1688).

MacDermott, Edward, T.M, *The History of the Forest of Exmoor* David and Charles reprint (Newton Abbot, 1973).

Markham, Clements R., *Major James Rennell and the Rise of Modern English Geography* (London: Cassell, 1895).

Thomas Michelmore, Junior, 'On the Value of the Farm Labourer' *Journal of the Bath and West of England Society* (London, 1855), 213–16.

Norden, John, *Surveyors Dialogue* (London: H. Astley, 1607).

Oliver, Bruce W., 'The Long Bridge of Barnstaple', *TDA* 70 (1938), facing 194.

Oliver, George, *Ecclesiastical Antiquities of Devon* 3 vols (Exeter: E. W.C. Featherstone, 1839).

Parkyns, G., *Monastic and Baronial Remains* 2 vols (London, 1816).

Peacham, Henry, *The Art of Drawing with the Pen and Limning with Water Colours* (London, 1606).

Phillimore, R.H., *Historical Records of the Survey of India* 1 (Dehra Dun, 1945).

Pamment, John and Bill Slater, 'An Eighteenth-century lead and silver mine near Newton St Cyres', *DAS* 48 (1988), 149–53.

Pigot's Directory.

Porter, J.H., 'The development of Rural Society' in *The Agrarian History of England and Wales, 1750–1850* G.E. Mingay, ed., (Cambridge, 1989), 836–63.

Prince, John, *The Worthies of Devon* (Samuel Farley: Exeter, 1701).

Pugsley, Steven, 'The Garden and Park in Devon' in *Devon Gardens: an Historical Survey* (Stroud: Alan Sutton, 1996), 1–20.

Pye, Andrew, 'Bideford Town Quay', *DAS* 50 (1992), 117–24.

Ravenhill, Mary R., 'Sir William Courten and Mark Pierce's Map of Cullompton 1633' in *Devon Documents*, Todd Gray, ed., *DCNQ* Special Issue (1996), xix–xxiii.

Ravenhill, Mary R., and Margery M Rowe, eds, *Early Devon Maps* (Exeter: Friends of Devon Archives, 2000).

Ravenhill, W.L.D., *Benjamin Donn A Map of the County of Devon, 1765* Facsimile and Introduction DCRS New Series 9, (Exeter: DCRS and University of Exeter, 1965).

Ravenhill, William, and Margery Rowe, 'A Decorated Screen Map of Exeter based on John Hooker's Map of 1587' in *Tudor and Stuart Devon* Todd Gray, Margery Rowe and Audrey Erskine, eds, (Exeter: University of Exeter Press, 1992), 1–13.

Ravenhill, William, *Christopher Saxton's 16th Century Maps* (Shrewsbury: Chatsworth Library and Airlife Publishing, 1992).

Ravenhill, William, 'Maps for the Landlord' in Peter Barber and Christopher Board eds, *Tales from the Map Room* (London: BBC Books, 1993), 96–7.

Ravenhill, W.L.D., 'Joel Gascoyne A Pioneer of Large-Scale County Mapping', *Imago Mundi* 26 (1972), 59–69.

Ravenhill, W.L.D. Ravenhill and O.J. Padel, *A Map of the County of Cornwall Newly Surveyed By Joel Gascoyne* Reprinted in Facsimile with an Introduction DCRS New Series 34, (1991).

Recorde, Robert, *The Grounde of Artes* (London: R. Wolfe, 1542).

Richards, John, *The Gentleman's Steward* (London: J. Senex & W. Innys, 1730), *Annuities on Lives* (London, 1739), *Cask Gauging Perfected* (1740).

Rowe, Margery M., and Andrew M Jackson, eds, *Exeter Freemen* DCRS (Exeter, 1973).

Russell, Percy, *Dartmouth* (London: B.T. Batsford, 1950).

Sherborne Mercury.

Singer, Charles, and others, *A History of Technology* III (Clarendon Press: Oxford, 1957).

Stuart, Elisabeth, *Lost Landscapes of Plymouth. Maps, Charts and Plans to 1800* (Stroud: Alan Sutton; Tring: Map Collector Publications, 1991).

Straton, Charles R., *Survey of the Lands of William First Earl of Pembroke* 2 (Oxford: Roxburghe Club, 1909).

Tapley-Soper', H., 'The Globe in Exeter', *DCNQ* 15 (1928–9), 240.

Taylor, E.G.R., *The Mathematical Practitioners of Hanoverian England 1714–1840* (Cambridge: Cambridge University Press, 1966).

Ternstrom, Myrtle, *Lundy Field Society Annual Report* No.52, 2001 (2002).

Thomas, A.H., notes in Royal Contract Estates/Conduit Meade Estate Papers 2.29 (1944).

Thompson, F.M.L., 'Landowners and the Rural Community', in *The Victorian Countryside* G.E. Mingay, ed., (London: Routledge, Kegan & Paul, 1981).

Tingey, J.C., Exeter Castle MSS.

Transactions of the Torquay Natural History Society 4.

Turner, G.L'E., 'Some Notes on the Development of Surveying and the Instruments used', *Annals of Science* 48 (1991), 313–17.

Universal British Directory.

Venn, John and J.A. Venn, eds, *Alumni Cantabrigiensis* Parts 1 and 2, 10 vols (Cambridge: Cambridge University Press, 1922–54).

Venn, T.W., Crediton, unpublished MS, no date.

Watkin, Hugh R., *Dartmouth* 1 (Devonshire Association, 1935).

Wood, E.C., and H. Tapley-Soper, transcribers & eds, *The Register of Marriages, Baptisms & Burials of the Parish of Widecombe=in=the=Moor, Devon* (Exeter: DCRS, 1938).

Worth, R.N. *Calendar of the Plymouth Municpal Records* (Plymouth, 1893).

Wright, D., 'William Boycott, Cartographer, in Devon', *Devon Historian* 12 (April, 1976), 10–13.

Youings, J., 'Landlords in England and Wales: the Church' in J. Thirsk, *The Agrarian History of England and Wales 1500–1640* 4 (Cambridge: Cambridge University Press, 1967), 306–56.

THE DEVON AND CORNWALL RECORD SOCIETY

7 The Close, Exeter EX1 1EZ
(founded 1904)

President:
General Sir Richard Trant KCB, DL

Officers (2002–3)

Chairman:
Professor I. A. Roots MA, FSA, FRHistS

Hon. Secretary:
J. D. Brunton LLB, BA

Hon. Treasurer:
J. H. Baldwin

Hon. Editor:
Prof. A. J. Thorpe BA, PhD, FRHistS

The Devon and Cornwall Record Society promotes the study of history in the South West of England through publishing and transcribing original records. In return for the annual subscription members receive the volumes as published (normally annually) and the use of the Society's library, housed in the Westcountry Studies Library, Exeter. The library includes transcripts of parish registers relating to Devon and Cornwall as well as useful genealogical works.

Applications to join the Society or to purchase volumes should be sent to the Administrator, Devon and Cornwall Record Society, c/o The Devon and Exeter Institution, 7 The Close, Exeter EX1 1EZ.

DEVON & CORNWALL RECORD SOCIETY PUBLICATIONS
ISSN/ISBN 0 901853

Obtainable from the Administrator, Devon and Cornwall Record Society, 7 The Close, Exeter EX1 1EZ

§ No longer available.   * Restricted availability: please enquire

New Series

1 §   *Devon Monastic Lands: Calendar of Particulars for Grants, 1536–1558*, ed. Joyce Youings, 1955   **04 6**

2   *Exeter in the Seventeenth Century: Tax and Rate Assessments, 1602–1699*, ed. W. G. Hoskins, 1957   **05 4**

3 §   *The Diocese of Exeter in 1821: Bishop Carey's Replies to Queries before Visitation*, vol. I, Cornwall, ed. Michael Cook, 1958   **06 2**

4 *   *The Diocese of Exeter in 1821: Bishop Carey's Replies to Queries before Visitation*, vol. II, Devon, ed. Michael Cook, 1960   **07 0**

5 §   *The Cartulary of St Michael's Mount*, ed. P. L. Hull, 1962   **08 9**

6   *The Exeter Assembly: The Minutes of the Assemblies of the United Brethren of Devon and Cornwall, 1691–1717*, as Transcribed by the Reverend Isaac Gilling, ed. Allan Brockett, 1963   **09 7**

7*,10*, 13*, 16*, 18* *The Register of Edmund Lacy, Bishop of Exeter, 1420–1455*. Five volumes, ed. G. R. Dunstan, 1963–1972   **10 0   12 7   15 1   02 X   17 8**

8 §   *The Cartulary of Canonsleigh Abbey*, calendared & ed. Vera London, 1965 **16 X**

9 §   *Benjamin Donn's Map of Devon, 1765*. Introduction by W. L. D. Ravenhill, 1965 **11 9**

11 §   *Devon Inventories of the Sixteenth and Seventeenth Centuries*, ed. Margaret Cash, 1966   **13 5**

12   *Plymouth Building Accounts of the Sixteenth and Seventeenth Centuries*, ed. Edwin Welch, 1967 **14 3**

14   *The Devonshire Lay Subsidy of 1332*, ed. Audrey M. Erskine, 1969   **00 3**

15   *Churchwardens' Accounts of Ashburton, 1479–1580*, ed. Alison Hanham, 1970   **01 1**

17 §   *The Caption of Seisin of the Duchy of Cornwall (1377)*, ed. P. L. Hull, 1971   **03 8**

19   *A Calendar of Cornish Glebe Terriers, 1673–1735*, ed. Richard Potts, 1974   **19 4**

20   *John Lydford's Book: the Fourteenth Century Formulary of the Archdeacon of Totnes*, ed. Dorothy M. Owen, 1975 (with Historical Manuscripts Commission) **011 440046 6**

21   *A Calendar of Early Chancery Proceedings relating to West Country Shipping, 1388–1493*, ed. Dorothy A. Gardiner, 1976   **20 8**

22   *Tudor Exeter: Tax Assessments 1489–1595*, ed. Margery M. Rowe, 1977   **21 6**

23   *The Devon Cloth Industry in the Eighteenth Century: Sun Fire Office Inventories, 1726–1770,* ed. Stanley D. Chapman, 1978   **22 4**

24, 26   *The Accounts of the Fabric of Exeter Cathedral, 1279–1353*, Parts I & II, ed. Audrey M. Erskine, 1981 & 1983   **24 0   26 7**

25, 27   *The Parliamentary Survey of the Duchy of Cornwall*, Parts I & II, ed. Norman J. G. Pounds 1982 & 1984   **25 2   27 5**

28   *Crown Pleas of the Devon Eyre of 1238*, ed. Henry Summerson, 1985   **28 3**

29   *Georgian Tiverton: the Political Memoranda of Beavis Wood, 1768–98*, ed. John Bourne, 1986   **29 1**

30   *The Cartulary of Launceston Priory* (Lambeth Palace MS.719): A Calendar, ed. P. L. Hull, 1987   **30 5**

31   *Shipbuilding on the Exe: the Memoranda Book of Daniel Bishop Davy (1799–1874) of Topsham, Devon*, ed. Clive N. Ponsford, 1988   **31 3**

32   *The Receivers' Accounts of the City of Exeter, 1304–1353*, ed. Margery M. Rowe and John M. Draisey, 1989   **32 1**

33   *Early-Stuart Mariners and Shipping: the Maritime Surveys of Devon and Cornwall, 1619–35*, ed. Todd Gray, 1990   **33 X**

34   *Joel Gascoyne's Map of Cornwall 1699.* Introduction by W. L. D Ravenhill and Oliver Padel, 1991   **34 8**

35   *Nicholas Roscarrock's 'Lives of the Saints': Cornwall and Devon*, ed. Nicholas Orme, 1992   **35 6**

36   *The Local Port Customs Accounts of Exeter, 1266–1321*, ed. Maryanne Kowaleski, 1993   **36 4**

37   *Charters of the Redvers Family and the Earldom of Devon, 1090–1217*, ed. Robert Bearman, 1994   **37 2**

38   *Devon Household Accounts, 1627–59, Part I: Sir Richard and Lady Lucy Reynell of Forde House, 1627–43, John Willoughby of Leyhill, 1644–6, and Sir Edward Wise of Sydenham, 1656–9*, ed. Todd Gray, 1995   **38 0**

39   *Devon Household Accounts 1627–59, Part II: Henry, Earl of Bath, and Rachel, Countess of Bath, of Tawstock and London, 1639–54*, ed. Todd Gray, 1996   **39 9**

40   *The Uffculme Wills and Inventories, 16th to 18th Centuries*, ed. Peter Wyatt, with an introduction by Robin Stanes, 1997   **40 2**

41   *Cornish Rentals and Surveys of the Arundell Family of Lanherne, Fourteenth to Sixteenth Centuries*, ed. H. S. A. Fox and Oliver Padel, 1998   **41 0**

42   *Liberalism in West Cornwall: The 1868 Election Papers of A. Pendarves Vivian MP*, ed. Edwin Jaggard, 1999   **42 9**

43, 45   *Devon Maps and Map-makers: Manuscript Maps before 1840*, ed. with introduction Mary R. Ravenhill and Margery M. Rowe, 2000 & 2002   **43 7, 45 3**

44   *Havener's Accounts of the Earldom and Duchy of Cornwall, 1301–1356*, ed. Maryanne Kowaleski, 2001   **44 5**

46   **(for 2003)**: *Death and Burial in Medieval Exeter*, ed. Nicholas Orme and David Lepine

Extra Series

1   *Exeter Freemen 1266–1967*, edited by Margery M. Rowe and Andrew M. Jackson, 1973   **18 6**

2   *Guide to the Parish and Non-Parochial Registers of Devon and Cornwall 1538–1837*, compiled by Hugh Peskett, 1979; supplement 1983   **23 2**

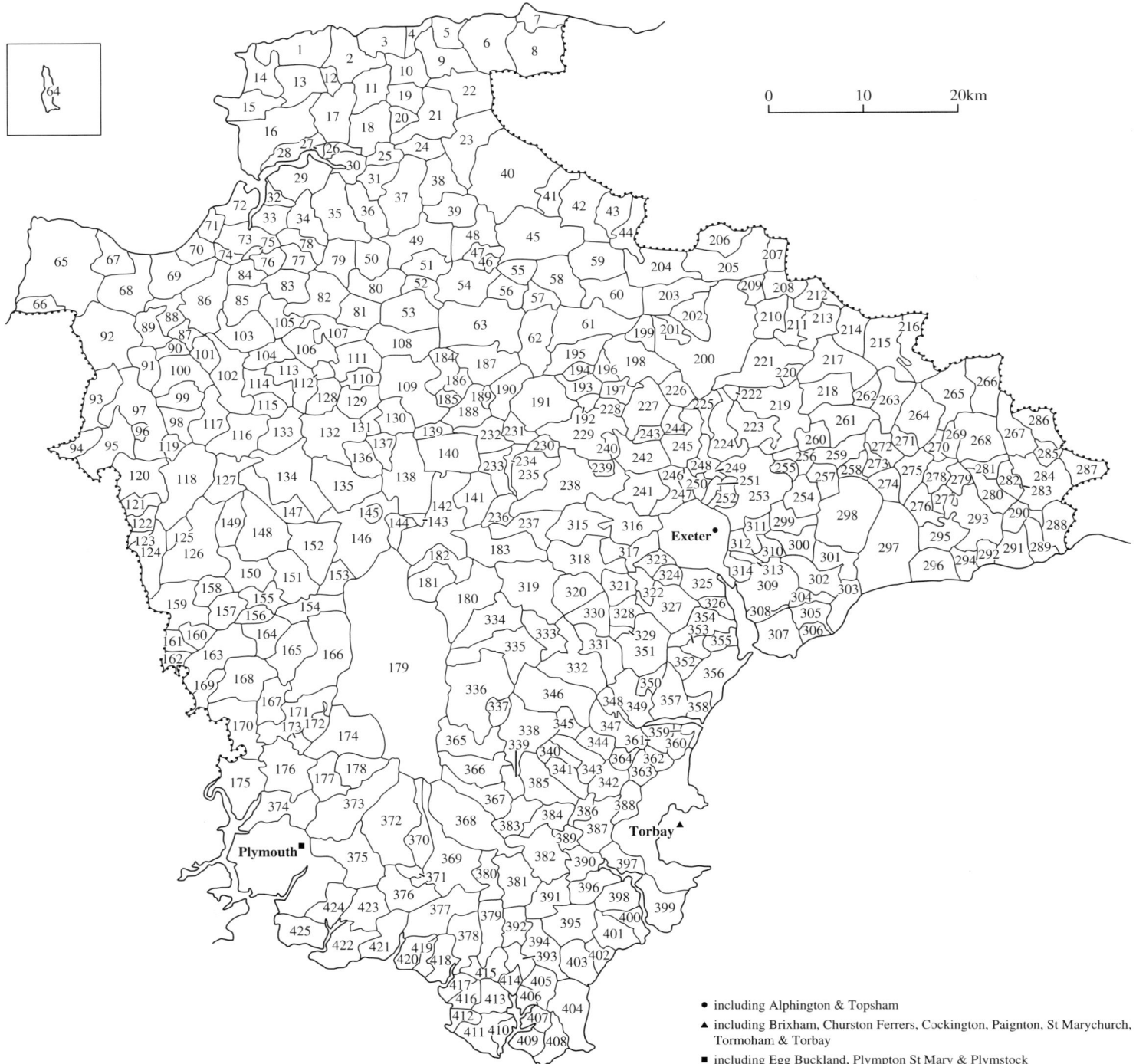

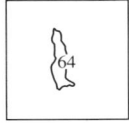
64

0   10   20km

• including Alphington & Topsham

▲ including Brixham, Churston Ferrers, Cockington, Paignton, St Marychurch,
  Tormoham & Torbay

■ including Egg Buckland, Plympton St Mary & Plymstock

Exeter •

Torbay ▲

Plymouth ■

1 Ilfracombe	72 Northam	144 Belstone
2 Berrynarbor	73 Bideford	145 Okehampton
3 Combe Martin	74 Littleham	146 Okehampton Hamlets
4 Trentishoe	75 Landcross	147 Beaworthy
5 Martinhoe	76 Weare Giffard	148 Bratton Clovelly
6 Lynton & Lynmouth	77 Huntshaw	149 Germansweek
7 Countisbury	78 Alverdiscott	150 Thrushelton
8 Brendon	79 Yarnscombe	151 Bridestowe
9 Parracombe	80 High Bickington	152 Sourton
10 Kentisbury	81 Roborough	153 Common to Bridestowe &
11 East Down	82 St Giles in the Wood	Sourton
12 Bittadon	83 Great Torrington	154 Lydford
13 West Down	84 Monkleigh	155 Lewtrenchard
14 Mortehoe	85 Frithelstock	156 Coryton
15 Georgeham	86 Buckland Brewer	157 Marystow
16 Braunton	87 Bulkworthy	158 Stowford
17 Marwood	88 East Putford	159 Lifton
18 Shirwell	89 West Putford	160 Kelly
19 Arlington	90 Abbots Bickington	161 Bradstone
20 Loxhore	91 Sutcombe	162 Dunterton
21 Bratton Fleming	92 Bradworthy	163 Milton Abbot
22 Challacombe	93 Pancrasweek	164 Brentor
23 Brayford (including	94 Bridgerule	165 Mary Tavy
Charles & High Bray)	95 Pyworthy	166 Peter Tavy
24 Stoke Rivers	96 Holsworthy	167 Tavistock
25 Goodleigh	97 Holsworthy Hamlets	168 Lamerton
26 Pilton West	98 Cookbury	169 Sydenham Damerel
27 Ashford	99 Thornbury	170 Gulworthy
28 Heanton Punchardon	100 Milton Damerel	171 Whitchurch
29 Fremington	101 Newton St Petrock	172 Sampford Spiney
30 Barnstaple	102 Shebbear	173 Horrabridge
31 Landkey	103 Langtree	174 Walkhampton
32 Instow	104 Peters Marland	175 Bere Ferrers
33 Westleigh	105 Little Torrington	176 Buckland Monachorum
34 Horwood, Lovacott,	106 Merton	177 Meavy
Newton Tracey	107 Beaford	178 Sheepstor
35 Tawstock	108 Ashreigney	179 Dartmoor Forest
36 Bishop's Tawton	109 Winkleigh	180 Chagford
37 Swimbridge	110 Dowland	181 Gidleigh
38 East & West Buckland	111 Dolton	182 Throwleigh
39 Filleigh	112 Huish	183 Drewsteignton
40 North Molton	113 Petrockstowe	184 Wembworthy
41 Twitchen	114 Buckland Filleigh	185 Brushford
42 Molland	115 Sheepwash	186 Eggesford
43 West Anstey	116 Black Torrington	187 Chawleigh
44 East Anstey	117 Bradford	188 Coldridge
45 Bishop's Nympton	118 Ashwater	189 Nymet Rowland
46 Queen's Nympton	119 Hollacombe	190 Lapford
47 George Nympton	120 Clawton	191 Morchard Bishop
48 South Molton	121 Tetcott	192 Kennerleigh
49 Chittlehampton	122 Luffincott	193 Woolfardisworthy
50 Atherington	123 Northcott	194 Washford Pyne
51 Satterleigh & Warkleigh	124 St Giles on the Heath	195 Thelbridge
52 Chittlehamholt	125 Virginstow	196 Puddington
53 Burrington	126 Broadwoodwidger	197 Poughill
54 King's Nympton	127 Halwill	198 Cruwys Morchard
55 Mariansleigh	128 Meeth	199 Templeton
56 Romansleigh	129 Iddesleigh	200 Tiverton
57 Meshaw	130 Broadwoodkelly	201 Loxbeare
58 Rose Ash	131 Monkokehampton	202 Washfield
59 Knowstone	132 Hatherleigh	203 Stoodleigh
60 Rackenford	133 Highampton	204 Oakford
61 Witheridge	134 Northlew	205 Bampton
62 East Worlington	135 Inwardleigh	206 Morebath
63 Chulmleigh	136 Jacobstowe	207 Clayhanger
64 Lundy	137 Exbourne	208 Hockworthy
65 Hartland	138 Sampford Courtenay	209 Huntsham
66 Welcombe	(including Honeychurch)	210 Uplowman
67 Clovelly	139 Bondleigh	211 Sampford Peverell
68 Woolfardisworthy	140 North Tawton	212 Holcombe Rogus
69 Parkham	141 Spreyton	213 Burlescombe
70 Alwington	142 South Tawton	214 Culmstock
71 Abbotsham	143 Sticklepath	215 Hemyock

216 Clayhidon	288 Uplyme	356 Dawlish
217 Uffculme	289 Combpyne Rousdon	357 Bishopsteignton
218 Kentisbeare	290 Musbury	358 Teignmouth
219 Cullompton	291 Axmouth	359 Shaldon
220 Willand	292 Seaton	360 Stokeinteignhead
221 Halberton	293 Colyton	361 Haccombe with Combe
222 Butterleigh	294 Beer	(Combeinteignhead)
223 Bradninch	295 Southleigh	362 Coffinswell
224 Silverton	296 Branscombe	363 Kingskerswell
225 Bickleigh	297 Sidmouth (including	364 Abbotskerswell
226 Cadeleigh	Salcombe Regis & Sidbury)	365 Holne
227 Cheriton Fitzpaine	298 Ottery St Mary	366 West Buckfastleigh
228 Stockleigh English	299 Rockbeare	367 Dean Prior
229 Sandford	300 Aylesbeare	368 South Brent
230 Copplestone	301 Newton Poppleford &	369 Ugborough
231 Down St Mary	Harpford	370 Harford
232 Zeal Monachorum	302 Colaton Raleigh	371 Ivybridge
233 Bow	303 Otterton	372 Cornwood
234 Clannaborough	304 Bicton	373 Shaugh Prior
235 Colebrooke	305 East Budleigh	374 Bickleigh
236 Hittisleigh	306 Budleigh Salterton	375 Sparkwell
237 Cheriton Bishop	307 Exmouth (including	376 Ermington
238 Crediton Hamlets	Littleham &	377 Modbury
239 Crediton	Withycombe Raleigh)	378 Aveton Gifford
240 Upton Hellions	308 Lympstone	379 Loddiswell
241 Newton St Cyres	309 Woodbury	380 North Huish
242 Shobrooke	310 Farringdon	381 Diptford
243 Stockleigh Pomeroy	311 Clyst Honiton	382 Harberton
244 Cadbury	312 Sowton	383 Rattery
245 Thorverton	313 Clyst St Mary	384 Dartington
246 Upton Pyne	314 Clyst St George	385 Staverton
247 Brampford Speke	315 Tedburn St Mary	386 Littlehempston
248 Nether Exe	316 Whitestone	387 Berry Pomeroy
249 Rewe	317 Holcombe Burnell	388 Marldon
250 Stoke Canon	318 Dunsford	389 Totnes
251 Huxham	319 Moretonhampstead	390 Ashprington
252 Poltimore	320 Bridford	391 Halwell & Moreleigh
253 Broadclyst	321 Doddiscombsleigh	392 Woodleigh
254 Whimple	322 Dunchideock	393 Buckland-tout-Saints
255 Clyst St Lawrence	323 Ide	394 East Allington
256 Clyst Hydon	324 Shillingford St George	395 Blackawton
257 Talaton	325 Exminster	396 Cornworthy
258 Feniton	326 Powderham	397 Stoke Gabriel
259 Payhembury	327 Kenn	398 Dittisham
260 Plymtree	328 Ashton	399 Kingswear
261 Broadhembury	329 Trusham	400 Dartmouth
262 Sheldon	330 Christow	401 Stoke Fleming
263 Dunkeswell	331 Hennock	402 Strete
264 Luppitt	332 Bovey Tracey	403 Slapton
265 Upottery	333 Lustleigh	404 Stokenham
266 Yarcombe	334 North Bovey	405 Frogmore & Sherford
267 Membury	335 Manaton	406 Charleton
268 Stockland	336 Widecombe in the Moor	407 South Pool
269 Cotleigh	337 Buckland in the Moor	408 Chivelstone
270 Monkton	338 Ashburton	409 East Portlemouth
271 Combe Raleigh	339 Buckfastleigh	410 Salcombe
272 Awliscombe	340 Woodland	411 Malborough
273 Buckerell	341 Broadhempston	412 South Huish
274 Gittisham	342 Ipplepen	413 West Alvington
275 Honiton	343 Torbryan	414 Kingsbridge (including
276 Farway	344 Ogwell	Dodbrooke)
277 Northleigh	345 Bickington	415 Churchstow
278 Offwell	346 Ilsington	416 South Milton
279 Widworthy	347 Newton Abbot (including	417 Thurlestone
280 Shute	Highweek & Wolborough)	418 Bigbury
281 Dalwood	348 Teigngrace	419 Ringmore
282 Kilmington	349 Kingsteignton	420 Kingston
283 Common to Axminster &	350 Ideford	421 Holbeton
Kilmington	351 Chudleigh	422 Newton & Noss
284 Axminster	352 Ashcombe	(Newton Ferrers)
285 All Saints	353 Mamhead	423 Yealmpton
286 Chardstock	354 Kenton	424 Brixton
287 Hawkchurch	355 Starcross	425 Wembury

D565656 1 509491